THE EVOLUTION OF
WALT WHITMAN
THE CREATION OF
A PERSONALITY

THE EVOLUTION OF
WALT WHITMAN
THE CREATION OF
A PERSONALITY

By

ROGER ASSELINEAU

THE BELKNAP PRESS
OF HARVARD UNIVERSITY PRESS
Cambridge, Massachusetts

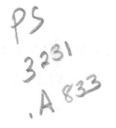

Distributed in Great Britain by Oxford University Press, London

Translated by Richard P. Adams and the author

Typography by Burton J Jones
Printed in the U.S.A. by Harvard University Printing Office
Bound by Stanhope Bindery, Inc., Boston

Library of Congress Catalog Card Number: 60-13297

TO THE MEMORY OF MY PARENTS

FOREWORD

THE French edition of this book having been warmly received in English-speaking countries and several reviewers having expressed the wish that it should be translated,* I have tried to satisfy their demands, and this is the result of my efforts. But I would never have carried out such a task without the help of Professor Richard P. Adams of Tulane University, who, during his stay in France as a Fulbright lecturer in 1959–60, worked with me on the translation with untiring devotion. I wish also to express my thanks to the Director and to the Syndics of the Harvard University Press, and more particularly to Professor Kenneth B. Murdock, for undertaking to publish an American edition of my book in spite of its length and bulkiness. They have shown admirable understanding.

As a matter of fact, *L'Evolution de Walt Whitman* is such a long book that it has seemed preferable to publish it in two volumes in the United States. But this dichotomy needs a few words of explanation. The first volume is practically a biography of Walt Whitman, whereas the second volume will be devoted to a critical study of his works. Such a division has fallen into disrepute. Yet, it offers undeniable advantages. It enables a critic to cover the whole field much more thoroughly than a so-called critical biography which in practice results in a loosely knit biography marred by inadequate critical dis-

* Gay W. Allen in *Etudes Anglaises*, October 1954; Sculley Bradley in *Modern Language Notes*, December 1955; and an anonymous reviewer in the *Times Literary Supplement*, January 27, 1956.

quisitions. I have preferred to follow the old pattern and treat the man and his works separately in order to give to each part its due.

Let me also add that, as Whitman scholars have been more active than ever since the French edition of this work appeared six years ago, I have brought the documentation of my notes up to date and corrected a few minor errors in the text.

When I undertook to write *L'Evolution de Walt Whitman,* there already existed a French doctoral dissertation on the author of *Leaves of Grass: Walt Whitman: la Naissance du Poète* by Jean Catel. But that work, so rich in original insight, studies only Whitman's youth and ends with the first edition of *Leaves of Grass,* and ignores the fact that nine other editions followed and that Whitman for the remaining thirty-seven years of his life did not cease to alter, to correct, and to enrich his book. Thus it seemed to me that there was room for a second work devoted to the growth of *Leaves of Grass* after its sudden birth in 1855.

Two authors had the same idea before: Frederik Schyberg, a Danish critic, and Gay Wilson Allen, Professor of English at New York University. Schyberg's *Walt Whitman* appeared in 1933, but since few Whitman scholars understand Danish, it was necessary to wait for Gay Wilson Allen's *Walt Whitman Handbook* (1946), which gave a summary of it, to know the general scope of that remarkable thesis. Finally, in 1951, the Columbia University Press published an English translation of it, done by Evie Allison Allen, and so the work became accessible to all. One finds there a penetrating study of the successive editions of *Leaves of Grass.* Thanks to a precise and close analysis of the poems and their variations, Schyberg brings out the true personality of Whitman, which so many of his biographers had, up to then, misunderstood, and he illumines the dramatic character of a grave crisis through which Whitman passed between 1855 and 1860. Gay W. Allen followed the same method and came to the same conclusions in his *Walt Whitman Handbook*. But, realizing the weaknesses of the analytic and chronological approach of the Danish critic, he tried, in a section of his work entitled "Fundamental Ideas," to go beyond the biographical to the critical level and to synthetize what the study of the variations revealed. Unfortunately, having too little space at his disposal, he could only begin that study. My debt to these two predecessors is naturally considerable. Thanks to them I have been able to push my analyses farther and to explore more minutely a domain which they had already pioneered.

An American Field Service Fellowship and a Smith-Mundt grant have permitted me to make two visits of a year each to the United States and to do my research there. I should like to express my gratitude to those organizations and I wish equally to thank Harvard University, where I worked under the expert guidance of Professors Kenneth B. Murdock and Perry Miller and which always opened wide to me the doors of its libraries. I must also give my thanks to the librarians of the universities of Pennsylvania, Yale, Brown, Columbia, and Duke and to the curators of the Berg Collection of the New York Public Library and of the Rare Book Division of the Library of Congress. Thanks to their generosity I have had access to original documents, some of which, still unpublished, were, with their permission, for the first time printed in the French edition of this book.

I cannot end this foreword without recalling the memory of Jean Catel, my French predecessor, who, during the German Occupation, at a time when I had no document whatever at my disposal, opened his library to me and lent me his books with that kindness and total disinterestedness that none of his friends can forget.

When the idea of beginning this study came to me, I was encouraged by Professors Louis Cazamian and Charles Cestre.

But I would especially like to express my gratitude to Professor Maurice LeBreton of the Sorbonne who directed my thesis with as much sympathy as competence. In the course of my stays in the United States I had the occasion to meet the most eminent Whitman specialists, the late Joseph C. Furness, Sculley Bradley, Emory Holloway, who were all very gracious to me, and, especially, I made the acquaintance of Professor Gay W. Allen, who did not hesitate to put his notes and his books at my disposal and with whom, in his charming house in New Jersey, I many times spent long hours discussing Whitman. He has been more than a guide for me, he has been a friend.

Before concluding, I must not forget to acknowledge my debt to Mrs. James E. Duffy of the Editorial Department of the Harvard University Press who, with admirable thoroughness, has prepared my typescript for the printer.

April 1960   R. A.

CONTENTS

THE EVOLUTION OF
WALT WHITMAN
THE CREATION OF
A PERSONALITY

INTRODUCTION

*I charge you forever reject those who would
expound me, for I cannot expound myself . . .*
("*Myself and Mine,*" line 27.)

T HE idea of writing this book came to me during the
gloomiest years of the German Occupation of France. Nothing
could have been more natural at that time, when every French-
man was a prisoner in his own country, than to try to escape
from that world of concentration camps into the vast spaces
of Whitman's universe where all is liberty and promise of
happiness. To avoid moral suffocation it was necessary to find,
in spite of an intolerable situation, some ground for hope and
for a renewal of faith in mankind. Whitman, in this respect,
was an ideal source of inspiration. Invaluable lessons of tenacious energy could be drawn from his *Leaves of Grass,* in
which with patient strength he overcame his anxieties and
doubts and repelled their repeated attacks over the years. The
presence of evil within him and around him never broke his
spirit. His faith and enthusiasm always brought him through.
But this invincible optimism was the result of a continual
struggle, and thus the serenity of his old age was a victory
over anguish. This is revealed by an attentive reading of his
works, as I shall try to show. The subject was in the air at
the time. As early as 1940, Jean Guéhenno wrote in his *Jour-*

nal, after commenting on the constantly enriched text of Montaigne's *Essays:*

> I know only one other book which in the same way has grown, ripened, matured along with its author: Whitman's *Leaves of Grass.* And it is no accident that both use almost the same formula:
> "Whoever takes my book in his hands takes a man."

At a distance of four centuries, the same individualistic zeal impelled them, drier and more intellectual in Montaigne, in Whitman, more generous and, as it were, in harmony with a new freedom, a new world in which the individual need not develop himself at the expense of others, but together with others, realizing that he benefits himself by becoming more fraternal.[1]

So I propose to study Walt Whitman's evolution from 1855 to his death. But why that initial date? Is it not arbitrary to set such a time limit to the inquiry? True, it is artificial, but it was imposed by the very nature of the subject. Why go back before 1855 to try to explain the birth of *Leaves of Grass?* The attempt would be doomed to failure. Nothing in the life of the author justifies any prediction of the sudden blossoming of such a strange masterpiece and nothing justifies any *a posteriori* deduction of its necessity. It seems wiser therefore to renounce the idea of clearing up the mystery and to attempt a humbler and more fruitful approach: a study of the years after 1855 during which the poet at last became himself and developed harmoniously rather than those in which he was still unsuccessfully searching for himself. Whitman, for that matter, was plainly aware of this superiority — at least so far as he was concerned — of middle age over youth, as is shown by this fragment found among his papers after his death:

> Between the ages of thirty-five and eighty may be the perfection and realization of moral life; rising above the previous periods in all that makes a person better, healthier, happier, more command-

moment, I wish merely to call attention to the difficulty of the subject, which results from the complexity of the revisions that Whitman made in *Leaves of Grass* and the scarcity of biographical documents. We must not forget that this unique collection was the object of his constant care throughout his poetic career and that in the course of thirty-seven years he brought out ten different editions. Moreover each edition not only contained new poems, but the old ones had been corrected, cut, and enriched; sometimes titles and punctuation had been changed and the arrangement of poems completely upset. The problem is to explain these changes and throw light on the obscurities of the poems, which are generally more allusive than explicit, with the help of what little we know about Whitman's life and personality. Paradoxically, this exuberant poet of comradeship was an extremely secretive man, and the passionate dithyrambs of his friends give us very little information about him. In a way, he is almost as mysterious as Shakespeare — no wonder he savored the mystery that surrounds the personality of Shakespeare and is still the despair of commentators. Since his own work was essentially lyric, its obscurity is even more troublesome, and it is important that we do our best to dissipate it. Unfortunately, the critic finds himself in the position of a paleontologist who, with only a few fossils, must try to reconstruct the whole evolution of the animal kingdom.

What is the best method to overcome these difficulties? In the absence of any critical edition of *Leaves of Grass,* I have had to collate the texts of the successive editions in order to determine each time the additions and the structural changes. At the same time I have had to study the variants, that is to say, the corrections made to previously printed poems.[3] Of course, I have also made full use of the facts of Whitman's biography and of the history of the time in order to interpret the results of the analysis correctly and to define their mean-

ing, more beloved and more a realisee of love. The mind matu
the senses in full activity, the digestion even, the voice firm,
walk untired, the arms and chest sinewy and imposing, the
joints flexible, the hands capable of many things, the complexi
and blood pure, the breath sweet, the procreative power ev
ready in man and the womb power in woman, the inward organ
all sweetly performing their offices — during those years the universe presents its riches, its strength, its beauty, to be parts of a
man, a woman. Then the body is ripe and the soul also and all
the shows of nature attained and the production of thought in
books.[2]

"At the age of thirty-five," he said; now in 1855 he was thirty-
six. He was obviously thinking of himself.

Accordingly my purpose is to follow the growth of *Leaves
of Grass* through the successive editions and not to attack the
insoluble problem of its genesis. This course seems all the
more appropriate since the youth of Whitman has already
been thoroughly and carefully studied by Jean Catel in his
Walt Whitman: La Naissance du poète (1929).

To be sure, it will often be necessary to go back in time
before the limit which I have assigned. However unexpected
the appearance of *Leaves of Grass,* it did not spring fully
armed from the brow of its author. Certain themes had been
sketched in the course of the preceding years in newspaper
articles, in stories, and in a few poems written along conventional patterns. The recapitulation of certain aspects of Whitman's career before 1855 will then compensate for the artificiality of the break I have made in his development.

But is it proper to speak of the evolution of Whitman? I
will try to show that it is and to describe the process. If the
subject has never been treated exhaustively, it has often been
touched on by critics, particularly by William Sloane Kennedy, Oscar Lovell Triggs, Floyd Stovall, Frederik Schyberg,
Irving C. Story, and Gay Wilson Allen. I will have occasion
to examine their theses and discuss their conclusions. At the

ing, more beloved and more a realisee of love. The mind matured, the senses in full activity, the digestion even, the voice firm, the walk untired, the arms and chest sinewy and imposing, the hip joints flexible, the hands capable of many things, the complexion and blood pure, the breath sweet, the procreative power ever ready in man and the womb power in woman, the inward organs all sweetly performing their offices — during those years the universe presents its riches, its strength, its beauty, to be parts of a man, a woman. Then the body is ripe and the soul also and all the shows of nature attained and the production of thought in books.[2]

"At the age of thirty-five," he said; now in 1855 he was thirty-six. He was obviously thinking of himself.

Accordingly my purpose is to follow the growth of *Leaves of Grass* through the successive editions and not to attack the insoluble problem of its genesis. This course seems all the more appropriate since the youth of Whitman has already been thoroughly and carefully studied by Jean Catel in his *Walt Whitman: La Naissance du poète* (1929).

To be sure, it will often be necessary to go back in time before the limit which I have assigned. However unexpected the appearance of *Leaves of Grass*, it did not spring fully armed from the brow of its author. Certain themes had been sketched in the course of the preceding years in newspaper articles, in stories, and in a few poems written along conventional patterns. The recapitulation of certain aspects of Whitman's career before 1855 will then compensate for the artificiality of the break I have made in his development.

But is it proper to speak of the evolution of Whitman? I will try to show that it is and to describe the process. If the subject has never been treated exhaustively, it has often been touched on by critics, particularly by William Sloane Kennedy, Oscar Lovell Triggs, Floyd Stovall, Frederik Schyberg, Irving C. Story, and Gay Wilson Allen. I will have occasion to examine their theses and discuss their conclusions. At the moment, I wish merely to call attention to the difficulty of the subject, which results from the complexity of the revisions that Whitman made in *Leaves of Grass* and the scarcity of biographical documents. We must not forget that this unique collection was the object of his constant care throughout his poetic career and that in the course of thirty-seven years he brought out ten different editions. Moreover each edition not only contained new poems, but the old ones had been corrected, cut, and enriched; sometimes titles and punctuation had been changed and the arrangement of poems completely upset. The problem is to explain these changes and throw light on the obscurities of the poems, which are generally more allusive than explicit, with the help of what little we know about Whitman's life and personality. Paradoxically, this exuberant poet of comradeship was an extremely secretive man, and the passionate dithyrambs of his friends give us very little information about him. In a way, he is almost as mysterious as Shakespeare — no wonder he savored the mystery that surrounds the personality of Shakespeare and is still the despair of commentators. Since his own work was essentially lyric, its obscurity is even more troublesome, and it is important that we do our best to dissipate it. Unfortunately, the critic finds himself in the position of a paleontologist who, with only a few fossils, must try to reconstruct the whole evolution of the animal kingdom.

What is the best method to overcome these difficulties? In the absence of any critical edition of *Leaves of Grass,* I have had to collate the texts of the successive editions in order to determine each time the additions and the structural changes. At the same time I have had to study the variants, that is to say, the corrections made to previously printed poems.[3] Of course, I have also made full use of the facts of Whitman's biography and of the history of the time in order to interpret the results of the analysis correctly and to define their meaning more accurately. Sometimes, however, the process was reversed: a careful study of the text and its development over the years permitted a clarification of certain obscure biographical points.

Naturally, this procedure calls for extreme prudence. I have been particularly careful not to read the early editions in the light of what I knew about the later ones. I have also been careful not to draw hasty conclusions from the examination of variant readings. A correction might very well be a matter of form and not the indication of a new attitude. An addition does not necessarily represent a new orientation of thought. It may merely fill a gap or supply an omission. I have constantly kept these various possibilities in mind and have tried to avoid the errors they might have occasioned.

My purpose was not to write a biography of Whitman or a chapter in the history of American literature, but rather to perform the critical task of bringing out the meaning of *Leaves of Grass* by continually confronting it with its own successive aspects and with Whitman's other works, as well as with what we know of the author and his time. It seemed to me that this study would promote a better understanding of *Leaves of Grass* and a deeper penetration into the mind of its author. The book is too often studied as a unit and critics tend to forget that it represents forty years of assiduous experimentation, that Whitman was thirty years old when he began, and that he was an old man when he stopped. They also forget that during the same period of time the United States made the transition from a rural to an industrial civilization after a terrible civil war. Whitman's book is therefore the fruit of a long life and the mirror of a crucial period of American history.[4] To use another image, it is not a plain of uniform nature and origin, but a plateau where layers of different geological periods have been brought to the surface by various upheavals and later eroded. It is true that Whitman wanted us to consider only the final result, that is to say, the text of 1892. He said so in a note prefixed to the "death-bed" edition:

As there are now several editions of L. of G., different texts and dates, I wish to say that I prefer and recommend this present one, complete, for future printing, if there should be any; a copy and fac-simile, indeed, of the text of these 438 pages.[5]

And Horace L. Traubel reports that he once said:

So far as you may have anything to do with it I place upon you the injunction that whatever may be added to the *Leaves* shall be supplementary, avowed as such, leaving the book complete as I left it, consecutive to the point I left off, marking always an un-mistakable, deep down, unobliteratable division line. In the long run the world will do as it pleases with the book. I am deter-mined to have the world know what I was pleased to do.[6]

Surely he has a right to try to impose a version to which he did his best to give a definitive structure, but we also have a right, which he recognized, to prefer a different approach, to try to rediscover behind the completed façade which he has left us the living presence of the author who slowly built up this work.

Here a problem arises: had Whitman conceived the defini-tive plan of *Leaves of Grass* as it appeared in the "deathbed" edition before 1855? He said so in 1881. For, when the 1881 edition was published, he declared to a Boston reporter:

It is now, I believe, twenty-six years since I began to work upon the structure; and this edition will complete the design which I had in mind when I began to write. The whole affair is like one of those old architectural edifices, some of which were hundreds of years in building, and the designer of which had the whole idea in mind from the first. His plans are pretty ambitious, and as means or time permits, he adds part after part, perhaps at quite wide intervals. To a casual observer it looks in the course of its construction odd enough. Only after the whole is completed one catches the idea which inspired the designer, in whose mind the relation of each part to the whole had existed all along. That is the way it has been with my book. It has been twenty-six years building. There have been seven different hitches at it. Seven different times have parts of the edifice been constructed sometimes in Brooklyn, sometimes in Washington, sometimes in Boston, and at other places. The book has been built partially in every part of the United States. And this edition is the completed edifice.[7]

As early as 1876 he had stated in an interview with one J.B.S. of the New York *World*: "I set out with a design as thoroughly considered as an architect's plan for a cathedral." [8]

What do these assertions mean? At first glance they are at least surprising. The book gives the impression, not of having developed harmoniously over the years, but of having undergone a series of Protean metamorphoses. A quick look at the different editions is enough to show this. The text of 1855 is a river of lava. Some of the poems in it, particularly the one which later became "Song of Myself," are interminable. They are not differentiated by titles, they are all indiscriminately called "Leaves of Grass." In 1856 the work was enriched with a large number of short pieces, and this time all the poems had titles. But it is only in 1860 that we find the first attempt at organization; most of the short poems now are grouped in sections with titles, but within each section, the poems lose their individuality; instead of titles they bear only numbers, as one numbers the panels of a frame house before taking it to pieces and moving it to another location. In 1867 the aspect of the book once more changed completely. Titles reappeared, each poem had its own, but now the sections in their turn lost their individuality. Except for "Children of Adam" and "Calamus" they were undifferentiated and all called "Leaves of Grass"; a partial return to the uniformity of the first edition. In 1871 the poems devoted to the Civil War were finally incorporated in the book. They formed three

groups interpolated among the existing sections, thus introducing an element of diversity and also giving the collection
a sort of skeleton. The edition of 1876 consisted for its part
of two volumes, but the first merely reproduced the edition
of 1871. For the new poems were not yet part and parcel of
Leaves of Grass proper. They were relegated to the second volume and mingled with pieces of prose. It was only in 1881
that they were allowed a place in the collection. Is it not
altogether remarkable that from 1867, that is to say, precisely
from the time Whitman tried to give his book a little order, he
was unable immediately to incorporate the poems which he
wrote? If he had really had a plan in mind, it would have
been easy for him to find a place for each of them. Even if
we concede that the Civil War surprised him and upset his
projects, how can we explain his failure to include in *Leaves
of Grass* the poems which in 1876 he was constrained to keep
apart provisionally in the miscellaneous volume entitled *Two
Rivulets*? Why, moreover, did he not announce his design
in the 1855 preface? And, if he had a plan from the beginning, why is it that he continued until 1881 to change the
order and the titles of the various poems? Why did his book
begin to be organized only in 1860 (and even then not tightly)?
As a matter of fact, in 1857, commenting in a letter on the
1860 edition which was almost ready, he made this very revealing statement:

> It is, I know Well enough, that *that* must be the *true Leaves
> of Grass* — and I think it has an aspect of completeness, and
> makes its case clearer. — The old poems are all retained. — The
> difference is in the new character given to the mass, by the addi-
> tions.[9]

According to this, he had as early as 1857 the impression that
the edifice was finished. But can we even speak of an edifice?
He was so reluctant to give his work an architectural aspect
that he used a word as little suggestive of order and harmony

as "mass" to describe the material of the volume to come. Besides, he made no allusion to any changes in structure; the difference he found between the two volumes was mainly quantitative; if the new edition was to produce a different impression, it would not be owing to a different arrangement, but to added material.

Several years later, on May 31, 1861, to be precise, he noted in the rough draft of a preface which he never had occasion to publish: "The paths to the house are made — but where is the house itself? At most only indicated or touched." [10] Could he say more frankly that there was no order in the work which he thus submitted to the reader and that he had not followed any plan? However he went on in these terms: "Nevertheless, as while we live some dream will play its part, I keep it in my plan of work ahead to yet fill up these *Whisperings*, (if I live & have luck) somehow proportionate to their original design." [11]

Thus, at the very time when he seemed to recognize that there was no trace of a plan in his *Leaves of Grass,* once more he asserted that he had one in his head. What precisely did he mean by "plan"? The interview which he gave in 1876 to the New York *World,* from which I have already cited a passage, may be of some help. For here he said among other things:

I set out to illustrate, without any flinching, actual humanity. I proposed to myself a series of compositions which should depict the physical, emotional, moral, intellectual and spiritual nature of a man.

— That man being yourself?

— That man for purposes of illustration, being myself . . . You can see I had first to deal with the physical, the corporal, the amative business — that part of our nature which is developed so strongly between the ages of 22 and 35. It is that part of my endeavor which caused most of the harsh criticism, and prevented candid examination of the ensuing stages of the design.[12]

We may compare this declaration with the one he made the same year in the Preface to *Two Rivulets*:

It was originally my intention, after chanting in *Leaves of Grass* the songs of the Body and Existence, to then compose a further, equally needed Volume, based on those convictions of perpetuity and conservation which, enveloping all precedents, make the unseen Soul govern absolutely at last. I meant, while in a sort continuing the theme of my first chants, to shift the slides, and exhibit the problem and paradox of the same ardent and fully appointed Personality entering the sphere of the re-sistless gravitation of Spiritual Law, and with cheerful face esti-mating Death, not at all as the cessation, but as somehow what I feel it must be, the entrance upon by far the greatest part of existence, and something that Life is at least as much for, as it is for itself. . .

Meanwhile, not entirely to give the go-by to my original plan, and far more to avoid a mark'd hiatus in it, than to entirely fulfil it, I end my books with thoughts, or radiations from thoughts, on Death, Immortality, and a free entrance into the Spiritual world. In those thoughts, in a sort, I make the first steps or studies toward the mighty theme, from the point of view necessitated by my foregoing poems, and by Modern Science. In them I also seek to set the key-stone to my Democracy's enduring arch.[13]

It is clear then that if Whitman had a plan in mind from the beginning, it was a singularly vague one — not a detailed and rigorous scheme with logical articulations clearly marked, but only two or three very general ideas which he proposed to develop. In other words, from the beginning, he knew where he was going and what he wanted, what great themes he was going to treat: the body, then the spiritual life, and then, by a natural progression, death and immortality, and finally, man no longer alone but in society, which for him was, of course, a democratic society. But he had no idea of the way in which he was to organize this rich material and compose his book. Only the goal toward which he was head-ing was fixed; the ways which he would take to attain it changed constantly, as his gropings and the frequent revisions he made in his poems indicate. In fact he admitted in the Preface of 1872:

When I commenced, years ago, elaborating the plan of my poems, and continued turning over that plan, and shifting it in my mind through many years, (from the age of twenty-eight to thirty-five,) experimenting much, and writing and abandoning much, one deep purpose underlay the others, and has underlain it and its execution ever since — and that has been the Religious purpose. Amid many changes, and a formulation taking far different shape from what I had first supposed, this basic purpose has never been departed from in the composition of my verses.[14]

It would therefore be more proper to speak of germs than of a plan. The word "plan" implies an architectural structure. But, as the evidence given above has shown, and as the detailed study of the different editions will prove, *Leaves of Grass* was not really constructed. Whitman allowed his book to grow within his mind little by little with an organic and almost vegetable growth. (In this sense the title of his book was particularly happy.) He did not intervene except to preserve a certain cohesion, a unity more organic than logical, which he defined himself in the "Notes on the Meaning and Intention of *Leaves of Grass*" published after his death by Richard Maurice Bucke: "My poems when complete should be *a unity*, in the same sense that the earth is, or that the human body, (senses, soul, head, trunk, feet, blood, viscera, man-root, eyes, hair) or that a perfect musical composition is." [15]

Or again, as John Burroughs said in his *Notes on Walt Whitman, Leaves of Grass* is "a series of growths, or strata, rising or starting out from a settled foundation or centre and expanding in successive accumulations." [16]

This comparison with the formation of a tree trunk is perhaps a little stiff, but at least it takes account of the instinctive, non-logical character of the development of *Leaves of Grass*. On the contrary, Oscar L. Triggs misses the point badly when he maintains that *"Leaves of Grass* has a marked tectonic quality. The author, like an architect, drew his plans, and the poem, like a cathedral long in building, slowly advanced to fulfilment. Each poem was designed and written with reference to its place in an ideal edifice." [17] Nothing could be more false, as we have seen. Such order as can be found in the later editions was imposed from the outside; it represents an intervention posterior to the act of creation.

At the beginning, then, Whitman had no plan; only a group of fairly general themes. It could hardly have been otherwise, given the subject which he had chosen. He was trying to express the inexpressible, an impossible task, never-ending, always to be resumed. He wanted his poems joyously to proclaim their "tidings old, yet ever new, untranslatable." [18]

He set off bravely in search of a new *Weltanschauung* that would be in harmony with the needs of his democratic and scientific century:

> . . . it is imperatively and ever to be borne in mind that *Leaves of Grass* entire is not to be construed as an intellectual or scholastic effort or Poem mainly, but more as a radical utterance out of the abysms of the Soul, the Emotions and the Physique — an utterance adjusted to, perhaps born of, Democracy and Modern Science. . .[19]

> Though from no definite plan at the time, I see now that I have unconsciously sought by indirections at least as much as directions, to express the whirls and rapid growth and intensity of the United States, the prevailing tendency and events of the Nineteenth Century, and largely the spirit of the whole current World, my time. . .[20]

Therefore he was only gradually aware of all the implications of his work:

> . . . I set out with the intention also of indicating or hinting

some point-characteristics which I since see (though I did not then, at least not definitely) were bases and object-urgings toward those "Leaves" from the first.[21]

This was hardly a rational process, or one that could be defined in rational terms. However, his subject being otherwise impossible to grasp, it was the only method that offered itself to him. Anyhow, he did not believe that anyone could ever succeed in pressing more closely into the mystery which lies at the heart of things:

> The best poetic utterance, after all, can merely hint, or remind, often very indirectly, or at distant removes. Aught of real perfection, or the solution of any deep problem, or any completed statement of the moral, the true, the beautiful, eludes the greatest, deftest poet — flies away like an always uncaught bird.[22]

Though the fowler in the course of successive editions tried to tighten the meshes of his net, he could never succeed in catching the bird.

Consequently, because of the fleeting nature of the subject and the peculiar progress of a way of thinking that proceeded by successive approximations, *Leaves of Grass* was slowly shaped by the interaction of two different processes, the one of instinctive growth and the other of rational and deliberate construction. As a result, the evolution of the work is difficult to trace in detail, as can be shown by the following example: in the edition of 1871 Whitman achieved with "Passage to India" a serenity and a mastery of himself he had never evinced before. Nevertheless this change had been announced as early as 1865–66 by a short poem ending with these lines:

> Ah think not you finally triumph, my real self has
>   yet to come forth,
> It shall yet march forth o'ermastering, till all lies be-
>   neath me,
> It shall yet stand up the soldier of ultimate victory.[23]

Thus a theme which appears at a given moment generally has its origin in a previous edition where it existed only as a germ. But the germ has invisibly developed in the interval and suddenly comes to light. It seems to be new, but it has been there for several years abiding its time. Whitman described this germination himself in one of his poems, "Unseen Buds." [24]

However, this slow, tenacious, and apparently regular evolution was actually interrupted by crises in the life of the poet. He himself compared his existence to a long sea voyage in the course of which the ship seemed several times about to sink: ". . . some lengthen'd ship-voyage, wherein more than once the last hour had apparently arrived, and we seem'd certainly going down — yet reaching port in a sufficient way through all discomfitures at last. . ." [25]

There was no exaggeration in that; as we shall see, each new edition marked a victory and was the resolution of a spiritual crisis. Accordingly I must precede my critical study with a biographical introduction in which I shall disentangle the complex relations that linked his life with his work. For if his life determined his work, his work in turn had an influence on his life. He tried to embody himself in *Leaves of Grass,* he hoped that his book would be inseparable from himself, that the one would be impossible to distinguish from the other.

> Camerado, this is no book,
> Who touches this touches a man. . .

he said at the end of "Songs of Parting." [26] His subject was first of all himself: "I celebrate myself, and sing myself. . ." he proclaimed in 1855 at the beginning of "Song of Myself"; [27] or, as he explained in 1888 in "A Backward Glance o'er Travel'd Roads":

"Leaves of Grass" indeed (I cannot too often reiterate) has

mainly been the outcropping of my own emotional and other personal nature — an attempt, from first to last, to put *a Person,* a human being (myself, in the latter half of the Nineteenth Century, in America,) freely, fully and truly on record. I could not find any similar personal record in current literature that satisfied me.[28]

But he dreamed of himself as a prophet of a new evangel and it was in that aspect that he portrayed himself; therefore it was necessary for him to try to resemble his own portrait if he wanted it to be a good likeness. He was obliged to shape both his life and his work at once. And he was very clearly aware of the duality of the task which he had imposed on himself, if we may believe what he said in a review of the first edition of *Leaves of Grass* that he himself wrote for the Brooklyn *Daily Times:* "First be yourself what you would show in your poem. . ." [29] Accordingly he was led to treat his life as a work of art, to make of his life and his book two parallel, always superimposable creations:

> On, on the same, ye jocund twain!
> My life and recitative, containing birth, youth, mid-
> age years,
> Fitful as motley-tongues of flame, inseparably twined
> and merged in one — combining all,
> My single soul. . .[30]

This is why W. B. Yeats in *A Vision* takes Whitman as an example of what he calls "an artificial personality." [31]

In order to resemble the mythical personage of the book, the one Whitman wanted to be but was not, he was often obliged to distort the facts somewhat. In particular, in his first edition, he completely suppressed his past as a journalist and a man of letters and passed himself off as an uneducated but inspired carpenter, as a "rough." [32] Is it then necessary to accuse him of duplicity and imposture, to reproach him for his "pose" as Esther Shephard has done? [33] This would be to misconceive the complexity of the problem. When Whitman made such affirmations, he was perfectly sincere. He really identified himself in imagination with the man he wanted to be. To a certain extent he became the ideal being of whom he dreamed and thus lived the part he had written for himself. He was so firmly persuaded of his own absolute sincerity that he made complete frankness one of the criteria for the recognition of great poets: "The great poets are . . . to be known by the absence in them of tricks and by the justification of perfect personal candor." [34]

There is no justification for speaking of a "pose" in the case of Whitman, for that would be to take up again the whole problem of sincerity and to affirm with J. P. Sartre that "a man is never anything but an imposture," [35] or with Valéry that "every work of art is a fake." [36] Let us say, then, quite simply that Whitman wanted to create a book and that in so doing he has created himself. His whole life was changed by his decision, thus illustrating Oscar Wilde's paradox that nature imitates art. He was tormented, unstable, storm-tossed; [37] his work allowed him to recover his equilibrium and achieve serenity. His poetry saved him. By its means he gradually escaped the dark and stormy chaos where he had been floundering and emerged in an orderly, peaceful universe where light overcame dark.[38]

These considerations explain why I have divided this work into two main parts, one a biographical introduction devoted to the "Creation of a Personality," the other a critical study in which I shall try to analyze the "Creation of a Book" and to examine the evolution of the great themes of *Leaves of Grass* and the development of Whitman's art.

CHAPTER I

YOUTH — THE UNSUCCESSFUL QUEST

 BEFORE arriving at the crucial years which saw the birth of *Leaves of Grass,* it will be well to examine briefly the youth of the poet in order to bring out certain elements which will contribute to a better understanding of his work — and project an indirect light upon it, clarifying some of its aspects, without, however, fully explaining it or determining with certainty the reasons for its extraordinary emergence. For, though we can follow the how of things, their why will escape us. True, we shall establish a certain number of causal relations to account for the more superficial aspects of the work, but the underlying cause will remain obscure; only the study of its later development will allow us to catch glimpses of that.

Walter Whitman was born at West Hills, a small country hamlet on Long Island, on May 31, 1819. (Walt Whitman was not to be born until some thirty-five years later at the same time as *Leaves of Grass.*) Through his mother, he was descended from Welsh Quaker sailors and Dutch farmers; through his father, from colonists of English origin.[1] Later, it was his Dutch ancestors whom he mentioned with greater pleasure, attributing to them some of the virtues of which he was most proud: his physical strength and perfect health, his taste for cleanliness, his moral seriousness, and a tenacity which at times amounted almost to stubbornness.[2] But he

probably owed something also to his English ancestors, his
mystic idealism for instance. He belonged therefore to a class
of simple rural people of plain manners, whose rough life he
described later in magazine articles and in his memoirs.[3] All
of his early childhood was spent in the country. Soon, however, his father sold the farm at West Hills (which still exists
hardly changed), and moved to Brooklyn, probably in the hope
of making a better living by practicing the trade of carpentering. The father, also named Walter, was a rather enigmatic
person; an admirer of Thomas Paine and Elias Hicks, a sub-
scriber to the *Free Inquirer* of Frances Wright, he seems to
have had a hard, self-contained, independent character,[4] ac-
commodating himself poorly to the ground rules of a mercantile
society. A mediocre and dissatisfied farmer, he apparently succeeded no better as a builder of frame-houses in Brooklyn.
Whitman's family was continually forced to abandon too
heavily mortgaged houses.[5] Whitman was probably thinking
of him when he described:

> The father, strong, self-sufficient, manly, mean, anger'd,
>   unjust,
> The blow, the quick loud word, the tight bargain, the
>   crafty lure. . .[6]

Hardly a flattering portrait, but, as he himself admitted,[7] Whitman preferred the women in his family. Still some of the traits
of his own character may be seen in this uncongenial father:
his instability, his relative indifference to worldly success, and
his taste for independence.

In those days Brooklyn was not yet connected by bridges to
New York; it was only an overgrown village and young Whitman continued to lead there the fairly rural life he has described in *Specimen Days*.[8] A seaside existence, too, marked
by frequent fishing or bathing parties on the coast and long
solitary walks on the immense deserted beaches.[9] One can im-

agine him silently absorbing the beauty of the countryside and all the sights it offered his eager eyes. He must have been somewhat like that child whose experiences he has recorded in one of his poems:

> The early lilacs became part of this child,
> And grass and white and red morning-glories, and white and red clover, and the song of the phoebe-bird,
> And the Third-month lambs and the sow's pink-faint litter, and the mare's foal and the cow's calf,
> And the noisy brood of the barnyard or by the mire of the pond-side,
> And the fish suspending themselves so curiously below there, and the beautiful curious liquid,
> And the water-plants with their graceful flat heads, all became part of him.
> The field-sprouts of Fourth-month and Fifth-month became part of him,
> Winter-grain sprouts and those of the light-yellow corn, and the esculent roots of the garden,
> And the apple-trees cover'd with blossoms and the fruit afterward, and wood-berries, and the commonest weeds by the road,
> And the old drunkard staggering home from the out-house of the tavern whence he had lately risen,
> And the schoolmistress that pass'd on her way to the school,
> And the friendly boys that pass'd, and the quarrelsome boys,
> And the tidy and fresh-cheek'd girls, and the barefoot negro boy and girl,
> And all the changes of city and country wherever he went.[10]

We may imagine him also barefoot at night on the shore of the sea, his hair blown by the wind, listening by moonlight to the sad song of the mockingbird like the child he describes in "Out of the Cradle Endlessly Rocking." [11]

These joys, however, were not unmixed, for he also had to go to school. But this bondage was short, for he stopped at the age of eleven,[12] with no regret if we may believe "Beginning My Studies." [13] This was the only formal education he ever received. In 1830, his parents, finding his upkeep a burden (he was the second of seven children),[14] placed him as an errand boy with a lawyer, then with a doctor. But young Whitman loved to read, and fortunately his first employer encouraged him by giving him a subscription to a circulating library. He was then able to plunge with delight into the *Arabian Nights* and the novels of Walter Scott. For the rest of his life he had a special affection for Scott, for the ballads as well as the fiction.[15]

A more important event in his education was his entry into journalism. It was, to be sure, by the back door, since he began very modestly as an apprentice-typesetter for the *Long Island Patriot* in Brooklyn, which then had about five hundred subscribers. Nevertheless this humble beginning was very important for Whitman.[16] He learned several things that were later useful to him, for in years to come each new edition of *Leaves of Grass* was planned not only poetically but also typographically. He attached the greatest importance to page make-up, to punctuation, to the choice of type. Once he even sacrificed nine verses to preserve a blank space, because, he said, he did not love his lines enough to let them spoil the effect of a page.[17] He always closely supervised the work of his printers, and when at the end of his life he could no longer go out, he sent them very detailed instructions in writing.

On the other hand, at that time when American journalism in the small towns was still a craft and not yet an industry, the workmen were not specialized and could be at the same time typographers and journalists.[18] Whitman's fellow-employees accordingly taught him writing as well as typesetting. We should also remember that the editorial room of a small-town newspaper was an ideal post of observation; there he could observe life and obtain a working knowledge of politics. There was in fact little news in these small papers. Most of the articles were devoted to political questions and campaign propaganda. He also had occasion to learn the history of his city and his country. An old printer on the *Patriot* had taken part in the Revolutionary War and had seen General Washington, and Whitman listened with fascination to his reminiscences.[19] Several of his historical poems are probably poetic transpositions of the stories of old Hartshorne.

Thus, between the ages of twelve and sixteen, Whitman worked for various papers in Brooklyn and New York, for he was soon drawn to New York, where he lived from May 1835 to May 1836.[20] When he described the misadventures of Franklin Evans, his temperance hero in search of a room in New York, he probably used recollections from this period of his life.[21] He no doubt preferred New York to Brooklyn because he was already a devotee of the theater,[22] and there was no theater in Brooklyn, then a suburban town of 30,000 inhabitants.[23] We may wonder why he did not stay in New York. The reason is apparently that he lost his job, like the hero of "The Shadow and the Light of a Young Man's Soul,"[24] as a result of the great fire which ravaged the city in 1835 and caused serious unemployment for several months.

He was therefore forced to return to Long Island and this time completely changed his occupation. He became a schoolmaster for nearly five years from 1836 to 1841, but he did not lead a completely sedentary life, for he taught in seven different schools and for several months was the sole publisher of a newspaper.

After a solid year of city life he thus found himself again in the country, for he taught in small village schools[25] and boarded in the homes of the farmers. This gave him a chance to mix more closely than he ever had before in the life of the country people on Long Island. He took part in their holidays if not in their work and joined them in fishing parties and boating excursions.[26] They accepted him as one of themselves. And yet he was already different, even in his methods of teaching. In particular, he did not believe in corporal punishment and refused to whip his students as much out of respect for humanity as out of his distaste for violence. He even wrote a very melodramatic story, "Death in a School-Room," to show the terrible dangers children might run from the brutality of a teacher.[27] He also disapproved of mechanical methods of teaching. His ideal, as he expressed it several years later in the Brooklyn *Eagle*,[28] was a good head rather than a full one. He tried above all to awaken his pupils' intelligence. Even at this time he wanted his disciples to be independent of their master and even to surpass him.[29]

He had at this period a well-established reputation as a shameless idler [30] and an incorrigible dreamer, if we are to believe the testimony of Mrs. Orvetta Hall Brenton, at whose stepmother's home in Jamaica he boarded for some time.[31] No doubt, like all adolescents, he was dreaming of the glorious future which awaited him. Since in his case some of these dreams came true, they are worth examining. We know the content of some, thanks to a series of articles he published in the *Long Island Democrat* in 1840. We find this in particular among his youthful effusions:

I think that if I should make pretensions to be a philosopher, and should determine to edify the world with what would add to the number of those sage and ingenious theories which do already so much abound, I would compose a wonderful and ponderous book. Therein should be treated on, the nature and peculiarities of men, the diversity of their characters, the means of improving their state, and the proper mode of governing nations. . . Nobody, I hope, will accuse me of conceit in these opinions of my own capacity for doing great things. In good truth, I think the world suffers from this much-bepraised modesty. Who should be a better judge of a man's talents than the man himself? I see no reason why we should let our lights shine under bushels. Yes: I *would* write a book! And who shall say that it might not be a very pretty book? Who knows but that I might do something very respectable? [32]

Evidently he already had in mind the project he undertook fifteen years later; however, the notion of the great book which he would write was still extremely vague; he speaks of a work in prose and was probably thinking of some political treatise, for at that time he was much interested in politics. This interest was natural since he had been initiated into it in the printing and editorial rooms of Brooklyn and New York. During the fall of 1840 he took an active part in the electoral campaign in Queens County [33] and made himself conspicuous in his zeal and a certain talent in public speaking; for on July 29, 1841, he was invited by the bosses of Tammany Hall to speak at New York before some ten thousand people.[34] He was only twenty-two, and it looked as if he had a brilliant career ahead of him. However he did not persist in this course. Probably his indolent temperament prompted him to abandon so absorbing an occupation, and it is likely also that he was too idealistic to be satisfied for long with the dirty work of local politics.

This period of his life was very full and in *Specimen Days* he emphasized its importance. It was especially rich in various human contacts, particularly when he was boarding with the parents of his students at their farms.[35] He also took advantage of the leisure his profession granted him for reading and beginning to write. From 1838 to 1841, he contributed to the *Long Island Democrat* a series of ten articles under the general title of "Sun-Down Papers — From the Desk of a School-master" [36] and also several poems.[37] He wanted to write, but the result of his efforts was still mediocre. The articles were naïve and artless, and the poems were unoriginal treatments of conventional feelings about death and the vanity of earthly glory. Their form was traditional and awkward. Nothing suggested the future author of *Leaves of Grass* except the frequency with which he recurred to the theme of death.

His need to write — or perhaps, more simply, his taste for journalism — was so strong that for eight or ten months he abandoned teaching completely and devoted all his time to a small biweekly, the *Long Islander*, which he edited, printed, and delivered himself. This adventure lasted from June 1838 to the spring of 1839.[38] Whitman, it seems, soon became tired of this much too regular work. The paper appeared at longer and longer intervals and finally stopped completely: a good example of his lack of perseverance in all the enterprises which require business sense; a proof also that he was able on occasion to shake his indolence and take the initiative. But at this time he was not only trying to express himself in writing, he was also training himself in the art of speaking. This effort began several years before he took an active part in political campaigns. When he was teaching school at Smithtown in 1837 he belonged to a debating society of which he even became secretary, and the minutes of the debates, which survive, show that he was one of the most eloquent members of this rural forum.[39] It was a symptom both of intellectual curiosity and of his constant desire to express himself and communicate with others.

Another striking trait of his youth which may be inferred from all this was his extreme love of independence. He left home when he was only fourteen and without any help or much education succeeded in establishing himself respectably outside his family. This must have been something of a wrench, for he was very attached to his brothers and sisters and he passionately loved his mother. It looks almost as if he were running away, and he probably was. Most of his biographers have painted his family in tender and idyllic tones, but recent investigations have revealed a much less attractive reality.[40] The elder Walter Whitman was, as we have already seen, a hasty and violent man, soured by failure, somber and morose. The mother was perfect in Whitman's eyes and he adored her, but she was often ill and, being illiterate, could not understand his ambitions. Edward, his youngest brother, born in 1815, was a congenital idiot, and the oldest, Jesse, was syphilitic and was to die in an insane asylum. Andrew, who was probably also infected, tried to forget his troubles by drinking and soon became a habitual drunkard. He later married a woman not much better than himself. After he died of tuberculosis or cancer of the throat, his widow sent their children out to beg in the streets and herself became a prostitute. Hannah, one of the sisters, after her marriage, became neurasthenic and probably showed signs of instability even during Whitman's youth. No wonder that he felt the need to escape and this flight for a time was his salvation.

In May of 1841 he ran away still farther and established himself once more in New York.[41] He threw himself wholeheartedly into the whirl of city life to make up for the long rustic interlude. His career was now as uncertain, if not as varied, as it had been in Long Island. He began as a typesetter for the *New World* and in 1842 worked as a reporter for various democratic papers, the *Aurora*, the *Sun*, the *Tattler*. In 1843 he was on the staff of the *Statesman*, a biweekly, and contributed at the same time to the *Democratic Review*.[42] The following year he campaigned in the *Democrat* for Silas Wright, a radical Democrat.[43] These continual shifts do not necessarily indicate his instability. They were due as much to the journalistic conditions of the time as to his own temperament. In this fast-growing city, newspapers started up and died with astonishing rapidity. Their polemic character made them extremely vulnerable to the reverses of politics. At any rate, the speed with which Whitman found a new job whenever he lost one shows that he was well thought of. Unfortunately nothing has survived of what he wrote in these ephemeral sheets, and we know this period of his life only by what he said of it later. There is also, to be sure, the description left by William Cauldwell, one of his colleagues on the *Aurora*:

> He was tall and graceful in appearance, neat in attire, and possessed a very pleasing and impressive eye and a cheerful, happy-looking countenance. He usually wore a frock-coat and a high hat, carried a small cane, and the lapel of his coat was almost invariably ornamented with a boutonnière.[44]

This description corresponds closely to the way Whitman looks in a daguerreotype apparently taken at about that time and which can still be seen today at his house in Camden.[45]

He had become very different from the country schoolmaster of a short time before or the editor-printer of the *Long Islander* who made the round of his subscribers in a cart. He was now almost a dandy. The change was complete. Instead of being in love with the open air and vast spaces, he seemed now to dream only of walks on Broadway, of cafés and theaters. He was transformed into a city-man and the crowd was his element. In 1846 he returned to Brooklyn as chief editor of the *Eagle* and he kept the job for two years, but every day after work he took the ferry early in the afternoon and passed the rest of the day in New York. He was interested in everything: the art exhibits, the new Egyptian museum, the theater, the opera, the fires, the movement of ships in the harbor, and above all, the countless crowds in the streets. His favorite pastime was to ride the Broadway omnibus seated beside the driver, gossiping familiarly with him or declaiming verses which were lost in the noise,[46] or observing with untiring interest the flood of humanity on the sidewalks which later inspired him to write the poem "Faces."[47]

He hoarded sensations, noted attitudes, gestures, cries, and

odors, and later poured them all out in long catalogues in the
first edition of *Leaves of Grass.* These loungings were not a
loss of time. They enriched him, allowed him to add to his
collection of picturesque sketches and develop the sense, which
was so strong in him, of the unanimous life of a great city, of
what he later called humanity "en-masse."

What part he himself took in that life cannot be known.
Was he simply a spectator or did he participate intensely?
There is no reliable information on this point. According to
Burroughs,

> Through this period (1840–1855), without entering into par-
> ticulars, it is enough to say that he sounded all experiences of life,
> with all their passions, pleasures and abandonments. He was
> young, in perfect bodily condition, and had the city of New
> York and its ample opportunities around him.

And he adds:

> I trace this period in some of the poems of "Children of Adam"
> and occasionally in other parts of his book, including "Calamus." [48]

Perhaps; but these are, as we shall see, only conjectures. The
Whitman of this period escapes our grasp. He was already
pregnant with his masterpiece, but nothing as yet in what he
wrote or did gave any indication of it.

There was nothing exceptional in his editorials for the
Brooklyn *Daily Eagle.*[49] They were honest articles, good journalism and nothing more. They do contain ideas that later
appeared in *Leaves of Grass*, but they were written in a sloppy
style without force or distinction, rather in the tone, as Canby
suggests,[50] of a talk on the radio. They are familiar asides to
the reader, not cries sounded "over the roofs of the world." [51]
Even the titles are flat and characterless. For example, he
wrote an editorial with the banal title "Morbid Appetite for
Money," [52] whereas he stigmatized the same vice with much

more vigor in *Leaves of Grass* as "the mania of owning things," in which his scorn and anger come through.[53]

If we compare his description of a New York fire in the Brooklyn *Eagle* [54] with its evocation in "Song of Myself," [55] we can hardly believe that the two are the work of the same author. The first was written by an idler gaping at the crowd and the firemen, afraid of tripping over the hoses, by a reporter short of copy who filled his article with commonplaces on human misfortune and with moral platitudes such as this:

And those crumbled ashes! what comforts were entombed there — what memories of affection and brotherhood — what preparation, never to be consummated — what hopes, never to see their own fruition — fell down as the walls fell down, and were crushed as they were crushed! [56]

There is no personal emotion in all this, only conventional phrases and sentimental banalities that do not involve the author's feelings. On the contrary, the poet who wrote "Song of Myself" was fully involved, he was at the center of the drama, he was the fireman buried in the debris, he was the fireman's comrades who feverishly dug to free him, he was the silent crowd who waited and trembled for him. Instead of the curious and detached idler recording all the details of some scene of the street, he intensely lived through a personal tragedy, he participated profoundly and succeeded in making us participate also. It may be symptomatic that the journalist used the past and the poet the present tense. The one reports and the other re-creates. The same comparison can be made between his descriptions of the Brooklyn ferry. The journalist in search of anecdotes amused himself watching people run when the bell rang for departure and good-naturedly mocked his contemporaries' habitual hurry. He gossiped familiarly with his "gentle reader," for, he said, "we like that time-honoured phrase." [57] He was still far from being the poet who, crossing the ferry, meditated on himself and on the future of the world, addressing all men and all women in all times.[58]

Nevertheless the journalist was the same man as the poet, and the editorial writer of the Brooklyn *Eagle* survived in the author of *Leaves of Grass*, which Emerson called "a combination of the *Baghavat-Gita* and the *New York Herald*." [59] The poet, in fact, owed something to the journalist: he often has the same familiarity and simplicity of expression. It is apparent that he has worked in editorial rooms and that this experience has freed him from the mannerisms and affectations which marred his early stories. He avoids literary effects, conventional expressions, and poetic clichés. Above all, journalism opened his mind. The young countryman of Long Island, the provincial Brooklynite, has had a revelation in New York of the immensity of his country and the world. It was probably there that he acquired that cosmic sense which characterizes his poetry and at the same time his lively feeling for the grandeur and the tremendous future of the United States. His political and social views were equally enlarged; many opinions of the chief editor of the Brooklyn *Eagle* are to be found in *Leaves of Grass*.

He kept his job for two years. It was the first time that he had remained so long in the same place. According to some reports [60] the paper lost subscribers during his editorship, and therefore the proprietor, one Isaac Van Anden, took the first opportunity to relieve himself of an unpopular editor. The occasion presented itself early in 1848. The Mexican War was about to end and the problem of the extension of slavery to the territories was posed with new sharpness. Whitman was not an abolitionist, but he wanted the West to be colonized only by free men who would not have to fear the competition of cheap slave labor. He became therefore a "free-soiler," that is, a Democrat who much to the horror of the Southern Democrats advocated the prohibition of slavery in the territories. Such a policy might have led to a schism in the Democratic camp. For this reason the conservatives in the party did their best to prevent the movement from developing, and that is probably why, according to some, Van Anden demanded that Whitman stop sustaining the free-soilers. But Whitman apparently refused and was dismissed in January 1848.[61]

If so, he lost his job — a job which he must have liked since he remained in it so long — for refusing to compromise on a question of principles: a fine case of disinterestedness and an early manifestation of an obstinacy of which he gave many further proofs. It was probably the only reason for his rupture with Van Anden, who, in all likelihood, would not have waited two years to get rid of him if his direction of the paper had been as disastrous as some biographers have thought. The theory of a political disagreement seems the best explanation of his sudden departure.[62]

At any rate, he had no difficulty in finding a new position. There had been some talk of his becoming editor of a barn-burner paper in Brooklyn,[63] but the project never materialized, probably for lack of funds. However, there was no need for Whitman to be disappointed, for in February, in the lobby of a New York theater, he met one McClure, who was part-owner of a New Orleans paper and who after a quarter-hour's conversation hired Whitman as an assistant editor and gave him an advance of two hundred dollars. This promised well, but in fact the paper, called the *Crescent*, did not yet exist and did not begin to appear until March. However, McClure, who had come North to procure the necessary equipment, had plenty of money at his disposal and success seemed sure.[64] Of course there was no question of Whitman's writing editorials. His free-soil articles would have been somewhat out of place in a southern newspaper. McClure needed a reporter, and more important, a journalist able to select and rewrite, as the custom was, articles from northern newspapers. He must have been delighted to have found a man with the experience of Whitman who for two years had competently directed the largest journal in a city of 60,000 inhabitants.

Thus, on February 11, 1848, Whitman left Brooklyn with his younger brother Jeff on his way to New Orleans. He was twenty-nine years old, but it was the first time that he had made so long a journey. It took him two weeks: the train went only as far as Cumberland, Maryland, and from there he had to take a stage-coach to Wheeling, from which point steamboats descended the Ohio and then the Mississippi. This trip must have been a revelation for Whitman, yet the account of it which he has left is rather dull. He did publish in the first three issues of the *Crescent* his notes on the stretch from Baltimore to Cairo. But they were extremely prosaic. He carefully recorded the prices of tickets and meals, but the descriptions were sketchy and prosaic and the picturesque details scarce.[65] He had not been insensible to the beauties of the countryside, for he deplored the fact that no American painter had yet turned it to account. In a way, he was already indicating his own program in this passage: an American artist, instead of trying to copy or imitate his European predecessors, should make an effort to express what was characteristic of his own country in an original way.[66] However, he had been sometimes disappointed. The Ohio in particular struck him as having been overpraised. This great river with its muddy water was decidedly unworthy of the poems which had been devoted to it.[67] But, if the landscape did not come up to his expectations, he was nevertheless favorably impressed by the quality of the men whom he met on the way: ". . . I was by no means prepared for the sterling vein of common sense that seemed to pervade them — even the roughest shod and roughest clad of all."[68]

This first contact with the West accordingly confirmed the hopes he had conceived before visiting it.[69] Moreover he was pleased with the prosperity of the region, the abundance which seemed to reign everywhere. His experience on this trip, even though it does not appear in the plain and dry notes which he published, must have reinforced his faith in democracy and in the future of the United States.

He was also sensitive to the beauty and grandeur of the Mississippi, which inspired him to write "The Mississippi at Midnight," but these stilted quatrains were still far from *Leaves of Grass*. The images were as conventional as stage props and only one stanza in which two present participles echo each other in an effort to suggest the incessant flow of the river and of life feebly foretells what was to come.[70]

But, if the West impressed him, New Orleans enchanted him. The climate, the vegetation, the people, the customs were all new to him and filled him with wonder. He never tired of walking through the town during the ample free time which his work on the *Crescent* allowed him. He found there an easy way of living unknown in New York and Brooklyn, and above all, it showed him a richer and healthier sensual life, unfettered by puritanism. He expanded in this freer atmosphere. A few years before he had hardly dared to speak of women, because, he said, "it behoves a modest personage like myself not to speak upon a class of beings of whose nature, habits, notions, and ways he has not been able to gather any knowledge, either by experience or observation." [71] He now devoted a whole article to Miss Dusky Grisette, a quadroon who sold flowers every evening in the open air close to where he lived. Her beauty and her charming smile delighted him.[72] In his old age he still spoke with admiration of the New Orleans octoroons, "women with splendid bodies — no bustles, no corsets, no enormities of any sort: large, luminous rich eyes: face a rich olive: habits indolent, yet not lazy as we define laziness North: fascinating, magnetic, sexual, ignorant, illiterate: always more than pretty — 'pretty' is too weak a word to apply to them." [73]

He was also pleased with the French quarter. He liked to walk in its narrow streets with their strange-looking houses and to hear the people around him speaking a language that he did not understand. He felt as if he had been transported into the Old World. He tried, through what he saw, to imagine Europe and its curious customs. He went, for instance, to the St. Louis Cathedral on Maundy Thursday, and although he had been reared in the simplicity and austerity of the Quaker faith, he never thought of criticizing the somewhat theatrical pomp of the catholic liturgy. On the contrary, he was struck by the fervor of the worshipers and immediately understood the underlying meaning of the bizarre ceremonies, namely that beauty might be an important aspect of religion.[74] This shows the openness of his mind and foretells the universal sympathy he was to proclaim in *Leaves of Grass*.

The taste for French and Spanish words with which he later sprinkled his poems probably also originated from this period. They were already appearing in his articles for the *Crescent*.[75] Even if he later borrowed from books the ones used in *Leaves of Grass*, they nonetheless had a sentimental value which dated back to his walks through the picturesque streets of New Orleans.

His visit to Louisiana was thus marked essentially by the discovery of a Latin culture of which he probably had no previous knowledge and of a semitropical vegetation, the splendor of which he celebrated several years later with nostalgia.[76] According to some biographers, he also had at this time a touching and almost tragic love affair. Henry Bryan Binns was the first to circulate this strange and tenacious myth by reporting in his biography that Whitman had had a liaison in New Orleans with a woman from a higher social rank than his own. He even said boldly that a child was born of this union, perhaps several children, but that, because of family opposition, Whitman was unable to marry the one he loved and even formally to recognize his children.[77] Binns unfortunately was unable to give any proof of this romantic tale, for it was nothing but a conjecture which he applied to a set of imprecise and hardly verifiable facts. The most plausible of the documents he invoked was the reply that Whitman later made to John Addington Symonds, who had urged him to clarify the meaning and scope of "Calamus." Whitman — and we will have occasion to return to this point — evaded the question with this avowal: "My life, young manhood, mid-age, times South, etc., have been jolly bodily, and doubtless open to criticism. Tho' unmarried I have had six children — two are dead — one living, Southern grandchild, fine boy, writes to me occasionally — circumstances (connected with their fortune and benefit) have separated me from intimate relations." [78]

He also alluded several times in talking with Horace Traubel — very vaguely however — to his illegitimate children,[79] but we shall see later what was behind this impudent falsehood which was apparently intended to camouflage one whole aspect of his life. At any rate, none of this evidence lends any credibility to the tale imagined by Binns. The hypothesis was certainly tempting, the more so as Binns supposed that the mysterious lady was a high-born Creole, romantic, sensual, noble, and passionate, who "opened the gates for him and showed him himself in the divine mirror of her love." [80]

Léon Bazalgette with his usual enthusiasm devoted one whole chapter of his biography to this pretty story under the enticing title of "Vers le sud et vers l'amour de la femme." [81] Even Basil de Selincourt let himself be seduced by this myth, and worse still, Emory Holloway, after successfully resisting the temptation in the preface to his edition of Whitman's uncollected papers,[82] succumbed in his turn when he wrote his biography.[83]

Another argument invoked by the partisans of this romance

is that Whitman did not really begin to be himself until after his return from New Orleans. They claim that the shock of this great passion suddenly made of him the poet that we know. I shall have to return to this question, but my purpose for the moment is only to indicate roughly the established exterior facts which marked Whitman's life up to the appearance of his masterpiece. It must be noted at this point that the earliest verses which he wrote in the manner of *Leaves of Grass* (that we know of) are found in a manuscript notebook dated 1847 — that is to say, a year before his departure for the South.[84] The love-affair hypothesis accordingly explains nothing and loses its *raison d'être*.

It seemed very convenient, though, because it furnished an explanation not only for the sudden birth of Whitman's genius but also for his hasty departure from New Orleans after a stay of exactly three months. But here again we can do very well without it. The facts explain themselves. Whitman recorded them in a notebook which has survived, and there is no reason to doubt the truth of his account since this memorandum was not intended for publication. According to him, after a time, Hayes and McClure, the proprietors of the *Crescent*, began to show a singular coldness toward him and an ungracious reluctance to discuss the politics of the paper with him. He became haughty in his turn, and finally, when they refused him an advance to which he thought he had a right, he offered his resignation, which they accepted.[85] He seems to have been surprised at their eagerness to get rid of him;[86] he was probably unprepared to lose so quickly a remunerative job in which he had hoped to make savings in order to buy a small farm on Long Island.[87] However, he made a virtue of necessity and decided to leave New Orleans at once. The reason for his departure was therefore purely professional and not at all sentimental. In all probability he was forced to leave not because of his work, but because of his political opinions. The articles he selected or rewrote for the paper must to some extent have reflected his convictions as a free-soiler, whether he so intended or not.[88] Hence, no doubt, the unwillingness of Hayes and McClure to discuss with him the policy of the *Crescent* as soon as they became aware of his intransigence. They very likely expected more flexibility on his part. Accordingly, when he asked for an advance, they may have refused it under the pretext that the two hundred dollars McClure had given him in New York was to be considered not as a payment for the expenses of the trip but as an initial advance on his salary. If they had wanted to keep him, they would have been more generous. Whitman must have realized this and preferred to leave — but not without regret, as is shown by the parenthesis added in pencil to his notes in which he referred to "some objections on the part of me."

Jean Catel speaks of Whitman's nostalgia and of his desire to return to his family.[89] This, I think, is an exaggeration. Certainly Whitman intended to return to Long Island, but not so soon. He had no intention of living permanently in the South, but for the moment it attracted him strongly. New Orleans had conquered him at once, and he enjoyed his work there. Nothing in either his personal journal or in what he published later suggests that he was in any hurry to leave. To speak of his nostalgia is to attribute to him the feelings of his brother Jeff, who did want to return as quickly as possible.[90] This is understandable since Jeff was only fifteen and was away from home for the first time. He felt very far from his family — all the more so since in those days a letter took several weeks to go from Brooklyn to New Orleans. The brothers were there for a whole month without receiving any mail.[91] Whitman recorded this fact in his notebook, but without any undue emotion. The theory of home-sickness does not seem to hold in his case, and the only possible reason for his sudden departure therefore must be simply and solely a disagreement with the owners of the paper, apparently on political grounds. This is a rather prosaic and matter-of-fact account which lacks the charm of Binns's romantic fable and which unfortunately offers no ready-made explanation for the genesis of *Leaves of Grass*, but it has the advantage of leaving the field clear for an unprejudiced study of the problem.

Whitman returned to Brooklyn, but without haste by way of the Great Lakes, Chicago, Buffalo, Niagara Falls, and Albany. Leaving New Orleans on May 26, he did not get home until June 15.[92] This leisurely progress does not seem to indicate an overwhelming nostalgia. It is rather the normal conduct of a man who has lost his job, but who is not greatly worried, knowing that he will easily find another.

And that is in fact what happened. By September he had again become chief editor of a Brooklyn free-soil paper, the *Freeman*, which had just been started by the wing of the Democratic Party with which Whitman was in sympathy. There was therefore no break in his career at this particular time. It was as if he had never left home. Apparently nothing in his life had changed, which is another indication that the supposed crisis of New Orleans very probably occurred only in the imagination of over-romantic biographers.

A year later, on September 11, 1849, Whitman resigned from the *Freeman*, and his farewell article to his readers vituperated the Old Hunkers, the conservatives of the Democratic Party.[93] He blamed them for the disunity of the Democrats and for their failure to live up to the hopes he had placed in them during his youth.[94] In fact it seems that at this time he did experience a rather serious political crisis. The exasperation shown by his resignation and by his farewell article apparently grew, for he was soon writing a whole series of political poems in an extremely violent tone. The first of these appeared on March 2, 1850, in Bryant's *Evening Post*, the "Song for Certain Congressmen," a brutal satire written under the pressure of indignation caused by the Compromise of Clay and the attitude of Webster.[95] The next was "Blood-Money," which Horace Greeley published in the New York *Tribune Supplement* on March 22 and which appeared again on April 30 in the New York *Evening Post.*[96] This was the cry of pain and anger of his idealism in revolt against the cowardice of the politicians who had allowed the Fugitive Slave Law to pass. The impetuosity of his inspiration on this occasion was such that the traditional poetic molds broke under the pressure and he used for the first time a kind of free verse which, in a rudimentary way, suggests the rhythm of *Leaves of Grass.* He must have felt that this experiment was a success, for two months later he used the new mode of expression to proclaim in "Resurgemus" his hatred of tyranny and his sympathy for the revolutionary movements of 1848 in Europe.[97] He had now found his voice. This poem was in fact the first of the *Leaves of Grass* and was included in the 1855 edition. All that Whitman needed to do in order to fit it in was to change the typography. In the version of 1850 the poem looks a little meager on the page, but two or three verses together made a line of the desired length in 1855.

Thus the signs multiplied. The masterpiece was on the way. The first rumblings of the coming eruption could already be heard. Let us try to discover what was going on in Whitman's mind without having recourse as yet to *Leaves of Grass.*

At the time of his return from New Orleans in 1848, as we have seen, nothing was changed. He was still a political journalist, and he took an active part in electoral campaigns. The Brooklyn *Freeman,* of which he was chief editor, reported that he was a member of the general committee of the free-soil faction in Ward 7. He was evidently the most influential member because his name was at the top of the list.[98] In August he had been sent by the Brooklyn free-soilers with a delegation of fourteen others to the party convention at Buffalo, where he spoke in favor of Martin Van Buren.[99] It was an exciting time. Everywhere, it seemed, the cause of liberty and democracy was triumphant. In all of Europe insurrectionist movements had been victorious, and tyrants had been overthrown or forced to make concessions to their subjects. In America free-soilers, full of illusions about the idealism of the people, hoped to win in the approaching presidential elections. Unfortunately disappointments soon multiplied. To begin with, Van Buren was not even nominated, and it was General Zachary Taylor, the Whig candidate, who won because of the schism in the Democratic Party. As a result of this defeat many free-soil politicians, feeling that the cause was lost, deserted to the right wing of the Democratic Party, doubtless to Whitman's great disgust. The free-soil minority quickly fell apart.

What was Whitman to do? He could not follow the opportunists and return to Democratic orthodoxy. He was too proud to recant and too much convinced of the justice of the cause to which he was devoted. We can see in this connection why several months earlier he had left the Brooklyn *Eagle* in a huff and why it had been impossible for him to remain longer in New Orleans on a paper that printed along with his articles announcements of slave auctions or descriptions of fugitive Negroes such as Dickens quotes in his *American Notes*.[100] Since there was no question of his becoming a Whig, he found himself without a party, completely left out. In the following months his disgust must have grown as the Dough-Faces increased their concessions to the advocates of slavery and of its extension. His feelings during these crucial years are expressed not only in his 1840 poems, but also in a short prose piece, "Origins of Attempted Secession," which he later reprinted in *Specimen Days*.[101] Even though some of its pages were written long after the period we are examining, they seem to have preserved all of the violent disgust which he had felt at that time.[102] He castigated the delegates to the Democratic convention with a force and virulence unusual for him. For twenty-five lines he throws insults at them, revealing the strength of his anger and hatred against those whom he held responsible for the collapse of all his dreams of peace and harmonious progress.[103] He had good reasons for this grudge, for his darkest forebodings were soon to be realized.

On March 7, 1850, Daniel Webster made his famous speech in support of Clay's compromise resolutions, and in September the Compromise was adopted by Congress. The federal authorities were henceforth required to pursue fugitive slaves in the North and return them to their masters. Many conscientious people rebelled because all citizens, whether they liked it or not, found themselves accomplices of the slave-owners of the South. There was a surge of indignation throughout the North. It was on this occasion that Whittier wrote "Ichabod" and described Daniel Webster's "bright soul" being "driven, fiend-goaded down the endless dark." [104] The gentle Emerson, who was not yet an abolitionist, noted in his Journal shortly after Webster's speech: "He has brought down . . . the free and Christian State of Massachusetts to the Cannibal level." And a little later, when the Fugitive Slave Law was passed, his despair knew no bounds.[105] The intractable Thoreau, though not yet an abolitionist either, had dissociated himself a year earlier from a government which he considered unjust by refusing to pay his poll tax and writing his essay on "Civil Disobedience," for which he had passed a night in the Concord jail. When the crisis came, his resistance, passive before, became active and he declared himself an ardent abolitionist.[106]

Whitman therefore was not the only one who suffered during this trying period. But, unlike Thoreau, he passed from action to inaction. Profoundly discouraged by the opportunism of the politicians, undoubtedly disappointed also by the voters' indifference to the ideas which were dear to him, he gave up active politics for good. He was never again seen on a platform among those

> Terrific screamers of Freedom,
> Who roar and bawl and get hot i' the face. . .[107]

He had been "wounded in the house of friends" [108] and had now realized his mistake. He had not reckoned with the love of money. He had thought all men were devoted to his ideal, but most men apparently wanted only material goods and nothing really touched their hearts without at the same time touching their pockets.[109] He had kept for a long time the illusions formed in his youth, but now his eyes were finally opened — a painful awakening. And yet, at the height of his pain and anger, he did not lose all hope. Let others despair of liberty, he never would.[110] The present was disappointing, so he took refuge in the future. In so doing he was not running away from reality, he was merely trying to nourish his faith with the image of its ultimate triumph. He was not a dilettante who evaded the present, but a visionary who defied it. He now knew the ugliness of reality, yet he did not condemn it. He courageously accepted it as it was. He did not try to beautify it or to forget its flaws and turpitudes, but he was not resigned. He protested, he revolted.

This was the result of the first crisis through which he passed — at least the first that we know of. He did not succumb; he surmounted it and emerged stronger and more sure of himself. He was now a different man from the sentimental and rather naïve dreamer he had formerly been, and different from everybody else too. He knew it, and therefore detached himself from the world in which he had developed thus far and which had seemed to give him complete satisfaction. Not only did he renounce active politics, but he almost completely abandoned journalism. After his resignation from the *Freeman*, his career is difficult to follow; documents are lacking. We know only that he contributed to various newspapers in Brooklyn and New York. In May and June of 1850, for instance, he wrote a series of articles entitled "Paragraph Sketches of Brooklynites" for the Brooklyn *Daily Advertizer*, a Whig paper (apparently he had become indifferent to political labels).[111] The following year he published in the same paper an article recommending that the city authorities undertake the construction of new water-works.[112] The subject is a little surprising, but Whitman had always been interested in such matters of health.[113] What is more surprising is that he maintained this interest during the time when he was working on *Leaves of Grass*. But this detail clearly shows that in spite of the crisis of 1850 there was no cleavage in his career and that there never would be. The journalist would always continue to coexist with the poet and the poet would never be indifferent to the fate of his city. He was not exaggerating when he declared in *Leaves of Grass*:

> This is the city and I am one of the citizens;
> Whatever interests the rest interests me. . . . politics,
>   churches, newspapers, schools,
> Benevolent societies, improvements, banks, tariffs,
>   steamships, factories, markets,
> Stocks and stores and real estate and personal estate.[114]

He demonstrated this interest in 1854 when he protested vigorously against the decision of the Brooklyn City Council to prohibit the running of street-cars and to force the closing of restaurants on Sunday in order to compel everyone willy nilly to observe the Sabbath. On this occasion he stated a principle which he was soon to proclaim in his poems: the representatives of the people must never forget that they are only representatives and that their duty is to act in the interest of all, not to tyrannize. The duty of the citizen, on the other hand, is not to obey but to make his will respected.[115]

Probably the most interesting piece that he wrote during

this period was his essay on "Art and Artists" which he read before the Brooklyn Art Union on March 31, 1851.[116] In this he raised, as an artist, the same protest that he had launched as a politician in "Blood-Money" against the materialism of the American people and their worship of the dollar. But it is evident that he had now found his way. It did not matter to him if others thought of nothing but running after honors and money; he preferred to be like that idler who lived in Persia hundreds and hundreds of years before and who replied when they asked him what he was good for: "to perceive [the] beauty [of this rose] and to smell its perfume." [117]

As a matter of fact this was not altogether his ideal. He did not want such an extreme detachment. He wanted to keep in touch with the rest of humanity, to share the life of the people, fighting along with them against their oppressors and guiding them in their struggle for liberty. The example he proposed was Socrates and, greater than Socrates, Christ.[118] The artist, according to him, should be the champion of the people and the advocate of the rights of man. That being so, there would be no divorce between art and society. Art would ennoble and sanctify the society that received it.[119] These ideas calmly expressed were those which would be developed more passionately in the 1855 Preface to *Leaves of Grass*.

This was his position after the crisis of 1850 when he was about to throw himself into his great poetic venture. On the one hand, he had a profound desire to live aside from the people and their base preoccupations in order to devote himself entirely to the contemplation of the world's beauty. On the other hand, he wanted to remain committed and to share the destiny of the society and the nation to which he belonged in spite of their unworthiness. In other ways also his life at that time showed his oscillations between the two extremes. As we have seen, he had not lost all contact with his contemporaries. If he no longer took part directly in their conflicts, he did intervene from time to time with newspaper articles. But for the most part he recoiled. He stayed with his family and made his living as a carpenter, working with his father and his brothers:[120] a strange and sudden change of direction. It is hard to say why he chose this trade. He never said himself. No doubt it was an easy way to supply his needs and protect his independence without having to mix in the political struggles with which he was disgusted. It seems to me that we need not see in this any profound desire to sink into the mass of the people or any mystic urge to identify himself with the proletariat by adopting the costume of a laborer and working with his hands, as his hagiographers, especially O'Connor, have supposed.[121] He was no Tolstoy and in any case such changes of status were not unusual in mid-nineteenth-century America. Society was neither very stable nor very stratified and no opprobrium attached to manual labor. It was therefore quite natural for Whitman to escape from the dilemma which his abandonment of journalism had placed him in by becoming a carpenter and thus helping his father whose health was declining (he died in 1855). True, he might have gone back to his old trade and taken a printer's job, but this would have been too close to the situation from which he wished to escape, and after the collapse of all his hopes he probably wanted a complete change of atmosphere.

At any rate, in practice, this solution proved to be ideal. Working with his family he could be at ease and, according to his fancy, either handle the plane and the hammer or step aside in order to dream. If we may believe his brother George, "he would lie abed late, and after getting up would write a few hours if he took the notion — perhaps would go off the rest of the day. We were all at work — all except Walt." [122]

Evidently he was not a very regular worker nor very strongly persuaded of the nobility of the craft he had chosen by chance and as an easy way out. But he probably soon realized how he could turn it to advantage — or rather, to describe the process in a somewhat less objective way, his imagination soon surrounded this prosaic occupation with a poetic halo. He wanted to be a poet of the people, a prophet of democracy, and here he was, dressed like a man of the people and apparently living by the labor of his hands. It was a fortunate coincidence. Circumstances had done away with the young dandy in the impeccable frock-coat who some years earlier had strolled down Broadway with a flower in his lapel and a cane in his hand. In his place was now a worker in canvas trousers and shirt sleeves whose open collar "ne se referma jamais plus, pas même dans la bière où il ful couché," as Bazalgette says with his usual romantic bombast.[123] So he appears in the engraved portrait on the frontispiece of the first edition of *Leaves of Grass*. He resembled then, without trying to at first, later consciously and intentionally perhaps, the man whom he wanted to be. Or it may be that the image of the man whom he wanted to be was formed in his mind under the influence of the man whom, without really intending it, he had already to some extent become. At any rate the work and the personality were taking shape together. The book he was writing in the ample leisure time allowed by his work as an amateur carpenter was subtly changing him. He modeled himself on his book and his book in its turn reflected him. It was a slow growth with many complex exchanges which we can guess at, but which it is impossible for lack of documentation to follow in detail or completely reconstruct. Only the result of this evolution has reached us, and it is toward this that we must now turn our attention.

But first let me recapitulate. We have followed Whitman from his childhood, we have observed his beginnings in journalism and literature, we have learned of his faith in democracy, his angry disappointments, his gropings for a poetic form and an individual style, but we will find it very difficult to arrive at a judgment of value on this early phase of his literary career. We cannot help recognizing that nothing which he had written was better than mediocre. The thinking is often dull and banal and the form undistinguished. No one would ever have exhumed his occasional poems or his newspaper articles if he had not later become the author of a masterpiece. Even his stories, which before 1855 would have been his most likely claim to fame, showed no originality though they had enabled him at an early age to see his name listed in the synopsis of the *Democratic Review* among those of Longfellow, Hawthorne, and Thoreau. He had been a good pupil, sometimes of Poe as in "The Angel of Tears," [124] sometimes of Fenimore Cooper or Hawthorne.[125] With great acumen Jean Catel has read in these stories confessions and thoughts which foretell Whitman's masterpiece, but, if they were examined outside the context of *Leaves of Grass*, none of these writings would have any interest. In themselves they are of no value; they mean something only in relation to what followed them. They precede, but they do not really foretell. They are only the dawn, not the sunrise.

And yet, for several years, an obscure process of germination had been going on — even though no outward sign had appeared. A face had been forming behind the mask of the journalist and of the man of letters — the face of a poet. In *Leaves of Grass* we will discover a new man to whom poetry had granted the power at last to become himself.

CHAPTER II

THE 1855 EDITION — BIRTH OF A POET

ON or about July 4, 1855, there appeared simultaneously in New York and Brooklyn a strange book entitled *Leaves of Grass*. Even its dimensions were unusual, for it was a quarto similar to those of the Elizabethan period. The cover was no less startling, not because of its deep green color, but because of its curious ornamentation. On the front and the back, which were identical, the title stood out in letters of gold. They were no ordinary letters. On close examination, they appeared to be alive, not merely inert characters, but plants with innumerable roots and leaves. The rest of the cover was similarly decorated with leaves and flowers.[1] Such a harmonious matching of the color and the decoration with the title gave notice that this was an exceptional work and a labor of love.[2] But whose? On the cover there was no author's name;[3] nor did it appear on the title page, which gave only this information: *Leaves of Grass*, New York, 1855. Not even a publisher's name. It was necessary to turn the page in order to find in very small print the name of Walter Whitman in the copyright notice. But even this was not the true signature of the work. Whitman had not wanted to be a name, but a presence; he wished to be a man rather than an author, and had therefore placed his portrait at the beginning of the book facing the title page.[4] Here we meet again the Brooklyn carpenter whom we have just left. He has not dressed up to meet his reader. He is wearing his everyday canvas trousers and workman's shirt. He has not even bothered to put on a necktie and the open collar reveals his undershirt. However he has kept his hat on his head, because he uncovers for no one.[5] He does not pose as a thinker. He stands before us in all simplicity, one hand in his pocket, the other on his hip, but not at all in a defiant attitude, for his eyes are those of a dreamer who looks without seeing. He certainly does not see his reader.

For a man who wanted to be so simple and easy the name of Walter is still a little too pretentious, so he renounces it. He uses it here only in the copyright notice. He does not want this barrier between him and us, and on page 29 of the book he presents himself by his nickname: Walt Whitman. Walter Whitman, the journalist, whom we have known thus far is dead; he is replaced henceforth by Walt Whitman, the poet, born on the fourth of July 1855.

As a matter of fact this birth had been in preparation for a long time, though no one knew it. For several years Whitman had been jotting in the little notebooks he always carried in his pockets germs and even long fragments of poems. One of these notebooks at least has survived — there may have been others before — carrying the date 1847. Whitman had therefore begun to use it during the time when he was chief editor of the Brooklyn *Eagle*; but, since the various changes of address he has recorded in it show that he was still using it in 1848, nothing proves that he had begun to write the long passage which foretells "Song of Myself" before his return from New Orleans.[6] The initial date of the gestation period cannot be fixed, but one thing is certain: the process was so slow and so secret that the unexpected appearance of *Leaves of Grass* in 1855 seems an inexplicable miracle. The fact that we are now aware of the beginnings of the book seven or eight years earlier does not change the problem. The mystery remains unsolved. Nothing can explain why, suddenly — or little by little — the idea occurred to this very ordinary journalist, this writer of mediocre accomplishment, to break with all his habits of expression — which were also those of his contemporaries and predecessors — and try to write as no one had ever written before on life and death, on God and men. The difficulty of the problem has stimulated the ingenuity of the critics and various theories have been advanced.

One of these hypotheses which is purely biographical I have already mentioned in passing, that which was invented by Binns [7] and taken up by Bazalgette,[8] Basil de Selincourt,[9] and Emory Holloway.[10] According to them, the explanation is simple: Whitman had in New Orleans the revelation of love; he was overwhelmed by it, and the shock transformed him. A simple journalist when he left New York, he returned four months later a poet of genius — a marvellous metamorphosis from caterpillar to butterfly. Unfortunately we cannot accept this tale. The evidence does not support it and his notebook of 1847–48 indicates that the change may have begun before he visited the South.[11]

The mystic hypothesis formulated by Maurice Bucke is more attractive.[12] According to him, there is not only a difference of degree, but a difference of kind between the pre-1855 Whitman and the author of Leaves of Grass. Whereas most authors develop by a gradual and regular evolution, the career of Whitman is marked by a sharp break, a sudden mutation. The man suddenly changed into a Titan. Bucke explains the mystery by comparing the case of Whitman to those of Buddha, St. Paul, and Mohammed.[13] Like them he had a vision. His soul was filled with joy and ineffable peace, and this ecstasy was accompanied by an illumination. He had the revelation of the presence of God in the world, of the immortality of the soul, of the continuity of creation, and of the universal brotherhood of all living things. This ecstasy marked him forever and was the first sign of the appearance in him of a new faculty which Bucke calls "cosmic consciousness" and which is more commonly designated as mysticism. Bucke estimates that Whitman had this revelation in June 1853 as he was entering his thirty-fifth year[14] and supports this hypothesis by referring to the passage in the 1855 edition of *Leaves of Grass* where the ecstasy is described.[15]

According to Bucke, this initial ecstasy was a consecration, and all of Whitman's works flowed from it. This extraordinary ability to see the spiritual reality behind material appearances never completely died in Whitman. To the very end, in spite of illness and old age, it remained alive. It can still be felt in "Prayer of Columbus" in 1874–75,[16] in "Now Precedent Songs Farewell" in 1888,[17] and even in one of the very last poems, "To the Sunset Breeze."[18] No doubt there is a relation between Whitman's mystical sense and his poetic activity, but this parallelism or coincidence in itself explains nothing. It replaces one mystery by another. To say that Whitman's genius was born of his mysticism does not solve the problem of its sudden appearance. Even if the principle of equivalence which Bucke invokes was just, it would be necessary to carry his analysis further and define more precisely what is meant by "cosmic consciousness." And in any case it would still be impossible to penetrate the mystery of the first ecstasy. Why did it happen in 1853 and not some other year? What spark suddenly set off the explosive mixture which had gradually accumulated in him? Such questions are probably unanswerable. Where mysticism is concerned we can only describe the how of things; the why always evades us. There is also another aspect of the problem that the mystical hypothesis does not account for: the transmutation of the vision into poetry, the reason why Whitman felt the need of translating his revelations poetically instead of merely experiencing them.

Other critics have thought that they could say with certainty

what caused this sudden explosion, notably Edward Hungerford.[19] According to him, everything can easily be explained.
Whitman hesitated, not knowing which way to go; he doubted
himself, and this doubt paralyzed him. He was suddenly re-
leased when in July 1849 he had himself examined by a
famous New York phrenologist, Lorenzo Niles Fowler.[20] Phrenology was then a very popular fad and Whitman partook of
the general infatuation. He was persuaded that a skillful
specialist could infallibly read the character and aptitudes of
an individual by feeling the bumps of his head.[21] In 1888 he
still believed it.[22] Experience, he thought, had confirmed his
faith. Now Fowler had found in Whitman a remarkable subject whose amativeness, philoprogctiveness, adhesiveness, in-
habitiveness, alimentiveness, self-esteem, and sublimity were
all equally prominent. And Whitman was so well pleased
with his "rugged phrenology"[23] that he took every occasion
to publicize it. He published it in a footnote to an article he
wrote for the Brooklyn *Times* reviewing his own *Leaves of
Grass* and reprinted it in some prospectuses of the 1855 edition
and again in *Leaves-Droppings* in 1856 and finally in *Leaves
of Grass Imprints* in 1860.[24] It is probable then, as Hungerford supposes, that his self-esteem was profoundly affected.
He had great projects in hand,[25] but he was not sure that he
had the qualities needed to carry them out, and here was
science bringing the strength of its authority to the support
of his ambitions. In a moment all his doubts vanished. After
Fowler's conclusions, he felt that success was sure. To use
the terms of Haniel Long, who has adopted Hungerford's
hypothesis, phrenology became a "spring of courage" for
Whitman.[26] It catalogued and recognized all of his traits, and
though it warned him against his indolence, it gave him an
exalted idea of his powers and especially of his mental balance
and moral health. He now considered himself as a type of
perfect humanity and threw himself joyously forward.[27] He

probably recognized himself in this cutting from a phrenological journal which was found among his papers:

Good taste consists in the appropriate manifestations of each and all of the faculties in their proper season and degree; and this can only take place from persons in whom there is no tendency for any one of them unduly to assume the mastery. When such a mind is prompted by some high theme to its fullest action, each organ contributes to the emotion of the moment and words are uttered in such condensed meaning, that a single sentence will touch every fibre of the heart, or, what is the same thing, arouse every faculty of the hearer. The power is known as Inspiration, and the medium in which it is conveyed is called Poetry.[28]

Such a passage must have been a source of great exaltation to Whitman. Certainly the moral support that Fowler's examination gave him cannot be denied, but its importance should not be exaggerated. It cannot be assigned a decisive role or even a predominant influence in his development. It was only one factor among many others. In particular, the intellectual encounters he happened to make during these crucial years must be taken into account.

The most important was probably that of Ralph Waldo Emerson. Haniel Long mentioned it,[29] but earlier it had been the subject of a lively controversy prompted by the contradictory declarations of Whitman himself. For, after addressing Emerson as "Master" half a dozen times in the open letter appended to the 1856 edition of *Leaves of Grass*,[30] Whitman later recanted. In 1867, through the medium of Burroughs' *Notes on Walt Whitman as Poet and Person*, he let it be known that

up to the time he published the quarto edition [of 1855] . . . [he] had never read the Essays or Poems of Mr. Emerson at all. This is positively true. In the summer following that publication, he first became acquainted with the Essays, in this wise: He was frequently in the habit of going down to the sea-shore at Coney Island, and spending the day bathing in the surf and rambling along the shore, or lounging on the sand; and on one of these excursions he put a volume of Emerson into the little basket containing his dinner, and his towel. There, for the first [time], he read "Nature", &c. Soon, on similar excursions, the two other volumes followed. Two years still elapsed, however, and after his second edition was issued, before he read Mr. E.'s poems.[31]

In *Specimen Days*, in 1882, speaking this time for himself, he mentioned offhand the reading which he might have done in Emerson during his youth, but pretended not to attach much importance to it:

The reminiscence that years ago I began like most youngsters to have a touch (though it came late, and was only on the surface) of Emerson-on-the-brain — that I read his writings reverently, and address'd him in print as "Master", and for a month or so thought of him as such — I retain not only with composure, but positive satisfaction. I have noticed that most young people of eager minds pass through this stage of exercise.[32]

Several years later, in 1887, in a letter to W. S. Kennedy, he was absolutely categorical:

It is of no importance whether I had read Emerson before starting L of G or not. The fact happens to be positively that I had *not*.[33]

Thus, after proclaiming himself a fervent disciple in 1856, he later denied any influence and his hagiographers took full advantage of the opportunity to maintain that he owed nothing to anyone.[34] In fact, the open letter of 1856 does not prove much. It might very well have been motivated by mere opportunism and desire for publicity.[35] But in 1902 John T. Trowbridge threw in a new piece of evidence, and the bases of the problem were completely changed. Whitman, he claimed, had made some sensational revelations to him in 1860, while staying in Boston to supervise the printing of the third edition of *Leaves of Grass*. One Sunday, in the course of a long conversation, he told the story of his life and spoke of Emerson in the following manner:

I was extremely interested to know how far the influence of our greatest writer had been felt in the making of a book which, without being at all imitative, was pitched in the very highest key of self-reliance. . . Whitman talked frankly on the subject, that day on Prospect Hill, and told how he became acquainted with Emerson's writings. He was at work as a carpenter (his father's trade before him) in Brooklyn, building with his own hands and on his own account small and very plain houses for laboring men; as soon as one was finished and sold, beginning another, — houses of two or three rooms. This was in 1854; he was then thirty-five years old. He lived at home with his mother; going off to his work in the morning and returning at night, carrying his dinner pail like any common laborer. Along with his pail he usually carried a book, between which and his solitary meal he would divide his nooning. Once the book chanced to be a volume of Emerson; and from that time he took with him no other writer. . .

He freely admitted that he could never have written his poems if he had not first "come to himself," and that Emerson helped him to "find himself." I asked him if he thought he would have come to himself without that help. He said, "Yes, but it would have taken longer." And he used this characteristic expression: "I was simmering, simmering, simmering; Emerson brought me to a boil" . . .

I make this statement thus explicit because a question of profound personal and literary interest is involved, and because it is claimed by some of the later friends of Whitman that he wrote his first Leaves of Grass before he had read Emerson. When they urge his own authority for their contention, I can only reply that he told me distinctly the contrary, when his memory was fresher.[36]

This looks like the answer to the problem. We wanted to know what spark set fire to the powder and here Trowbridge shows it to us. But, should we believe his testimony? He claims to remember the conversation of that day vividly in all its details;[37] but, after all, the meeting took place forty years earlier, and we might well doubt the exactness of his memory. However, he is probably right, for we know from the Brooklyn *Eagle* that Whitman had read Emerson before 1855. In the issue for December 15, 1847, Whitman quoted a whole paragraph from one of the "inimitable lectures" of Ralph Waldo Emerson.[38] Moreover, he was certainly interested in everything Emerson wrote, for reviews of Emerson's books were found among his papers, dating back to 1847 and carefully annotated in his own hand.[39] Besides, as a contributor to the *Democratic Review*, he could hardly have ignored the long articles on Emerson in that magazine.[40] Whitman not only went through the published works, but he had also heard some of Emerson's lectures in New York. In *Good-Bye My Fancy* he reports that he had been present at antislavery meetings addressed by Wendell Phillips, Emerson, and others, and that he had heard in a room at the Athenaeum on Broadway "two or three addresses by R. W. Emerson." [41] He remembered this occasion vividly enough to evoke later in a poem not published during his lifetime the figure of Emerson speaking from a platform: "And there, tall and slender, stands Ralph Waldo Emerson, of New England, at the lecturer's desk, lecturing . . ." [42]

From all this we may conclude that Whitman knew the writings of Emerson at least second-hand from 1847 at the latest and that he read them with enthusiasm as he admits in the passage from *Specimen Days* quoted above.[43] But we see no trace of the lightning-stroke mentioned by Trowbridge which would explain everything. On the contrary, if Emerson's ideas and philosophy were familiar to him for so long, it is very unlikely that they suddenly overwhelmed him in 1854 and were then imposed on him with the force of an unexpected revelation. It seems therefore that Emerson was one of the many influences which helped Whitman find himself rather than the spark that made it possible for him to achieve at one stroke the synthesis of hitherto inert elements.

Many another scholar discovering in his turn one of these influences has thought that he had finally found the key to the mystery. Fred Manning Smith has thus tried to explain everything by the influence of Carlyle.[44] He points out that if it is true that Whitman had read very little Emerson before 1855, he might very well have felt the impress of Carlyle, with whom after all Emerson had much in common. The transcendentalist themes and phraseology which are found in *Leaves of Grass* consequently might come, not from the poems and essays of the Sage of Concord, but directly from the works of his Scottish predecessor. Whitman had published in the Brooklyn *Eagle* reviews of several books of Carlyle, *Sartor Resartus, Heroes and Hero-Worship*, and *Past and Present*.[45] He could very well have found in *Heroes and Hero-Worship* the idea of becoming a poet-prophet and of giving the world a new Bible.[46] He merely followed the example of Mohammed, Luther, and Knox.[47] His poems often evoke ecstatic states which suggest that he was visited by the same kind of inspiration as, according to Carlyle, was Odin.[48] His writing of poems in free verse which he calls "chants" brings to mind Carlyle's remarks in his chapter on "The Hero as Poet" that "all passionate language does of itself become musical . . ." and that "Rhyme that had no inward necessity to be rhymed; — it ought to have told us plainly, without any jingle, what it was aiming at." [49]

Like the heroes of Carlyle, Whitman prefers Nature to Art, which has always seemed to him to be marred by artifice.[50] And again, like them, he embraces all men in the same fraternal love. Like Mohammed, he is the "equalizer" of men.[51] And, like Knox and Luther, he refuses to bow his head to worldly powers. For him all men are equal. He despises wealth and practices the trade of carpentry instead of making a brilliant career in journalism, as if prompted by this passage in which Carlyle praises poverty:

On the whole one is weary of hearing about the omnipotence of money. I will say rather that, for a genuine man, it is no evil to be poor; that there ought to be Literary Men poor, — to show whether they are genuine or not.[52]

Moreover, this notion of the man of letters, of the "Literatus," as Whitman says, strongly resembles the ideas that Carlyle expresses in his chapter on "The Hero as Man of Letters." [53] In the same way as Carlyle he believes that all religions are true, that they all in their time have expressed a part of the essential verity, but that the poet must go beyond them.[54] Finally, the world which our senses perceive was for Carlyle the permanent proof of the presence of God beyond material appearances.[55] This is the very source of Whitman's poetic wonder. Certainly there is no lack of correspondences between the two writers. F. M. Smith in his second article is able to devote one whole page to a double-column list of striking analogies between *Leaves of Grass* and *Sartor Resartus*.[56] From all this he concludes that Carlyle was at least as much a master of Whitman as Emerson was. However he does not go quite so far as in his first article. At the end of his inquiry he is content to maintain, taking up Trowbridge's image, that if Emerson had brought Whitman to a boil, it was certainly Carlyle who began to make him simmer.[57] Thus, in spite of the great hopes which he had conceived for his hypothesis at the beginning, he is forced to recognize that it is impossible to demonstrate more than a diffuse and very distant influence. This is not at all the sudden illumination, the heavy and decisive shock which in itself would allow us to explain satisfactorily the unexpected appearance of *Leaves of Grass*. The work of Carlyle is only one of the sources on which Whitman drew; it was not at all the direct, immediate cause of his conversion.

In her book entitled *Walt Whitman's Pose*, Esther Shephard has unfortunately failed to show the same moderation as F. M. Smith.[58] Overjoyed at having caught Whitman in the act of imitating, she undertakes to demonstrate that *Leaves of Grass* is nothing but a shameless plagiarism from the works of George Sand and that even Whitman's attitude was copied from that of certain heroes of the French novelist and is therefore nothing but a pose. According to her, the source of *Leaves of Grass* is quite simply the epilogue of *La Comtesse de Rudolstadt,* which Whitman could have read in a translation by Francis G. Shaw.[59] There is, in fact, in this novel a "rhapsode vagabond" dressed as a peasant or a worker,[60] who, during a mystic trance, composes "the most magnificent poem that can be conceived." [61]

This mysterious personage is at the same time a poet and a prophet,[62] a magus and a philosopher,[63] whom Spartacus, the revolutionary and the man of action, consults with respect as an oracle. Like Whitman in the 1855 edition of *Leaves of Grass* he wants to be anonymous: "My name is *man,* and I am nothing more than any other man." [64] It is the soul of the whole of humanity that speaks through him.[65] He interprets all the religions of the past and brings out what is living and true in them, for he believes in the continuity of human history and in progress.[66] In this evolution each has his part, however humble: no effort is vain; nothing is lost. [67] Is not that precisely what Whitman proclaims in his "Song of Prudence"? [68] To the poet-prophet everything is beautiful — life, nature, humanity. The only evil is tyranny, which goes against nature and ignores the fact that all men are born brothers in freedom and equality.[69] Surely all this is remarkably similar to certain themes in *Leaves of Grass*, and therefore Esther Shephard concludes that Whitman was inspired, not by a transcendentalist mysticism, but by very conscious and carefully concealed borrowings from the work of George Sand.[70] She is indignant to find him writing in the 1855 Preface: "The great poets are also to be known by the absence in them of tricks and by the justification of perfect personal candor." [71]

Why then did he conceal his sources? she demands. Why did he never mention *The Companion of the Tour of France*, which he had reviewed in the Brooklyn *Eagle* in 1847 [72] and which must have influenced him? In this volume George Sand had told the story of a young carpenter, as handsome and noble as Christ, who worked with his father but used his leisure to read and talk about art. Although he dressed as a laborer, he was always impeccably clean. One day he experienced an ecstasy — like Whitman — and, when he was moved, he spoke with such eloquence that his friends saw him as a potentially great orator or writer.[73]

The analogy is certainly striking. But, even if we admit that Whitman, giving way to a somewhat puerile desire to identify himself with a fictional hero, sometimes modeled his dress and behavior on the Count of Rudolstadt and Pierre Huguenin, the Companion of the Tour of France, is that sufficient to explain the birth of his masterpiece? It seems unlikely, for it is not possible to find anything more than very vague suggestions in these verbose novels, and these suggestions probably did no more than confirm tendencies already present and living in him. Many of the analogies that Esther Shephard points out are in fact more apparent than real. In spite of what she says the ecstasy of Pierre Huguenin has nothing in common with the rapture that Whitman describes in "Song of Myself." [74] The resemblance is purely superficial. The trance into which the Count of Rudolstadt falls when questioned by Spartacus is of a totally different kind.[75] It permits him to prophesy, to express his ideas and dreams with passion and eloquence. It illustrates in general the romantic concept of inspiration, but this was not at all in practice Whitman's method of composition. With him the ecstasy was the source of inspiration. It put him in a state of poetic grace, but it was not immediately translated into poetry. It preceded the poem instead of accompanying it and creating it on the spot, as in the case of George

Sand's "rhapsode vagabond." On this point at least Whitman differs notably from his model. As for the philosophical and social ideas of these heroes whom Esther Shephard accuses him of copying, he could equally well have found them in the works of Carlyle and Emerson. They were not the exclusive property of George Sand. They were in the air, and Whitman may certainly be forgiven if he forgot where he found them.[76] A possibility remains that Pierre Huguenin and the Count of Rudolstadt inspired Whitman's attitude at the time of his return from New Orleans. Their example gave him the courage to become what he had dreamed of being. He may have felt less lonely in their company and less abnormal. These precedents were reassuring. Others had taken before him the way which he wanted to follow — fictional heroes, it is true, but that fact did not deter him. It seemed quite natural for him to try to become a poet-prophet like the Count of Rudolstadt and, to begin with, to make his living as a carpenter in the manner of Pierre Huguenin and of his own father. The fact that his own father was also a carpenter probably appeared to him as a striking and portentous coincidence.

This is in fact the limit of George Sand's influence. It seems almost certain that she helped and encouraged Whitman in fashioning the curious personality which he was trying to develop during the years from 1850 to 1855 in order to bring his life into harmony with his work. Perhaps she also suggested some of the ideas he took up in his poems, but this is by no means certain. At any rate it is clear that she did not provide the great and decisive shock which critics are looking for and which would by itself explain the birth of *Leaves of Grass*.[77]

Esther Shephard's hypothesis thus proves on analysis to be as disappointing as the others. The most reasonable conclusion would probably be a confession of failure. Jean Catel is close to this when, at the end of his book, he formulates his theory of the "I" in Whitman's poetry. He rejects both the hypothesis of mysticism and that of a sexual awakening in New Orleans; according to him, Walt Whitman was merely a misfit; he had thus far encountered nothing but disappointments and finally, tired of the continuous struggle, he retreated to an interior world where he was the sovereign creator, where his "I" was master and this "I" imposed itself on him to the point that he forgot the existence of the discontented journalist, of the loveless young man that he had been until then.[78] Artistic creation was for him a compensation, a making up for the deficiencies of life. This is a penetrating interpretation. Gay Wilson Allen has taken it up and expressed it with vigor in his *Walt Whitman Handbook*.[79] But the attempt to explain a work by reference to the slow and mysterious and almost undefinable operations of the unconscious amounts to a renunciation of the effort to discover the origin of the *fiat* which gave it birth.

Thus all the hypotheses that have been suggested for the origin of *Leaves of Grass* prove equally unsatisfactory. Their number alone shows the complexity of the problem. Their defect is precisely their failure to recognize this complexity. Each of these theories is too partial and accounts for only one aspect of the question. Each of these critics imagines that he has discovered Ariadne's thread, but one thread is not enough, for there is really a cluster of causes. The most reasonable course is perhaps to refrain from attacking this difficult problem and frankly admit to an inability to penetrate the mystery. To use the image of Whitman in his conversation with Trowbridge,[80] he simmered from 1847 to 1855, but no one knows what finally brought him to a boil. He probably did not know himself. His mind at that time might be described as a supersaturated solution very rich in elements borrowed from life and from books: childhood dreams, adolescent disturbances, ecstasies, memories of Long Island, scenes of Brooklyn and New York, unsettling impressions of New Orleans, recollections of Carlyle, Emerson, and George Sand. All this was probably full of eddies, but it remained amorphous until a sudden crystallization occurred. This crystallization is as inexplicable as that of the glycerine sent to Russia in a barrel which was found solidified at the end of the journey. No one ever knew how this first specimen of solid glycerine came into the world. The birth of *Leaves of Grass* is an enigma of the same kind. No one has discovered the crystal which served as a "germ," and probably no one ever will.

It might be tempting to examine the notebooks that Emory Holloway has published,[81] some of which go back to 1847–48, in the hope of discovering the secret there, but they contain nothing that is not more clearly and more forcefully set forth in *Leaves of Grass*. These documents are interesting only because they permit us to attribute an earlier date to the thoughts and feelings Whitman expressed in his poems. The only remaining possibility is to examine the work itself as it was revealed to Whitman's contemporaries in 1855.

The earliest version of *Leaves of Grass* is different from the others not only in format, but also in form. One of its peculiarities is that an important role is played by prose. Of the ninety-five quarto pages, the Preface alone takes ten, printed in very small type. At first glance the work appears to be twofold and consist of a prose manifesto and a collection of poems. But in the reading, the differences diminish; for in the unusual prose of the Preface, there are hardly any subordinate constructions. Whitman proceeds by series of independent clauses, by the juxtaposition of affirmations which he makes no attempt either to prove by logic or to integrate into a well-constructed whole. He is content to affirm. This is the reason for the peculiar punctuation that he uses both in the Preface and in the poems. Instead of commas and semicolons, we find only points of suspension varying in number from two to eight.[82] He uses them to indicate the rhythm of the sentences and to mark the places where the reader, if he were reading aloud, would need to take breath. This is the normal concern of a poet or an orator. He does not try to convince by argument, but rather to affect emotionally. He wants his text to be an incantation or a rhapsody. Therefore his prose is very close to his verse. It looks as if he had not had time to versify the ideas of the Preface. As we shall see, it required only a rapid revision in the following year to turn this long piece of prose into the poem later called "By Blue Ontario's Shore." [83] And the book thus gained at once in richness and homogeneity.

Here we see the essential character of the first edition, which is its lack of finish. It is very close to the primitive magma. It has the appearance of a flow of lava which nothing could stop and which has remained formless. The twelve poems the book contains are part of the same amorphous mass. Outwardly nothing distinguishes one from another. To be sure, they are separated by double horizontal lines, but this typographical device is not sufficient to give them any individuality. They have no titles and must be considered indiscriminately as "Leaves of Grass." The 1855 edition is undoubtedly the least organized of any. Thus it is not surprising that the poems do not entirely fulfill the promise of the Preface. The subject of the Preface is mainly America and democracy, whereas in the poems these themes are hardly touched upon. [84] In the Preface the accent is on politics; in the poems it is on metaphysics. The poet had not yet completely absorbed the political journalist, or rather, since the political journalist would never completely disappear, the poet was not yet able to transmute into poetry the political ideal with which he was pregnant and of which he had been aware since the crisis of 1850. [85]

The *Leaves of Grass* of 1855 is then a heterogeneous and rather poorly constructed book. The composition is more musical than architectural, but the content is already extremely rich. The title itself is worth dwelling on. Why did Whitman

call the book *Leaves of Grass* instead of "Blades of Grass"? [86]
He evidently wanted this play on words. These "leaves" would
be at the same time the leaves of his book and those of the
grass. Thus the work would be a bunch of leaves consisting of
poems which were already written when he gathered them,
as he was soon to explain in "Spontaneous Me":

> And this bunch pluck'd at random from myself,
> It has done its work — I toss it carelessly to fall where
>   it may. [87]

Others — Fanny Fern in particular — had already played
on the word, [88] but with Whitman it was no longer a banal
pun designed to make the reader smile; it was the expression
of a symbolic relationship suggesting mystical correspondences.
These pages, these "leaves," are both himself and his work
since he incorporates himself in the book:

> Camerado, this is no book,
> Who touches this touches a man. [89]

But at the same time they are actual leaves, not only the leaves
of graminaceous plants, but the leaves of any herbaceous
plants, as is shown by the designs on the cover. [90] These *Leaves
of Grass* therefore include the poet and his song and all the
vegetation which covers the earth. He has chosen grass, the
anonymous mass of herbaceous plants, because it symbolizes
for him the universal presence of life, not only in space, [91]
but also in time, even beyond death:

> This is the grass that grows wherever the land is and
>   the water is . . . [92]

> And it means, Sprouting alike in broad zones and
>   narrow zones,
> Growing among black folks as among white,
> Kanuck, Tuckahoe, Congressman, Cuff, I give them
>   the same, I receive them the same . . . [93]

Tenderly will I use you curling grass,
It may be you transpire from the breasts of young men,
It may be if I had known them I would have loved
them,

. . . . .

The smallest sprout shows there is really no death . . .[94]

Thus *Leaves of Grass* represents the universal brotherhood of all living things permeated in all places and times by the same immortal burning force. The title admirably characterizes this book and fairly sums up one of its essential themes, the eternal cycle of life.[95]

Since the book purports to be above all a man, let us look for the man who hides behind these strange *Leaves of Grass*. To be sure, when the book is opened, he does not hide at all; on the contrary he sings himself and celebrates himself [96] and he presents us several times in "Song of Myself" with his full-length portrait. He introduces himself as a man of the people:

Walt Whitman, an American, one of the roughs, a kosmos,
Disorderly fleshy and sensual. . . . eating drinking
and breeding,
No sentimentalist. . . . no stander above men and
women or apart from them. . . . no more modest
than immodest.[97]

He wished first of all to give an impression of physical vigor. The image he tries to impose is that of a laborer, solidly built, proud of his strength and of his carnal appetites, whose sensual instincts are not paralyzed by any inhibition. He is no "gentleman" distant and reserved. He wears no mask. He gives free rein to his emotions; he is not ashamed of the needs of his body and, above all, he does not stand apart from the other people; he is, as he loudly proclaims, a part of the mass.

These are the two aspects of his personality that he seems to value most: a vigorous animality and a highly developed sense of human brotherhood. He returns to them constantly. "The friendly and flowing savage"[98] he describes a little farther along is no other than himself. There is so much force in him and so much love for his fellow-men that all feel irresistibly drawn toward him as if his body radiated a secret magnetism:

> Wherever he goes men and women accept and desire
> him,
> They desire he should like them and touch them and
> speak to them and stay with them.[99]
>
> He has the passkey of hearts . . . to him the response
> of the prying of hands on the knobs.
> His welcome is universal . . .
> . . . the mechanics take him for a mechanic,
> And the soldiers suppose him to be a captain. . . .
> and the sailors that he has followed the sea,
> And the authors take him for an author. . . . and the
> artists for an artist,
> And the laborers perceive he could labor with them and
> love them . . .[100]

He makes common cause with all the oppressed; [101] no social barrier stops him:

> To the drudge of the cottonfields or emptier of privies
> I lean. . . . on his right cheek I put the family kiss
> . . .[102]

He moves through life and among men with sovereign ease. He is "not different" and fraternizes with everyone. He is not embarrassed with anyone and no one is embarrassed with him. He lives democracy. Wherever he goes, equality and fraternity are immediately realized, thanks to his wonderful faculty of speaking with the first to come without reserve or constraint and of giving himself entirely to each one.

If he is not at all a "gentleman," he is no more an intellectual. He exalts physical power and life in the open air. He avoids libraries and prefers the rude, bronzed, bearded face of the vagabond always on the go to the smooth-shaven face of the city man:

> I tramp a perpetual journey,
> My signs are a rain-proof coat and good shoes and a
>   staff cut in the woods;
> I lead no man to a dinner-table or library or exchange
> . . .[103]

He passionately loves the countryside and sometimes takes part in the work of the fields — as a dilettante, for he is more a spectator than an actor. Nothing pleases him more than to return to the farmyard lying on a wagon-load of hay, or to roll in the dried grass stored in the mow.[104] He takes part in fishing parties and spends whole days at the seaside digging clams,[105] or he wanders alone in the woods and gazes after the wild ducks who fly away at his approach.[106] He is

> . . . enamoured of growing outdoors,
> Of men that live among cattle or taste of the ocean or
>   woods,
> Of the builders and steerers of ships, of the wielders
>   of axes and mauls, of the drivers of horses . . .[107]

He needs the open spaces of the American countryside in order to feel at ease and breathe freely. His vigorous body needs air and movement. In this sense he retains the tastes of the country boy which he had acquired in his childhood at West Hills. He is fully aware of this background and in one of the last poems of the book he describes his youthful wonder before the ever-new beauty of all things that struck him as a child.[108]

This is the portrait of the artist by himself which emerges from the 1855 edition of *Leaves of Grass*, his "Me myself" [109] insofar as it is possible to disentangle it from the mystical metamorphoses which it underwent in imagination while he was writing "Song of Myself." He wanted first of all to appear as an apostle of democracy and as an uncultured man filled with masculine force and a powerful animality. He was especially proud of his "perfect health," [110] of his "reckless health." [111] He gave an impression of firmness and complete confidence in himself bordering on arrogance. He chanted at the top of his lungs his joy in living and in creating, and his nonchalance, it seems, was the sign of a perfect physical and moral equilibrium.

At least that was the image which he wished to impose on us, but a more attentive reading of "Song of Myself" brings out strange dissonances. First of all there is the admission that he had not always possessed the faith and the certitude which now prompted his exultant optimism:

> Backward I see in my own days where I sweated
> through fog with linguists and contenders . . . [112]

> Down-hearted doubters, dull and excluded,
> Frivolous sullen moping angry affected disheartened
> atheistical,

> I know every one of you, and know the unspoken in-
> terrogatories,
> By experience I know them. [113]

> Be at peace bloody flukes of doubters and sullen mopers,
> I take my place among you as much as among any. [114]

Moreover, when he thought of the suffering of the oppressed and of all those who were ill and about to die, he still sometimes paled and trembled:

> Agonies are one of my changes of garments . . . [115]

> I am less the jolly one there, and more the silent one
> with sweat on my twitching lips. [116]

So he was not simply the happy extrovert of his portrait. His exuberance concealed agonies and secret doubts. His personality was less simple than he wanted his reader to think, less normal. That was to be expected. The mystical overtones of "Song of Myself" and the extreme sensuality of some passages indicated an exceptional temperament.[117] For, surprisingly, as soon as Whitman stops talking directly about himself, the hearty, superficial man of the people of the self-portraits gives way to the dreamy poet of the frontispiece who looks without seeing, his gaze lost in the clouds:

> Apart from the pulling and hauling stands what I am,
> Stands amused, complacent, compassionating, idle, unitary,
> Looks down, is erect, bends an arm on an impalpable certain rest,
> Looks with its sidecurved head curious what will come next,
> Both in and out of the game, and watching and wondering at it.[118]

Other passages permit this analysis to be pushed still further. In a notebook which he used about 1848–49 the following reflections are found:

> I am not glad to-night. Gloom has gathered round me like a mantle, tightly folded.
> The oppression of my heart is not fitful and has no pangs; but a torpor like that of some stagnant pool.
> Yet I know not why I should be sad.
> Around me are my brother men, merry and jovial . . .
> No dear one is in danger, and health shelter and food are vouchsafed me.
> O, Nature! impartial, and perfect in imperfection
> Every precious gift to man is linked with a curse — and each pollution has some sparkle from heaven.
> The mind, raised upward, then holds communion with angels and its reach overtops heaven; yet then it stays in the meshes of the world too and is stung by a hundred serpents every day . . .
> Thus it comes that I am not glad to-night.–

I feel cramped here in these coarse walls of flesh.
The soul disdains its [incomplete]
O Mystery of Death, I pant for the time when I shall
    solve you! [119]

We do not have enough information for a diagnosis of this
incurable sadness which he suffered on occasional evenings
and could not exorcise,[120] but we now know with certainty
that there were discordant elements at the heart of his exuberant optimism and his triumphant health. We suspect that
the joy which uplifts his poems has a secret corollary in moments of depression that, he claims, are without cause. It is
clear that he had never learned to analyze himself, for he
indicates in passing, without realizing it, two very plausible
reasons: the presence of evil in the world and the weakness of
the flesh. These probably account for some of his melancholy
and echo the crisis described in the preceding chapter which
caused him to withdraw from the world into himself. The
crisis persisted. He was not completely cured. In spite of his
assurance and his apparent equilibrium, he had not yet attained the serenity of faith. His personality still contained
elements of instability disquieting for the future.[121]

This analysis shows at any rate that there was a wide gap
between the image of himself which he tried to impose on us
and the person whom the documents permit us to reconstruct
and whose character we can infer from the poems. The jolly
fellow of the official portrait was actually very unstable, passing back and forth between exaltation and gloom. The man of
the people who claimed that he had never sat on a platform
among the notables forgot the political speeches he had made
when he had fought in the ranks of the Democratic Party and
the free-soil faction.[122] By his account he had never associated
with men of letters or read any books.[123] He ignored his contributions to the *Democratic Review* and all the book reviews
that he had published in the various newspapers on which he

had worked. He never even breathed a word of his journalistic career.[124] One would think by his testimony that he had spent his life in the fields.

Does this mean that he was deliberately trying to deceive us? Probably not, for the portrait includes a number of authentic features. In any case, as we have already noticed, the working clothes which he was now wearing were not a disguise put on for the occasion.[125] He had adopted this costume about 1850 when he decided to change his way of life, to break with his past and renounce the world with all its pomp and circumstance in order to devote himself entirely to his ideal.[126] He took the vow of poverty and that alone is sufficient evidence of his sincerity. There is no justification for reproaching him with the fact that he did not altogether resemble his portrait. He had described the kind of person he wanted to be rather than the one he really was. We will see how he kept on trying to approximate more and more closely the model he had set for himself. There is certainly no reason for accusing him of charlatanism. He had no intention of deceiving; he was attempting rather to impose a new personality on himself.

He wanted to become manful, expansive, and normal, and he began by claiming that he already had these qualities. He wanted to play in real life the role he had given himself in his book. He was, however, obscurely aware of the distance that still separated the dream from the reality. He wrote in one of his notebooks in 1848 or 1849: "I cannot understand the mystery, but I am always conscious of myself as two — as my soul and I: and I reckon it is the same with all men and women." [127] He was evidently more naïve than deceptive, less the player than the man incapable of seeing clearly what passed within himself.

His contemporaries, naturally, were somewhat disconcerted by this book which pretended to be a man and by this strange man who wanted so much to identify himself with his book.

Many critics reacted violently, some to the point of gratuitous insults. For example, R. W. Griswold wrote slanderously in the New York *Criterion*: ". . . it is impossible to imagine how any man's fancy could have conceived such a mass of stupid filth, unless he were possessed of the soul of a sentimental donkey that had died of disappointed love." [128] And the critic of the Boston *Intelligencer*, after citing this edifying passage, saw fit to add on his own account: ". . . the author should be kicked from all decent society as below the level of the brute. There is neither wit nor method in this disjointed babbling, and it seems to us he must be some escaped lunatic, raving in pitiable delirium." [129]

Those who condescended to give reasons for their judgment made in general two main accusations: lack of art in the form and obscenity in the contents. What the reviewer in the London *Critic* said was typical of the reproaches commonly made:

But what claim has this Walt Whitman . . . to be considered a poet at all? We grant freely enough that he has a strong relish for nature and freedom, just as an animal has; nay, further, that his crude mind is capable of appreciating some of nature's beauties; but it by no means follows that, because nature is excellent, therefore art is contemptible. Walt Whitman is as unacquainted with art, as a hog is with mathematics. His poems — we must call them so for convenience . . . are innocent of rhythm, and resemble nothing so much as the war-cry of the Red Indians . . . Or rather perhaps, this Walt Whitman reminds us of Caliban flinging down his logs, and setting himself to write a poem . . .[130]

After these amiable remarks, the reviewer went on to the second complaint:

The depth of his indecencies will be the grave of his fame, or ought to be if all proper feeling is not extinct . . . we who are not prudish, emphatically declare that the man who wrote page 79 of the *Leaves of Grass* deserves nothing so richly as the public executioner's whip.[131]

In conclusion he slyly quoted the line, "I talk wildly . . . I have lost my wits," which he affected to take literally as a confession. Another gratuitous insult.

The London *Examiner*, equally shocked by the formal deficiencies, paid particular attention to the long catalogues which Whitman loved: "Three-fourths of Walt Whitman's book is poetry as catalogues of auctioneers are poems. . ." [132] Likewise the *Crayon* in New York: ". . . according to Walt Whitman's theory, the greatest poet is he who performs the office of camera to the world, merely reflecting what he sees — art is merely reproduction." [133] Although this critic admitted that Whitman had a certain power, he concluded with an unfavorable verdict: "With a wonderful vigor of thought and intensity of perception, a power, indeed, not often found, *Leaves of Grass* has no ideality, no concentration, no purpose — it is barbarous, undisciplined, like the poetry of a half civilized people. . ." [134]

The critic of the London *Leader* mainly complained that "The poem is written in wild, irregular, unrhymed, almost unmetrical 'lengths' . . . by no means seductive to English ears. . ." And, like the others, he condemned the lack of modesty:

. . . much . . . seems to us purely fantastical and preposterous; much . . . appears to our muddy vision gratuitously prosaic, needlessly plain-speaking, disgusting without purpose, and singular without result. There are so many evidences of a noble soul in Whitman's pages that we regret these aberrations, which only have the effect of discrediting what is genuine by the show of something false; and especially do we deplore the unnecessary openness with which he reveals to us matters which ought rather to remain in sacred silence. [135]

The New York *Times* protested similarly in an otherwise favorable article: "If . . . to roam like a drunken satyr, with inflamed blood, through every field of lascivious thought . . .

is to be a Kosmos then indeed we cede to Mr. Walt Whitman his arrogated title. Like the priests of Belus, he wreathes around his brow the emblems of the Phallic worship." [136]

The gross violence of some of these articles was not, however, the general rule. Even the most hostile critics were often courteous and even occasionally mingled praise with blame. The publication of *Leaves of Grass* did not provoke a universal outcry. On the contrary a surprising number of reviews were, if not enthusiastic, at least frankly sympathetic.

One of the most favorable was that of Charles Eliot Norton, published anonymously in *Putnam's Monthly Magazine* for September 1855. He praised "this gross yet elevated, this superficial yet profound, this preposterous yet somehow fascinating book." It was, he said,

a mixture of Yankee transcendentalism and New York rowdyism, and, what must be surprising to both these elements, they here seem to fuse and combine with the most perfect harmony . . . there is an original perception of nature, a manly brawn, and an epic directness in our new poet, which belong to no other adept of the transcendental school.

To be sure, he made some reservations, such as: "the introduction of terms, never before heard or seen, and of slang expressions, often renders an otherwise striking passage altogether laughable." But in general the book thrilled him, as his conclusion shows: "Precisely what a kosmos is, we hope Walt Whitman will take early occasion to inform the impatient public." [137]

Edward Everett Hale in the *North American Review* was equally fascinated by the naturalness and vigor of this new poetry: ". . . one reads and enjoys the freshness, simplicity, and reality of what he reads, just as the tired man, lying on the ground, lying on the hillside in summer, enjoys the leaves of grass around him,– enjoys the shadow,– enjoys the flecks of sunshine,– not for what they 'suggest to him', but for what they are." [138]

The *Christian Spiritualist,* which had been founded by a group of Swedenborgians, welcomed *Leaves of Grass* with enthusiasm and recommended it as containing — without the author's knowledge — echoes of the Master's doctrines. The reviewer was apparently so pleased with these correspondences that he easily pardoned the obscenities and unreservedly praised the style, which hardly anyone had dared to do thus far:

His style is everywhere graphic and strong, and he sings many things before untouched in prose or rhyme, in an idiom that is neither prose nor rhyme, nor yet orthodox blank verse. But it serves his purpose well. He wears his strange garb, cut and made by himself, as gracefully as a South American cavalier his poncho . . .

A "remarkable volume," he concluded.[139]

These commendations were pale beside the hymn of praise intoned by Fanny Fern in the New York *Ledger: "Leaves of Grass* thou art unspeakably delicious, after the forced, stiff, Parnassian exotics for which our admiration had been vainly challenged. Walt Whitman, the effeminate world needed thee. . ." This tone pervaded the whole article. She even absolved Whitman of the accusation of grossness and sensuality which had been brought against him: "My moral constitution may be hopelessly tainted or — too sound to be tainted, as the critic wills, but I confess that I extract no poison from these "Leaves" — to me they have brought only healing. Let him who can do so shroud the eyes of the nursing babe lest it should see its mother's breast. . ." [140]

And this was not an isolated article. Others could be cited, particularly that of William Howitt in the London *Dispatch.* The English critic, less impulsive than Fanny Fern, was able to praise Whitman's peculiar style with intelligence and analyze it with finesse:

> They [these poems] are destitute of rhyme, measure of feet and the like — every condition under which poetry is generally understood to exist, being absent; but in their strength of expression, their fervor, hearty wholesomeness, their originality, mannerism, and freshness, one finds in them a singular harmony and flow, as if by reading they gradually formed themselves into melody, and adopted characteristics peculiar and appropriate to themselves alone.

He predicted for Whitman a great and lasting success: "He will soon make his way into the confidence of his readers, and his poems in time will become a pregnant text-book, out of which quotations as sterling as the minted gold will be taken. . ." [141]

The reviews in the *Monthly Gazette*,[142] the *National Intelligencer*,[143] and the Brooklyn *Daily Eagle* [144] were also flattering. On the whole, then, in spite of the cries of anger and indignation of part of the press, the critical reception was favorable. This, it must be added, was the impression, from a distance, of the commentator in the London *Critic* who wrote:

> We should have passed over this book, *Leaves of Grass*, with indignant contempt, had not some few Transatlantic critics attempted to "fix" this Walt Whitman as the poet who shall give a new and independent literature to America — who shall form a race of poets as Banquo's issue formed a line of kings.[145]

The English critic in writing these lines may have been thinking of the extremely enthusiastic and almost dithyrambic articles which had appeared in the Brooklyn *Daily Times*, the *American Phrenological Journal*, and the *United States Review*,[146] but Whitman himself was the author of these. His desire to achieve a great success in publishing *Leaves of Grass* was such that he had neglected no means of drawing public attention to his book. Apparently dissatisfied with the reviews it had received, he undertook to compose a certain number himself for anonymous publication in friendly periodicals. The ruse was promptly uncovered, and Whitman was sharply criticized for the indelicacy of this procedure.[147] Certainly such methods were inelegant and bordered on dishonesty, but it should be remembered that Whitman had no publisher or publicity agent and that he had to do the necessary advertising himself. He did what he could. And, besides, as he pointed out, he was not the first to do so. Leigh Hunt following Spenser's example had also reviewed his own poems.[148] Whitman was then in very good company; however, he did not have the excuse which he later claimed: that he had been obliged to write these articles to defend himself against the insults of his enemies and to clear up misunderstandings.[149] He tried to establish this legend in his old age, but as we have seen, it is not founded on fact.[150]

There is another legend which ought to be destroyed, that of the commercial failure of the first edition. It was also invented by Whitman. In 1886 he declared in an interview published by the Brooklyn *Eagle*: "The edition was 1,000 copies — the ordinary edition of new books in those days. But there wasn't a single copy sold, not a single copy. I couldn't even give them all away. Many of them were returned to me with insulting letters." [151] A little later he repeated this story to Horace Traubel, and, when Traubel incredulously demanded what had become of all these copies, he replied, "It is a mystery: the books scattered, somehow, somewhere, God knows, to the four corners of the earth . . ." [152] — a most evasive reply and indeed a contradiction of his first assertion. He was forced to admit that the first edition had disappeared and that not a single copy remained in his possession. This is, in fact, the conclusion toward which all the pertinent evidence leads.

First of all, it must be granted that *Leaves of Grass* was

printed in an edition of 1,000 copies. There is no reason to doubt Whitman's word on that point. It was, as he said, the usual number for a first edition at the time. In 1836 Emerson's first book, *Nature*, had been issued in only 500 copies, which had taken thirteen years to sell. And in 1849 only 2,000 copies of *Walden* were printed.[153] It is true, however, that the first edition of *Leaves of Grass* was not immediately sold out. Ralph Adimari,[154] studying the advertisements that Fowler and Wells, who handled the book, placed in the New York *Tribune* has been able to show that there were three successive issues — which is confirmed by an examination of the copies still in existence.[155] The first and handsomest, with gilding on the cover, was put on sale from July 6 to the end of September for two dollars — which was a very high price for the time (*Hiawatha* sold for only one dollar and *The Scarlet Letter* for seventy-five cents). Most of the surviving copies are of this issue. After September 26, the price was cut in half and the cover lost part of its gilding; this was the second issue.[156] Then on November 24 and 25 Fowler and Wells announced the sale of paper-covered copies for seventy-five cents — which constituted the third issue. In spite of this the sales must have dropped; for, on February 18 of the following year, Fowler and Wells ran the following announcement in the *Tribune*: "Walt Whitman's Poems — *Leaves of Grass* — This work was not stereotyped; a few copies only remain, after which it will be out of print." This announcement continued until March 1.

It seems unlikely that this last announcement can have been a mere publicity trick. If the book had failed to sell, Fowler and Wells would hardly have spent so much money on advertising. Adimari has calculated that these announcements in the *Tribune* cost them $84.30. They were too commercial-minded to risk so much without being sure of getting their money back. It would seem, then, that *Leaves of Grass* had a fair success with the critics and the public. On this point, the best testimony is not that of Whitman in his last years, but that of the young author proud of the victory which he had just won and which he proclaimed in his open letter to Emerson in 1856: "I printed a thousand copies and they readily sold." [157] If the public and critical reaction had been what he later described, he could hardly have had the courage to continue. Yet, in less than a year, as we shall see, his book was to double in size. Such an intensive output would be difficult to explain if the 1855 edition had been a failure. It was to some extent the demand which encouraged the supply.

Whitman, it is true, might have done without this success, for, shortly after the appearance of *Leaves of Grass*, he had received an encouragement beside which all the others faded: Emerson had sent him an enthusiastic letter that had gone straight to his heart and that must have aroused boundless hopes. Emerson had said:

I greet you at the beginning of a great career . . . I find [your book] the most extraordinary piece of wit and wisdom that America has yet contributed . . . I have great joy of it. I find incomparable things said incomparably well, as they must be . . .[158]

The Master, in other words, had recognized the ideal American poet whose coming he had looked for and predicted.[159] Whitman could not help being stimulated by such a warm tribute. He had not perhaps achieved the triumph he had hoped for,[160] but he had at least obtained enough of a victory to preserve all his confidence in himself and all his faith in the genuineness of his inspiration. All that he had to do was to persevere, to respond to Emerson's letter and the encouragements of the critics with an even richer and more vigorous work. That was what he did. Several months later a second edition appeared.

CHAPTER III

THE 1856 EDITION

IN June of 1856 [1] there appeared in Brooklyn and New York a small sextodecimo of nearly four hundred pages entitled *Leaves of Grass*. The thin quarto of 1855 had thus undergone a curious metamorphosis. On the outside, except for the color, the two books were completely different. Not only was the format greatly reduced, but also the cover had lost a large part of its ornamentation. The vegetation which had flourished there had almost completely disappeared; there remained only some small floral motifs confined to the four corners. Similarly the letters of the title had lost their former luxuriance; they were no longer half-letters, half-plants, but large thin characters without life or mystery. The backstrip had also become much simpler. *Leaves of Grass* was repeated there, and discreetly recalling the mystic interlacings of the 1855 title, the *a* of "Grass" extended itself into a leaf and the last leg of the *m* of "Whitman" was adorned with a clover leaf. For this was by far the greatest innovation: the name of the author, which had been so carefully hidden in the first edition, now followed the title as on any other book.

This, then, was no longer an anonymous pamphlet presented in such a way as to intrigue and arouse curiosity, but an ordinary commercial edition, economically and plainly bound, signed by an author already known to the public. Moreover,

the book sold for only one dollar instead of two, which confirmed this impression. It was no longer the work of an amateur
published at his own expense. Although their names were not
on the title page, the publication this time had been undertaken by Fowler and Wells,[2] who, having acted as distributors
of the first edition, performed the same function for this one,
as is shown by the fact that the last page was used for their
advertisements.[3]

The commercial character of this second edition also appeared in another detail. On the backstrip, in letters of gold,
one of the most flattering sentences in Emerson's letter was
reproduced: "I greet you at the beginning of a great career." [4]
This advertising was in doubtful taste,[5] though it would not
surprise a modern reader accustomed to the highly colored
dust-jackets of today's popular novels.

When the book was opened, the reader found as the
frontispiece the same portrait used in the 1855 volume, and
the title page, also recalling the preceding edition, did not
carry the name of the author. But this omission was no longer
significant since his name now appeared on the backstrip.
Curiously enough, on the next page, in the copyright notice,
the first name was no longer Walter as in 1855, but Walt. He
was consistent this time: Walter was really dead.

Leafing through the book, the reader would be struck by a
notable difference between it and the first edition. The book
was now organized — there was even a table of contents —
and the poems were differentiated and classified. Each of
them had been given a title and a number. It is true that these
titles were rather monotonous and singularly lacking in distinction — they all contained the word "poem" — and these
poems were merely juxtaposed rather than really grouped, as
we shall see; but one thing is certain, they no longer gave the
impression of a continuous tide that had characterized the
1855 edition.[6] The composition of the pages, moreover, had

also changed. With the reduced format, the long verses had lost their amplitude and the punctuation had become more conventional. The points of suspension had disappeared; commas and semicolons had replaced them. Decidedly *Leaves of Grass* had been vulgarized. In appearance at least it was a book like any other.

However, it was considerably enriched. It had contained only twelve poems in 1855; the table of contents listed thirty-two this time, and they occupied about 340 pages. None attained the exceptional length of the first poem, which had now become "Poem of Walt Whitman, an American." But the fact remains that the work had nearly doubled in size, a sure sign of vigor and fecundity.

If the presentation showed a certain number of concessions to the public, the text nevertheless remained equally novel and bold. Whitman had even introduced a new theme, the sexual theme which in 1855 had been hardly sketched and which he now developed extensively. There had previously been allusions and occasional images, but now he had written whole poems on this subject: "Poem of Women" (later "Unfolded out of the Folds"), "Poem of the Body" (later "I Sing the Body Electric"),[7] "Poem of Procreation" (later "A Woman Waits for Me"), "Bunch Poem" (later "Spontaneous Me").[8] Moreover, he proclaimed in his reply to Emerson's letter his intention of celebrating henceforth, with complete freedom and without reserve, all that pertained to the sexual life:

I say that the body of a man or woman, the main matter, is so far quite unexpressed in poems; but that the body is to be expressed, and sex is. Of bards for These States, if it come to a question, it is whether they shall celebrate in poems the eternal decency of the amativeness of Nature, the motherhood of all, or whether they shall be the bards of the fashionable delusion of the inherent nastiness of sex, and of the feeble and querulous modesty of deprivation. This is important in poems, because the whole of the other expressions of a nation are but flanges out of its great poems. To me, henceforth, that theory of any thing, no matter what, stagnates in its vitals, cowardly and rotten, while it cannot publicly accept, and publicly name, with specific words, the things on which all existence, all souls, all realization, all decency, all health, all that is worth being here for, all of woman and of man, all beauty, all purity, all sweetness, all friendship, all strength, all life, all immortality depend. The courageous soul, for a year or two to come, may be proved by faith in sex, and by disdaining concessions.[9]

It appears from the warmth of the tone that this topic was close to his heart, even though he had not breathed a word of it in the 1855 Preface and nothing in any of his previous writings had given any hint of it. He had, it would seem, suddenly decided to reveal this secret aspect of his personality. The enterprise required a certain amount of courage in the face of the extreme prudishness which at that time characterized American society. As the last sentence indicates, Whitman expected resistance and protests. However, in spite of that, he considered it his duty to go ahead and make the most complete frankness in sexual matters a basic aspect of his message,[10] for reasons which we will try to specify later.

Another new theme, or at least one to which he gave a new emphasis, for it already existed as a germ,[11] was that of the journey. He devoted an entire poem to it, "Poem of the Road," [12] one of the longest in the collection, in which he sang of a strange and purely symbolic *Wanderlust* (since his return from New Orleans he had not left New York). This journey on the open road to which he invited his reader was first of all a renunciation of the comforts of routine and conformity, an uprooting similar to that which he had effected for himself when he had decided to abandon his journalistic career in order to consecrate himself to his poetry. Thus, he discovered an aspect of himself that he had hardly alluded to before, and he erected his own spiritual adventure into a general rule of conduct. But he added something else. With this theme of the journey was mingled and associated the theme of the universe contemplated in its totality or in its perpetual becoming. This was the subject not only of the "Poem of the Road," but also of the "Sun-Down Poem" (later "Crossing Brooklyn Ferry"); [13] for, in order to perceive the total becoming of the world, one need not get away from Brooklyn or Manhattan. The eternal ebb and flow of life were visible to any who could see. It was enough to look at the water, the passing boats, and the crowds of people. Whitman had feasted his eyes on these every day, and it was probably for that reason that he could issue his fervent invitation to the journey without being aware of any inconsistency with his own sedentary habits. He traversed the infinities of space and time without moving. He had succeeded in uprooting himself on the spot, but, if others wished to do so, they would first have to depart. For himself he had achieved a higher liberty than could be obtained by motion in space, which is the most elementary form of liberty; he was now able to evoke cosmic visions merely by taking the ferry to New York; he did not even need, in order to place himself in a state of grace, to catalogue for pages and pages everything that was happening in the world, as he had recently done in "Song of Myself." [14]

However, side by side with the mystic and visionary poet, there was still the rowdy Walt in love with publicity, who the year before had hesitated at nothing in order to launch his book. The quotation from Emerson's letter which he had put on the backstrip of his volume was a sufficient symptom. But there was more: the complete text of this letter was printed in an appendix,[15] and Whitman answered it with a long twelve-page proclamation that served as a postscript to the book. The tone was extremely declamatory, — at least at the outset:

. . . these thirty-two Poems I stereotype, to print several thousand copies of. I much enjoy making poems . . . the work of my life is making poems. I keep on till I make a hundred, and then several hundred — perhaps a thousand. The way is clear to me. A few years, and the average annual call for my Poems is ten or twenty thousand copies — more, quite likely. Why should I hurry or compromise? [16]

Apparently the success of the first edition had intoxicated him with delusions of grandeur. But the naïveté of his swagger should not be allowed to obscure the value of this manifesto which has been too often underestimated, perhaps because bibliophiles for sentimental reasons place a high value only on the 1855 edition. This reply to Emerson is a document of equal importance with the 1855 Preface. First of all, he stated the reasons why he intended henceforth to celebrate sex in all frankness. Then he took up again the problem, which he had attacked in the 1855 Preface, of the relations between the poet and the public; but, this time, he adopted a less subjective point of view. Instead of trying to define the American poet of the future as he conceived him, he now attempted rather to define the conditions of his success and the qualities which, in his opinion, the American public should have. It was now less a matter of the poet than of the nation. Whereas in the 1855 Preface the constantly recurring words had been "the poet," "the great poet," the keynote of this letter was "These States," "America." The new manifesto was less personal and much more national. He advocated, in short, a less egocentric and more democratic poetry. He was less "Myself" and more the "Bard of Democracy." Another detail shows the same tendency: the 1855 Preface had completely disappeared; it had been converted into poems,[17] the most important of which was significantly entitled "Poem of Many in One," [18] in which he celebrated the mystic participation of everyone in democracy. In the following edition, he placed this poem at the head of his "Chants Democratic." [19] The center of interest was therefore shifting. Nevertheless he

still exalted the individual who remained an end in himself
and not a means. It is clear that he was passing gradually from
his initial subjectivism into his faith in democracy simply by
generalizing his own experience.[20]

It is evident from all this that the version of 1856 was in
many respects richer than that of 1855. It emphasized several
of the deeper preoccupations of Whitman which could only
be glimpsed a year earlier, such as his concern with sex. It
vigorously developed the theme of the journey, which inspired one of his finest poems, the future "Song of the Open
Road." It brought into full development his cosmic poetry,
which instead of being monotonously analytic achieved a
powerful synthetic form in the poem that later became "Crossing Brooklyn Ferry." And, finally, it definitely initiated a puri-
fication of his previous egotism, which henceforth shifted
more and more toward a passionate affirmation of his faith in
democracy.

It seems therefore that Malcolm Cowley is mistaken when
he says:

Some of the pure intensity of emotion that produced the first
edition was carried over into the 20 new poems of the second,
in 1856; but by then Whitman was less visionary and more
calculating in his methods. If these new poems have one quality
in common, it is that whether good or bad they are all inflated.
One feels in reading them that Whitman had some kinship with
the manufacturers and promoters of his busy era. Having created
a new poetic personality — in the same way that a businessman
might acquire a new invention — he was determined to exploit
it and, as we can see from his notebooks, to produce more and
bigger poems each year, like a thriving factory . . . but all of
them, even the best, are padded out with lists of things seen or
done, things merely read about, anatomical details and geographi-
cal names.[21]

But we have already noted that the 1856 edition, on the
contrary, marks a definite enrichment of the material, if not

by a complete change, at least by a more profound treatment of certain themes; and, in the form, it is not inferior, for the 1855 edition already contained some very long catalogues which weighed it down considerably.[22] There is no reason therefore to consider the first edition superior to the second.

By far the most interesting poem — or at least the most revealing — in the 1856 edition happens to be one of the last in the collection, the "Poem of the Propositions of Nakedness" (later called "Respondez," which disappeared from *Leaves of Grass* after 1876).[23] Its tone is bitterly ironic in contrast to the exuberant and joyful lyricism of the other poems. It recalls "A Boston Ballad," [24] but the subject is infinitely greater. The title is Carlylean: it concerns the tearing away of appearances, which, like clothes, cover and conceal the essential reality, in order to show the real in all its nakedness.[25] But the method that Whitman used was strictly his own. He sought, by means of a long series of fiats which in the end reach blasphemy,[26] to provoke in the reader a reaction of revolt, not against the speaker of the blasphemy, but against the present condition of things; for the reader could not fail to realize before long that these were not really blasphemies, that Whitman, in fact, was only evoking reality in all its ugliness in order to arouse disgust, because he was disgusted himself. He had good reasons. The world in which we live has its seamy side. Evil triumphs.[27] "Infidels" — that is to say, unbelievers, those who have neither ideal nor love — impose their law on the rest of mankind.[28] And they seem to be justified, for men think neither of themselves (by that Whitman means that they do not think of their essential identity), nor of the death which will nevertheless prolong their lives to infinity.[29] They repress love and live in the dark.[30] They prefer respectability to life, appearances to reality.[31] It is a desperate scene. Everywhere the wicked triumph over the good, and indeed one looks in vain for the good. To make things worse,

democracy, which might have saved humanity, has not succeeded in building in the United States the ideal society of
which Whitman among many others had dreamed. There are
still castes and differences between men. Liberty is not yet
everyone's inalienable right.[32] Worse still, some men are sold
like cattle. In the country which should be a model, slavery
is not yet abolished.[33]

The long enumeration of Whitman's complaints continues
thus for several pages. With bitter humor he describes things
as they are and pretends to believe that they are as they should
be. He goes even further by calling for things which exist
already — and thus introduces irony. He seems tormented and
unable fully to express the pain and impotent rage which
smoulder in him (for this poem is extremely awkward and
that is probably one of the reasons why he suppressed it in
1881). Here at any rate is a denial of the cry of joy which he
utters in "Poem of the Heart of the Son of Manhattan Island":
"And who has been happiest? O I think it is I — I think no
one was ever happier than I. . ." [34]

How could he have been as happy as he pretended with all
these causes for sadness? Wherever he turned he found only
occasions for suffering. On the metaphysical plane, he was
troubled by the predominance of evil in the world; on the
moral plane, he was shocked by the apathy and worthlessness
of most men, seduced by the vanity of appearances, insensi-
tive to the dazzling realities of life and love; and finally, on
the political plane, the United States inflicted a cruel disappointment on him by betraying the cause of democracy.

Here again are some of the symptoms that we had detected
in the 1855 edition. The crisis had not yet ended, the wound
had not closed. Apparently he was reconciled with the world,
but in his inmost heart there still was the same indignation,
and the spectacle of evil in all its forms continued to obsess

and afflict him. He himself participated in the universal corruption and in the misery of mankind:

> It is not you alone who know what it is to be evil,
> I am he who knew what it was to be evil,
> I too knitted the old knot of contrariety,
> Blabbed, blushed, resented, lied, stole, grudged,
> Had guile, anger, lust, hot wishes I dared not speak,
> Was wayward, vain, greedy, shallow, sly, a solitary
> committer, a coward, a malignant person,
> The wolf, the snake, the hog, not wanting in me,
> The cheating look, the frivolous word, the adulterous
> wish, not wanting. . .[35]

A strange confession, which is certainly not mere rhetoric, but rather a sincere avowal and a lyrical confirmation of the moral indignation and satirical sarcasms of "Respondez." Instead of scourging others, he castigates himself, but again we find the same obsession with evil and the same torments of an unquiet soul. Moreover, in spite of his habitual assurance, he admits that he has known moments of doubt and despair when it has seemed to him that his work was ridiculous and worthless. There could hardly be a better proof of his secret instability. This passionate optimist was haunted by the idea of evil. This arrogant Walt Whitman trying to impose his faith on the rest of the world was sometimes doubtful of himself and his mission.

But these hesitations and these painful uncertainties, which in any case occupy only a very minor place in the book, probably escaped his contemporaries, judging by the reviews that appeared in periodicals at the time. As in 1855, what mainly struck the critics was the impression of "manly vigor" and "brawny health" that emerged from the book.[36] And in general the reaction of the press seems to have been the same as in the preceding year, in spite of the somewhat different character of the new edition. The positions were unchanged. The Puritans, of course, again protested with utmost violence against the indecency of the work. The critic of the Boston *Christian Examiner*, for instance, wrote:

. . . in point of style, the book is an impertinence towards the English language; and in point of sentiment, an affront upon the recognized morality of respectable people. Both its language and thought seem to have just broken out of Bedlam . . . he has no objection to any persons whatever, unless they wear good clothes, or keep themselves tidy . . . an ithyphallic audacity that insults what is most sacred and decent among men.[37]

But curiously, in spite of the augmented importance of the sexual theme in the second edition, those who liked Whitman continued to offer their praise and encouragement. The New York *Times*, for example, printed these flattering comments:

Still, this man has brave stuff in him. He is truly astonishing. The originality of his philosophy is of little account . . . In manner only can we be novel, and truly Mr. Whitman is novelty itself. Since the greater portion of this review was written, we confess to having been attracted again and again to *Leaves of Grass*. It has a singular electric attraction . . . We look forward with curious anticipation to Mr. Walt Whitman's future works.[38]

The review in the Boston *Times* was more subtle and included some reservations, but recognized nevertheless the exceptional value of the book.[39]

Again, in spite of some attacks, the critical reception was far from discouraging. But, however flattering the praises which were occasionally offered, this was not yet the immense success that Whitman had dreamed of. Though several lines from *Leaves of Grass* had been quoted by way of preface in a collection of tales and sketches as early as 1856,[40] Whitman had had higher hopes for his book, if we may believe the ambitious declarations of his open letter to Emerson.

It is possible, however, that he had resigned himself to a

more modest success. Certain scattered allusions in the new poems seem to indicate that he had accepted the idea of being only a precursor:

> I am willing to wait to be understood by the growth of
> the taste of myself . . .[41]

> Say on, sayers!
> Delve! mould! pile the words of the earth!
> Work on, age after age, nothing is to be lost,
> It may have to wait long, but it will certainly come in
> use,
> When the materials are all prepared, the architects shall
> appear.
> I swear to you the architects shall appear without fail!
> I announce them and lead them! [42]

In any case, the triumph on which perhaps he had counted in spite of these prudent reservations never materialized. The second edition was no more successful commercially than the first. Even if it was stereotyped, as he claimed, it was probably not printed in more than a thousand copies, and sales were slow.[43] But he was prepared for this; his readings had informed him of similar failures; he knew that Wordsworth, for instance, had had to wait many years for recognition by the public.[44] So he bravely continued his work, persevering in the way which he had chosen, refusing to be discouraged by disappointments.

CHAPTER IV

NEW UNCERTAINTIES:
CONTEMPLATION OR ACTION?
JOURNALISM OR POETRY?

FOR an impression of the way Whitman lived at the time of the second edition of *Leaves of Grass*, some very good evidence is offered by Bronson Alcott in his report of the visit which he made to him in Brooklyn at the end of 1856:

> He receives us kindly, yet awkwardly [Alcott was accompanied by Thoreau], and takes us up two narrow flights of stairs to sit or stand as we might in his attic study — also the bed-chamber of himself and his feeble brother, the pressure of whose bodies was still apparent in the unmade bed standing in one corner, and the vessel scarcely hidden underneath. A few books were piled disorderly over the mantelpiece, and some characteristic pictures — a Hercules, a Bacchus, and a satyr — were pasted, unframed, upon the rude wall . . .

> He took occasion to inform us . . . of his bathing daily through the mid-winter; said he rode sometimes a-top of an omnibus up and down Broadway from morning till night beside the driver, and dined afterwards with the whipsters, frequented the opera during the season, and "lived to make pomes", and for nothing else particularly.

> He had told me on my former visit of his being a house-builder, but I learned from his mother that his brother was the house-builder, and not Walt, who, she said, had no business but going

out and coming in to eat, drink, write and sleep. And she told how all the common folks loved him. He had his faults, she knew, and was not a perfect man, but means us to understand that she thought him an extraordinary son of a fond mother.[1]

This unpremeditated page tells us many things — first of all, Whitman's total indifference to his environment. (This was one of the constants of his life and explains in particular how he was able to spend his old age in Camden without suffering from the ugliness of that industrial city with its dirt and smoke.) He had no need for beautiful surroundings: the sordid attic [2] shared with an infirm brother sufficed him. He lived there in disorder and discomfort, but he did not care. He was a Bohemian — and a stay-at-home at the same time, so much so that at the age of thirty-seven he had not yet completely detached himself from his family — which is rather a remarkable fact. The situation had its advantages. Though he lived at home, he enjoyed complete freedom of movement and everyone respected his independence. Free of material cares, he was able to consecrate himself entirely to his work and to follow his dreams without the risk of being brutally recalled to reality by material considerations.

However, he did not live in an artificial vacuum. He was indifferent to beauty, but he needed to be surrounded by some human warmth, and this was not lacking in Brooklyn. He had the affection of his mother and the friendship of ordinary people: his neighbors, the men he met on the street and with whom he took the ferry to New York, and the omnibus drivers on Broadway.[3] He had really become the democratic poet, the friend of all, whom he had evoked in the self-portraits of his 1855 edition, as Alcott's testimony shows.

But, above all, Alcott tells us that Whitman, at the end of 1856, had practically ceased to work as a carpenter. We already know that he had never been very industrious in pursuing this trade,[4] but it seems that now he had completely given

up earning his living by manual labor. Is it necessary to conclude that he was living as a parasite on his family? Although
it is impossible to know what *modus vivendi* he had come to
with his relatives, such an eventuality seems improbable because later on he regularly sent small sums of money to his
mother and contributed to the support of Edward, his infirm
brother. He had a strong sense of family solidarity. It is much
more reasonable to suppose that he lived on his savings and on
the income from the sales of *Leaves of Grass*. Unfortunately,
since the book sold poorly, this inaction could not last for ever.
Sooner or later his lack of money [5] would inevitably force him,
if not completely to renounce a life of contemplation, at least
to seek some kind of work which would enable him to supply
his material needs and still remain faithful to his ideal. Probably for this reason he thought very seriously of becoming an
orator. It might be the best solution.[6] He would travel through
the country giving lectures, spreading the message of his poems
everywhere and at the same time making his living. This
attractive idea had occurred to him even before he had found
himself again obliged to work for a living. In his open letter to
Emerson he had already declared:

> Other work I have set for myself to do, to meet people and The
> States face to face, to confront them with an American rude
> tongue . . . In poems or in speeches I say the word or two
> that has got to be said, adhere to the body, step with the count-
> less common footsteps, and remind every man and woman of
> something.[7]

Some months later, disappointed by the public reception of
his book, he had recompensed himself in imagination by dreaming that he might some day become a great orator, the champion
and supreme arbiter of American democracy:

> The strong thought-impression or conviction that the straight,
> broad, open, well-marked true vista before, or course of public
> teacher, "wander-speaker", — by powerful words, orations, ut-

tered with copiousness and decision, with all the aid of art, also the natural flowing vocal luxuriance of oratory. That the mightiest rule over America could be thus — as for instance, on occasion, at Washington, to be, launching from public room, at the opening of the session of Congress — perhaps launching at the President, leading persons, Congressmen, or Judges of the Supreme Court. That to dart hither and thither, as some great emergency might demand — the greatest champion America ever could know, yet holding no office or emolument whatever, — but first in the esteem of men and women. *Not* to direct eyes or thoughts to any of the usual avenues, as of official appointment, or to get such anyway. To put all those aside for good. But always to keep up living interest in public questions — and *always to hold the ear of the people.*[8]

This great prophet, this hero of the people, though he was not named, was no other than himself and it was to himself that these recommendations were addressed. For a long time, moreover, he had cherished the dream of influencing his contemporaries through the medium of speech because it always gives an impression of direct contact and tremendous power. Journalism was only a poor substitute. In 1837, as an obscure country school-master on Long Island, he had already launched himself in public speaking, taking an active part in the meetings of the Smithtown debating society.[9] Later, but when still very young, he had had occasion to speak in political meetings before large audiences — [10] though we do not know with what success. In any case, in 1855, he still thought of becoming a great political orator. In one of the reviews of *Leaves of Grass* which he himself wrote, he said: "Doubtless in the scheme this man has built for himself, the writing of poems is but a proportionate part of the whole. . . In politics he could enter with the freedom and reality he shows in poetry." [11]

He had made preparations for this career; according to his brother George, he had composed " 'barrels' of lectures," [12] and among his papers many notes have been found which prove that he had often reflected on the art of oratory and on the techniques of lecturing, and had already assembled materials for these future speeches.[13] He had not limited himself to politics. He had attacked all the subjects that interested him, particularly art, literature, and above all, religion.[14] He wanted, in short, to take up in a simpler, more direct, and explicit form some of the essential themes of his poems. This would have been one way of familiarizing the public with his thinking and of imparting to it a taste for his poetry. For, according to him, every poet had himself to create his public if he wished to be appreciated or even merely accepted.[15] His oratorical activity would thus have been a supplement to his poetic creation and his speeches would have been more than a mere source of income. Eloquence and poetry would have been two parallel modes of expression: "Henceforth two co-expressions. They expand, amicable from common sources, but each with individual stamps by itself. First POEMS, *Leaves of Grass*, as of INTUITIONS. . . Second, Lectures, or Reasoning. . ."[16]

In addition he contemplated publishing his lectures in the form of a book that would be a sort of companion-piece to *Leaves of Grass*,[17] and it seems that his project of becoming a lecturer or an orator (for he continually confused the two ideas)[18] developed as the failure of *Leaves of Grass* became more apparent and his need for money more pressing.[19] Thus in 1858 he thought of undertaking a lecture tour throughout the United States, particularly in the West and South, and into Canada. In this way he would be able to live on his fees and on the income from the sale of his printed lectures.[20]

But this fine project was never realized, probably because it was easier to dream about it[21] than to put it into execution, and perhaps also because Whitman, although he delighted in imagining the triumph which he would obtain as an orator, knew very well that in practice he would inevitably fail. His voice was too weak, his delivery monotonous; he lacked fire; he would never be able to move an audience — as was proved later when he gave commemorative addresses on the death of Lincoln. He was therefore constrained to resign himself again to being a mere journalist.

In May 1857 he became in fact the editor-in-chief of the Brooklyn *Daily Times*.[22] His experimental period had apparently ended. He had given up carpentry.[23] It is true that the portraits of this period still show him dressed as a laborer. He had not resumed the costume of the dandy, but he bowed for the time being to bourgeois taste and consented to wear a necktie.[24] Since the editorials in the *Daily Times* were not signed, it is impossible to tell exactly when he took office. However, it seems almost certain that his first regular contribution was dated the first of May 1857.[25]

The *Daily Times* was the youngest and most important of the Brooklyn newspapers. It had come to the fore after very humble beginnings, thanks to the skill of its proprietors and also to its political neutrality.[26] The fact that the direction of such a paper was confided to Whitman proves that its owners had complete faith in his competence. Moreover, a glance through *I Sit and Look Out*, in which the articles he wrote at this time have been collected, shows that he acquitted himself creditably. In his editorials he attacked the most various subjects, from Washington's birthday [27] to liquor legislation [28] by way of the education of teachers.[29] A comparison of these articles with those written nine years earlier for the Brooklyn *Eagle* shows how much he had matured in the interval. He no longer had the same illusions. Previously, he had violently opposed capital punishment; [30] now he admitted that it was a necessary evil.[31] He knew more of life. He had lost his former youthful naïveté and his belief in utopias. On occasion he even made fun of overenthusiastic reformers — though he recognized their importance as forerunners.[32] His earlier absolute idealism had given way to a somewhat disillusioned realism. He condemned the blind fanaticism of those who wanted to impose temperance on the rest of the nation.[33] This was far from the conventional clichés of *Franklin Evans*; he even went so far as to propose the supervision of prostitution which he did not believe could be suppressed.[34] Generally speaking he was hostile to any radical measure. He had realized that human nature could not be changed by decree and that progress could be made only as the result of a slow and gradual evolution,[35] depending not on a reform of society but on the moral improvement of individuals.[36] Even his patriotism was shaken. Formerly so proud of his country, he now denounced the anarchical taste for violence in some of his compatriots — [37] which Dickens had so severely criticized in *American Notes*. Ten years earlier, Whitman had been an enthusiastic partisan of the Mexican War,[38] but now he came out in the *Daily Times* against the imperialistic visions of those who would have liked to see the United States annex the South American republics.[39]

This apparent eclipse of his faith in man and his country was probably due to a new political crisis which he had just gone through and which had begun in 1856. In that year, the presidential campaign had been particularly violent. In 1854, under Franklin Pierce's administration, the Democrats led by Douglas denounced the Missouri Compromise and authorized the introduction of slavery into the Territory of Kansas, and this measure provoked the immediate indignation of all those in the North who were opposed to slavery, or even, more simply, to its extension into the new territories of the West. In 1856 the dissatisfied politicians organized a new party, the Republican Party, which proposed to bring Kansas into the Union as a free state. Their candidate for the presidency was John C. Frémont, the famous explorer. The old parties chose professional politicians as their candidates. The Whigs named Millard Fillmore, who had served as President from 1850 to

1853 after the death of Zachary Taylor, and the Democrats nominated James Buchanan. Whitman, apparently as much revolted by the tergiversations and compromises of the two traditional parties as he had been in 1850, cried out his indignation and rage in an unusually violent pamphlet: *The Eighteenth Presidency.*[40] He addressed himself "to each young man in the Nation, North, South, East, and West"; to "mechanics, farmers, sailors, etc.," who "constitute some six millions of the inhabitants of These States"; to "merchants, lawyers, doctors, teachers and priests," whom he opposed to the 350 owners of slaves and to the handful of corrupt politicians who managed to govern the country without taking account of its profound aspirations.[41] He began by proclaiming his faith and absolute confidence in the honesty and genius of the people:

There is more rude and undeveloped bravery, friendship, conscientiousness, clear-sightedness, and practical genius for any scope of action, even the broadest and highest, now among the American mechanics and young men, than in all the official persons in These States, legislative, executive, judicial, military, and naval, and more than among all the literary persons. I would be much pleased to see some heroic, shrewd, fully-informed, healthy-bodied, middle-aged, beard-faced American blacksmith or boatman come down from the West across the Alleghanies and walk into the Presidency, dressed in a clean suit of working attire, and with the tan all over his face, breast and arms; I would certainly vote for that sort of man, possessing the due requirements before any other candidate.[42]

After this measured and almost solemn preamble, he hastened to the attack. Carried away by anger, he could hardly control himself; he let go more and more insults: "traitors . . . prostitutes . . . dough-faces, office-vermin, kept-editors. . ."[43] And shortly after, for a whole page,[44] he heaped abuse on his enemies the politicians, some of it gratuitous ("body-snatchers"), some probably deserved. He was disheartened by the mediocrity of Buchanan and Fillmore,[45] and he called for a "Redeemer President" who would be the representative of all and not just of some. It seemed to him that Frémont might play this role.[46] In any case, he felt that slavery had to be abolished at whatever cost, lest it abolish the liberties of the people.[47] Such was the essential message of this passionate pamphlet — generous and fervent when it addressed the American people, full of hate and contempt when it scourged those who had betrayed the democratic ideal. Its language was firm and bare; he had instinctively adopted a clear and energetic polemic style that contrasted vividly with the habitual imprecision of the prose he had been writing at this period — the prose of the 1855 Preface, for example, or of the open letter to Emerson or of his projected lectures. He seems to have been tense and fully in control of himself (except, of course, in the several passages where he indulged in insults); but under this contained vehemence, an unshakable conviction can be felt. Moreover, the last paragraph was a tranquil affirmation of his faith in the continued progress of humanity and in the final victory of democracy. The argument expanded, it was not a matter only of the United States but of the destiny of mankind and of the struggle for liberty which was raging throughout the world:

Freedom against slavery is not issuing here alone, but is issuing everywhere. The horizon rises, it divides, I perceive, for a more august drama than any of the past . . . Everything indicates unparalleled reforms. . . Never was justice so mighty amid injustice; never did the idea of equality erect itself so haughty and uncompromising amid inequality, as today. . . Never was the representative man more energetic, more like a god than to-day. . . What whispers are these running through the eastern Continents, and crossing the Atlantic and Pacific? What historic denouements are these we are approaching? On all sides tyrants tremble, crowns are unsteady, the human race restive, on the watch for some better era, some divine war. . .[48]

A cosmic vision of the future of humanity in which the pamphleteer rejoined the poet.

It is clear that in spite of the severe disappointments that Whitman had experienced in 1850, his faith in democracy had remained intact. He saw a new crisis coming, and he wanted to speak his mind and to play an active part. He longed to join the fray. He was again tempted to action, but he stopped short of actual intervention. He did not really act, he contented himself with dreaming that he acted — or was about to act. For this violent pamphlet, which might have had a certain influence and created a great stir, was not published. He prepared it with the greatest care and went so far as to set it in type in order to print some proofs, but at the last moment he refrained from having it published himself. He abandoned to others the responsibility of diffusing it. Just before the conclusion he inserted this appeal:

To the editors of the independent press, and to rich persons. Circulate and reprint this Voice of mine for the workingmen's sake. I hereby permit and invite any rich person, anywhere, to stereotype it, or reproduce it in any form, to deluge the cities of The States with it, North, South, East and West.[49]

Apparently he hoped that someone else would publish his pamphlet. It is not even known whether he sent any copies to the newspapers. At any rate, no one seems to have read it during Whitman's lifetime, and if two specimens had not been found among his papers, nothing would be known today of his velleity of intervening in the electoral campaign of 1856.

Could this powerlessness to act have been caused by a lack of practical ability? Did he not know how to set about publishing his diatribe? Or was it a lack of courage, a fear of making enemies? It is possible, but not probable. He had already given proof of his courage by making no concessions to his detractors in the second edition of *Leaves of Grass*. Whatever the cause,

there was a strange failure in this, which is the more difficult
to understand since the passionate tone of the pamphlet indicates a wholehearted adhesion to the cause which he extolled.

There can be no doubt of his sincerity, for otherwise how
can the bitter realism and the disillusioned skepticism of some
of his editorials in the *Daily Times* be explained, except on the
ground of the pain that the defeat of Frémont must have given
him? Reality had once again inflicted a harsh reproof to the
incorrigible dreamer. It must have been heartbreaking for him
to be obliged once more to postpone the realization of his ideal.
It seems likely that he experienced, at least temporarily, some
disgust for the blindness of the majority of his fellow-countrymen and some fear for the immediate future. Cruelly disappointed in his dearest hopes, he could do nothing except
retire for a time into his tent. And so he did — which accounts
for the neutrality of his articles in the Brooklyn *Daily Times*.
He deliberately kept away from the party battles, the senseless-
ness of which he had realized. This is the line of conduct he
laid out for himself in a short poem written at this time, "To
the States. To identify the 16th, 17th or 18th Presidentiad." [50]
He was speaking here of his disillusionment and his decision
to withdraw for a time until the American people should awake
from their torpor:

> Are those really Congressmen? are those the great
>   Judges? is that the President?
> Then I will sleep awhile yet, for I see that these States
>   sleep, for reasons;
> (With gathering murk, with muttering thunder and
>   lambent shoots we all duly awake,
> South, North, East, West, inland and seaboard, we will
>   surely awake.) [51]

But this painful political crisis had by no means extinguished
the poet in him. A few months later, he wrote in his journal:

The Great Construction of the New Bible. Not to be diverted

from the principal object — the main life work — the three hundred and sixty-five. — It ought to be ready in 1859 (June '57).[52]

This passage refers of course to *Leaves of Grass*. He had not stopped working at it. Even while he trembled for the future of democracy, his poetic activity was not diminished, for, on June 20, 1857 (when he had been editor of the *Daily Times* for nearly two months), he wrote to a friend:

Fowler and Wells are bad persons for me. — They retard my book very much. — It is worse than ever. — I wish now to bring out a third edition. — I have now a *hundred* poems ready (the last edition had thirty-two.) — and shall endeavor to make an arrangement with some publisher here to take the plates from F.&W. and make the additions needed, and so bring out the third edition. — F.&W. are very willing to give up the plates — they want the thing off their hands. — In the forthcoming Vol. I shall have, as I said, a hundred poems, and no other matter but poems — (no letters to or from Emerson — no Notices or any thing of that sort.) — It is, I know Well enough, that *that* must be the *true Leaves of Grass*.[53]

So in the space of about a year he had composed some seventy poems. His creative power was still as great — at least quantitatively — as at the time when he had been preparing the first edition. Since 1855, in spite of setbacks and disappointments, the flow of his poems had been uninterrupted. It looked as if he were immune to the influence of exterior events. Although he became excited over the political battles of these crucial years, and to some extent participated in them — more as a dreamer than as a man of action — in his innermost being something escaped the vicissitudes of life and resisted all the assaults of experience. He hoped and despaired by turns, but at the center of himself, the poet looked out, an imperturbable spectator whose faith in mankind and in his own destiny could not be shaken by any contradictory experience.

One might also ask why he did not publish a new edition of his poems in 1857, but the reason was probably that his efforts to find a publisher interested in the venture did not succeed. He was therefore obliged to remain a journalist and to write mediocre editorials in the Brooklyn *Daily Times*. He was, in short, living a double life; for no reader of his articles could have suspected that their author was a poet. Nothing in their style or their language recalls *Leaves of Grass*, and only on rare occasions can a parallelism between his journalistic productions and his poems be discovered.[54]

Apparently this kind of existence suited him, for he remained with the *Daily Times* for nearly two years. The job of chief editor required no great expense of physical energy, and it evidently allowed him a great deal of leisure. As he had done when he was editing the Brooklyn *Eagle*, he passed his time running about New York whenever he had a free moment. He had taken up again with his friends, the omnibus drivers, and rode along Fifth Avenue or Broadway, seated beside them, watching the innumerable crowds on the sidewalks and half lost in his dreams:

A fine warmish afternoon — and Broadway in the full flow of its Gulf Stream of fashion. . . Omnibuses! — There they go incessantly — the Broadway line, Yellow Bird, Twenty-Third Street. . . Everything appertaining to them is a study. — One man appears to think so at any rate — Do you mind him, as the driver of the handsome Fifth Avenue pulls up casting at the lounger a friendly and inquiring glance, as much as to say, come take a ride, Walt Whitman? For none other than Walt is it who in response turns off from the pave, and seizes the handle, swings himself up with spring and elastic motion, and lights on the off-handside of the stage, with his hip held by the rod as quietly as a hawk swoops to its nest.

That man is the subject for the whole of this week's Plaza Sketch — that pet and pride of the Broadway stage-drivers.

As onward speeds the stage, mark his nonchalant air, seated

aslant and quite at home — Our million-hued, ever-changing panorama of Broadway moves steadily down; he, going up, sees it all, as in a kind of half-dream. — Mark the salutes of four out of each five of the drivers, downward bound; — salutes which he silently returns in the same manner — the raised arm, and the upright hand.[55]

When he had enough of such promenading, he took refuge at Pfaff's. This famous Swiss restaurant on Broadway was at that time the favorite haunt of literary Bohemia in New York. In particular Whitman found there Henry Clapp, founder of the *Saturday Press*, who became one of his more faithful allies and who lost no occasion to praise him in his review at the expense of Longfellow, whom he detested.[56] There he also met William Winter, Clapp's assistant, a Bostonian and an admirer of Longfellow — with whom Whitman got along less well — and Ada Clare, nicknamed Queen of Bohemia, a rich adventuress who had come back from Paris with the ambition of re-creating in New York the atmosphere of the Latin Quarter.[57] William Dean Howells, who visited Pfaff's in 1860, tells how Whitman on seeing him

leaned back in his chair and reached out his great hand to [him] as if he were going to give it to [him] for good and all. He had a fine head, with a cloud of Jovian hair upon it, and a branching beard and moustache, gentle eyes that looked most kindly into [his], and seemed to wish the linking which [he] instantly gave him, though [they] hardly passed a word, and [their] acquaintance was summed up in that glance and the grasp of his mighty fist upon [his] hand.[58]

Two details stand out: Whitman's Olympian majesty and his taciturnity. He never really mingled with the New York Bohemians. He was there as a spectator. Instead of taking part in the conversation, he preferred to look on in silence or to think about the Broadway crowds whose uninterrupted flood passed a few yards away:

> The curious appearance of the faces — the glimpse
>   first caught of the eyes and expressions as they flit
>   along,
> O You phantoms! oft I pause, yearning to arrest some
>   one of you!
> Oft I doubt your reality whether you are real — I sus-
>   pect all is but a pageant.[59]

The problem of the reality of the exterior world preoccupied him more than the remarks exchanged around him. His curiosity was metaphysical rather than psychological. Therefore he never became a regular member of the group. "My own greatest pleasure at Pfaff's," he declared to Traubel, "was to look on — to see, talk little, absorb. I never was a great discusser, anyway — never. I was much better satisfied to listen to a fight than take part in it." [60]

This aloofness is characteristic of his attitude toward life. He wrote in a sketch for a poem dating from this time:

> But that shadow, my likeness, that goes to and fro
>   seeking a livelihood, chattering, chaffering,
> I often find myself standing and looking at it where it
>   flits —
> That likeness of me, but never substantially me.[61]

During this whole period, his life was in general extremely calm, he worked in the morning for his paper and idled all afternoon. But in 1859, toward the end of June, he lost his job as chief editor of the Brooklyn *Times*. The exact circumstances are not known,[62] but very probably it was because he had written two articles which must have provoked the anger of the clergy of the town. On June 20, the columns of his paper contained an article on "A Delicate Subject," namely, prostitution, a tabooed topic which he should never have brought up, especially since he declared himself in favor of a realistic solution of the problem and hoped that the authorities would recognize the existence of prostitution in New York instead of hypocritically pretending that there was no such thing.[63] The second article, two days later, discussed celibacy. "Can All Marry?" he asked, and he took occasion frankly to dilate on the dangers of sexual repression.[64] It seems probable that after this, because of the indignation of some of his readers, Whitman was obliged to resign or that the proprietor of the paper found it necessary to part company with him. Anyhow, he was again unemployed, and on June 29, he wrote in one of his notebooks: "It is now time to *stir* first for *Money* enough, *to live and provide for* M——. *To Stir* — first write stories and get out of this Slough." [65]

Who was this mysterious M——? Emory Holloway has proposed several explanations. Perhaps it was his mother, or his sister Mary? But why did he not write out the name in full? Or it may have been some mistress, perhaps the woman he had loved in New Orleans.[66] Canby believes that it must have been his mother, whom he had supported since the death of his father in 1855.[67] It is impossible to arrive at any certainty here. We are coming into a very obscure period in Whitman's life. There is at this time a gap in the recollections which he had recorded in *Specimen Days*,[68] and no notebook has been found among his papers to fill in the hiatus.[69] We can only make conjectures. It seems almost certain, however, that during this time he went through a severe moral crisis. The two articles that caused his resignation or dismissal from the Brooklyn *Times* were perhaps symptoms of it. Sexual problems were beginning to trouble him to the point that he could not refrain from discussing them in his editorials in spite of the reprobation which he was sure to encounter.[70] He was to treat them poetically with still more boldness in the 1860 edition of his book.[71] Moreover this edition shows unequivocal traces of a painful emotional disappointment. It seems that he experienced in 1858–59 (the exact date is uncertain) a great passion for a man about whom nothing is known, not even his name.[72] This passion was so violent and so exclusive that it superseded everything that concerned him previously. He was in love, nothing else mattered:

> . . . now take notice, land of the prairies, land of the
>   south savannas, Ohio's land,
> Take notice Kanuck woods — and you Lake Huron —
>   and all that with you roll toward Niagara — and
>   you Niagara also,
> And you, Californian mountains, — That you each
>   and all find somebody else to be your singer of songs,
> For I can be your singer of songs no longer — One who
>   loves me is jealous of me, and withdraws me from
>   all but love,
> With the rest I dispense — I sever from what I thought
>   would suffice me — it is now empty and tasteless to
>   me,
> I heed knowledge, and the grandeur of The States, and
>   the example of heroes, no more,
> I am indifferent to my own songs — I will go with him
>   I love,
> It is to be enough for us that we are together — We
>   never separate again.[73]

Drunk with love, he experienced moments of extraordinary exaltation in which his usual apathy completely disappeared. Normally a stay-at-home, he now dreamed of setting out with the one he loved on the open road of which he had formerly sung platonically in the 1856 *Leaves of Grass* — at least if it is possible to believe the following poem composed at this time, which probably reflects the feelings that he then experienced:

> We two boys together clinging,
> One the other never leaving,
> Up and down the roads going — North and South
>   excursions making,
> Power enjoying — elbows stretching — fingers clutch-
>   ing,

Armed and fearless — eating, drinking, sleeping, loving,
No law less than ourselves owning — sailing, soldiering, thieving, threatening,
Misers, menials, priests alarming — air breathing, water drinking, on the turf or the sea-beach dancing,
With birds singing — With fishes swimming — With trees branching and leafing,
Cities wrenching, ease scorning, statutes mocking, feebleness chasing,
Fulfilling our foray.[74]

But this great love was probably not returned, and soon Whitman found himself alone, abandoned by his loved one and broken-hearted.

Hours continuing long, sore and heavy-hearted,
Hours of dusk, when I withdraw to a lonesome and unfrequented spot, seating myself, leaning my face in my hands,
Hours sleepless, deep in the night, when I go forth, speeding swiftly the country roads, or through the city streets, or pacing miles and miles, stifling plaintive cries;
Hours discouraged, distracted — for the one I cannot content myself without, soon I saw him content himself without me;
Hours when I am forgotten, (O weeks and months are passing, but I believe I am never to forget!)
Sullen and suffering hours! (I am ashamed — but it is useless — I am what I am;)
Hours of my torment — I wonder if other men ever have the like, out of the like feelings?
Is there even one other like me — distracted — his friend, his lover lost to him?
Is he too as I am now? Does he still rise in the morning, dejected, thinking who is lost to him? and at night, awaking, think who is lost?
Does he too harbor his friendship silent and endless? harbor his anguish and passion?

> Does some stray reminder, or the casual mention of a
>   name, bring the fit back upon him, taciturn and
>   deprest?
> Does he see himself reflected in me? In these hours,
>   does he see the face of his hours reflected.[75]

This remarkably poignant cry of pain seems to come from the
depth of his being. He moans like a wounded animal. His
suffering was still so keen in 1860 that he could not refrain
from giving it a place in his book, but the confession was too
intimate, the revelation too compromising; therefore in the
next edition he suppressed this poem and also the preceding
one. The terrible despair he had experienced was probably
rendered still more painful by an awareness of his singularity
— of his inversion of which I will speak again. He was to
some extent ashamed of it and did not dare to complain or to
confess as much as he would have liked:

> Sullen and suffering hours! (I am ashamed — but it is
>   useless — I am what I am;)
> . . . I wonder if other men ever have the like, out of
>   the like feelings?

In this connection it is possible to understand the quality
of despair of certain poems of the 1860 edition, notably "A
Word Out of the Sea," [76] the extremely personal overtones of
which he later tried to minimize. There was this admission in
particular:

> O throes!
> O you demon, singing by yourself — projecting me.[77]

Clearly the bird weeping for the loss of its companion was the
poet himself and the major theme of the fragment was originally abandonment, not death.[78] "My love soothes not me,"
says the bird, and thinking it sees its mate, it cries: "Hither,
my love! Here I am! Here! . . . Do not be decoyed else-

where!" [79] And it is the abandoned poet, not the child, the fictitious witness of a tragedy of nature, who exclaims:

O a word! O what is my destination?
O I fear it is henceforth chaos!
O how joys, dreads, convolutions, human shapes, and
    all shapes, spring as from graves around me!
O phantoms! you cover all the land, and all the sea!
O I cannot see in the dimness whether you smile or
    frown upon me;
O vapor, a look, a word! O well-beloved!
O you dear women's and men's phantoms! [80]

This macabre evocation provides a measure of Whitman's dismay when he suddenly found himself alone once more after having loved so deeply. It also accounts for the despair of "As I Ebb'd with the Ocean of Life," [81] whose topic is the desolation and vanity of life and in which he inaugurates the theme of the shipwreck resumed more tragically in "Thoughts." In his pain he almost goes so far as to doubt the immortality of the soul:

Are souls drown'd and destroy'd so?
Is only matter triumphant? [82]

Life itself became suspect to him, and he was obsessed with the idea of death, the tragic irreversibility of which weighed on his mind now that he had suffered the experience of separation. He could see nothing but graves around him, but he searched them in vain; nowhere could he find the body of the one he loved. Death was dissolution and annihilation, and the dust of the dead was mingled with the living:

Of him I love day and night, I dreamed I heard he was
    dead,
And I dreamed I went where they had buried him I
    love — but he was not in that place,
And I dreamed I wandered, searching among burial-
    places, to find him,

And I found that every place was a burial-place,
The houses full of life were equally full of death,
    (This house is now,)
The streets, the shipping, the places of amusement, the
    Chicago, Boston, Philadelphia, the Mannahatta, were
    as full of the dead as of the living,
And fuller, O vastly fuller, of the dead than of the
    living. . .
And if the memorials of the dead were put up in-
    differently everywhere, even in the room where I
    eat or sleep, I should be satisfied,
And if the corpse of any one I love, or if my own corpse,
    be duly rendered to powder, and poured in the sea,
    I shall be satisfied,
Or if it be distributed to the winds, I shall be satisfied.[83]

Nevertheless there were moments when he could not believe
that separation in space or time could be permanent. It sometimes seemed to him that his friend was again by his side, but
the phantom, alas, soon vanished away:

I thought I was not alone here by the shore,
But the one I thought was with me, as now I walk by
    the shore,
As I lean and look through the glimmering light — that
    one has utterly disappeared,
And those appear that perplex me.[84]

His grief was so keen that at the age of forty he anticipated
nothing more from life. He could only say "so long" to his
readers and die:

It appears to me I am dying. . .
Dear friend, whoever you are, here, take this kiss,
I give it especially to you — Do not forget me,
I feel like one who has done his work — I progress on,
The unknown sphere, more real than I dreamed, more
    direct, darts awakening rays about me — *So Long!*

> Remember my words — I love you — I depart from
> materials,
> I am as one disembodied, triumphant, dead.[85]

And it is probably his own face that he describes in this profoundly melancholy little poem:

> What weeping face is that looking from the window?
> Why does it stream those sorrowful tears?
> Is it for some burial place, vast and dry?
> Is it to wet the soil of graves? [86]

In 1855 he had exclaimed in his joy before the spectacle of the universe:

> It is not chaos or death. . . . it is form and union
> and plan. . . . it is eternal life. . . . it is happi-
> ness.[87]

Now he commented, sad and disillusioned:

> . . . O what is my destination?
> O I fear it is henceforth chaos! [88]

His former exuberant and triumphant pantheism had given way, as Frederik Schyberg notes,[89] to a desperate pantheism — at least in his moments of depression, for it seems to me that Schyberg exaggerates the morbid character of the 1860 edition. According to him, after the emotional crisis that had brought Whitman to the brink of suicide (which is probable, though not demonstrable), Whitman had led in New York a life of debauchery from which he did not succeed in extricating himself until 1861, at the outbreak of the Civil War.[90] But in that case how can the publication of the 1860 edition be explained? The mere existence of this edition would seem to prove that Whitman had by that time regained his equilibrium, otherwise how could he have found the courage to publish a new version of his book? Moreover the tranquil tone of the letters he wrote from Boston during that year [91] permit no doubt that he had recovered his serenity. Once again he had triumphed over his despair. In spite of his anguish and doubts, he had resumed his creative work and art had saved his life. The 1860 *Leaves of Grass* is the indication and the proof of this new victory over himself. The words with which he concludes:

> . . . I depart from materials,
> I am as one disembodied, triumphant, dead [92]

are not those of a defeated or desperate man.

CHAPTER V

THE 1860 EDITION

THE 1860 edition of *Leaves of Grass* represented for Whitman a double victory, for not only did he emerge successfully from a lacerating crisis, but again he won an unexpected victory over circumstances. For the first time his book had been brought out by a publisher and not by himself. This was a dream which he had cherished for a long time, but which he had not yet realized.[1] In December 1859, however, his luck had begun to turn; he had succeeded in publishing a poem, "A Child's Reminiscence," in the New York *Saturday Press* edited by his friend Henry Clapp.[2] It was shortly after this that the young Boston publishers, Thayer and Eldridge, agreed to bring out a new edition of his book.[3] In the following March, Whitman was in Boston supervising the composition and printing of his volume with the care and competence one would expect from a former typographer. He spent three months there, and as his proofreading left him plenty of leisure, he took the opportunity to see the sights.[4] For example, he went to hear Father Taylor, a former seaman, who preached in a vigorous and picturesque language, at once familiar and Biblical, whose eloquence was greatly appreciated by Whitman. Every time, he tells us, Father Taylor's prayers moved him to tears.[5] He also attended the trial of Frank Sanborn, who was being prosecuted for complicity in John Brown's raid on Harper's Ferry. He was one of a group of abolitionists ready to intervene if the judge decided to surrender Sanborn to the federal authorities.[6] He made many friends during this visit, notably C. Q. Eldridge, one of his publishers, with whom he maintained friendly relations for the rest of his life. It was probably owing to Eldridge that "Bardic Symbols" (later "As I Ebb'd with the Ocean of Life") was published in April in the *Atlantic Monthly*, then edited by W. D. Howells.[7] The poem appeared anonymously, as was the custom in that magazine, but Whitman's style was easily recognizable. Eldridge also introduced him to William D. O'Connor, whose antislavery novel, *Harrington*, he was publishing at the time. Later, O'Connor became one of the most fanatical champions of *Leaves of Grass*. Whitman became equally friendly with John T. Trowbridge, who has left an account of their relations.[8] It is remarkable that none of those with whom he became acquainted noticed anything abnormal in him. On the contrary, they were all impressed by his physical vigor and his perfect equilibrium. Apparently he had completely recovered.

His book appeared at the end of June. It was a thick, strongly bound duodecimo of 456 pages.[9] As in the earlier editions, the name of the author was not given on the title page.[10] In order to find it, the reader had to refer to a copyright notice on the second page or to the title of the second poem, proudly called "Walt Whitman." (In 1856 this poem, which had been the introductory piece in the 1855 edition, was already entitled "A Poem of Walt Whitman, an American.")

As in 1855, he used his portrait instead of his name. He wanted his reader to see him not as an abstract entity, but as a living reality, a presence. Therefore, we find facing the title page a steel-engraving by S. A. Schoff after a portrait by Charles Hine. This time it was no longer the nonchalant and somewhat affected workingman of 1855, but the dreaming face of an artist or of a prophet. The vague and distant look remained, but the visage had aged. It gave the impression now of a fully matured man. His forehead was wrinkled. The beard and the abundant hair looked gray — and in fact they were. Whitman had become gray very early. Only the eyebrows were still brown. He was no longer in shirt sleeves as in 1855. He wore a coat, but the collar of his white shirt was still wide open. He had made one further concession, however: he had negligently tied a cravat round his neck, with the knot hanging low on his breast.

The vegetable motifs that had decorated the previous editions had completely disappeared. They were recalled only by the tendrils which prolonged the *L* and the *a*'s of *Leaves of Grass* on the cover and in all the letters of *Grass* on the title page. The color of the binding had also changed. Some of the copies were green, the rest were reddish-brown. Otherwise vegetable symbolism tended to be replaced by other themes in the decoration. The front cover showed the globe with the two Americas resting on clouds, and the back cover showed the sun rising — or setting — on the sea, and these motifs were repeated several times inside the book, as if to emphasize the cosmic character of the poet's inspiration. On the spine appeared a butterfly perched on a hand. It was also to be found on the last page and was meant to suggest the "magnetism" of Whitman, to which even the insects were susceptible. It made him comparable to Buddha or St. Francis of Assisi. Perhaps this butterfly also represented the soul, the "psyche" of the Ancient Greeks.[11]

The 1860 edition contained 154 poems, of which 122 were new, for the 1856 edition had included thirty-two. As he had announced in June 1857 that he had a hundred poems ready,[12] he must have composed some fifty poems since then — that is to say, probably all of "Calamus" and the greater part of "Children of Adam." [13]

A striking aspect of the book is its structure. Whereas in

1856 the poems were all placed on the same level and numbered in sequence from 1 to 32, Whitman had tried this time to introduce an order and a hierarchy into his work. Appropriately, the first poem, entitled "Proto-Leaf," presents the author and announces the essential themes: Love, Religion, and Democracy.[14] Then came "Walt Whitman," which had been placed at the beginning in the first two editions and which like "Proto-Leaf" is essentially an introduction. It was followed by a group of poems collectively entitled "Chants Democratic and Native American" and differentiated only by numbers. This is one of the characteristics of the new presentation, for there were several other similar groups: "Leaves of Grass" (which was thus at the same time the title of the whole book and of one of its parts), "Enfans d' Adam;" "Calamus," and "Messenger Leaves." Among these groups, which were still in a nebulous state, Whitman intercalated clearly individualized poems that were given titles — "Salut au Monde," "Poem of Joys," "A Word out of the Sea," *et cetera*, down to "So Long!" which, being a farewell poem, very naturally brought the book to a close. For the first time, then, Whitman tried to impose an architectonic structure on his work. In the table of contents his intention is clear. He had even had the section titles printed in boldface type, as if he wanted to make them the pillars upon which the rest of the edifice would stand. And there is a remarkably close correspondence between them and the themes announced in "Proto-Leaf." The "Chants Democratic" develop the theme of democracy, "Leaves of Grass" that of religion (God, death, evil, nature), "Enfans d'Adam" and "Calamus" two aspects of love. In "Messenger Leaves" the intention is less clear, but it seems probable that Whitman wanted to present himself as a new Messiah: the three principal themes are here repeated and regrouped.

Thus, although *Leaves of Grass* had hardly any structure

yet, the poems now followed a plan, the main lines of which were clear and immediately perceptible. The form of the book had become much more vigorous. It had been musical in the first two versions; this time it was more architectural. The themes formerly had been mingled and interlaced; they were now separated and distinguished. Compared to this, the previous editions were incoherent. Whitman recognized this fact himself when he announced:

We are able to declare that there will also soon crop out the true *Leaves of Grass*, the fuller-grown work of which the former two issues were the inchoates — this forthcoming one, far, very far ahead of them in quality, quantity, and in supple lyric exuberance. . . Walt Whitman, for his own purpose, slowly trying his hand at the edifice, the structure he has undertaken, has lazily loafed on, letting each part have time to set, — evidently building not so much with reference to any part itself, considered alone, but more with reference to the ensemble, — always bearing in mind the combination of the whole, to fully justify the parts when finished.[15]

He wanted this volume to be a finished work, self-sufficient and clear to all: "It is, I know well enough, that *that* must be the *true Leaves of Grass* — and I think it has an aspect of completeness and makes its case clearer." [16] If he had disappeared or stopped writing at that time — these were eventualities which he envisaged in "Leaves of Grass n°20" [17] and in "So Long!" [18] — no matter, he had formulated his essential message, his Bible was written.[19]

But the presentation was not the only novelty in this edition. This third version of *Leaves of Grass* had a different character from the others. The essential themes were those found already in the text of 1856, but they were expressed with more vigor. The disposition and structure of the book gave them an emphasis they had not possessed before. And, moreover, their relative importance had changed. The accent was placed on democracy since the "Chants Democratic" came at the beginning, just after the introductory poems, and occupied nearly ninety pages of the book — comprising by far the longest group of poems. Previously *Leaves of Grass* had been much more personal. Its subject had been the poet in his relation with the universe. The center of interest had now shifted. The poet had partly given place to the prophet, as can be seen in "Proto-Leaf" and in the embryonic "Messenger Leaves." At the same time, however, a very personal theme — and one which was generally considered taboo — had acquired a new importance along with the democratic theme: that of physical love or of sex. It had been announced as early as 1855:

> Through me forbidden voices,
> Voices of sexes and lusts. . . . voices veiled, and I
>   remove the veil,
> Voices indecent by me clarified and transfigured.[20]

The fifth poem of that collection, besides, had already treated it to some extent.[21] In 1856 this theme recurred more insistently. Three new poems scattered through the book were devoted to it: "Poem of Women," "Poem of Procreation," and "Bunch-Poem." [22] But in 1860, as if Whitman could no longer contain himself,[23] two whole groups of poems, "Enfans d'Adam" and "Calamus," chanted the violent joys of love with a crudity that prompted Thoreau to say: "It is as if the beasts spoke." [24] "Enfans d'Adam" celebrates the love of woman and "Calamus," more obscurely, but with greater force and tenderness, homosexual love. Whitman seems to have put together "Enfans d'Adam" after "Calamus" both to counterbalance [25] and to camouflage the abnormal character of his instincts. Dr. Bucke discovered the following note among his papers: "A string of poems, (short etc.) embodying the amative love of woman — the same as Live Oak Leaves [such was originally the title of "Calamus"] do the passion of friendship for man." [26]

"Calamus," then, was an echo of the great emotional crisis which he had just gone through [27] and which would otherwise be unknown. None of the biographical documents establish the date or the circumstances, but there can be no mistake: the tone of "Calamus" is so vehement, so passionate, that it leaves no possible doubt of the sincerity of this confession. We shall have occasion to return later to this delicate problem. The internal evidence of the work is enough for the time being. Up to this point Whitman's sexual desires had been very vague, as if they had not yet found their object. In 1855 he was still exclusively preoccupied with the troubled emotions of adolescence:

> I have perceived that to be with those I like is enough,
> To stop in company with the rest at evening is enough,
> To be surrounded by beautiful curious breathing laughing flesh is enough,
> To pass among them. . to touch any one. . . . to rest my arm ever so lightly round his or her neck for a moment. . . . what is this then?
> I do not ask any more delight. . . . I swim in it as in a sea.[28]

The following year he had loudly celebrated the duty and joys of procreation in "Poem of Procreation," [29] but he had declared at the same time in "Bunch-Poem":

> The greed that eats in me day and night with hungry gnaw, till I saturate what shall produce boys to fill my place when I am through. . .[30]

If we are to believe this statement, he had not yet encountered the ideal woman who could give him children worthy of him and his line. Where he had written "A Woman Waits for Me," [31] it would be more correct to read "I Wait for

a Woman." His early poems clearly show his disquietude and
the torments his sexual nature caused him. In 1860, on the
contrary, he had found himself. True, he had expanded the
"Poem of Procreation," which later became "Enfans d'Adam,"
but he did so from a sense of duty; his heart was elsewhere.
He had in the meantime suddenly discovered what his body
was longing for. It seems probable that a brief homosexual
affair had given him a revelation of love and also of the abnormal character of his desires.[32] Hence the passionate vehemence and at the same time the reserve of "Calamus," and
his desire, already clear, to reconcile this theme with that of
democracy.

Although these admissions were veiled, they touched nonetheless on a subject that had never before been treated with
so much frankness, and it required great courage — or an
extremely pressing need for confession — for Whitman to
dare to celebrate these forbidden desires and joys. In spite of
the fact that he had already been criticized for obscenity in
his two previous editions, he still persisted in the course he
had chosen. This stubbornness clearly shows the importance
which he attached to the sexual theme. He himself tells us
how, during February of 1860, while he was supervising the
printing of his book in Boston, Emerson, in the course of a
long conversation tried to dissuade him from publishing
"Enfans d'Adam":

More precious than gold to me that dissertation — it afforded
me, ever after, this strange and paradoxical lesson; each point of
Emerson's statement was unanswerable, no judge's charge ever
more complete or convincing, I could never hear the points better
put — and then I felt down in my soul the clear and unmistakable
conviction to disobey all, and pursue my own way. "What have
you to say to such things?" said Emerson, pausing in conclusion.
"Only that while I can't answer them at all, I feel more settled
than ever to adhere to my own theory, and exemplify it," was my
candid response. Whereupon we went and had a good dinner.[33]

Another theme which also gained in importance was that of life in the great cities. The germs of this can be found in the 1855 *Leaves of Grass*, but now the theme had grown. Whitman was already the "lover of populous pavements, dweller in Mannahatta my city," [34] as he proclaimed in 1867. And perhaps he insisted more than ever before on the theme of America:

> You bards of ages hence! when you refer to me, mind
>   not so much my poems,
> Nor speak of me that I prophesied of The States, and led
>   them the way of their glories. . .[35]

> And then, to enclose all, it came to me to strike up the
>   songs of the New World.[36]

Moreover, the full title of "Chants Democratic" is "Chants Democratic and Native American." [37] And in "Proto-Leaf" Whitman devoted some forty lines to the immensity and wealth of his country.

This new edition therefore presents a subtler and more complex image of the poet himself than the previous ones. The shadows were deeper, the relief sharper. To be sure, he was still "free, fresh, savage, fluent, luxuriant, self-content, fond of persons and places," [38] but he also was the one who loved to step aside to "muse and meditate in some deep recess, far from the clank of crowds . . . rapt and happy." [39]

"Rapt"? — perhaps, but "happy"? That seems doubtful since he sometimes thought of giving up his writing, not because he was discouraged by the indifference of the public, but because, having dreamed of being the poet of ideal democracy, he regarded the results obtained thus far with despair:

> So far, and so far, and on toward the end,
> Singing what is sung in this book, from the irresistible
>   impulses of me;
> But whether I continue beyond this book, to maturity,

Whether I shall dart forth the true rays, the ones that
wait unfired,
(Did you think the sun was shining its brightest?
No — it has not yet fully risen;)
Whether I shall complete what is here started,
Whether I shall attain my own height, to justify these,
yet unfinished,
Whether I shall make THE POEM OF THE NEW
WORLD, transcending all others — depends, rich
persons, upon you,
Depends, whoever you are now filling the current Presi-
dentiad, upon you,
Upon you, Governor, Mayor, Congressman,
And you, contemporary America.[40]

He was not at all sure that this passionate appeal would be
heard. He despaired to the point of saying good-by to his
reader in "So Long!" [41] Above all, he trembled for the Union.
If it should be broken through the fault of a few, what would
become of American democracy or of democracy anywhere?
It would be the collapse of his dreams and the death of all his
hopes:

O, as I walk'd the beach, I heard the mournful notes
foreboding a tempest — the low, oft-repeated shriek
of the diver, the long-lived loon;
O I heard, and yet hear, angry thunder; — O you
sailors!
O ships! make quick preparation!
O from his masterful sweep, the warning cry of the
eagle!
(Give way there all! It is useless! Give up your spoils;)
O sarcasms! Propositions! (O if the whole world should
prove indeed a sham, a sell!)
O I believe there is nothing real but America and free-
dom!
O to sternly reject all except Democracy!
O imperator! O who dare confront you and me?
O to promulgate our own! O to build for that which
builds for mankind! [42]

Although he exclaimed a little later in the same poem:

> O Libertad! O compact! O union impossible to dissever!

he nevertheless feared a secession of the southern states:

> And I will make a song that there shall be comity by
> day and by night between all The States, and be-
> tween any two of them,
> And I will make a song of the organic bargains of These
> States — And a shrill song of curses on him who
> would dissever the Union;
> And I will make a song for the ears of the President,
> full of weapons with menacing points,
> And behind the weapons countless dissatisfied faces.[43]

The following poem has been found in one of his notebooks:

> Why now I shall know whether there is anything in
> you, Libertad,
> I shall see how much you can stand
> Perhaps I shall see the crash — is all then lost?
> What then? Have those thrones there stood so long?
> Does the Queen of England represent a thousand years?
> And the Queen of Spain a thousand years?
> And you
> Welcome the storm — welcome the trial — let the
> waves
> Why now I shall see what the old ship is made of
> Any body can sail with a fair wind or a smooth sea
> Come now we will see what stuff you are made of Ship
> of Libertad
> Let others tremble and turn pale — let them? [sic]
> I want to see what? [sic] before I die
> I welcome this menace, I welcome thee with joy Ship
> of Libertad
> Blow mad winds!
> Rage, boil, vex, yawn wide, yeasty waves
> Crash away
> Tug at the planks, make them groan — fall around,
> black clouds of death

Ship of the world — ship of Humanity — Ship of the
ages? Ship that circlest the world
Ship of the hope of the world — Ship of promise.[44]

But these were only muffled echoes of the severe crisis he
had undergone in 1856–57; [45] in spite of these fears, he had
confidence in the future. A few selfish and petty-minded
politicians might indulge in underhand intrigues and, for a
time, deceive the people, but sooner or later people would see
through these deceptions and impose their will. Democracy
would triumph:

Thought
Of public opinion
Of a calm and cool fiat, sooner or later, (How impas-
sive! How certain and final!)
Of the President with pale face asking secretly to him-
self, *What will the people say at last?*
Of the frivolous Judge — Of the corrupt Congressman,
Governor, Mayor — Of such as these, standing help-
less and exposed.
Of the New World — Of the Democracies, resplend-
ent, en-masse,
Of the conformity of politics, armies, navies, to them
and to me,
Of the shining sun by them — Of the inherent light,
greater than the rest. . ." [46]

Of these years I sing — how they pass through con-
vulsed pains, as through parturitions. . .
Of how many hold despairingly yet to the models departed, caste, myths, obedience, compulsion, and to
infidelity;
How few see the arrived models, the Athletes, The
States — or see freedom or spirituality — or hold
any faith in results,
(But I see the Athletes — and I see the results glorious
and inevitable — and they again leading to other
results;) [47]

> . . . of seeds dropping into the ground — of birth. . .
>   of the growth of a mightier race than any yet. . .
> Of cities yet unsurveyed and unsuspected. . .
> Of immense spiritual results. . .[48]

In order to proclaim his faith and emphasize his credo, Whitman gathered together, as we have seen, all his poems inspired by democracy under the title of "Chants Democratic." He even went so far as to date all the historical events, including the publication of his book,[49] from the year 1776, which had the same importance to him as the Hegira to a Mohammedan. He regarded it as the beginning of a new era for humanity, the promise of a millennium.

But the gravity of the political situation was not his only torment, there were many other reasons for distress. The dangers menacing democracy were after all only one aspect among many of an infinitely greater problem, the problem of evil. In one of the purely political poems which we have just quoted, he declared: "America. . . illustrates evil as well as good," [50] and it was this omnipresence of evil in creation and in himself which obsessed him. Already in 1856 this thought had disturbed him,[51] but it returned now with greater insistence than ever:

> I own that I have been sly, thievish, mean, a prevaricator, greedy, derelict,
> And I own that I remain so yet.
> What foul thought but I think it — or have in me the stuff out of which it is thought. . .
> Beneath this face that appears so impassive, hell's tides continually run,
> Lusts and wickedness are acceptable to me,
> I walk with delinquents with passionate love,
> I feel I am of them — I belong to those convicts and prostitutes myself,
> And henceforth I will not deny them — for how can I deny myself.[52]

> This is curious, and may not be realized immediately —
>   But it must be realized;
> I feel in myself that I represent falsehood equally with
>   the rest,
> And that the universe does . . .
> And henceforth I will go celebrate anything I see or am,
>   and sing and laugh, and deny nothing.[53]

He suffered from it, but apparently resigned himself to it:

> I sit and look out upon all the sorrows of the world,
>   and upon all oppression and shame [then follows a
>   rather long list of the ills of humanity]. . .
> All these — All the meanness and agony without end,
>   I sitting, look out upon,
> See, hear, and am silent.[54]

But whence came this keen perception of evil and this apparently new sense of guilt? Its origin seems to have been almost physiological: the uneasiness and remorse that follow the sexual act:

> I hear secret convulsive sobs from young men, at anguish
>   with themselves, remorseful after deeds done.[55]

This is probably an echo of the intense emotional crisis which had tortured him a little earlier and which had perhaps revealed to him how abnormal his instincts were. He was ashamed of himself. He suffered because he was different from others:

> Who is now reading this?
> May-be one is now reading this who knows some wrong-
>   doing of my past life. . .
> Or may-be one who is puzzled at me.
> As if I were not puzzled at myself!
> Or as if I never deride myself! (O conscience-struck!
>   O self-convicted!) [56]

The relation between his obsession with evil and his sexual life is evident here. It accounts for the sadness and reticence

of many passages in "Calamus," the modest tone of which is
surprising after the triumphant proclamations of "Enfans
d'Adam." [57] He felt so depressed at times that he longed for
death. Thus far, only life had counted for him, and death
had been merely a distant prospect, an abstraction, a conception of the mind. Now, on the contrary, life was of little importance; death seemed lovely and sweet:

> Yet you are very beautiful to me, you faint-tinged roots
> — you make me think of Death,
> Death is beautiful from you — (what indeed is beauti-
> ful, except Death and Love?). . .
> Death or life I am then indifferent — my Soul declines
> to prefer. . .) [58]

Sometimes he even surrendered himself to death, and as
in "As the Time Draws Nigh" or in "So Long!" he calmly and
almost indifferently envisaged his approaching end.[59]

This seems a strange passivity and a surprising sadness in
a poet who had lately been singing the joy of life at the top
of his voice. Should we conclude that he had sunk into pessimism and that he was tired of life? That would be an extremely simplistic interpretation of the 1860 *Leaves of Grass*.
For these melancholy and resigned strains coincide with paeans
of victory such as "Proto-Leaf" [60] and the "Poem of Joys" [61]
in which resounds the same gladness as in "Song of Myself."
Moreover, the tenth poem in the group entitled "Leaves of
Grass" is no different in tone from those which precede or
follow it, and which were present in the earlier editions:

> It is ended — I dally no more,
> After to-day I inure myself to run, leap, swim, wrestle,
> fight,
> To stand the cold or heat — to take good aim with a
> gun — to manage horses — to beget superb children,
> To speak readily and clearly — to feel at home among
> common people.

And to hold my own in terrible positions, on land and
  sea. . .
After me, vista!
O I see life is not short, but immeasurably long,
I henceforth tread the world, chaste, temperate, an
  early riser, a gymnast, a steady grower,
Every hour the semen of centuries — and still of cen-
  turies.[62]

The crisis was definitely ended. He felt in himself now an
excess of energy [63] that he wished to expend; he longed for a
more active life; he launched himself confidently into the
future; the idea of death no longer disturbed him; he looked
forward to eternity.

It seems then that Schyberg — and after him Gay W.
Allen [64] — have greatly exaggerated the pessimism of the 1860
edition. Certainly Whitman in his moments of despair sometimes had the impression that his *Leaves of Grass* were nothing
but a handful of "dead leaves," [65] but he did not let himself
be discouraged for long (otherwise how could he have so
quickly prepared this new edition?); soon the "leaves of grass"
became green again:

Tomb-leaves, body-leaves, growing up above me, above
  death,
Perennial roots, tall leaves — O the winter shall not
  freeze you, delicate leaves,
Every year shall you bloom again.[66]

. . . these are not to be pensive leaves, but leaves of
  joy. . .[67]

Malcolm Cowley makes the same mistake [68] when he undertakes to show that the "word unsaid" [69] by means of which
Whitman in 1855 promised to explain the world had become
in 1860 the word "death" in "A Word Out of the Sea." [70] But
this is to underestimate the importance of "Poem of Joys"; it
ends with these lines which (probably not by accident) immediately precede "A Word Out of the Sea":

O to have my life henceforth my poem of joys!
To dance, clap hands, exult, shout, skip, leap, roll on,
   float on,
An athlete — full of rich words — full of joys.[71]

Besides, although the mockingbird in "A Word Out of the Sea" sends forth his desperate cry, in "Proto-Leaf," at the very beginning of the book, Whitman describes the same bird "inflating his throat and joyfully singing." [72] Even if he wrote "Proto-Leaf" before "A Word Out of the Sea," as all the evidence indicates, the fact that he let it stand in 1860 is sufficient assurance that he had overcome his pessimism of 1859. Neither did he try to diminish the impression of infinite happiness that emerges in many of the "Calamus" poems,[73] a happiness which was at the same time a blossoming and a relief since it sprang from the profound satisfaction of his instincts at last free and in possession of the object for which they had been so long and vainly searching.[74] He made no effort either to conceal the signs of the optimism that he had attained in the fulness of his joy when, during his homosexual liaison, he had had the belated revelation of love; all the metaphysical problems that had previously been torturing him had suddenly been resolved:

> I cannot answer the question of appearances, or that of
>   identity beyond the grave,
> But I walk or sit indifferent — I am satisfied,
> He ahold of my hand has completely satisfied me.[75]

And this serene certainty survived the terrible disappointment which the liaison brought him: betrayed by one lover, he extended his love to all the potential lovers whom the world held in store,[76] and not only to them, but to the entire universe:

> Sometimes with one I love, I fill myself with rage, for
>   fear I effuse unreturned love;
> But now I think there is no unreturned love — the pay
>   is certain, one way or another,

> Doubtless I could not have perceived the universe, or
> written one of my poems, if I had not freely given
> myself to comrades, to love.[77]

By celebrating in this way the love that he had experienced,
he generalized his emotions and at the same time purified and
transcended them. It was not a matter now of the great passion that had torn him, but a very pure and noble transport
which brought men together and which would assure the unity
of his country and later of the world. In short, he proposed to
support democracy on a universal web of homosexual friendships — giving it in this way an indestructible physiological
basis [78] (we shall have occasion to return to this point). In his
usual fashion he trusted in the future. The present disappointed
him, but the future, he felt sure, would justify him by realizing his dream of a universal love among men. What had been
an abnormal liaison became, by virtue of this sublimation, the
point of departure for a great democratic utopia. The hope
born of his songs and the songs born of this hope had saved
him. By the time he published the 1860 edition he had recovered; the wound had healed and he was able to proclaim in
the closing poem of "Calamus":

> Full of life, sweet-blooded, compact, visible,
> I, forty years old the Eighty-third Year of The
> States. . .[79]

The trials and disappointments he had experienced did not
matter to him. After his pains and sufferings he had attained
a perfect serenity:

> O Soul, we have positively appeared — that is enough.[80]
>
> Quicksand years that whirl me I know not whither,
> Your schemes, politics, fail, lines give way, substances
> mock and elude me,
> Only the theme I sing, the great and strong-possess'd
> soul, eludes not,

> One's-self must never give way — that is the final sub-
> stance — that out of all is sure,
> Out of politics, triumphs, battles, life, what at last
> finally remains?
> When shows break up what but One's-Self is sure.[81]

He was henceforth "imperturbe"; contingencies no longer
affected him:

> Me imperturbe,
> Me standing at ease in Nature,
> Master of all, or mistress of all — aplomb in the midst
> of irrational things,
> Imbued as they — passive, receptive, silent as they,
> Finding my occupation, poverty, notoriety, foibles,
> crimes, less important than I thought. . .
> Me, wherever my life is to be lived, O to be self-bal-
> anced for contingencies!
> O to confront night, storms, hunger, ridicule, accidents,
> rebuffs, as the trees and animals do.[82]

Accordingly, he found it easy to resign himself to the public's lack of enthusiasm. It is true that his book showed — provisionally — the marks of moments of bitterness, [83] but it also
included poems in which he renewed the optimism of his
1856 "Sun-Down Poem" [84] and affirmed his faith in the ap-
preciation of future generations.[85] He knew that the great
innovators had always been misunderstood by their contemporaries. Besides, he had not altogether renounced his hope
of achieving immediate recognition. The East misunderstood
him, but perhaps he would be triumphantly welcomed in the
West as soon as his work was known there. The pioneers, he
thought, were pure of heart and despised money.[86] He had
faith in them.

But there is another aspect of the 1860 edition which even
more emphatically shows his recovered equilibrium: in the
whole group of partly new poems entitled "Messenger

Leaves," [87] he presented himself as a Messiah and Redeemer. Here it looks as if, having cured himself, he now felt able to liberate and cure others. Not content with being a poet, he wanted to be a prophet and equal to Christ, whom he called his "dear brother" and his "comrade." [88] They would go through the world together, bringing to all men the same message of pity and consolation. For his part, he addressed himself more particularly for the moment "To One Shortly to Die" [89] or "To a Common Prostitute." [90] He had long had this ambition in an embryonic form,[91] but what had so far been a vague and confused aspiration now became a categorical assertion. He described himself as a savior. He seems really to have had a great power, a reservoir of spiritual energy on which anyone might draw. He even proposed to found a new religion that would synthetize and surpass all others:

> I too, following many, and followed by many, inaugu-
> rate a Religion — I too go to the wars,
> It may be I am destined to utter the loudest cries there-
> of, the conqueror's shouts,
> They may rise from me yet, and soar above everything.[92]

> . . . now a third religion I give. . . I include the
> antique two. . . I include the divine Jew, and the
> Greek sage. . . More still — that which is not con-
> science, but against it — that which is not the Soul,
> I include
> These, and whatever exists, I include — I surround all,
> and dare not make a single exception.[93]

In other words, democracy would be his religion.

These pretensions might appear exorbitant, but they probably seemed quite natural to him. Thanks to the power that was in him, he had succeeded in emerging from the abyss of despair into which he had fallen. By his example and his songs he could help those who were too weak to save themselves.[94]

In spite of these exalted virtues, the critical reception of the 1860 *Leaves of Grass* was substantially the same as that which had greeted the preceding editions. It was easy to make jokes at Whitman's expense. Many reviewers did so.[95] Thus the author of a review published by the *Southern Field and Fireside*:

Five years ago we recollect to have seen the first edition of it, and to have made up our mind that if it did not proceed from a lunatic, it was designed as a solemn hoax upon the public. The extravagance of the style, the beastliness of the sentiments. . . its frequent indecency of language, all suggested Bedlam. The bizarre appearance of the book also indicated a crazy origin. The page, about half the size of our own, was printed in type as large as a playbill, the presswork seemed to have been done with a sledge-hammer. . . he can perceive no difference between Bacon and a Berkshire pig. . . Among the Heenan-ities of the day, his verse may find admirers, but with all the votaries of a pure literature, he must be greeted with a "Procul, procul, este profani!" [96]

Here again were the usual reproaches: indecency, obscurity, and lack of art and rhythm. The critic who reviewed "A Child's Reminiscence" in the Cincinnati *Commercial* gave a good summary of these complaints in the following passage:

. . . we grieve to say he revived last week, and although somewhat changed, changed very little for the better. We do not find so much that is offensive, but we do find a vast amount of irreclaimable drivel and inexplicable nonsense. . . It ["A Word Out of the Sea"] has neither rhythm nor melody, rhyme nor reason, metre nor sense.[97]

But luckily for Whitman, not all the critics shared that opinion. A certain number of favorable articles appeared — notably in the Brooklyn papers where he still had friends [98] and in the New York press.[99] Henry P. Leland in the Philadelphia *City Item* recognized him as undoubtedly a poetic genius:

He is the Consuelo for the poor man, the friendless, the outcast. . . in spite of a belief that poetry can only be appreciated by the few, he goes in for giving it to the "oi polloi". . . There are two thousand roses to a drachm of the otto, there are untold thousands of poems in this duodecimo. . .[100]

So, in spite of the violent attacks of which he was always the object, Whitman was beginning to be appreciated. The critic in the London *Saturday Review* realized the fact with surprise and was further astonished that a book which he had condemned four years before appeared in such a handsome edition: "It is startling to find such a poet acquiring popularity in a country where piano-legs wear frilled trousers. . ." [101]

In fact, Whitman had become popular — in a relative but quite real way. According to Burroughs, several thousand copies of the 1860 edition were sold.[102] The figure is open to doubt, for the evidence on which it was founded is not known; still it is certain that the book achieved a very decent success.[103] Unfortunately, when the Civil War broke out, Thayer and Eldridge, some of whose assets were frozen in the South, suddenly found themselves deprived of part of their capital and went bankrupt. Their equipment, their stock, and their plates were sold at auction. That was the end of the first commercial edition of *Leaves of Grass*. And so Whitman lost the only chance he had had to reach a large public. He found himself again thrown back on his own resources, and he had to wait twenty years before finding another commercial publisher for his book.[104]

CHAPTER VI

THE WOUND DRESSER

IT is probable that after his return from Boston in June 1860 Whitman resumed his indolent existence and divided his time between Brooklyn, where he continued to live with his family, and New York, where he rejoined his friends at Pfaff's. But we know absolutely nothing for certain concerning this period of his life. He says nothing about it in *Specimen Days,* and we are reduced to conjectures. One thing, however, seems sure: he had no regular employment. Rather than submit to the daily servitude of a job, he preferred to live poorly on the income from the sale of his poems. He preferred complete independence to security and comfort. Yet, he would probably have been glad to accept the help of a patron in order to be able to consecrate himself entirely to his work without any concern for the future. He had declared in one of the poems of the 1860 edition:

> Whether I shall make THE POEM OF THE NEW
> WORLD, transcending all others — depends, rich persons,
> upon you,
> Depends, whoever you are now filling the current Presi-
> dentiad, upon you,
> Upon you, Governor, Mayor, Congressman,
> And you, contemporary America.[1]

So long as he was free to create, it mattered little to him

whether his patron was a rich man or a politician. He would not have felt at all humiliated by this apparent dependence:

> What you give me, I cheerfully accept,
> A little sustenance, a hut and garden, a little money —
>   these as a rendez-vous with my poems,
> A traveller's lodging and breakfast as I journey through
>   The States — Why should I be ashamed to own
>   such gifts? Why to advertise for them?
> For I myself am not one who bestows nothing upon
>   man and woman,
> For I know that what I bestow upon any man or
>   woman, is no less than the entrance to all the gifts
>   of the universe.[2]

Unfortunately this appeal went unheard; Whitman found no William Calvert on his road, and he would perhaps have continued to share the rather artificial Bohemian life of New York if the war had not wrenched him out of it. On April 12, 1861, less than a year after his return from Boston, the federal troops who occupied Fort Sumter in Charleston harbor were bombarded by Confederate batteries and surrendered two days later. Whitman recounts in *Specimen Days* with what emotion he heard the news in New York on April 13.[3] The event was not unexpected. For several years the trial of force between the two camps seemed imminent and almost inevitable. Whitman, because of his hatred for dishonorable compromises, had sometimes almost wanted it. But now that the time had come, he felt profoundly shaken and upset. On April 18, he jotted in one of his private notebooks:

I have this hour, this day resolved to inaugurate a sweet, clean-blooded body by ignoring all drinks but water and pure milk — and all fat meats, late suppers — a great body — a purged, cleansed, spiritualized invigorated body.[4]

This strange resolution looks like the program of an ascetic who proposes to do penance in order to redeem the sins of mankind. At the deepest level, without ostentation, Whitman, it seems, associated himself with his contemporaries and intended secretly to participate in their trial.

However, by a curious contradiction, there was no immediate change in his life. To be sure, he renounced the joys of nature in order to devote himself to New York and participate more intensely than ever in the life of Manhattan, but he continued nevertheless shamelessly to enjoy all the pleasures which a great city has to offer:

> Keep your splendid silent sun;
> Keep your woods, O Nature, and the quiet places by
> the woods;
> Keep your fields of clover and timothy, and your corn-
> fields and orchards;
> Keep the blossoming buckwheat fields, where the Ninth-
> month bees hum;
> Give me faces and streets! give me these phantoms in-
> cessant and endless along the trottoirs!
> Give me interminable eyes! give me women! give me
> comrades and lovers by the thousand!
> Let me see new ones every day! let me hold new ones
> by the hand every day!
> Give me such shows! give me the streets of Manhattan!
> . . . . .
> O such for me! O an intense life! O full to repletion,
> and varied!
> The life of the theater, bar-room, huge hotel, for me!
> The saloon of the steamer! the crowded excursion for
> me! the torch-light procession!
> The dense brigade, bound for the war, with high piled
> military wagons following. . .[5]

Thus he thought about the war, but it was only one preoccupation among many others, and he seems to have been remarkably attracted by the "comrades and lovers" whom he encountered on the sidewalks and in the bars. His private notebooks confirm this impression; we find indications such as these:

> Victor Smith — Evening June 30 '62 — met a man who introduced himself to me as V. Smith — in the government employ on the Pacific Coast . . . Afternoon July 3rd in front of Hospital Broadway Aaron B. Cohn — talk with — he was from Fort Edward Institute — appears to be 19 years old — fresh and affectionate young man. . . William Robinson, Brooklyn lad (Socratic nose) Aug. 16 — driving on 23rd St. is going to enlist — said he would enlist with me in two minutes.[6]

Strange encounters to which we will have occasion to refer again. However that may be, it is clear by now that, for all his ascetic resolutions, Whitman continued to lead a carefree life. The only notable change that can be seen in his existence is that he ceased to be completely unemployed and became active again in journalism. He was probably constrained to this by circumstances, the failure of his publishers having suddenly deprived him of the income from the sale of *Leaves of Grass.*

Contrary to what might be expected, instead of writing about the war, he published in the Brooklyn *Standard*[7] a series of twenty-five articles on the past and present of the city — a form of escape literature which would seem remarkably inappropriate in such a historic context. It may be said in his defense that perhaps he could find nothing better to do. He needed money, and he was probably forced to accept the assignment. The series was nothing but a pot-boiler which he never mentioned afterwards, although the copyright was in his name, which was rare at that time for such articles. On the other hand, if he was able to choose his own topic, his natural indolence must have prompted him to take the easy way out, for he had written about Brooklyn several years before in the Brooklyn *Daily Times,*[8] and he would merely have to draw on his memory or his notes.

Nevertheless, in spite of the inappropriateness of these articles, Whitman was not unaware of the war. At the time of the disaster at Bull Run on July 21, 1861, and during the several days when everything seemed lost,[9] he found himself brusquely recalled to reality. The shock was so brutal that he ceased for several months to work on his "Brooklyniana." It is true that once the alarm had passed, he resumed his routine, and nothing in his articles reflected the grave events occurring at the time. In fact, his chronicle became a reportage and gave him a pretext to revisit the small villages of Long Island which he had known in his youth and to take part in a fishing party at Montauk Point.[10] But he may have foreseen the more and more tragic turn that the war would take and the role that he himself would come to play in it. This happy excursion was in some ways a pilgrimage and a farewell visit to the countryside which he had loved so much.

It may seem surprising, however, that after having celebrated the departure of the troops for the front with so much enthusiasm and patriotic fervor in several of his poems,[11] he did not sign up himself in a New York regiment. Certain critics have accused him of cowardice and inconsistency on this ground. But this is to forget that Whitman was forty-two years old; the average age of volunteers was a great deal less, especially at the beginning of the war.[12] And it is remarkable that none of his contemporaries thought of blaming him for this supposed defection and that it never occurred to any of his enemies to use it against him. Besides his age, there were many other reasons for his abstention: First of all, his temperament, which had always made him avoid action; his stay-at-home tastes; his placid disposition; and his natural horror of violence, reinforced by his Quaker education. It is hard to imagine him as a warrior, even though, on principle, he was heartily in sympathy with those who fought for the Union.

His true vocation was to sing and celebrate the Union and the indissoluble compact which bound the various states together:

> From Paumanok starting, I fly like a bird,
> Around and around to soar, to sing, the idea of all. . .
> To sing first, (to the tap of the war-drum, if need be,)
> The idea of all — of the western world, one and insepa-
>   rable,
> And then the song of each member of These States.[13]

In 1855 he had already defined the role of the poet in wartime: "In war he is the most deadly force of the war. . . Who recruits him recruits horse and foot . . . he fetches parks of artillery the best that engineer ever saw . . . he can make every word he speaks draw blood." [14]

His family situation must also be considered. His father was dead. Two of his brothers, Eddie and Jesse, were unable to support themselves. George, ten years his junior, had left among the first volunteers. Another of his brothers, Andrew, was drafted a little later. Whitman therefore found himself, with Jeff, the only support of all the women and children remaining in the Portland Street house. Hence his uneasiness in 1863 at the possibility that Jeff might be drafted in his turn,[15] or that he himself might be drafted too.[16] And yet, for a moment in 1864 he thought of volunteering and confided to his mother: "The war must be carried on, and I could willingly go myself in the ranks if I thought it would profit more than at present, and I don't know sometimes but I shall as it is." [17]

In any case, up to the end of 1862, he continued to lead a quiet existence in New York — quite comparable to that which most Americans of his age had in the two world wars. He was far from the theater of operation. He certainly followed the war news with eagerness, but however great his power of sympathy may have been, the fighting could only have been for him an unreal abstraction that did not deeply affect him. War cannot be imagined, it must be seen. He soon had occasion to see it.

On December 13, 1862, he heard that his brother George had been seriously wounded during an attack, and without hesitation, he took the train for the South to try to find him. He stopped first for two days at Washington, where he thought George had already been brought. And during those two days he searched feverishly in all the hospitals in the city without success. Very fortunately, a few hours after his arrival, he met William O'Connor whose acquaintance he had made in Boston and who was now employed in the Lighthouse Bureau. Without O'Connor's help he would have been much embarrassed, for he had been robbed of his wallet in Philadelphia, while changing trains, and had no money.[18] Thanks to him, Whitman was able to learn where his brother was and to continue his journey, furnished with papers and the necessary cash. On December 19 he arrived at Falmouth, Virginia, on the left bank of the Rappahannock River, where the 51st New York Regiment, to which his brother belonged, was bivouacking.[19] George, whose wound was less serious than had been feared, was already out of danger. Walt's presence was therefore superfluous, but he nevertheless remained at Falmouth until the end of the month, spending about eight days on the front-lines with the troops. It was an unforgettable adventure. He shared the hard life of the soldiers, subsisting like them on salt pork and sea biscuits and sleeping in the mud and snow, rolled up in a blanket. And, above all, for the first time, he saw the war close up, in all its horror. He did not actually participate in any fighting, but he did see some of the immediate results. He visited the improvised hospital where the more serious cases were treated. Outside, at the foot of a tree, was a pile of feet, legs, arms, and hands freshly amputated and waiting for a cart to take them away.[20] He saw even more horrible things: the wounded being cared for at the dressing-stations, often lying on the ground under tents. He was immediately overcome by a great pity for all these young soldiers who were suffering so atrociously and some of whom seized on him convulsively and constrained him to stay beside them for hours.[21] By his own testimony, on one occasion, he even helped the stretcher-bearers to remove the dead from the battle-field and to give first-aid to the wounded during a truce.[22]

This accidental encounter with the war changed the course of his life. At the end of December he left Falmouth with a convoy of wounded soldiers whose sufferings he tried to relieve during the trip,[23] and instead of returning home to Brooklyn, he established himself in Washington in order to remain close to his beloved soldiers. From then until the end of the war, he was to pass as much time as possible in the military hospitals. The letters that he wrote to his family and friends and the pages of *Specimen Days* that he devoted to this period allow us to follow him in his charitable rounds.[24] Although he sometimes helped the doctors and nurses to change bandages, he was never, in a literal sense, a "wound-dresser," as Bucke called him.[25] Nevertheless this title suited him perfectly; for, if he did not attend the wounds of the body, he brought to the wounded or sick soldiers something which was as necessary to their recovery as medical care, but for which the regulations had not provided: the comfort of a loving presence, the sweetness of an almost maternal affection, the delicate attentions of an ingenious kindness. He had already rehearsed this role in the New York hospitals where he had often visited sick omnibus drivers.[26] He fulfilled it with perfect tact. He tried to explain it in these terms in a letter:

The work of the army hospital visitor is indeed a trade, an art, requiring both experience and natural gifts, and the greatest judgment. A large number of the visitors to the hospitals do no good at all, while many do harm. The surgeons have great trouble from them. . . there are always some poor fellows, in the crises of sickness or wounds, that imperatively need perfect quiet — not to be talked to by strangers. Few realize that it is not the mere giving of gifts that does good; it is the proper adaptation. Nothing is of any avail among the soldiers except conscientious personal investigation of cases, each for itself; with sharp critical faculties, but in the fullest spirit of human sympathy and boundless love. The men feel such love more than anything else. I have met very few persons who realize the importance of humoring the yearnings for love and friendship of these American young men, prostrated by sickness and wounds.

To many of the wounded and sick, especially the youngsters, there is something in personal love, caresses, and the magnetic flood of sympathy and friendship, that does, in its way, more good than all the medicine in the world. . . Many will think this merely sentimentalism, but I know it is the most solid of facts. I believe that even the moving around among the men, or through the ward, of a hearty, healthy, clean, strong, generous-souled person, man or woman, full of humanity and love, sending out invisible, constant currents thereof, does immense good to the sick and wounded.[27]

These are the principles that he put into practice. He went from bed to bed, distributing oranges, lemons, sugar, jam, preserved fruit, tobacco (which the soldiers rarely had, for none of the welfare workers sent by the various churches brought any to them),[28] and even small sums of money which permitted them to buy some comforts. But, above all, he paused at the bedside of one or another to listen to their stories. He was passionately interested in the fate of each one[29] and recorded in his notebooks the more remarkable cases.[30] Many of the young soldiers felt abandoned and deprived of affection, and he performed the function of a family and gave them back the will to live. He had for them, it seemed,[31] a fatherly affection, and some of them called him "Uncle"[32] or even "Pa." He wrote letters for them to their mothers or their wives:

"When eligible, I encourage the men to write, and myself, when called upon, write all sorts of letters for them (including love letters, very tender ones)." [33]

Sometimes also he read them passages from the Bible [34] or poems — but never his own, a surprising abnegation for a poet.[35] To those who were too ill to listen or to speak, he offered his silent presence, the presence of a body which from the first days of the war he had consecrated to purity and health.[36] He remained at their bedside for hours if necessary. Thus took place a mysterious transfusion of strength. It was as if his serenity and health were contagious; at his contact the wounded regained hope. He gave them the desire to recover. In short, he was the mystical healer whom he had described in the first edition of *Leaves of Grass*:

> To any one dying. . . . thither I speed and twist the
>   knob of the door,
> Turn the bedclothes toward the foot of the bed,
> Let the physician and the priest go home.
> I seize the descending man. . . . I raise him with
>   resistless will.
> O despairer, here is my neck,
> By God! you shall not go down! Hang your whole weight
>   upon me.
> I dilate you with tremendous breath. . . . I buoy you
>   up;
> Every room of the house do I fill with an armed
>   force. . . . lovers of me, bafflers of graves:
> Sleep! I and they keep guard all night;
> Not doubt, not decease shall dare to lay finger upon you,
> I have embraced you, and henceforth possess you to
>   myself,
> And when you rise in the morning you will find what I
>   tell you is so.
> I am he bringing help for the sick as they pant on their
>   backs.[37]

Once more then nature imitated art and his life conformed

to his work. He was becoming more and more that which he had dreamed of being in 1855. At any rate, one thing is certain: his presence and care sometimes worked miracles. Doctors themselves were obliged to admit it,[38] and in a letter to his mother, he told the story of a cure which he had effected in 1865 after several days' battle with death:

One soldier brought here about fifteen days ago, very low with typhoid fever, Livingston Brooks, Co. B. 17th Penn. Cavalry, I have particularly stuck to, as I found him to be in what appeared to be a dying condition, from negligence and a horrible journey of about forty miles, bad roads and fast driving; and then, after he got here, as he is a simple country boy, very shy and silent, and made no complaint, they neglected him. . . I called the doctor's atttention to him, shook up the nurses, had him bathed in spirits, gave him lumps of ice, and ice to his head; he had a fearful bursting pain in his head, and his body was like fire. He was very quiet, a very sensible boy, old fashioned; he did not want to die and I had to lie to him without stint, for he thought I knew everything, and I always put in of course that what I told him was exactly the truth and that if he got dangerous I would tell him and not conceal it. The rule is to remove bad fever patients out from the main wards to a tent by themselves, and the doctor told me he would have to be removed. I broke it gently to him, but the poor boy got it immediately in his head that he was marked with death, and was to be removed on that account. It had a great effect upon him, and although I told the truth this time it did not have as good a result as my former fibs. I persuaded the doctor to let him remain. For three days he lay just about an even chance, go or stay, with a little leaning toward the first. But, mother, to make a long story short, he is now out of immediate danger. He has been perfectly rational throughout — begins to taste a little food (for a week he ate nothing; I had to compel him to take a quarter of an orange now and then), and I will say, whether anyone calls it pride or not, that if he *does* get up and around again it's me that saved his life.[39]

By the power of patience and tenderness he had in fact succeeded in tipping the balance toward the side of life. And he saved the lives of many sick and wounded soldiers in the same way:

> Mother, [he wrote a few months later,] I have real pride in telling you that I have the consciousness of saving quite a number of lives by saving them from giving up — and being a good deal with them; the men say it is so, and the doctors say it is so — and I will candidly confess I can see it is true, though I say it of myself.[40]

It was above all to his marvellous health that Whitman attributed these miraculous results. In a letter of 1863 he said:

> I believe I weigh about 200, and as to my face, (so scarlet,) and my beard and neck, they are terrible to behold. I fancy the reason I am able to do some good in the hospitals among the poor languishing and wounded boys, is, that I am so large and well — indeed like a great wild buffalo, with much hair.[41]

He felt full of strength, and yet, knowing how unhealthy his existence in the pestilential atmosphere of the hospitals was, he began, after several months, to take better care of himself:

> I keep about as stout as ever, and the past five or six days, I have felt wonderful well, indeed never did I feel better. . . I generally go to the hospitals from twelve to four — and then again from six to nine; some days I only go in the middle of the day or evening, not both — and then when I feel somewhat opprest, I skip over a day, or make perhaps a light call only, as I had several cautions by the doctors, who tell me that one must beware of continuing too steady and long in the air and influences of the hospitals. I find the caution a wise one.[42]

His uneasiness and these warnings were justified, for, in June, he began to complain for the first time of symptoms of illness: "Mother, I have had quite an attack of sore throat and distress in my head for some days past, up to last night, but today I feel nearly all right again." [43] In October this concern had been forgotten and he boasted of his excellent health as if nothing had happened:

I feel so tremendously well myself — I will have to come and show myself to you, I think — I am so fat, good appetite, out considerably in the open air, and all red and tanned worse than ever. You see, therefore, that my life amid these sad and death-stricken hospitals has not told at all badly upon me, for I am this fall so running over with health I feel as if I ought to go on, on that account, working among all who are deprived of it.[44]

The following month, however, he left his wounded friends and did not return for several weeks.[45] Ostensibly, he went in order to vote at Brooklyn, but he was apparently very glad of this relief, for he remained until December 2 and took advantage of his visit to attend the opera and the theater,[46] of which pleasures he had been deprived for a year. But, however greatly he may have been tempted to indulge again in this careless life, he did not give way. The memory of those he had left in the hospitals pursued him:

I do not think [he wrote to one of them] one night has passed in New York or Brooklyn when I have been at the theatre or opera or afterward to some supper party or carousal made by the young fellows for me, but what amid the play and the singing I would perhaps think of you, — and the same at the gayest supper-party of men where all was fun and noise and laughing and drinking, of a dozen young men and I among them I would see your face before me. . . and my amusement or drink would be all turned to nothing. . .[47]

Therefore he returned to Washington. Two months later he left again for Culpeper, Virginia, with a paymaster, Major Hapgood, for whom he was working as a clerk. Again he found himself very near the front, but the sector was fairly calm; [48] the troops were in winter quarters and no action was under way. He tried however, in talking with the men, to learn as much as possible about their life; for, he said, "I can never cease to crave more and more knowledge of actual soldier's life and be among them as much as possible." [49] But this second visit to Virginia was very brief and less dramatic than the first. Perhaps also Whitman had become more accustomed to the horrors of war.

By March he had resumed his visits to the Washington hospitals, apparently always in excellent health,[50] but in June he felt very depressed:

> Mother, if this campaign was not in progress I should not stop here, as it is now beginning to tell a little upon me, so many bad wounds, many putrefied, and all kinds of dreadful ones, I have been rather too much with. . .[51]

A few days later, he complained of headaches and fits of dizziness,[52] and since the symptons instead of abating became worse,[53] he was obliged on the advice of doctors to return to his family in Brooklyn for a rest. He remained there from the end of June to the middle of January 1865. However, thanks to the rest and the change of climate, he recovered quickly. He was even able during these six months to work on his *Drum-Taps* and prepare them for publication.[54]

For all that, he did not interrupt his visits to the wounded. He still went regularly to the military hospitals in Brooklyn and New York.[55] And after his return to Washington he resumed his charitable rounds as if nothing had happened. Even peace did not immediately put an end to his voluntary service. Until April 1867 he was still going almost every Sunday to see the invalids who remained in the hospitals of the capital.[56] He himself had apparently completely recovered, but the symptoms which he had noticed during these last few years were the advanced signs of the stroke of paralysis which he suffered in 1873.

But how did he make his living during his stay in Washington? And how, without any regular income, could he afford his charities to the soldiers in the hospitals? The fact is that the money which he distributed or which he used to buy small gifts was furnished for the most part by friends who wanted to help him relieve the misery of the wounded.[57] But he had to make his own living also, and therefore he had to look for work. He found some quickly, thanks to Eldridge, his former Boston publisher, also in difficulty, who served as deputy-paymaster to Major Hapgood. Whitman was hired as part-time assistant. He worked three or four hours a day copying payrolls and earned enough to support himself without giving up his freedom of movement.[58] From time to time he also sent articles to New York or Brooklyn newspapers,[59] which brought him a little money. But all this did not amount to much. He would have liked to earn a great deal more in order to be able to help the wounded without the support of others and at the same time relieve the needs of his relatives by purchasing a small farm for them on Long Island.[60] To make these fine dreams come true, he thought for a time of undertaking one of the lecture tours he had had in mind since 1856, but he quickly gave it up, probably realizing that circumstances were less favorable than ever and that his project would have no chance of success.[61] He also cherished for some time the hope of publishing a book of memories of the war, but he was probably unable to find a publisher interested in the venture.[62]

During this period in any case he could have found a more lucrative employment in some government office through the agency of influential friends such as Emerson,[63] but he preferred the humbler tasks which left him more freedom to dispose of his time as he wished. Instead of trying to increase his income, it probably seemed to him worthier of a free man to simplify his life, like Thoreau, and reduce his wants.[64] During the war years he lived very cheaply, almost in destitution. At first, he rented a small room in the same house as the O'Connors for seven dollars a month and took his meals with them — free of charge, for the O'Connors refused to let him pay, although they did allow him after a time to provide some of the food at his own expense.[65] J. T. Trowbridge, who paid him a visit during this time, has left a description of his lodgings:

Walt led the way up those dreary stairs, partly in darkness, found the keyhole of a door which he unlocked and opened, scratched a match, and welcomed us to his garret.

Garret it literally was, containing hardly more furniture than a bed, a cheap pine table, and a little stove in which there was no fire. A window was open and it was a December night. But Walt, clearing a chair or two of their litter of newspapers, invited us to sit down and stop awhile, with as simple and sweet hospitality as if he had been offering us the luxuries of the great mansion across the square. . . Two mornings after this I went by appointment to call on Walt in his garret. . . he was cutting slices of bread from a baker's loaf with a jackknife, getting them ready for toasting. The smallest of tin-kettles simmering on the stove, a bowl and spoon, and a covered tin cup used as a teapot comprised with the aforesaid useful jackknife his entire outfit of visible housekeeping utensils. His sugar-bowl was a brown paper-bag. His butter plate was another piece of brown paper, the same coarse wrapping in which he had brought home his modest lump from the corner grocery.[66]

He moved several times,[67] but he always took a room as miserable as the first in order to save as much money as possible for the wounded and perhaps also in order to remain faithful to the ascetic vow he had made at the beginning of the war.[68] He suffered however. He suffocated during the humid, stifling summers that prevail in Washington, and he complained sometimes in his letters,[69] but he held out until the end and never occupied more comfortable quarters. He had always lived in an attic in Brooklyn in the home of his family,[70] so it was not as much of a trial as Trowbridge may have thought. It remains true nevertheless that he could have lived more comfortably if he had wished, and that he deliberately chose poverty.[71]

Such was his life during the Civil War — seen from the outside. We must now try to determine what effects all these events had on his personality and works.

When war broke out in 1861, Whitman immediately chanted his joy and enthusiasm. It was the end of the revolting compromises. The war would cut at one stroke the Gordian knot of the political intrigues. He rejoiced; all the plots of the Democrats in league with the slave-merchants of the South would be thwarted. They had tried to impose their will on the mass of the nation, but these events had silenced them. Now the people had the floor, and not their corrupt representatives. Selfish plotters had tried to put the country to sleep and sell its soul to preserve a senseless peace, but, at the first cannon shots fired on Fort Sumter, the country had awakened. Its soul had been saved. All the doubts which had tortured Whitman were dissipated when he saw how enthusiastically the volunteers responded to the government's appeal.[72] Carried away by the same patriotic fervor as all these young men, he set himself to vindicate the war:

> Long, too long, O land,
> Traveling roads all even and peaceful, you learn'd from
>   joys and prosperity only;
> But now, ah now, to learn from crises of anguish —
>   advancing, grappling with direst fate, and recoiling
>   not;
> And now to conceive, and show to the world, what your
>   children en-masse really are;
> (For who except myself has yet conceived what your
>   children en-masse really are?) [73]

He now felt that events were justifying him; he had been right. The masses were not enamoured of peace at any price as the politicians had maintained and believed.[74] They accepted the trial. The "too long" which escaped him in the first line marks his impatience at the delay which he had been obliged to endure. According to him, peace was not always best for a country, for it was in war that a nation took form and consciousness and the true character of a people revealed itself.[75] A strangely idealistic conception.

In another poem, entitled "1861," he celebrated war because it was for him the synonym of energy, of manly vigor and generous spirit.[76] He refused to sing the sweetness of a debilitating peace; [77] he meant to consecrate himself from now on to the war. No matter to him if it lasted months or years, it was a virile undertaking.[78] He considered it as a fresh and joyous adventure:

> And ever the sound of the cannon, far or near, (rousing, even in dreams, a devilish exultation, and all the old mad joy, in the depths of my soul;) [79]

At the time he was acquainted only with that aspect of war, not having seen it at close range. He had made no progress since 1860 when he sang in "Poem of Joys":

> O the joys of the soldier!
> To feel the presence of a brave general! to feel his sympathy!
> To behold his calmness! to be warmed in the rays of his smile!
> To go to battle! to hear the bugles play; and the drums beat!
> To hear the artillery! to see the glittering of the bayonets and musket-barrels in the sun!
> To see men fall and die and not complain!
> To taste the savage taste of blood! to be so devilish!
> To gloat over the wounds and deaths of the enemy.[80]

He was soon to have occasion "to see men fall and die and not complain" with very different feelings, but for the moment, absorbed in his dream of glory and heroic death, he wanted total war. Everyone should renounce his peaceful occupations and take part in the struggle. No one had the right to remain behind when the drums beat.[81] He earnestly called for the mobilization of all men old enough to bear arms — without any exception, for thus the nation would cease to be an abstraction and become a living reality.[82]

In "Song of the Banner at Daybreak" — which may have been written before the outbreak of the war, but which he revised for inclusion in *Drum-Taps* [83] — he contrasted peace with war; the father represents the love of peace and material riches, whereas the child, the banner, and the poet embody an opposing aspiration to the ideal that Whitman defined as "out of reach, an idea only, yet furiously fought for, risking bloody death. . ." [84] In short, then, he did not glorify all wars, or war in general, but this particular one which involved an ideal — his ideal, the cause of democracy which he had always placed above everything else. It was for him, as we say today, an ideological war. He heard Liberty,[85] armed Liberty,[86] and Democracy advancing in a sound of thunder,[87] and he indissolubly linked the government at Washington, the cause of the North, with the cause of democracy. Above all, the Union must be saved. For, if the links uniting the various members of the federation should be broken, it would be the end of democracy in the world; the United States, henceforth disunited, would be too weak to defend itself against attacks from without and nowhere else would democracy be able to triumph over tyranny. So he exalted the Union because it had become for him a sacred and mystical notion to which everything, if necessary, must be sacrificed:

> See the Identity formed out of thirty-eight spacious and
>   haughty States, (and many more to come,). . .[88]

The parenthesis is important, he attached less importance to the political bonds that united the thirty-eight states in a single federation than to the promise of future grandeur of which that unity was the pledge. What mattered was the profound unity of this new race on the way to a glorious destiny. This is the theme of "Pioneers! O Pioneers!" which originally was part of *Drum-Taps* and which he later detached in order to give it a more general significance. Originally the poem was an appeal for unity in the name of the great tasks that awaited the whole American nation without distinction by states, North or South:

> From Nebraska, from Arkansas,
> Central inland race are we, from Missouri, with the
>   continental blood intervein'd;
> All the hands of comrades clasping, all the Southern,
>   all the Northern,
>   Pioneers! O pioneers! [89]

This war, the purpose of which was to save the Union, was therefore indispensable to the future of the nation, and by way of consequence, to the progress of the whole human race of which the American people were the vanguard: "We, the youthful sinewy races, all the rest on us depend." [90] and Whitman, who was a pioneer among the pioneers in the vanguard of the American nation, could not but throw himself wholeheartedly into the conflict — at least in imagination.

That was his first reaction; but, at the touch of harsh reality, his illusions were quickly dissipated; his idealistic concepts of a sacred and redeeming war collapsed as soon as he had a close view of the horrors with which it was inevitably accompanied, and he quickly passed from enthusiasm to disillusion: [91]

> Arous'd and angry, I'd thought to beat the alarum, and
>   urge relentless war,
> But soon my fingers fail'd me, my face droop'd and I
>   resign'd myself,
> To sit by the wounded and soothe them, or silently
>   watch the dead. [92]

One day, during a visit to friends, he became angry and began to pace the floor and cry out: "I say stop this war, this horrible massacre of men!" [93] and no opposing argument could make him give in. A little later, on September 8, 1863, he wrote to his mother: "Mother, one's heart grows sick of war, after all, when you see what it really is; every once in a while I feel so horrified and disgusted — it seems to me like a great slaughter-house and the men mutually butchering each other." [94]

So, from then on, instead of celebrating the exaltation of the volunteers going into combat, he chanted his infinite pity for the young men whose death made him think of Christ on the cross,[95] or the sufferings of the wounded who had been operated on near the front-lines [96] and of the dying on the battlefields.[97] Instead of glorifying the drunken excitement of the fighting, he described the poignant pain of the families when the terrible news arrived of the death of a son.[98] He no longer exalted the proud bearing and discipline of the troops, he criticized the officers and condemned their class-feeling and lack of democratic spirit.[99]

This complete reversal was caused not only by the spectacle of the evils engendered by the war, but was also the fruit of the terrible disappointment which he had experienced when, contrary to his expectation, the Confederate armies at first inflicted defeat after defeat on the armies of the Union. After the first battle of Bull Run in July 1861 he recorded his discouragement and despair:

The dream of humanity, the vaunted Union, we thought so strong, so impregnable — lo! it seems already smash'd like a China plate. . . the hour was one of the three or four of those crises we had then and afterward, during the fluctuations of four years, when human eyes appear'd at least just as likely to see the last breath of the Union as to see it continue.[100]

Year that trembled and reel'd beneath me!
Your summer wind was warm enough — yet the air I
    breathed froze me:

A thick gloom fell through the sunshine and darken'd
   me;
Must I change my triumphant songs? said I to myself;
Must I indeed learn to chant the cold dirges of the
   baffled?
And sullen hymns of defeat? [101]

This would have been unendurable for Whitman if it had
meant that the North would lose the war; it would have been
the ruin of his great democratic dream and the destruction
of his faith.

But this crisis did not last long. His faith in democracy was
so firmly anchored that he could never altogether despair of
final victory. At the very moment when he was assailed by
doubts he affirmed the necessity of pursuing the war. In the
letter to his mother which has just been quoted he continued
immediately in these terms: "I feel how impossible it appears
. . . to retire from this contest, until we have carried our
points." He was himself perfectly aware of the inconsistency
of his position and he was troubled by it: "It is cruel to be
so tossed from pillar to post in one's judgment." [102]

But little by little the agony this harrowing crisis caused
him subsided, and a year later he was able to write to his
mother: "After first Fredericksburg [December 1862] I felt
discouraged myself, and doubted whether our rulers could
carry on the war — but that has passed away. The war must
be carried on. . ." [103] The victories won in the interval had
revived his courage and renewed his hope. In the spring of
1863, he declared to a young friend: ". . . but for all our
bad success at Charleston and even if we fail for a while
elsewhere I believe this Union will conquer in the end as
sure as there's a God in heaven. This country can't be broken
up by Jeff Davis and all his damned crew." [104]

This assurance quickly hardened him and extinguished all
the pity which he had felt up to that time. He became accus-

tomed to the idea that the sacrifice of human lives was necessary to secure the victory of democracy. When the draft riots broke out in New York in July 1863, he was at first prejudiced in favor of the demonstrators,[105] but soon, recognizing his error, he declared himself in favor of vigorous government action to crush the resistance of the disloyal.[106] Although he had lately mourned the death of young soldiers in "Vigil Strange I Kept on the Field One Night" and in "A Sight in Camp in the Daybreak Gray and Dim," [107] he was now resigned; for the young soldiers were not really dead, they survived in the trees and the grass and in the aromas exhaled by the soil which would perfume the air for ages and ages.[108] This pantheistic vision of the eternal cycle of life reconciled him to the horror of the present. Besides, it seemed to him that he heard above the carnage a prophetic voice announcing the final triumph of the love of comrades and the reconciliation of the states in liberty and equality.[109] He tended — and he would tend more and more — to see only the happy consequences of this war [110] and, if not to close his eyes on the sufferings which it had brought, at least to accord them only a relative importance. He thus recovered little by little, not without struggles and hesitations, the serene optimism expressed in certain poems of the 1860 edition.[111]

After the war, true, he did not forget the dead; he celebrated their heroism and their sacrifice,[112] but he preferred the splendor of the future to the sorrow of the past. His optimism knew no bounds: [113]

> Years of the unperform'd! your horizon rises. . .
> I see not America only — I see not only Liberty's
>   nation, but other nations preparing. . .
> I see Freedom, completely arm'd, and victorious, and
>   very haughty, with Law by her side. . .[114]

Borders would disappear; thanks to the steamship and the

telegraph, distances would be abolished. The world would achieve unity and universal democracy:

> Are all nations communing? is there going to be but one
>   heart to the globe?. . .
> Years prophetical! the space ahead as I walk, as I vainly
>   try to pierce it, is full of phantoms; . . .
> The perform'd America and Europe grow dim, retiring
>   in shadow before me,
> The unperform'd, more gigantic than ever, advance,
>   advance upon me.[114]

He dreamed and prophesied of the infinite potentialities of human grandeur. The war had confirmed and reinforced his faith in the average man: "Never was average man, his soul, more energetic, more like a God." [114] He had witnessed the courage of the soldiers who freely accepted their trials [115] and bravely confronted death in the hospitals. It was this, above all, which impressed him:

To me the points illustrating the latent personal character and eligibilities of these States, in the two or three millions of American young and middle-aged men, North and South, embodied in those armies — and especially the one-third or one-fourth of their number stricken by wounds or disease at some time in the course of the contest — were of more significance even than the political interests. (As so much of a race depends on how it faces death and how it stands personal anguish and sickness. . .) [116]

Those three years [spent in the hospitals] I consider the greatest privilege and satisfaction. . . and, of course, the most profound lesson of my life. . . It has given me my most fervent view of the true *ensemble* and extent of the *States*.[117]

But it was necessary first, in order that this dream of universal democracy [118] might come true, that the North and the South forget their fratricidal struggles. Therefore he launched an appeal for reconciliation at the end of his *Sequel to Drum-Taps*.[119] During the war, in spite of his hatred for the Copperheads [120] and his profound antislavery convictions, he had never had anything but pity and sympathy for the Confederate soldiers. In the hospitals he had cared for them with as much devotion as for the others.[121] They had, after all, the same essentially American qualities as the soldiers of the federal armies, [122] and they were equally heroic: "Was one side so brave? the other was equally brave." [123] And had they not been reconciled by death? [124] It is therefore easy to understand his pain and his concern when Lincoln was assassinated by a fanatical southerner. What would happen? Would the North in anger and despair indulge in bloody reprisals? Such acts would be the end of the Union. Fortunately, there were none, and Whitman exulted. This was another proof of the political maturity of the American people:

We must own to a feeling of pride that the hand of summary vengeance was stayed under such an ordeal of wrath, and justice allowed to work out her own unfailing purposes. Surely the calm hour of reflection, following on the first heat of passion, marked us pre-eminently as a self-governing people.[125]

Thus, at the end of the war, after a period of disillusion, doubt, and despair, he recovered the fervor by which he had been carried away in 1861, but this was mingled with sadness at the memory of the sufferings he had witnessed and shared vicariously. In short, his evolution had followed a Hegelian pattern: thesis, antithesis, synthesis; and he was probably aware of such a threefold movement when he constructed about this time three of the sides of his "Square Deific." [126] We shall return to this topic later.

Drum-Taps appeared in New York in November 1865 as a pamphlet of seventy-two pages printed, like *Leaves of Grass*, at the author's expense.[127] It contained fifty-three poems, none of which had previously been published. Although there is no way of dating them precisely, these poems clearly were composed throughout the duration of the war, and some of them must have been written even before the outbreak of hostilities. One feels this in reading them, and we have tried to reconstruct their chronological order as accurately as possible in describing Whitman's development during these tragic years.[128] Besides, we do know that, even before his departure for Washington in 1862, Whitman had among his papers a small notebook entitled "Drum-Taps." Writing to his mother on March 31, 1863, he asked her to take the greatest care of it [129] (and this is a further proof of the profound interest which in spite of appearances he had in the war at that time). He tried very early to publish it. A year later, on April 10, 1864, he announced to his mother: "I want to come on in a month and try to print my *Drum-Taps*. I think it may be a success pecuniarily, too." [130] Trowbridge had already tried, vainly, to find a publisher for it in Boston.[131] Whitman was no more successful and finally, as usual, had to resign himself to being his own publisher.

He felt, however, that he had made great progress since his latest edition of *Leaves of Grass*:

> It is in my opinion superior to *Leaves of Grass* — certainly more perfect as a work of art, being adjusted in all its proportions, & its passion having the indispensable merit that though to the ordinary reader let loose with wildest abandon, the true artist can see it is yet under control.[132]

And he was very proud of the discipline he had succeeded in imposing on himself:

> But I am perhaps mainly satisfied with *Drum-Taps* because it delivers my ambition of the task that has haunted me, namely, to express in a poem (& in the way I like, which is not at all by directly stating it) the pending action of this *Time & Land we swim in*, with all their large conflicting fluctuations of despair & hope, the shiftings, masses, & the whirl & deafening din, (yet over all, as by invisible hand, a definite purport and idea). . .[133]

To be sure the material was less subjective and easier to handle;[134] however, according to him, *Drum-Taps* was also superior to *Leaves of Grass* in another way: the style was purer and less heavy.

> I see I have said I consider *Drum-Taps* superior to *Leaves of Grass*. I probably mean as a piece of art, & from the more simple and winning nature of the subject, & also because I have in it succeeded to my satisfaction in removing all superfluity from it, verbal superfluity I mean, I delight to make a poem where I feel clear that not a word but is indispensable part thereof & of my meaning.[135]

He was right in that this feeling for conciseness and economy of means was something new in his work. But the formal simplicity was largely owing, as he realized, to the simplicity of the subject, since most of the poems were descriptive and anecdotal.[136] In spite of what he said, the direct method of expression used in *Drum-Taps* naturally resulted in a clarity which the indirect suggestions of his earlier poems could not attain. But it remains to be seen whether this was a progress, as he seems to have thought, or an impoverishment and a loss of power. This can only be shown by his later development. It seems in any case that he became more and more resigned to the idea of making concessions to the public. He even thought of expurgating *Leaves of Grass*:

> *Drum-Taps* has none of the perturbations of *Leaves of Grass*. I am satisfied with *Leaves of Grass*. . . but there are a few things I shall carefully eliminate in the next issue, & a few more I shall considerably change.[137]

He did not go quite so far as to repudiate his great work, but he seems now to have regretted some of the things which had hampered its sale. He retained them out of stubbornness and for the sake of the past, but it is clear that he was not quite the same man as he had been:

Still *Leaves of Grass* is dear to me, always dearest to me, as my first born, as daughter of my life's first hopes, doubts, & the putting in form of those days' efforts & aspirations — true, I see now, with some things in it I should not put in if I were to write now, but yet I shall certainly let them stand, even if but for proofs of phases passed away.[138]

We shall see how far in 1867 he pushed his expurgation of *Leaves of Grass* and to what extent he remained faithful to himself.

Most copies of *Drum-Taps* included under the same cover another small booklet of twenty-four pages entitled "When Lilacs Last in the Door-Yard Bloom'd and Other Pieces," dated Washington, 1865–66. This collection is more commonly referred to by its subtitle "Sequel to Drum-Taps," which also appeared at the top of each page.[139] It is a natural extension of *Drum Taps*. When Lincoln was assassinated, Whitman was in Brooklyn supervising the printing of *Drum-Taps*. The war had just ended; it was early spring and the lilacs were in bloom in the yard of the family home; joy was everywhere. But when he heard the shocking news, he was overcome. For him Lincoln was more than the savior of the Union, he was a friendly and familiar presence; for though they had never met, Whitman had often had occasion to see him in Washington.[140] In the first intensity of pain, he wrote a short poem, "Hush'd Be the Camps To-Day," commemorating the martyred President's funeral at Springfield,[141] and he held up the printing of *Drum-Taps* to include it, probably in the place of another poem of equal length. On his return to Washington, his friend Peter Doyle, who had witnessed the assassination at the Ford Theater, told him the story of what he had seen. It was probably then that Whitman composed "When Lilacs Last in the Door-Yard Bloom'd." [142] This long and moving threnody is generally regarded by critics as Whitman's masterpiece.[143] In it he demonstrates the greatness of his art in a very personal way. On the whole, he repeated the formula he had used in 1860 for "Out of the Cradle Endlessly Rocking." The poem is first of all a symphony of interlacing musical and symbolic themes, but the pattern is simpler than that of 1860 and shows greater mastery — though, perhaps, less power.

It was now too late to include "When Lilacs Last. . ." in *Drum-Taps*, the printing of which was in progress, if not completed, at New York. Whitman was therefore obliged to have the poem printed separately in Washington. He took advantage of the occasion to put a certain number of other poems in with it. Some, such as "I Heard You, Solemn-Sweet Pipes of the Organ," "Not My Enemies Ever Invade Me," "O Me! O Life!" and "Ah Poverties, Wincings and Sulky Retreats," [144] were essentially personal and, later, either disappeared from *Leaves of Grass* or were transferred to sections other than "Drum-Taps." Whitman probably included them for good measure, but it seems likely that they had been written much earlier and that they referred to the emotional crisis of 1859–60.[145] The others, however, concerned the end of the war and did belong to *Drum-Taps*. At any rate they remained in *Leaves of Grass* under that title, which shows the fundamental unity of the two books — with the exception of "O Captain! My Captain!" [146] which commemorates Lincoln and was later put in a separate group with "When Lilacs Last. . ." The case of "Chanting the Square Deific" [147] is a little peculiar, and we shall take it up later.

Whitman had hoped that *Drum-Taps* would sell rapidly and bring him some money.[148] Unfortunately we do not know to what extent this hope was realized, but there is no doubt that the book was much better received than *Leaves of Grass*.[149] Critics in fact were sometimes embarrassed at having to recommend a book by Whitman after having treated him so rudely up to that time. George William Curtis, for instance, in *Harper's* apologized in these terms for mentioning him at the same time as Tennyson and Jean Ingelow:

> If any reader is appalled by seeing that name in so choice a society, let us not argue the matter, nor express any opinion, but ask whether there is no poetry in this wail upon the death of Lincoln and in the Song of the Drum.[150]

Whitman's friends multiplied their efforts in the reviews and the newspapers to dissipate such prejudices, especially William O'Connor, who became his acknowledged champion and boldly broke lances with all assailants in the columns of the New York *Times* and the *Round Table*.[151] John Burroughs, a friend of more recent date, less fiery and more judicious, wrote articles for the *Boston Commonwealth* and *Galaxy*, in which with a more discerning enthusiasm he praised Whitman for being a difficult poet who made no concessions to the public — a judgment which, as we have seen, was beginning to be less true:

> . . . let it be understood we are dealing with one of the most tyrannical and exacting of bards — one who steadfastly refuses to be read in any but his own spirit. It is only after repeated readings and turning to him again and again that the atmosphere he breathes is reached. . . The poem may disappoint on the first perusal. The treatment of the subject is so unusual, so unlike the direct and prosy style to which our ears have been educated — that it seems to want method and purpose.[152]

In this concert of praises there were, however, two discords: the articles of W. D. Howells and Henry James. Howells recognized that on this occasion the poet could not be accused of obscenity, but he still reproached him for a lack of art:

> . . . there is no indecent thing in *Drum-Taps*. The artistic method of the poet remains, however, the same, and we must think it mistaken. . . it is unspeakably inartistic. On this ac-

count it is a failure. . . Art cannot greatly employ itself with
things in embryo. . . *Expression* will always suggest; but mere
suggestion in art is unworthy of existence, vexes the heart and
shall not live. . . There are such rich possibilities in the man
that it is lamentable to contemplate his error of theory. . . A
man's greatness is good for nothing folded up in him, and if
emitted in barbaric yawps, it is not more filling than Ossian or the
east wind.[153]

Howells in spite of the prejudices owing to his education
seems to have felt a certain sympathy for Whitman. It was
otherwise with Henry James, for whom "it [had] been a
melancholy task to read this book." [154] He too condemned the
lack of art, but his analysis went further than that of Howells.
Art for him was not only a matter of technique, it was also a
way of life, a discipline which governed the artist as well as
his art and implied a lucid awareness of himself and others.
Surely there was nothing of this sort in Whitman, whose lack
of restraint James found repelling:

We find a medley of extravagances and commonplaces. We
find art, measure, grace, sense sneered at on every page, and
nothing positive given us in their stead. To be positive one must
have something to say; to be positive requires reason, labor and
art; and art requires, above all things, a suppression of one's self,
a subordination of one's self to an idea. . . It is not enough to
be rude, lugubrious and grim. You must also be serious. You must
forget yourself in your ideas. Your personal qualities — the vigor
of your temperament, the manly independence of your nature,
the tenderness of your heart — these facts are impertinent.[155]

Thus, even the severest critics no longer complained of anything except Whitman's lack of form. But in spite of this
greater sympathy, no one seems to have seen what constituted
the real value and originality of *Drum-Taps*. The image of
war which emerged from it was quite unconventional, though.
The opening poems were warlike enough, praising warfare as
a fine and noble adventure,[156] and Whitman sometimes cele-

brated acts of heroism in the best tradition of epic poetry, as in "The Centenarian's Story" and "I Saw Old General at Bay." [157] He also sang the glory of battles and the beauty of troops on the march,[158] but in general, in spite of his vibrant call to arms and his cries of triumph, the tone of the book is melancholy, as he knew perfectly well himself.[159] This is because, as we have seen,[160] after his first contact with the realities of war he had been, if not repelled (once begun, the conflict could not be stopped), at least profoundly moved by the martyrdom of the young soldiers, by what Wilfred Owen was later to call "the pity of War." [161] He was, in short, the first poet of modern war as we know it, the war of masses, of large-scale massacres, where heroism has become anonymous and courage more passive than active, the individual having lost all independence and initiative. Whitman was thus the first and the only poet of his time who dared to do what we call the debunking of war.[162] Herman Melville, in his *Battle-Pieces*, in spite of his sense of evil and original sin, in spite of his great sympathy for Confederate soldiers (as men, for he detested their cause as much as Whitman did), offers only weak stories of individual acts of heroism.[163] Lacking personal experience, he could not vividly imagine the terrible sufferings of the hundreds of thousands of wounded and sick. He was therefore reduced to treating the war in the traditional epic fashion. In *Drum-Taps*, on the contrary, Whitman removed the poetry of war from the epic and infused it with the more human and subjective tones of lyric poetry. Instead of celebrating heroes and supermen, he described the sufferings of ordinary men.

Even though more lyric than epic, it is remarkable that *Drum-Taps* at first occupied a place apart in Whitman's work. For the time being it did not occur to him to include the poems in *Leaves of Grass.* So he made them into a separate volume which he believed would always remain distinct from the other poems.[164] It was only gradually that he decided to incorporate them in *Leaves of Grass*. In the fourth edition in 1867, they were relegated to an appendix. It was not until 1871 that he succeeded in fitting them into the body of the book, but even then they formed a distinct group (or rather three groups), and in the definitive edition, they are still almost all grouped together. Moreover, as O. L. Triggs has noted, unlike the rest of *Leaves of Grass*, *Drum-Taps* remained almost completely unrevised.[165] The arrangement changed, but the original text underwent few alterations, as if Whitman feared that in revising his war poems he might weaken them. It seems that he particularly wanted to preserve the primitive character of these poems. One has the impression, in short, that he was never entirely able to assimilate the extraordinary adventure and tragic trial which the Civil War had been for him. When *Drum-Taps* first appeared, he was still dazed by his emotions and could not as yet absorb such exceptional experiences or integrate such new and overwhelming feelings into the web of his life. These circumstances explain the autonomy he gave at first to *Drum-Taps*. The war was an intrusion which he had not foreseen and which compelled him to modify the organization of *Leaves of Grass*. Even if he had a plan in mind at the beginning, the irruption of war into his work forced him to change it.

The Civil War, then, exercised on his life and on his poetic career a considerable influence, the importance of which he further exaggerated later on. In 1888, casting "a backward glance o'er travel'd roads," he went so far as to declare:

It is certain, I say, that, although I had made a start before, only from the occurrence of the Secession War, and what it show'd me as by flashes of lightning, with the emotional depths it sounded and arous'd (of course, I don't mean in my own heart only, I saw it just as plain in others, in millions) — that only from the strong flare and provocation of that war's sights and scenes the final reasons-for-being of an autochthonic and passionate song definitely came forth. . .

I went down to the war fields of Virginia (end of 1862), lived thenceforward in camp — saw great battles. . . Without those three or four years and the experiences they gave, *Leaves of Grass* would not now be existing.[166]

The exaggeration is striking. With the passage of time he had almost succeeded in persuading himself that he had taken part in the great battles of the Civil War, or at least that he had witnessed them, although the most he had actually seen — and that at a distance — was a few skirmishes.[167] As to the statement that *Leaves of Grass* could not have existed without the War of Secession, if we take it literally, it is absurd, since most of the poems in *Leaves of Grass* were written before 1860. It should be interpreted as meaning that without the impetus of the war his career would have ended, and he would have had nothing further to say. At the end of the 1860 edition he had indeed made his farewell to his readers.[168] Nevertheless, even in this restricted sense, there is still a patent exaggeration; for when the 1860 edition appeared, he had already surmounted the crisis which had inspired the pessimistic poems written during that period.[169] The war had not caused him to find himself, since his poetic birth took place in 1855; and neither had it saved him, since he had saved himself at least twice before 1862; but it had consolidated the victories which he had won by definitively confirming his reasons for belief in and hope for mankind. For he knew now that the human character was essentially made up of heroism and love. He had seen the proof of this in the hospitals. Evil was only accidental.[170] Thus reassured, he lived henceforth with the conviction that his democratic ideal was attainable. It was no longer for him a utopian dream, but a certainty founded on facts that he had been able to verify daily during more than three years.

But that was not all. The years he had passed in the hospitals had brought him other revelations, more precious still. He had served an apprenticeship there to brotherhood and friendship. Up to that time he led a very solitary existence. True, he lived with his family, but none of them could understand him, and he came and went among them without really living in the same world.[171] In New York, he had many acquaintances among the journalists and comrades among the omnibus drivers, but no real friends. His rides along Broadway on the roofs of coaches symbolize the solitude in which he lived in the midst of the noisy crowds of the great city.[172] At Pfaff's he was equally isolated. He sat there among the rest, affable and smiling, but as far away from them as if he had lived on another planet.[173] In Washington everything changed; he was finally able to step outside himself and fraternize with the wounded and the sick without fear of scandal. He was at last permitted to lavish every day the treasures of unused affection which had accumulated in him and to lay the foundations of that democracy of comrades of which he had dreamed for ten years.[174] He expanded in the new atmosphere. He became for the first time, it seems, capable of friendship, and it was then that he linked himself with William O'Connor and his wife Ellen, with John Burroughs, and on a different level, with Peter Doyle. From then on, he ceased to be alone in life. In addition to his mother, he had his friends. Even when he was separated from them, he wrote to them very simple letters, very direct, without ornaments, the only purpose of which was to maintain relations. He also wrote for several years to some of the soldiers whom he had known in Washington.[175] This correspondence, part of which has survived, shows how precious these friendships were to him in permitting him to escape from his original solitude. Thanks to his young comrades of the hospitals, and to his new friends, he participated more fully in the life of his contemporaries and mingled more effectively than before in the society of his time.

The war was responsible for another change: his sensuality, at least in appearance, subsided. He was less tormented by his homosexual leanings, which his visits to the hospitals permitted him to satisfy in part without incurring social disapproval or even suspicion. His vocation as "wound-dresser" was certainly not a pose. He was undoubtedly motivated by charity, but, unconsciously at least, he was also moved by his desire and his need to be among young men. He experienced not only pity for them, but a tremendous affection, and he was happy because it seemed to him that this affection was reciprocated. He had the very strong impression that these young soldiers, like himself, needed manly affection — [176] a reassuring discovery since it furnished proof that his instincts were more normal than he had thought. Having dreamed of "the comrade's long-dwelling kiss" in the City of the Future,[177] he now had occasion every day to kiss the wounded who were eager for affection and caresses:

> Lots of them have grown to expect, as I leave at night, that we should kiss each other, sometimes quite a number; I have to go round. There is very little petting in a soldier's life in the field, but . . . I know what is in their hearts, always waiting, though they may be unconscious of it themselves.[178]

So, again, nature imitated art and his life was modeled on his work. At any rate, these marks of affection, innocent as they may have seemed, indicated the violent desires he was obliged to repress:

> O beloved race in all! O my breast aches with tender love for all. . .[179]

> These and more I dress with impassive hand — (yet deep in my breast a fire, a burning flame.) [180]

> How good they look as they tramp down to the river, sweaty, with their guns on their shoulders!

How I love them! how I could hug them, with their
brown faces and their clothes and knapsacks cover'd
with dust.[181]

It was, then, their beauty which moved him. When he
described the nation mourning its dead, he made it say in
its prayer to the earth: "My dead absorb — my young men's
beautiful bodies absorb. . ." [182] Curiously enough, the adjective "beautiful" later disappeared, as if Whitman had been
afraid of betraying his secret thoughts. In fact, these very
discreet avowals revealed his sensual stirrings. We shall have
occasion later to examine further the nature of these amorous
instincts and to determine how far he let them go. One thing
seems certain: he did not at this time do anything which
society would disapprove. He was sometimes tempted to enter
into more intimate relations with some of the soldiers, but
his dreams of peaceful domestic life with them never came
true.[183] He learned to content himself with much less; a pressure of the hand, an exchange of kisses, or even a mere loving
look were enough to satisfy him.[184] Moreover, it seems that,
without any sensual satisfaction during the war years, his
homosexual passion was gradually purified and idealized. His
troubled desires were succeeded by an ardent but ethereal
and completely Platonic emotion:

I have been and am now, thinking so of you, dear young man,
and of your love, or more rightly speaking, our love for each
other — so curious, so sweet, I say so *religious* — We met there
in the Hospitals — how little we have been together — seems to
me we ought to be some together every day of our lives — I don't
care about talking, or amusement — but just to be together, and
work together, or go off in the open air together.[185]

Such were, in all likelihood, the sentiments which he wished
to express in one of the most mysterious poems of *Drum-Taps*,
"Out of the Rolling Ocean the Crowd":

> "Out of the rolling ocean, the crowd, came a drop gently
>   to me,
> Whispering, *I love you, before long I die,*
> *I have travel'd a long way, merely to look on you, to*
>   *touch you,*
> *For I could not die till I once look'd on you,*
> *For I fear'd I might afterward lose you.*
> Now we have met, we have look'd, we are safe;
> Return in peace to the ocean my love;
> I too am part of that ocean, my love — we are not so
>   much separated;
> Behold the great rondure — the cohesion of all, how
>   perfect!
> But as for me, for you, the irresistible sea is to separate
>   us,
> As for an hour carrying us diverse — yet cannot carry
>   us diverse for ever;
> Be not impatient — a little space — know you, I salute
>   the air, the ocean and the land,
> Every day, at sundown, for your dear sake, my love.[186]

Thus, by a strange transmutation, doubtless under the influence of his pity for the young wounded soldiers, his homosexual feelings were sublimated during these three years, and transformed into a mystical kind of love, so pure of all carnal desire that he could sometimes speak of it in terms of paternal or fraternal love.[187] The war permitted him in some degree to realize that democracy of comrades founded on "manly love" which he had announced in 1860 [188] and for which he always longed, although he knew that its realization would encounter innumerable difficulties:

> . . . Dear camerado! I confess I have urged you on-
>   ward with me, and still urge you, without the least
>   idea what is our destination,
> Or whether we shall be victorious, or utterly quell'd
>   and defeated.[189]

The war also had another effect on Whitman. It brought

about his final reconciliation with death. Already in 1860, in "Out of the Cradle Endlessly Rocking," he had celebrated the sweetness of "the low and delicious word death." [190] But death, in spite of this acceptance in principle, was still associated at this time with the angry moans of the sea [191] and with the infinitely dolorous theme of the separation of two loving creatures. For all its promises it concealed an obscure menace, since, who knows, it might be nothing but chaos.[192] In 1865 it had lost its tragic halo; it was the certainty of peace and repose. It brought deliverance and redemption instead of chaos and despair:

> Come lovely and soothing Death. . .
> Approach, encompassing Death — strong Deliveress!
> When it is so — when thou hast taken them, I joyously
>   sing the dead,
> Lost in the loving, floating ocean of thee,
> Laved in the flood of thy bliss, O Death,[193]

sings the bird from a distance at the time of Lincoln's funeral, because, in the interval, Whitman had lived familiarly with death. In the hospitals he had seen so many young soldiers meet it so bravely that it no longer had either horror or mystery for him: [194]

> For I have seen many wounded soldiers die,
> After dread suffering — have seen their lives pass off
>   with smiles. . .[195]

This then, what frightened us so long. Why, it is put to flight with ignominy — a mere stuffed scarecrow of the fields. Oh death, where is thy sting? Oh grave, where is thy victory? [196]

Those who die, no longer suffer. Death was a deliverance in those days. It freed thousands and thousands of young men. It was those who remained, the living, who suffered.[197]

The joy with which Whitman had welcomed peace and the victory of democracy and the serenity with which he regarded

death were therefore tempered with sadness, even though
he now almost preferred the repose of death to the life he had
so passionately loved before. This was undoubtedly a sign of
lassitude, probably due to the accumulated physical fatigue
from the long months in the hospitals and also to the moral
distaste aroused by all the horrors and turpitudes which he had
witnessed [198] and which are perhaps echoed in "O Me! O Life!"
— unless that poem was written before the war.[199] The elegy
on Lincoln, besides, includes a casual admission of his nervous-
ness and restlessness at this time: ". . . something I know
not what kept me from sleep." [200]

So the same battle between doubt and hope went on. He
wavered endlessly between suffering and serenity, but once
more he emerged victorious — thanks to his art. He was
perfectly aware of it himself, since he said to the fraternal
bird who sang sorrowfully in the distance:

> . . . well dear brother I know,
> If thou wast not granted to sing thou wouldst surely
> die.[201]

He knew that his victory was precarious and that the
battle would have to be continually renewed. Peace, he fore-
saw, would be another struggle. So he gathered his forces in
the expectation of new trials to come:

> Weave in! weave in, my hardy life!. . .
> We know not what the use, O life! nor know the aim,
>   the end — nor really aught we know;
> But know the work, the need goes on, and shall go on —
>   the death-envelop'd march of peace as well as war,
>   goes on;
> For great campaigns of peace the same, the wiry threads
>   to weave;
> We know not why or what, yet weave, forever weave.[202]

CHAPTER VII

HAPPY BUREAUCRAT AND
TORMENTED POET

ONE day, during the war, a New York newspaper correspondent named Swinton, finding Whitman on time for an appointment, exclaimed: "Well, Walt, I have known you dozens of years, and made hundreds of appointments with you, but this is the first time that I ever knew you to keep one. I thought that I saw signs of decay." [1]

This is the general impression which the evidence gives of Whitman at the end of the war. He had never before been settled but had continually changed from one paper, and even from one profession, to another; now, on the contrary, he had installed himself in Washington, and he did not leave it until he was forced to do so by illness in 1873, after a stay of nearly ten years. Besides, he had even renounced his independence and consented to become a civil servant. The vagabond always ready to take the open road now resigned himself to the monotonous routine of a clerk's life in an office. At first glance, this appears a strange downfall.

In January 1863, soon after his return from Falmouth, he had sought a job in the government service in order to make a living; [2] but his efforts were unsuccessful and he soon became tired of waiting in antechambers. So he contented himself with the modest position of part-time assistant that

Major Hapgood had offered him. But at the end of the war, vigorously supported by J. Hubley Ashton, Assistant Attorney General, whose acquaintance he had made at the home of the O'Connors, and by Assistant Secretary W. T. Otto of the Department of the Interior, he obtained a clerkship in the Indian Bureau at a salary of twelve hundred dollars a year.[3] He amply deserved it, as the poet of *Drum-Taps* and the indefatigable wound-dresser, the two claims that he had advanced in support of his request — taking care at the same time not to mention *Leaves of Grass*.[4] If James Harlan, the Secretary of the Interior, had known him as the author of that book, Whitman would probably never have obtained the position. Harlan was a narrow and fanatical Methodist who could live only in an atmosphere of virtue and purity. Unfortunately, through some zealous employee, he soon learned that Whitman had written an indecent book. In June 1865, to make certain, he searched the suspect's desk after office hours and seized a copy of *Leaves of Grass* which he found there.[5] What he read in it must have horrified him, for the next day Whitman was dismissed without explanation.[6] Ashton quickly intervened and protested against this unjustified dismissal of his protégé, who, strangely enough, had been promoted the month before.[7] But Harlan was inflexible and claimed that it was impossible for him to keep such an immoral author among his subordinates. He would resign rather than reconsider his decision. Ashton gave up the attempt and found a job for Whitman in the Department of the Interior.

The incident was closed and the crisis resolved without damage to Whitman, but the ebullient and generous O'Connor, always ready to fly to the help of the weak and the oppressed, did not take that view. In his opinion, Harlan had shown a criminal intolerance in persecuting a poet and deserved to be punished. In a few weeks, Whitman's fearless champion composed a virulent and lyrical pamphlet attacking Harlan and lauding the author of *Leaves of Grass*. *The Good Gray Poet* [8] is a masterpiece of its kind.[9] O'Connor gave free rein to his virtuosity in invective and hyperbole. He represented Whitman as a superman equal, if not superior, to Homer, Shakespeare, Dante, and Christ and acclaimed *Leaves of Grass* as one of the world's great books. At the same time, with a great deal of skill, he praised Whitman for having tried to found a specifically American literature completely free from all European influence, and in taking this line, he was sure to gain sympathy for Whitman. Besides, in representing Whitman's dismissal as an infringement on freedom of thought and a manifestation of obscurantism, he further enlarged the argument and made his hero a martyr whom every liberal in the land would feel bound to support.

For these reasons the pamphlet created a certain stir when it was published in 1866.[10] It helped to draw attention to *Drum-Taps* and their *Sequel*, which appeared about the same time. It was favorably mentioned in the reviews,[11] and it gave rise to a current of sympathy for Whitman. Even those who found O'Connor's dithyrambic eulogies exaggerated were obliged to respect the work Whitman had done in the hospitals and to recognize the value of his war poems. It was impossible henceforth to ignore him or to abuse him as certain critics had done before the war. The obscene author of *Leaves of Grass* had now become "the Good Gray Poet." He was no longer merely a poet but a legendary personage.

While O'Connor stormed, Whitman took things easy.[12] His work in the office was not exacting and left him a great deal of leisure.[13] Theoretically, his working day began at nine o'clock and finished at four, but he always came late in the morning after having gossiped with his friends for a long time at breakfast,[14] and he generally left early in the afternoon.[15] Thus he had long evenings to himself, which he spent idling, chatting, or reading. When he wished to read after dinner, he returned to his office and there, comfortably installed, warmed, and lighted at government expense, he devoured the books of the departmental library.[16] Moreover, it is probable that even during working hours he occupied himself more with literary than with governmental matters.[17] Bureaucratic customs were then much easier than they are today, and his career as a civil servant in no way hampered his activity as a writer. He was in fact given a leave of absence whenever he wanted one in order to supervise the printing of his books. Thus it was that in April 1865 (only three months after his appointment and one month after his first promotion) he was in Brooklyn preparing *Drum-Taps* for publication.[18] And he obtained the same favor each time he had a book to publish.[19] This did not prevent his advancement, since in November 1866 he was promoted to the status of third class with a salary of sixteen hundred dollars a year.[20] He had never been so rich before.[21] He began to live less frugally and moved to a somewhat more comfortable boardinghouse at the corner of M and Twelfth Streets.[22] He occupied an attic as usual, but in his letters to his mother, he repeatedly praised the abundant food.[23] His tastes were decidedly becoming more bourgeois.

What a difference indeed between the untidy Whitman of 1855 and the well-behaved, conventional personage whose image he now tried to convey to his English readers through the medium of Moncure D. Conway and William Rossetti:

. . . personally the author of *Leaves of Grass* is in no sense or sort whatever the "rough," the "eccentric," "vagabond," or queer person that the commentators (always bound for the intensest possible statement,) persist in making him. He has moved and moves still along the path of his life's happenings and fortunes, as they befall or have befallen him, with entire serenity and decorum, never defiant even to the conventions, always bodily sweet and fresh, dressed plainly and cleanly, a gait and demeanor of antique simplicity, cheerful and smiling, performing carefully all his domestic, social and municipal obligations, his demonstrative nature toned very low but eloquent enough of eye, posture and expression, using only moderate words, and offering to the world, in himself, an American Personality and real Democratic Presence, that not only the best old Hindu, Greek and Roman worthies would have at once responded to, but which the most cultured European from court or academy would likewise on meeting to-day, see and own without demur.[24]

He had come a long way in ten years, from the superb arrogance with which in the 1855 Preface he had affirmed the superiority of America and of American poets,[25] an arrogance which perhaps arose from an obscure feeling of inferiority. But now American democracy had emerged victorious from a terrible struggle and no one could doubt its solidity. He no longer needed to shout its praises, he could be content to affirm them quietly. Similarly he no longer needed to call attention to himself by means of eccentric clothing or revolutionary appeals. He had succeeded in compelling recognition; he could now afford to give up the "rough," the vagabond of the "Song of the Open Road" who had never existed anyhow, except metaphorically. He shed the personality which he had once wanted to embody (which he had perhaps believed he did embody), but which had never really been his. The more conventional portrait of himself that he presented in 1866 placed the accent on equilibrium and serenity rather than on passion and dynamism.[26] A trait of the earlier portrait remained however: perfect physical health. It was unfortunately the most illusory.

In fact, during the summer of 1866, the symptoms which had bothered him during the war recurred: fits of dizziness, violent headaches, and insomnia.[27] He complained of them constantly in his letters to his mother. Over the years his condition, instead of improving, grew worse. In 1896 he had several attacks of this mysterious illness, each of which lasted three or four days and left him prostrate and powerless.[28] The heat overcame him. He who had once taken sunbaths on the Long Island beaches was now obliged to walk with a parasol in the summer.[29] In 1870 he felt better, but for several weeks his sight failed so rapidly that he had to wear spectacles for reading and writing.[30] In 1872, after several months of good health, his apparently causeless maladies recurred [31] and worried him so much that he made a will and sent it to his brother George, telling him not to be alarmed, but not to laugh either.[32]

His presentiments were in fact well founded. On January 23, 1873,[33] as he was quietly reading a novel by Bulwer-Lytton before a good fire in his office, he suddenly felt ill and hurried home as fast as he could. When he woke up next morning he realized that his left side was paralyzed. He had had a stroke during the night.[34] The poet of perfect health had suddenly become an invalid. After having emerged from so many psychological crises, he was now brought low — defeated by his own body.

There has been much speculation concerning the causes of this sudden physical collapse. For Whitman and his friends, the explanation was simple: he had lost his health in the military hospitals during the war; overwork and continual strain had finally broken his resistance to the infections to which he was exposed. They recalled also that he had had blood poisoning from a cut on the hand by the scalpel of a surgeon during an operation,[35] and they did not wonder that he had finally succumbed. Accordingly this paralytic attack became for Whitman a new claim to glory. It made a martyr of him and a victim of the war which he had extolled. He wrote of it proudly in the Preface to the 2nd Annex of *Leaves of Grass* in 1891.[36] But soon after his death, the iconoclasts began to express their doubts. In March 1892, Thomas Wentworth Higginson, to the indignation of Whitman's admirers, advanced the hypothesis that his stroke was probably caused

not by his heroic conduct in the hospitals, but by the irregu-
larities of his sexual life.[37] And several years later, the German
critic Eduard Bertz, comparing Whitman's case to that of
Nietzsche, inquired whether this attack was not the result
of a hereditary taint.[38] There was no lack of arguments in
favor of such an explanation. Edward (Eddie), his youngest
brother, was feeble-minded, subject to epileptic fits, and
paralyzed on the left side (perhaps as a result of a difficult
delivery and a violent attack of scarlet fever); Jesse, his oldest
brother, was syphilitic and died insane in an asylum (but his
insanity may have been due to a fall or to a blow on the head);
another brother, Andrew, died at the age of thirty-seven from
cancer or tuberculosis of the throat; his younger sister, Hannah,
was a neurotic, incapable of keeping house and also had a
paralytic attack in 1892; finally, one of his brothers had died
six months after birth.[39] Certainly, the picture is dark, but
it should be pointed out that Mary and George Whitman both
led perfectly normal lives and died, like their mother, at an
advanced age. So there is nothing to prove, even if there was
actually a taint in the family, that Walt Whitman was affected.
Moreover, a physician, Dr. J. C. Trent, who analyzed Whitman's case in 1948,[40] withholds his opinion and seems to lean
toward the hypothesis of a stroke due to hypertension.[41] This
diagnosis by a practitioner acquainted with recent medical
theories is also confirmed by the opinion of John Burroughs
who knew Whitman well.

In any case, whatever the cause of his illness, the uneventful
life Whitman had thus far led in Washington was brutally
interrupted. Had he been truly happy during the years following the intoxication of victory and the joy of renewed peace?
It seems not. He had been very lonely and his solitude had
weighed upon him. "As to me, I lead rather a dull life here. . .
I do not associate much with the department clerks, yet many

appear to be good fellows enough," he wrote in 1866 to a young soldier whom he had known in the hospitals.⁴² Two years later, he expressed himself in almost the same terms: "I am leading a quiet monotonous life, working a few hours every day very moderately. Have plenty of books to read but few acquaintances. I spend my evenings mostly in the office." ⁴³

This is a long way from the vigorous and happy vagabond that he had imagined himself to be in 1855 and that he had presented in his self-portrait, the friend of all whose friendship all had sought as if drawn by his secret magnetism.⁴⁴ There were no more wounded soldiers to visit and to comfort.⁴⁵ Peace had left a great emptiness which nothing came to fill. Now he was no longer living with the O'Connors, he saw them infrequently. He was able to visit John Burroughs only on Sundays.⁴⁶ He therefore felt terribly isolated — in spite of the friendship of Peter Doyle — and he was sometimes at the point of tears. It was at this time that he wrote the poignant little poem entitled "Tears," one of the few new poems of the 1867 edition:

> Tears! tears! tears!
> In the night, in solitude, tears,
> On the white shore dripping, dripping, suck'd in by the sand,
> Tears, not a star shining, all dark and desolate,
> Moist tears from the eyes of a muffled head;
> O who is that ghost? that form in the dark, with tears?
> What shapeless lump is that, bent, crouch'd there on the sand?
> Streaming tears, sobbing tears, throes, choked with wild cries;
> O storm, embodied, rising, careering with swift steps along the beach!
> O wild and dismal night storm, with wind — O belching and desperate!
> O shade so sedate and decorous by day, with calm countenance and regulated pace,

But away at night as you fly, none looking, — O then
the unloosen'd ocean,
Of tears! tears! tears! [47]

Who is this tragic phantom if not himself, a model employee
by day and a desperate man at night when he found himself
alone? The serenity which he had attained at the end of the
war was thus, it seems, once more endangered. In appearance,
as always, he gave an impression of perfect balance,[48] but in
the depth of his mind a tempest raged. He was passing through
a new crisis.

It is true that very little is known about his emotional life
at this time. According to Emory Holloway, in his introduction to the *Uncollected Poetry and Prose of Walt Whitman*,[49]
and Frances Winwar, in her fictional biography,[50] Whitman
had been torn by an unhappy passion for a married woman,
Mrs. Juliette H. Beach, in whose honor he had written "Out
of the Cradle Endlessly Rocking." But Clifton J. Furness has
proved that this romantic story is totally unfounded,[51] and
Holloway himself later recanted; the biography of Whitman
which he published in 1926, several years after his *Uncollected
Poetry and Prose,* makes no mention of Juliette Beach.[52] All
that we know for certain is that Whitman was again obsessed
by ambiguous sexual desires which he tried to suppress. One
of his private notebooks, dated July 15, 1870, furnishes evidence of his secret troubles:

. . . fancying what does not really exist in another, but is all
the time in myself alone — utterly deluded & cheated by *myself*
& my own weakness — REMEMBER WERE I AM MOST WEAK, &
most lacking. Yet always preserve a kind spirit & demeanor to 16.
But PURSUE HER NO MORE. . .

It is IMPERATIVE, that I obviate & remove myself (&
my orbit) *at all hazards* [away from] this *incessant
enormous* & . . . . PERTURBATION

To GIVE UP ABSOLUTELY & *for good, from this present hour,* [all] this FEVERISH, FLUCTUATING, *useless undignified pursuit of 164 — too long, (much too long)* persevered in, — so humiliating — *it must come at last* & had better come now — *(It cannot possibly be a success)*

LET THERE FROM THIS HOUR BE NO FALTERING, . . NO GETTING . . . at all henceforth, (NOT ONCE, *under any circumstances) — avoid seeing her, or meeting her, or any talk or explanations —* or ANY MEETING WHATEVER, FROM THIS HOUR FORTH, FOR LIFE.[53]

This curious resolution recalls the one that he made at the beginning of the Civil War,[54] but it is much more revealing and its tone much more urgent. It is not a matter of sobriety, but of continence. It shows to what degree his feelings were agitated by sexual desires. He felt disabled. He was no longer master of himself and felt ashamed. In his poems he had sung the joys of the flesh and celebrated the sexual act; now he blushed for his desires. The "child of Adam" had been driven from the earthly paradise and had discovered shame. To what should this change be attributed? Probably to the loss of vitality which we have already noted. His appetites were less ardent, his instincts less imperious, and he controlled them more easily. Formerly their violence had frightened him too,[55] but they were too powerful then and their force carried him away. Now he curbed them, or at least he tried to do so; for the struggle was long and difficult, and he was constantly tossed between his desires and the denials which he endeavored to impose on them. Apparently a sedentary bureaucrat, he was actually the young helmsman who prudently steered through dangerous reefs a ship that threatened at any moment to sink:

Aboard, at the ship's helm,
A young steersman, steering with care.
A bell through fog on a sea-coast dolefully ringing,
An ocean-bell — O a warning bell, rock'd by the waves.
O you give good notice indeed, you bell by the sea-
reefs ringing,
Ringing, ringing, to warn the ship from its wreck-place.
For, as on the alert, O steersman, you mind the bell's
admonition,
The bows turn, — the freighted ship, tacking, speeds
away under her gray sails,
The beautiful and noble ship, with all her precious
wealth, speeds away gaily and safe.
But O the ship, the immortal ship! O ship aboard the
ship!
O ship of the body — ship of the soul — voyaging,
voyaging, voyaging. [56]

But what was the danger that menaced him and that he
must at all costs escape? A close examination of the manuscript
of this resolution reveals it. The cause of these troubles was
not a woman, but a man. All the masculine pronouns of the
text have been erased and replaced by their feminine equiva-
lent, but under the superscription they can still be very clearly
seen.[57] There can be no doubt: Whitman deliberately camou-
flaged his private notes. Moreover, one of the pages is missing,
and it was probably Whitman himself who tore it out,[58] finding
his admission too compromising. If he feared the judgment of
posterity to this extent, how much more must he have feared
the scandal that would have broken out if anyone had known
the true nature of his passion. This would explain the panic
that seems to have seized him and his frantic efforts to smother
such dangerous tendencies.

Besides the shame which this inadmissible instinct [59] caused
him, there was the fear that he could not succeed in his amorous attempt; "useless, undignified pursuit . . . it cannot pos-

sibly be a success," he noted. Since the failure of his love affair in 1859–60, he feared rebuff. In short, he was afraid of life and very far now from the attitude of defiance he glorified in "One Hour to Madness and Joy": "To court destruction with taunts, with invitations." [60] The time of madness had apparently passed. His vitality had obviously decreased.

He had, of course, gone through similar crises in the past. In the edition of 1865–66 in particular there is a poem dealing with exactly the same struggles and the same agonies:

> Ah poverties, wincings, and sulky retreats!
> Ah you foes that in conflict have overcome me!
> (For what is my life, or any man's life, but a conflict
>   with foes — the old, the incessant war?)
> You degradations — you tussle with passions and
>   appetites;
> You smarts from dissatisfied friendships, (ah wounds,
>   the sharpest of all;)
> You toil of painful and choked articulations — you
>   meannesses;
> You shallow tongue-talks at tables, (my tongue the
>   shallowest of any;)
> You broken resolutions, you racking angers, you
>   smothered ennuis. . .[61]

We find the same disappointed love, the same efforts to control himself in the notebook of 1870 and in the poem. The same disgust with himself and the others is pushed to the point of a condemnation of the innocent pleasures of conversation.[62] There is the same revulsion from love. He had already depicted himself in a poem of the same period as "utterly abject, grovelling on the ground" before the one he loved.[63] Whether these poems were written during the war, or as is more likely, in 1860–61,[64] it is clear that whatever was tormenting him recurred at regular intervals and seized on him periodically. But each time, with a prodigious effort of will, he succeeded in freeing himself. His notebook of 1870 shows him appealing to the stoicism of Epictetus and the wisdom of Heine to help him through the crisis [65] and hoping eventually to live in full harmony with nature and to attain the age of Merlin "strong & wise & beautiful at 100 years old." [66]

Once again he succeeded effectively in controlling himself and regaining his equilibrium. Yet nothing in his behavior seems to have indicated that his serenity was menaced at this time. These struggles and this distress were all internal. Outwardly they did not appear. Peter Doyle, the young Irish streetcar conductor whose acquaintance Whitman had made in 1866 [67] and who may have been the cause of his despair, probably suspected nothing. We have the letter which Whitman wrote to him from Brooklyn on July 30, 1870, only two weeks after recording his resolutions in his notebook; its tone is calm, it gives the impression of an unclouded friendship.[68] Whitman had apparently succeeded in repressing and sublimating the passion that was torturing him.

The edition of *Leaves of Grass* which came out in 1871–72 confirms both his moral recovery and his physical fatigue. The new poems show him tired of life and of its perpetual struggles. He would have like to escape from his body and launch himself with his soul in search of God, a God almost transcendent to the creation, but in whom he could lose himself and find rest and peace. All this is symbolically suggested in "Passage to India":

> Passage — immediate passage! the blood burns in my
>   veins!
> Away, O soul! hoist instantly the anchor! . . .
> Have we not grovell'd here long enough, eating and
>   drinking like mere brutes? . . .
> Sail forth! steer for the deep waters only!
> Reckless, O soul, exploring, I with thee, and thou with
>   me. . .

> O my brave soul!
> O farther, farther sail!
> O daring joy, but safe! Are they not all the seas of God?
> O farther, farther, farther sail! [69]

The same joyful certainty of an immortal happiness after death is expressed in "On the Beach at Night," which, over the intervening years, answers the despair of "As I Ebb'd with the Ocean of Life" and renews with more human warmth the pantheistic affirmation of "On the Beach at Night Alone":

> Something there is more immortal than the stars, . .
> Something that shall endure longer even than lustrous
>   Jupiter,
> Longer than sun, or any revolving satellite,
> Or the radiant sisters, the Pleiades. [70]

When the lilacs bloomed in the spring, he no longer thought of Lincoln or his former sorrow; he wished to go away, to lose himself, to leave this world:

> Thou, Soul, unloosen'd — the restlessness after I know
>   not what;
> Come! let us lag here no longer — let us be up and
>   away!
> O for another world! O if one could but fly like a bird!
> O to escape — to sail forth, as in a ship!
> To glide with thee, O Soul, o'er all, in all, as a ship
>   o'er the waters! [71]

To the problems posed by his body he had thus finally found a spiritual solution. He wanted to separate himself from matter and to die. In this connection, the new passage which he inserted in the "Poem of Joys" (later entitled "Song of Joys") is quite revealing:

> Yet, O my soul supreme!
> Know'st thou the joys of pensive thought?
> Joys of the free and lonesome heart — the tender,
>   gloomy heart?

Joy of the solitary walk — the spirit bowed yet proud —
the suffering and the struggle?
The agonistic throes, the ecstasies — joys of solemn
musings, day or night?
Joys of the thought of Death — the great spheres Time
and Space?
Prophetic joys of better, loftier love's ideals — the
Divine Wife — the sweet, eternal, perfect Comrade?
Joys all thine own, undying one — joys worthy of thee,
O Soul.[72]

The poem is still quivering from the battles Whitman had
fought with his instincts during the preceding years. He had
had to wrestle like an athlete in the arena, but happiness had
finally escaped him. He was lonely and depressed, but his
spirit was indomitable ("the spirit bowed yet proud"). He had
no reason to despair after all. Later, after his death, he would
have the consolation of knowing, in a nobler form, the love
which had been refused him on earth, an ideal, imperishable
love. His poems henceforth would build a bridge between
life and death,[73] between the world of matter where he had
suffered and the infinite spaces where his soul would have the
revelation of the highest spiritual joys.

Whereas in 1860 he had stood on the beach and listened
with fear to the moaning of the sea, he now imagined himself
sailing far from shore in the supreme adventure of death. The
image of embarkation and departure on the high seas haunted
him. As early as 1867, in "Aboard at a Ship's Helm," [74] he had
braved the dangers of the ocean, but his ship had stayed close
to shore; now, on the contrary, he threw himself out to sea
toward India and farther than India. Joy accompanied him on
his quest ("Joy, Shipmate, Joy"),[75] and he said a last farewell
to the land: "Now Finale to the Shore." [76]

The untold want, by life and land ne'er granted,
Now, Voyager, sail thou forth, to seek and find.[77]

So he prepared to depart with his soul, ". . . accepting, exulting in Death, in its turn, the same as life." [78]

With exultation, he said; with resignation too. He realized himself that his powers had diminished. He no longer felt the same urge to write and to create as when his imperious vocation had made him renounce any temporal occupation. He probably also felt the approach of the death which in a few months was to strike its first blow and leave him half-paralyzed. He had even made his will.[79] It seemed to him that his life and work were ended. As in 1860 he said farewell to his reader:

One song, America, before I go.[80]

However, once again, he underestimated his energy and his will to live.

But, before proceeding, we must examine more closely the works produced during this period of trouble and crises. In 1867, less than two years after *Drum-Taps,* a new edition of *Leaves of Grass* came out, the fourth, very different in appearance from that of 1860.[81] Its binding was remarkably sober: the boards were without decoration, the corners and backstrip were of black leather, and only the title, *Leaves of Grass,* and "Ed'n 1867" appeared on the latter. No author's name. The title page was equally plain: "Leaves of Grass — New York, 1867." The author's name appeared only in the copyright notice and at the head of the poem later called "Song of Myself," but which in 1860 had already carried the title "Walt Whitman." There was thus a return to the relative anonymity of the first edition, but for the first time, the author's portrait was missing. The appearance of the book was on the whole rather poor; the paper was mediocre and the number of variants in details of binding seems to indicate that copies were bound as orders came in. It is probable that Whitman, who this time no longer had a publisher as in 1860, was having difficulty in financing the publication of a book of over 400 pages. This, in fact, represented a heavy investment. The work included not only *Leaves of Grass* proper, but *Drum-Taps* and *Sequel to Drum-Taps,* and, in some copies, "Songs before Parting," each with its own pagination and each printed separately on different kinds of paper.[82] These appendices were not yet assimilated into *Leaves of Grass.* They were only superimposed, but Whitman's intention was clearly to attach them to the main body. Besides, "Songs before Parting" were also called "Leaves of Grass"; in Whitman's mind they were therefore already part and parcel of *Leaves of Grass.* It is not clear why he had detached them, for they do not include a single poem which had not already appeared in the 1860 volume. Perhaps he had intended at some time to reject them. At any rate, there is no way of explaining the reasons for this wavering in Whitman's plan.

As for *Leaves of Grass* proper, the organization had changed, as the table of contents immediately shows. Moreover, all the poems now had titles, and not, as they often had in 1860, mere numbers. However, almost all of them had been published in the earlier edition. There were only seven new ones:[83] "Inscriptions,"[84] "The Runner,"[85] "Tears! Tears! Tears!"[86] "Aboard at a Ship's Helm,"[87] "When I Read the Book,"[88] "The City Dead-House,"[89] and "Leaflets."[90]

They are all very short and, with the exception of the third and fourth which we already have had occasion to examine, they are rather trivial. The originality of the 1867 edition does not reside in these almost negligible additions, but in the revisions undergone by the old poems, the meaning and character of which were often considerably altered. The war had not only inspired *Drum-Taps,* it had also had repercussions on *Leaves of Grass.* In the first lines of "Starting from Paumanok," which as in 1860 opened the book, Whitman now mentioned among his imaginary avatars "a soldier camp'd or carrying [his] knapsack and gun,"[91] and throughout the book he took the same meticulous care to bring his poems up to date by introducing allusions to the recent past and by suppressing all references to slavery.[92] But this was not all; the war, as we have seen, had fortified his faith in democracy and accordingly he celebrated it with renewed fervor. "As I Sat Alone by Blue Ontario's Shore," which in 1860 had exalted above all the role of the poet-prophet of democracy (that is, his own role),[93] now celebrated the Democracy of which the prophet was the poet. The emphasis this time is placed on democracy rather than on the poet.[94] He added whole paragraphs [95] in which he chanted the victory of the "great Idea," of democracy with its marvellous inventions and its armies on the march.[96] There could be no question now of its "defections"; [97] he was entirely reassured about its future. The inspiration of the poems is thus more frankly democratic and less exclusively personal, more plainly political and less preoccupied, at least in principle, with poetic expression. Whereas in 1856 he wanted only "to speak beautiful words," in 1867 he aspired, or so he claimed, "to sing the songs of the great Idea." [98]

However (this was an unexpected consequence of his exaltation), having become more modest about himself, he now showed an outrageous arrogance about everything concerning his country. His patriotism sometimes takes the form of a challenge to the rest of the world, as in these two lines:

> We stand self-pois'd in the middle, branching thence
>   over the world,
> From Missouri, Nebraska, or Kansas, laughing attacks
>   to scorn.[99]

And at other times it takes the form of a narrow and scornful nationalism, as in this tirade:

> America isolated I sing;
> I say that works made here in the spirit of other lands,
>   are so much poison to These States.

> How dare these insects assume to write poems for
> America?
> For our armies, and the offspring following the
> armies.[100]

Later, in 1881, realizing that such haughty isolationism was in contradiction with his aspirations to universality, he suppressed this awkward passage.

On the personal level, the 1867 edition also presented some new aspects, of a rather negative character to be sure. Several poems of "Calamus" which contained intimate and hardly disguised confessions were now excluded from the book. Among these were Number 8, in which he proclaimed his great love for a man ("Long I thought that knowledge alone would suffice"); Number 9 ("Hours continuing long sore and heavy-hearted"), in which he lamented his lover's desertion; and Number 16 ("Who is now reading this?") in which he deplored his abnormal instincts.[101] There were in these poems too many transparent allusions to the emotional crisis he had undergone just before the war. He probably suppressed them out of prudence, but perhaps also because his feelings had changed in the interval. These confessions corresponded to a stage which he may have thought he had passed, since he had to some extent succeeded in sublimating his homosexual instincts in the course of his visits to the hospitals. Besides, the suppressions are not limited to these three poems. Here and there, even outside of "Calamus" and "Children of Adam" [102] where the more sensual pieces were concentrated, he discreetly eliminated a certain number of inessential sexual allusions; in "Song of Myself," for instance, where he canceled such verses as:

> We hurt each other as the bridegroom and bride hurt
> each other.[103]

Or:

> The most they offer for mankind and eternity less than
> a spirit of my own seminal wet.[104]

He had already begun this work of expurgation in the edition of 1860,[105] but the changes were very few; in 1867 the tendency was confirmed and amplified. Was this a denial of one part of himself? It seems not, since "Calamus" and "Children of Adam" remained almost unchanged. Perhaps he sometimes regretted his former aggressive frankness, but he was much too stubborn to erase the past and disavow what he had been. In 1860 he had refused to give way to Emerson's exhortations and he was now bound by that refusal. It seems in any case that in 1867 he endeavored to suppress whatever might have been too morbid in his book and that he wanted once again, as in the first two editions, to place the accent on the poet-prophet rather than on the lover.[106]

This partial submission to the exigencies of conventional morality which the 1867 *Leaves of Grass* reveals explains how the English edition of the book came to be published. A volume entitled *Poems by Walt Whitman* appeared in 1868 in London, under the imprint of J. C. Hotten and selected and edited by W. M. Rossetti.[107] The book contained none of the poems which at the time of their publication had brought down on Whitman so many reproaches and insults. In the classification adopted by Rossetti, there were no groups entitled "Calamus" or "Children of Adam"; from these two sections he kept only four poems, the most innocent and least sensual of all.[108] The problem of an expurgated edition had been posed from the moment that the question of publishing *Leaves of Grass* in England came up. Moncure D. Conway, whom Whitman had asked to sound out the publishers,[109] wrote to O'Connor that Swinburne, W. M. Rossetti, and J. C. Hotten were agreed that publication of the complete text was impossible. The publisher would immediately be prosecuted. Whitman, who very much wanted to be published in Great Britain, was rather easily persuaded to make the necessary concessions. On November 1, 1867, he wrote to Conway:

My feeling and attitude about a volume of selections from my *Leaves* by Mr. Rossetti, for London publication, are simply passive ones, yet with decided satisfaction that if the job is to be done, it is to be by such hands. . . I have no objection to his substituting other words — leaving it all to his own tact — for "onanist", "father-stuff", &c. &c. Briefly, I hereby empower him (since that is the pivotal affair and since he has the kindness to shape his action so much by my wishes — and since, indeed, the sovereignty of the responsibility is not mine in the case) to make verbal changes of that sort wherever, for reasons sufficient for him, he decides that they are indispensible.[110]

Thus he fully accepted the principle of changes such as those which he himself in 1867 had made in the 1860 text. But two months later he became panicky and felt that he had gone too far. He wrote directly to W. M. Rossetti this time to try to withdraw the authorization which he had given:

I hasten to write you that the authorization in my letter of Nov. 1st to Mr. Conway, for you, to make verbal alterations, substitute words, &c. was meant to be construed as an answer to the case presented in Mr. Conway's letter of Oct. 12. Mr. Conway stated the case of a volume of selections, in which it had been decided that the poems reprinted in London should appear verbatim, and asking my authority to change certain words in the preface to first edition of poems, &c. . . . I penned that authorization, and did not feel to set limits to it. But abstractly, and standing alone, and not read in connection with Mr. C.'s letter of Oct. 12, I see now it is far too loose, and needs distinct guarding. I cannot and will not consent, of my own volition, to countenance an expurgated edition of my pieces. I have steadily refused to do so here in my own country, even under seductive offers, and must not do so in another country. . . And now, my friend, having set myself right, in that matter, I proceed to say, on the other hand, for you and for Mr. Hotten, that if, before the arrival of this letter, you have practically invested in and accomplished, or partially accomplished, any plan, even contrary to this letter, I do not expect you to abandon it, at loss of outlay, but shall *bona fide* consider you blameless if you let go on and be carried out as you may have arranged. It is the question of the authorization of an expurgated edition proceeding from me that deepest engages me.[111]

It is clear that the outcome of this intervention mattered little to him and that he was ready to accept any conditions in order that the book might appear. He was really concerned only with the question of principle and wanted at all cost to avoid seeming to authorize the publication of an expurgated edition. He went so far as to add: "It would be better, in any introduction, to make no allusion to me as authorizing, or not prohibiting; &c." [112]

Finally, it *was* an expurgated edition that appeared, but Rossetti alone was responsible for it; Whitman had saved face. He would certainly have preferred that the complete 1867 text be published, but he had every reason to be satisfied with this partial victory, since without any cost to his self-esteem or any concession on his part, his collection had been relieved of the more compromising poems which would have limited its distribution in England as they had done in the United States. What is more, in his preface, Rossetti openly sided with Whitman against the absurd prudery of the public — though at the same time, to be sure, he condemned the sexual poems for aesthetic reasons. Not eager to acquire the reputation of a new Bowdler he had at any rate refused to mutilate a single poem. He had preferred to omit completely all those at which a delicate reader might have had to blush, and he was thus able to claim with some appearance of justice that his edition was not strictly speaking expurgated, but rather abridged.[113] However, this subtle distinction did not satisfy Whitman for long. In 1871 he attacked the problem again and tried to find another publisher who would agree to print the complete version, but F. S. Ellis, whom he had approached, shied off invoking exactly the same reasons as Conway.[114] The only edition of his poems to appear in England during his lifetime was therefore that of Rossetti, which in his old age he could not help referring to with bitterness and regret, forgetting the success it had achieved and the friendships it had brought him.[115]

But Whitman had other things on his mind besides these literary preoccupations. Political questions continued to interest and even to torment him. In 1867 he published in *Galaxy* an essay entitled "Democracy," in which he tried to refute the objections that Carlyle had raised against democratic principles in *Shooting Niagara.*[116] The following year he published in the same review an essay on what he called "Personalism," that is, on his conception of the relations between the individual and society in a democracy.[117] Finally, in 1871, he returned to the same problems in a small pamphlet of some eighty pages entitled *Democratic Vistas.*[118] This title was particularly well chosen; his gaze was turned away from the present and lost itself in the infinite perspectives of the future:

> The boundless vista and the horizon far and dim are
> all here. . .[119]

He was once more disappointed by reality, and this was precisely the reason why he felt the need of solemnly reaffirming his faith in democracy. Before the war, he had already had some doubts, but the heroism of the soldiers had dissipated them. Unfortunately, once the war was over, during the period of Reconstruction, corruption was more manifest than ever and politicians happily gave themselves up to it. Whitman had no illusions on this point. In *Democratic Vistas,* with ruthless lucidity, he unveiled all the hidden vices of American society and left out none of its turpitudes.[120] Carlyle himself had not been more pitiless. But, whereas Carlyle concluded that democracy was impossible, Whitman proclaimed that these flaws were accidental and that some day all would be well. He did not give up his dream; he only postponed its realization to a later time, and by that means, avoided pessimism and despair. This bold extrapolation enabled him to calm his fears and gracefully resolve the political problem which had again begun to trouble him. *Democratic Vistas* thus replied to certain cries of pain which had escaped him in the 1871 edition of *Leaves of Grass*. For instance:

> (Stifled, O days! O lands! in every public and private
> corruption!
> Smother'd in thievery, impotence, shamelessness, moun-
> tain-high;
> Brazen effrontery, scheming, rolling like ocean's waves
> around and upon you, O my days! my lands!
> For not even those thunderstorms, nor fiercest lightnings
> of the war, have purified the atmosphere;) [121]

Logic as well as chronology leads us now to a discussion of the fifth edition of *Leaves of Grass*,[122] which appeared the same year as *Democratic Vistas,* in 1871.[123] Like the 1867 edition, it lacked cohesion and consistency. Some copies consisted only of *Leaves of Grass* proper; others contained, besides *Leaves of Grass*, an annex called "Passage to India," with independent pagination, which however was also entitled "Leaves of Grass." [124] In some copies, there was also a second annex, "After All Not to Create Only," [125] which had already been published separately as a small pamphlet of twenty-four pages. The physical appearance of the book was again mediocre; it had a green cloth binding on the spine of which was stamped *Leaves of Grass — Complete —* and nothing else. The place and date were given on the title page: Washington, D.C., 1871, or 1872,[126] for there were two printings of this edition a year apart; but since they are identical, we will not distinguish them. As in some of the previous editions, the name of the author appeared only in the copyright notice. And, as in 1867, there was no portrait, perhaps again for reasons of economy, but the paper was of better quality.

Although the external appearance of the book was not much changed, the contents had undergone certain modifications. In the first place, the work of expurgation had quietly continued. For instance, this particularly disturbing verse of a "Song of Joys" disappeared from a passage which was to be completely suppressed in 1881: "O of men — of women toward me as I pass — The memory of only one look — the boy lingering and waiting." [127] The short poem entitled "To You" was also removed. [128]

But there were more important changes. This edition shows that the memory of the war was still haunting Whitman. He kept thinking about it. *Drum-Taps*, which in 1867 still remained outside the main body of the work, were now definitively incorporated and mingled in *Leaves of Grass*. [129] Not only that, but he had written new poems on the subject of the war. He had not forgotten those who had taken part in it, as is shown by "Adieu to a Soldier." [130] He still heard the "echoes of camps with all the different bugle-calls," the "sounds from distant guns with galloping cavalry." [131] He evoked again

> the sobs of women, the wounded groaning in agony,
> The hiss and crackle of flame, the blacken'd ruins, the
>   embers of cities,
> The dirge and desolation of mankind. [132]

And he anathematized war and its devastations:

> Away with themes of war! away with war itself!
> Hence from my shuddering sight to never more return
>   that show of blacken'd, mutilated corpses!
> The hell unpent and raid of blood, fit for wild tigers or
>   for lop-tongued wolves, not reasoning men. . . [133]

But he did not consistently maintain this purely negative attitude, which was merely a return to the pessimism of the darkest hours of 1863. He also celebrated the greatness of the Union which the war had saved, and he preached the reconciliation of the North and South. [134] This was nothing new, but this time, he went much further. He no longer treated the war from a local or national point of view; he gave it a universal value. Instead of being a mere accident, it became an eternal symbol; for he considered it now as an episode in the perpetual struggle that humanity must carry on for liberty and the triumph of democracy, for the "good old cause":

> To thee, old Cause!
> Thou peerless, passionate, good cause!
> Thou stern, remorseless, sweet Idea!
> Deathless throughout the ages, races, lands!
> After a strange, sad war — great war for thee,
> (I think all war through time was really fought, and
>   ever will be really fought, for thee;)
> These chants for thee — the eternal march of thee.[135]

He now saw life itself as a struggle and a continual war:

> I . . . sing war — and a longer and greater one than
>   any,
> . . . The field the world;
> For life and death, for the Body, and for the eternal
>   Soul. . .[136]

This is the underlying reason for the integration of *Drum-Taps* into *Leaves of Grass*. Whitman now considered war — war in general and not only the Civil War, war no longer in its military form, but as an act of violent revolt — as a form of human progress, as an aspect of life; and as such it became one of the essential themes of his book. Accordingly he entitled one of the new sections, "Marches Now the War is Over" [137] and included in it some of the poems formerly in *Drum-Taps*. After the war, the forward march was resumed, or rather continued.

While this important transmutation was going on, the democratic character of *Leaves of Grass*, already strongly marked in 1867,[138] was further accentuated, as is seen at the beginning of the book if one compares the introductory poem, "One's

Self I Sing," with its original version, entitled "Inscription" in 1867. He considerably attenuated its individualism:

> Small is the theme of the following Chant, yet the greatest — namely ONE'S SELF — that wondrous thing, a simple, separate person. That, for the use of the New World, I sing.

became in 1871:

> One's self I sing, a simple separate person. . .[139]

And the last line in which he had tried to establish a personal and almost physical contact, man to man, with the reader was dropped.[140] The essential ideas are the same in the two versions, but in 1871 the accent was clearly on man "en-masse"; the separate man, the individual, had, by comparison, almost disappeared. This was no accident. Whitman was fully aware of the new orientation of his work as is shown by this passage from the 1872 Preface:

> *Leaves of Grass* already published, is, in its intentions, the song of a great composite *Democratic Individual*, male or female. And following on and amplifying the same purpose, I suppose I have in my mind to run through the chants of this Volume, (if ever completed,) the thread-voice, more or less audible, of an aggregated, inseparable, unprecedented, vast, composite, electric *Democratic Nationality*.[141]

It was probably to strengthen this voice that he regrouped a certain number of poems under the title of "Songs of Insurrection" [142] and wrote by way of introduction some unusually violent lines:

> Still though the one I sing,
> (One, yet of contradictions made,) I dedicate to Nationality,
> I leave in him revolt, (O latent right of insurrection! O quenchless, indispensable fire!) [143]

This glorification of revolt can be explained by reference to the historical context. The edition of 1871–72 appeared in the midst of the "Gilded Age." [144] Taking advantage of the unprecedented prosperity of the United States after the Civil War, employers engaged in a shameless exploitation of their workers, who had no legal protection whatever. Whitman was aware of it, and it disturbed him, as is shown by this note which he seems at one time to have considered publishing as an introduction to his "Songs of Insurrection":

Not only are These States the born offspring of Revolt against mere overweening authority — but seeing ahead for Them in the future, a long, long reign of Peace with all the growths, corruptions and tyrannies & formalisms of Obedience, (accumulating, vast folds, strata, from the rankness of continued prosperity and the more and more insidious grip of capital) I feel to raise a note of caution (perhaps unneeded alarm) that the ideas of the following cluster will always be needed, that it may be worth while to keep well up, & vital, such ideas and verses as the following.[145]

Thus the nascent social problem was already beginning to trouble him. He was apparently thinking less and less of himself and more and more of the human society of which he was a member. This is far from the subjectivism of *Leaves of Grass* in 1855 — or even in 1860. The starting-point is no longer himself, but frequently an event outside himself. Several of the new poems are occasional. This is a new aspect in the development of *Leaves of Grass*, but one which was to grow in importance in the years to come. For example the long poem entitled "After All Not to Create Only" was composed expressly to be read during the inaugural ceremony of the 40th Annual Exhibition in New York at the invitation of the sponsors.[146] "Passage to India," though its inspiration was personal, was written on the occasion of the opening of the Suez Canal, the completion of the North American railroad, and the laying of the Atlantic marine cable.[147] "Brother of All, with Generous Hand" was a tribute to the memory of a philan-

thropist, George Peabody,[148] and "The Singer in Prison" com-
memorated a concert given by the soprano, Parepa Rosa, at
Sing-Sing.[149] "A Carol of Harvest for 1867" [150] was also an
occasional poem, as the title indicates.[151]

"As a Strong Bird on Pinions Free." [152] must also be added
to this list, since Whitman, on the invitation of a group of
students, was to read it at the Dartmouth College Commencement on June 26, 1872. He had written the poem especially
for the occasion, and he published it separately in 1872 [153]
with several others composed since the publication of the
1871 edition.[154] Among these was another occasional piece,
"O Star of France," particularly moving to the French since
it expressed his pity and admiration for France at the time of
her defeat by Prussia.[155]

From the frequency of such poems one might ask oneself
whether it was a question of a voluntarily more democratic
poetry or whether the inspiration of the poet was declining.
Apparently Whitman himself was aware of a certain loss of
power, for he wrote in the preface to "As a Strong Bird on
Pinions Free": ". . . the present and any future pieces from
me are really but the surplusage forming after that Volume
[*Leaves of Grass*] or the wake eddying behind it. . . it may
be that mere habit has got dominion of me, when there is no
real need of saying anything further. . ." [156]

He no longer had the health or the vigor of old; he was
tired. Sometimes, as we have seen, he even felt death approaching.[157] But, in general, he did not let himself be discouraged,[158]
and in his preface, after having expressed his fears concerning
the value of his present inspiration, he announced his decision
to continue writing on new themes and particularly on the
prodigious development of contemporary America: "I have
the ambition of devoting yet a few years to poetic composition. . . . The mighty present age! To absorb, and express
in poetry any thing of it. . ." [159]

Thus, in spite of his fatigue and of the decline of his inspiration, he did not lose heart. The old fighter was not yet vanquished. To the personal crisis which he went through in the course of these postwar years and to the political crisis which the country was undergoing, he opposed the same tenacious will to live, the same steadfast faith in the future. The personal optimism of "In Cabin'd Ships at Sea" is matched by the political optimism of "One Song, America, before I Go."

> One song, America, before I go. . .
> For thee — the Future.
> Belief I sing — and Preparation;
> As Life and Nature are not great with reference to the
>   Present only,
> But greater still from what is to come. . .[160]

echoes:

> In cabin'd ships at sea,
> The boundless blue on every side expanding. . .
> Or some lone bark buoy'd on the dense marine,
> Where joyous full of faith, spreading white sails,
> She cleaves the ether mid the sparkle and the foam of
>   day. . .
> Here not the land, firm land, alone appears. . .
> We feel the long pulsation, ebb and flow of endless
>   motion. . .
> The boundless vista and the horizon far and dim are
>   all here. . .
> Then falter not O book, fulfil your destiny. . .
> You too as a lone bark cleaving the ether, purpos'd I
>   know not whither, yet ever full of faith. . .[161]

In both cases the solution of the crisis is the same: Whitman took refuge in the future, or more precisely — for it was not a question of cowardly flight, but of a journey toward something — he threw himself with impatient fervor forward in the direction of his destiny and that of his country.

This was the nature of his work during the period of Reconstruction, but how was it received? Immediately after the war, his good works in the hospitals had earned him the respect of everyone, while the scandal of his dismissal by Harlan and the violent campaign conducted in his favor by O'Connor had given him a certain notoriety. *Drum-Taps* had been praised by the critics. He thought for a time that he was about to receive the recognition he felt he deserved. During a visit in 1867 to F. P. Church, the editor of *Galaxy*, he had the impression that he was being given special consideration, as if he were regarded as one of the great forces in American literature:

. . . the Galaxy folks have received and treated me with welcome warmth and respect. . . The indirect and inferential of his tone and words in speaking to me would have satisfied your highest requirements — they evidently meant that in his opinion I was, or was soon to be, "one of the great powers." [162]

Following this interview he was able to publish his two articles on democracy [163] in *Galaxy*; and Church had earlier published "A Carol of Harvest for 1867." [164] It was the first time since his contributions to the *Democratic Review* that he had succeeded in publishing anything in a magazine. His joy was understandable. He must have thought that the quarantine in which he had been placed by the *literati* was at an end.[165]

When the 1867 edition appeared, the reviews were again favorable. There were still a few sullen critics to renew the habitual reproach of obscenity — such as the reviewer of the *Round Table* who compared "To a Common Prostitute" with a licentious poem by Catullus — [166] but in general they preferred not to dwell on that aspect of his inspiration or on his lack of art; but tried rather, like the reviewer in *The Nation*, to emphasize his democratic message, which indicates that they were aware of the change of direction in his work and that they appreciated it.[167] This approval can easily be explained. The Civil War had brought the victory of the democratic North over the aristocratic South, and the North, as a result of the conflict, had become more clearly aware of the meaning and value of its civilization. In short, Whitman had in this respect merely followed the general development of his country — or more precisely, since in spite of his pessimism in 1859–60 his faith in democracy had always been strong — the war had prepared his country for a better understanding of his political doctrine.

However, in spite of the increased understanding of the critics and the larger public thus drawn to his work, he still did not obtain the triumphant success of which he had dreamed. And, paradoxically, it was not in the United States, the chosen land of democracy, but in England, a country which he had hitherto regarded as feudal, that he found at this time his most fervent admirers.[168] On July 6, 1867, W. M. Rossetti published in the London *Chronicle* an enthusiastic article in which he described *Leaves of Grass* as the poetical masterpiece of the century.[169] This compliment must have been particularly pleasing to Whitman, for Rossetti attributed to his poetry all the artistic qualities that most of the American critics had denied him. When the English edition of *Leaves of Grass* appeared a few months later, it was enthusiastically welcomed by the press, and Whitman was profoundly moved: ". . . it flushed my friends and myself too, like a sun dash, brief, hot, and dazzling," [170] he wrote to Hotten, his publisher, with reference to a review in the London *Morning Star*. He had already expressed his gratitude to Conway:

Indeed, my dear friend, I may here confess to you that to be accepted by these young men of England, and treated with highest courtesy and even honor, touches me deeply. In my own country, so far, — from the press, and from authoritative quarters, I have received but one long tirade of impudence, mockery, and scurrilous jeers. Only since the English recognition have the skies here lighted up a little.[171]

Here he darkened the picture somewhat, for "the press . . .

and authoritative quarters," had never, as we have again and again noticed, been unanimous in condemning his poetic experiments. It is true that his public had never been large, and that he had sometimes been violently attacked, but the connoisseurs from 1855 on had supported and encouraged him. His complaints were therefore exaggerated, but during his remaining years we will encounter other manifestations of this strange self-pity, an after-effect of his wounded pride.

Whitman had some reason to be proud of the success he had achieved in England, for as soon as Rossetti's selected *Poems* appeared, a strong movement in his favor sprang up in English literary circles. Writers as different as Robert Buchanan [172] and Swinburne [173] took up his cause. Soon afterwards, Alfred Austin, in his book on contemporary poetry, devoted a whole chapter to him under the title of "The Poetry of the Future." [174] Mrs. Herbert Gilchrist, seeing in *Leaves of Grass* a declaration of love to the world in general and to herself in particular, published in May 1870 in the *Boston Radical* "A Woman's Estimate of Walt Whitman," a passionate and unreserved tribute. Its principal merit in Whitman's eyes was probably that it absolved him of the charge of obscenity. She had written:

> Nor do I sympathize with those who grumble at the unexpected words that turn up now and then. . . If the thing a word stands for exists by divine appointment (and what does not so exist?), the word need never be ashamed of itself.[175]

Most of the American critics had condemned him either for his lack of art or for his grossness, and now Rossetti and Mrs. Gilchrist in turn justified him on both counts. It must have been a pleasant balm for his wounded self-esteem. He was so delighted with this unexpected succour that he immediately arranged to have these articles distributed to the American newspapers and magazines.[176]

Also his fame began to extend beyond the frontiers of the

English-speaking world. In 1868, Ferdinand Freiligrath published three articles accompanied by translations in the *Augsburger Allgemeine Zeitung*.[177] In France, as early as 1868, Amédée Pichot spoke of him in the *Revue Britannique* [178] and a few years later Mme Bentzon presented him to the general public in the *Revue des Deux Mondes* under the somewhat ironic title, "Un Poète Américain, Walt Whitman: Muscle and Pluck Forever." [179] Emile Blémont devoted several pages to him in his *Renaissance Littéraire et Artistique*.[180] He was even discussed in Denmark, where Rudolf Schmidt saw him as the bard of American democracy.[181]

All these articles were very encouraging to Whitman; he had them translated and he circulated them as widely as he could.[182] He probably regarded them as a means of persuading the American public that outside the United States he was considered as the spokesman and representative of America.[183] And, in many ways, the victories which he had enjoyed in Europe consoled him for the relative indifference of his fellow-countrymen. He needed this comfort. It was at this time that he wrote "My Legacy," in which, comparing his own life to that of a rich businessman, he concluded with a rather bitter resignation under the apparent idealism:

> But I my life surveying,
> With nothing to show, to devise, from its idle years,
> Nor houses nor land — nor tokens of gems or gold for
>   my friends,
> Only these Souvenirs of Democracy.[184]

Still, even in America, he also had warm admirers, particularly his friend John Burroughs who, in 1867, published his *Notes on Walt Whitman as Poet and Person*, [185] an apologetic work in which Whitman collaborated shamelessly, for it has been demonstrated that he wrote the first few chapters himself.[186] William O'Connor, who had already shown his mettle in *The Good Gray Poet*, went even further. In 1868, in a story entitled *The Carpenter*, he presented Christ as having the physical and moral traits of Whitman.[187] In this instance apologetics had turned to hagiography.

Thus, in spite of the temporal failure which he lamented in "My Legacy," Whitman had no reason for despair. Since the war his position had greatly improved. The "good gray poet" had acquired a universal esteem, and from this time on it was impossible to treat him with contempt. Some critics regarded him as the greatest poet or one of the greatest poets of the century. To some fanatics he appeared as a saint or a prophet, as the equal of Christ or Buddha. In the space of a few years his renown had become international.

Moreover, the 1871 edition of *Leaves of Grass* sold well, and Whitman congratulated himself on this fact in a letter to Peter Doyle in July of the same year: "I am doing well, both in health and *business prospects* here — my book is doing first rate — so everything is lovely." [188]

The book succeeded so well that he issued a second printing the following year. In Great Britain this new edition attracted the attention of an academic critic, Edward Dowden, who devoted an entire essay to it.[189] Whitman was very pleased with this tribute. He appreciated its measured but in general very flattering tone.[190]

This notoriety however still fell short of true fame. As John C. Dent noted in an essay on "America and Her Literature":

It is within the bounds of probability that Walt Whitman will be compelled to pass through quite as fiery an ordeal in America as erewhile fell to the lot of Wordsworth in England; but, if so, we here beg to record our sincere conviction that the ultimate result in his case will be the same as was that in the case of Wordsworth.[191]

But, before undergoing this trial, Whitman was to experience another, a more cruel one, that of illness and suffering.

CHAPTER VIII

THE HEROIC INVALID (1873–1876)

ON January 23, 1873, Whitman woke up paralyzed on the left side and threatened with death if another attack should occur. But instead of sinking into despair, he accepted the tragic situation,[1] and without complaining or lamenting, clung with all his strength to what life remained in him. Slowly, very slowly, he recovered. He was attended by one of the best physicians in Washington, Dr. W. B. Drinkard, who treated him according to the newest methods with electricity.[2] In a few weeks, his improvement was evident; and at the end of March he went back to his office, but he was still unable to work regularly. Then bad news came from Camden. His mother, who was now living with George, was very ill. Although he was hardly in a condition to travel, Whitman went to her bedside at once on May 20. Three days later his mother was dead, and he was plunged into intense grief. In August he wrote to Peter Doyle: ". . . it is the great cloud of my life — nothing that ever happened before has had such an effect on me. . ."[3]

And, in 1875, when he published the sixth edition of *Leaves of Grass*, he was still thinking of her:

I occupy myself arranging these pages for publication, still envelopt in thoughts of the death two years since of my dear Mother, the most perfect and magnetic character, the rarest combination of practical, moral and spiritual, and the least selfish, of all and any I have ever known — and by me O so much the most deeply loved. . .[4]

This loss was all the more cruel as it came only a few weeks after the death of his sister-in-law, Martha, for whom he always had a great deal of affection.[5]

Destiny seemed set against him: 1873 was for him a terrible year. Still he kept up his courage. Ten days after his mother's death, he returned to Washington [6] and discharged his duties as well as he could, though he was still under medical care. But, in June, when hot weather came, he was obliged to ask for two months' leave. He hoped to find rest and fresh air on the New Jersey coast, but he fell ill on the way, at Philadelphia, and had to take refuge with George at Camden.[7] Thus he was led by chance to the city where he was to reside until his death.

In spite of this relapse, probably caused by his family losses, he again recovered little by little. His slow progress can be followed in the letters that he regularly sent to Peter Doyle. In July, the headaches from which he had been suffering abated and became less frequent.[8] He had good hope of regaining his health, but he sometimes thought of death with great courage and complete resignation.[9] In September, he began to feel much better. His strength was returning. He was thought to be suffering from cerebral anaemia, and this diagnosis reassured him: his life was not in danger, all that he needed was patience. He took no medicine, but he was careful to guard against any excess.[10] Although he moved only with difficulty, he refused to let himself go and went out as often as he could, even as far as Philadelphia.[11] But sometimes the slow pace of his progress discouraged him, and the frequency with which he noticed announcements of deaths due to paralytic attacks in the newspapers troubled him.[12] He went so far as to make a new will.[13] Still he never lost hope.[14] His courage was steadfast and his morale high. He suffered most from loneliness, although he lived with his brother, and his sister-in-law took very good care of him. He missed his Washington friends. He knew no one at Camden as yet and was so lonesome at times that he felt the need of a dog to keep him company.[15]

The setting must also have been depressing. Camden was, and still is, to a large extent a gray, dirty, industrial suburb. He could not but feel severely deprived after having known the nobly designed avenues of Washington, the vibrant life of New York, and the open spaces of Long Island. Yet he did not complain and seems to have accepted the situation calmly. In this, his natural passivity was a great help. Instead of worrying and chafing, he bore the trial calmly. When his brother moved to Stevens Street, not far from the railroad track, Whitman, as usual, took possession of the attic in the new house [16] and spent his time watching the trains go by.[17] Perhaps it was at this time that he wrote "To a Locomotive in Winter," [18] which shows that he quickly became aware of the powerful beauty of steam-engines, which none of the poets of his time had as yet been able to see. Thus he succeeded in escaping the apparent ugliness of his surroundings.

But he soon had other reasons for uneasiness. When he found himself unable to resume his duties in Washington, he obtained permission to hire a substitute, one Walter Godey. After paying Godey's salary, he still had enough money to live on. But this arrangement could not last for ever. At the end of a year, in July 1874, though Whitman had tried an appeal to the President, the post which he occupied was abolished,[19] and he suddenly found himself without resources.

True, he was not condemned to absolute poverty, for he had some savings; but deprived from then on of any steady income, he could not help being worried about the future, even though, in the letter announcing this bad news to Peter Doyle, he pretended to be indifferent.[20]

Interminable illness, spiritual isolation and lack of sympathy, ugliness of the surroundings in which he was obliged to live, financial insecurity — the picture was gloomy. "Ah, the physical shatter and troubled spirit of me the last three years!" he exclaimed in *Specimen Days*.[21] And it was at that time that he wrote "Prayer of Columbus," [22] in which he identified himself with the "Great Admiral" "near the close of his indomitable and pious life," when in Jamaica in 1503 "death seem'd daily imminent." [23]

Like Christopher Columbus, he was "a batter'd, wreck'd old man," "sicken'd and nigh to death," "sore" and with a "heavy heart"; [24] and the prayer that Columbus offered up to God was undoubtedly his own:

> Thou knowest the prayers and vigils of my youth,
> Thou knowest my mandhood's solemn and visionary
> meditations,
> Thou knowest how before I commenced I devoted all to
> come to Thee,
> Thou knowest I have in age ratified all those vows and
> strictly kept them,
> Thou knowest I have not once lost nor faith nor ecstasy
> in Thee. . .[24]

Whitman was forgetting his moments of doubt and his crises of despair, as he had the right to do since he had always surmounted them. And, once more, his faith sustained him; he reaffirmed it emphatically:

> The urge, the ardor, the unconquerable will,
> The potent, felt, interior command, stronger than
> words,
> A message from the Heavens whispering to me in sleep,
> These sped me on.[25]

He too, though his body betrayed him, though his hands and limbs were powerless and his brain was tortured, clung to God as his supreme and only certainty.[26] It was not only Whitman who was identified with Columbus, but Columbus who was confused with Whitman, since he is decribed as "old, poor and paralyzed," [27] which in reality he was not.

At the same time, Whitman identified himself with a great sequoia being cut down by lumberjacks, and he said farewell to the world:

> Farewell my brethren,
> Farewell O earth and sky, farewell ye neighboring
>   waters,
> My time has ended, my term has come.[28]

He felt death coming, but it did not matter, he was ready to disappear since he would survive in the "race" he would leave behind and whose triumph was assured:

> . . . a superber race. . .
> For them we abdicate, in them ourselves. . .[29]

This certainty of animistic survival reassured him. The errors that had formerly tormented him were only "passing errors, perturbations of the surface." [30]

Thus, in 1874, one year only after his paralytic attack, he had regained his equilibrium and his serenity. He had emerged victorious from the terrible trial imposed on him by his illness. Though he wrote in 1875, "O how different the moral atmosphere amid which I now revise this Volume [*Two Rivulets*], from the jocund influences surrounding the growth and advent of *Leaves of Grass*," [31] the danger had been left behind and the crisis ended several months earlier. Suffering, in any case, is soon forgotten, and in writing these lines he greatly exaggerated the joy out of which his work had grown; for, as we have seen, each single edition of *Leaves of Grass* had been born of pain rather than of happiness.

His renewed optimism was not for himself alone; it extended equally to politics, in which nevertheless occasions for worry and despair were not lacking. It was the period of the Crédit Mobilier frauds, the Salary Grab, the Sanborn contracts, and

the Whisky Ring. Political circles seemed hopelessly corrupt.[32]
But Whitman preferred to ignore these turpitudes:

> Nay, tell me not to-day the publish'd shame,
> Read not to-day the journal's crowded page,
> The merciless reports still branding forehead after fore-
> head,
> The guilty column following guilty column.[33]

The poem in which he thus expressed his discouragement
was not incorporated into *Leaves of Grass* during his lifetime;
he published it in *Lippincott's Magazine* for March 5, 1873,
and then put it out of his mind and his work. It is now found
only in the posthumous section entitled "Old Age Echoes."
All these scandals were to him merely temporary accidents,
ripples on the surface; the deeper water was pure and tranquil; these blemishes did not affect the truth or the essential
validity of democracy:

> Your million untold manly healthy lives, or East or
> West, city or country,
> Your noiseless mothers, sisters, wives, unconscious of
> their good. . .
> (Plunging to these as a determin'd diver down the deep
> hidden waters,)
> These, these to-day I brood upon — all else refusing,
> these will I con. . .[34]

In March 1874 he wrote in the same vein to Mrs. O'Connor:

Nelly, your last letter is very blue, mainly about political and
public degradation. Sumner's death and inferior men etc. being
rampant etc. I look on all such states of things exactly as I look on
a cloudy and evil state of weather, or a fog, or a long sulk meteoro-
logical — it is a natural result of things, a growth of something
deeper, has its uses and will hasten to exhaust itself and yield to
something better.[35]

And, during the same period, in an article for the New
York *Graphic*, he could claim, this time without restriction:

The present! Our great Centennial of 1876 nigher and nigher at hand — the abandonment, by tacit consent, of dead issues — the general readjustment and rehabilitation, at least by intention and beginning, South and North, to the exigencies of the Present and Future — the momentous nebulae left by the convulsions of the previous thirty years definitely considered and settled by the re-election of General Grant — the Twenty-second Presidentiad well-sped on its course — the inevitable unfolding and developments of the tremendous complexity we call the United States. . .[36]

In this context the optimistic conclusion of the "Song of the Reedwood Tree" is not surprising:

> Fresh come, to a new world indeed, yet long prepared,
> I see the genius of the modern, child of the real and
>   ideal,
> Clearing the ground for broad humanity, the true
>   America, heir of the past so grand,
> To build a grander future.[37]

What gave him confidence above all was that it seemed to him on reflection that the worst was over:

> Within my time the United States have emerged from nebulous vagueness and suspense, to full orbic, (though varied,) decision. . . and are henceforth to enter upon their real history — the way being now (i.e. since the result of the Secession War,) clear'd of death-threatening impedimenta.[38]

Reasoning by analogy in one of his poems,[39] he compared his country to a thrush which transformed the loathsome worms that nourished it into songs of ecstatic joy. For him comparison was synonymous with reason: the United States would also some day transform the meannesses and the scandals which for the moment its citizens fed on into harmony and beauty. Then their "joyous trills" would "fill the world."

This grandiose future which awaited America reassured him concerning his own destiny and that of his work:

Shadowy vast shapes smile through the air and sky,
And on the distant waves sail countless ships,
And anthems in new tongues I hear saluting me.[40]

Thus, oppressed by illness, confined to Camden and to the present by his paralysis, he consoled himself by imagining his coming apotheosis in a radiant future. It was an effective consolation, since it freed him from the worry which his health and the political situation might otherwise have caused.

At the end of 1875, in spite of his occasional uneasiness,[41] he was feeling distinctly better. He was able to undertake, in the company of John Burroughs, a three-week trip to Washington and to Baltimore, where he attended the reburial of Poe's remains.[42] In the spring, he felt restless and planned other trips; he even declared himself ready to go to England.[43]

As usual, however, the clearest sign of his recovery was the publication of a new edition of *Leaves of Grass*, the sixth, which he called the "Centennial Edition," in honor of the centennial of the United States for which he was waiting with so much impatience in 1874. The new edition was ready by the end of 1875 [44] and appeared in 1876; of course, at the author's expense. It consisted of two volumes priced at ten dollars. The first volume was merely a reprint of the fifth edition. Only the second volume included new pieces, and curiously, it was not entitled *Leaves of Grass*, but *Two Rivulets*. It was made up of several pamphlets with separate pagination: first, "Two Rivulets" proper, which consisted of a preface and a collection of new poems accompanied by prose passages printed as notes to the poems; then "Democratic Vistas," a reprint of the 1871 text; four poems under the title "Centennial Songs," three of which were new; "As a Strong Bird on Pinions Free," a mere reprint; "Memoranda during the War," previously printed in the New York *Graphic*; and finally "Passage to India," which had appeared in 1871-72 as an appendix to *Leaves of Grass*.[45]

This volume was therefore truly a "melange," as Whitman said.[46] But what did the title mean? *Two Rivulets,* as he explained in various places,[47] referred first to the duality of form, since he sometimes used prose and sometimes poetry; and also, more important, to the duality of the subject, since the prose notes were devoted to politics, that is, to the actual, and the poems to immortality or the ideal. In short, the prose was objective and the poetry subjective.

The most striking aspect of the new poems was the importance attributed to death. It dominated the volume, and Whitman knew it. He recognized the fact in the Preface.[48] Whereas in *Leaves of Grass* the accent was placed on life and the body,[49] here he was obsessed by the thought of death and immortality. In this connection, the placing of "Passage to India" is symptomatic. In 1872 he had added it almost fortuitously as an appendix to the rest of *Leaves of Grass;* this time, he deliberately made it his farewell song to the reader and the conclusion of his two volumes. Certainly, as we have often noticed, death had always been an important theme in his work — he was perfectly aware of it himself — [50] but it is nonetheless true that this was the first time he had purposely given it so much emphasis.

This preoccupation is also related to a more general tendency. He was detaching himself more and more from the actual, from the material, in order to devote himself exclusively to the spiritual. This tendency to spiritualization is particularly marked in the poem with the curious title "Eidólons" where objects are replaced by their eternal archetypes. Evanescent material appearances give way to the true reality which is spiritual.[51] The ideal triumphs over the real. Instead of celebrating the vigor and magnificent nonchalance of the oxen as in 1855, Whitman now reserved his admiration for the old farmer who dominates them with all the spiritual force which is in him.[52]

In the ideal world in which he was now living, he was no longer as sensitive as before to the ugliness of reality. Thus, in "Song of the Universal," he eliminated the problem of evil by giving it a Hegelian solution:

> In spiral routes by long detours
> (As a much-tacking ship upon the sea,)
> For it the partial to the permanent flowing,
> For it the real to the ideal tends.[53]

This process of idealization was general and even affected politics:

> Has not the time come, indeed, in the development of the New World, when its Politics should ascend into atmospheres and regions hitherto unknown — (far, far different from the miserable business that of late and current years passes under that name) — and take rank with Science, Philosophy and Art?. . .[54]

He similarly idealized his whole past life. He remembered only the moments of happiness: "the jocund influences surrounding the growth and advent of *Leaves of Grass*." [55] He neglected to speak of the painful crises through which he had passed, and he may really have forgotten them, unless he was making a distant allusion to them in "Out from Behind This Mask":

> (Tragedies, sorrows, laughter, tears — O heaven!
> The passionate teeming plays this curtain hid!). . .
> This film of Satan's seething pit. . .[56]

This idealization particularly affected the "adhesiveness" which Whitman had celebrated in "Calamus" and the purely sexual significance of which we have noted. That which had originally been, as he himself recognized, an "irresistible and deadly urge" became now a "never-satisfied appetite for sympathy," a "boundless offering of sympathy" and "universal democratic comradeship." [57] Thus he belatedly took cognizance in 1876 of the transformation which we have seen in his personality since the period of the Civil War. In the same way "Calamus," which had been at first an expression of his own Self, now acquired an essentially political meaning that it certainly had not had before.

> Besides, important as they are in my purpose as emotional expressions for humanity, the special meaning of the *Calamus* cluster of *Leaves of Grass*. . . mainly resides in its Political significance. . .[58]

Thus Whitman changed the whole character of the book by emphasizing the importance of the theme of democracy at the expense of the theme of individuality. He tried to make his work seem more impersonal and less egoistic than it had been in the beginning by attributing to some of his earlier poems a significance that properly belonged only to his most recent writings.

In addition, as the Preface of *Two Rivulets* shows, he was becoming more clearly aware of the basic premises of *Leaves of Grass*. In particular he distinguished two themes on which he had not previously passed judgment, science and industry, even though he had long ago included them in his poems. He was now, he claimed, "joyfully accepting Modern Science, and loyally following it without the slightest hesitation," [59] and on occasion he drew his inspiration from the great industrial expositions, "the majestic outgrowths of the Modern Spirit and Practice." [60]

Such were in 1876 the new characteristics of Whitman's book, but the fact is that the new material in *Two Rivulets* was meager. There were only seventeen new poems (most of them, besides, were very short) since 1872, that is to say, in four years, though he had no longer to spend his time making a living. His productiveness had greatly declined. His illness, although he had conquered it, had weighed on him heavily;

he found it very difficult now to do any creative work; he hardly did more than revise and rearrange what he had already written. But, at least, he did not renounce anything that he had done — a proof that he remained essentially himself. Upon rereading his book, he declared himself well pleased:

> Ere closing the book, what pride! what joy, to find them,
> Standing so well the test of death and night! [61]

And, we might add, of illness and suffering.

His fatigue — already apparent in 1871–72 — was betrayed in particular, as in the preceding edition, by the frequency of occasional poems. There are two in *Two Rivulets*: "Spain, 1873–'74" [62] and "An Old Man's Thought of School," [63] which was read at Camden on October 31, 1874, at the inauguration of a public school. "Centennial Songs" contained another, much more important, "Song of the Universal," which Whitman composed for the Tufts College Commencement in June 1874.[64] He was, of course, unable to attend; he could only send the poem, which was read for him.[65]

Another symptom of the decline of his creative power is the increasingly intellectual tone of his poems. "Eidólons" is characteristic of his new manner. He no longer concerned himself now with the concrete details which swarmed in "Song of Myself"; he preferred to philosophize. His instinctive pantheism has become a kind of dessicated Hegelianism. This intellectualization can be seen also in the suddenly increased proportion of prose in his work. In the second volume of the Centennial Edition it almost smothered the poetry, and in the section entitled "Two Rivulets" it even intrudes into the poems in the form of footnotes running parallel to the poetic text, but unrelated to it.

The two volumes of the Centennial Edition appeared at the beginning of March 1876. As usual, Whitman, incorrigibly optimistic, hoped that they would sell well and that the

profits would permit him to repair his finances and even to
buy a small house where he would be completely independent.[66] It seemed to him that the occasion was propitious and
that people would celebrate the centenary of the American
Republic by purchasing the works of the spokesman of democracy. Unfortunately, the Centennial Edition was very coolly
received by American critics. They no longer insulted him —
since the Civil War the fashion had changed — but they
affected to treat him with contempt as a second-rate poet.
This was the tone, for instance, of the review in *The Hour,*
though it was in general favorable enough: "No doubt he
overrates himself, and his friends overrate him. But still the
man has a touch of something uncommonly like poetic fire." [67]
A few weeks later, Charles F. Richardson expressed almost
the same opinion in the New York *Independent*: "His gold
is very bright; but its tiny nuggets are embedded in dispropor-
tionate masses of earth and organic matter . . . He is a poet of
the second rank among American bards . . ." [68]

This reception must have discouraged Whitman somewhat.
In an anonymous article printed by the *West Jersey Press,*
May 24, 1876 — which, if he did not write it himself, he at
least inspired — he complained not bitterly, but sadly of having been the victim of a veritable conspiracy of silence:

Down to the present time, and to this hour, not one leading
author of the United States (Whitman says grimly he is "getting
to be rather proud of it") is friendly in either a personal or professional mode to *Leaves of Grass* or Whitman himself. Will it
not prove a pretty page of the history of our literature a couple of
decades hence, that in 1874–5 Emerson, Bryant and Whittier
each made great Omnibus-gatherings of all the current poets and
poetry — putting in such as Nora Perry and Charles Gayler and
carefully leaving Walt Whitman out? Not a magazine in America
— not a single well-established literary journal — will to-day, on
the usual terms, accept and issue his productions. Not a publisher

will bring out his book (which to this hour has never been really published at all). . .[69]

The facts which he mentioned were generally correct. Although the 1860 edition of *Leaves of Grass* had been issued by a publisher, the venture, as we have seen, had turned out badly because of the Civil War. Also, *Harper's Monthly* in 1874 had accepted the "Song of the Redwood Tree" and "Prayer of Columbus," [70] but these favors had not lasted; the editors had soon rejected his contributions like the others. The only periodical which had offered Whitman the hospitality of its columns during this period had been the New York *Graphic*, [71] but it was a daily newspaper with no prestige and the consolation was slight.

This was the situation when, unexpectedly, Robert Buchanan, having read in the London *Athenaeum* [72] the article of the *West Jersey Press* of January 26, 1876, published in the London *Daily News* for March 13, in the form of a letter to the editor, a violent attack against American writers who, in his opinion, were guilty of neglecting the greatest poet of the United States and even of conspiring against him. He compared them to a flock of crows harrying an old eagle.[73] These insulting insinuations raised a general outcry in the American press. On March 28 (the London papers at the time took two weeks to get to the United States), Bayard Taylor and G. W. Smalley protested in the New York *Tribune* against the subscription which was being taken up in England for Whitman, claiming that he had no need of financial assistance. On March 30 and April 12 Bayard Taylor renewed his attack, even going so far as to revive against Whitman the old charge of obscenity. Naturally, Whitman's friends did not remain inactive. On April 13, Burroughs came to his defense in a long letter which occupied an entire column of the *Tribune*. Then, on April 22, O'Connor in his turn came into the lists, striking at Whitman's enemies with an article of two columns, to which Taylor replied in the same issue.[74] The battle then spread and was soon raging in other papers. The New York *Herald,* after having published on April 1 an article by John Swinton which described Whitman's poverty and called on the public to help him, contained the next day an anonymous protest, the author of which, though praising Whitman for his faith in democracy, condemned his "naked nastiness" and concluded, "even Mr. Buchanan will admit that in a country where women can read, it would be hard to circulate his prophet." [75] This attack was the more perfidious in that it pretended to be impartial. During the same month, an equally hostile article was published in *Scribner's* by J. G. Holland, to whom Charles A. Dana replied on April 28 in the New York *Sun,* defending Whitman against "Tupper Holland," as he ironically called him.[76]

It appears from all this that even in the United States, Whitman had about as many friends as he had enemies, since whenever he was attacked, someone rose in his defense. Moreover, though some of the critics tended to dig up forgotten grievances which might adversely have affected the sale of *Leaves of Grass,* this controversy had on the whole the good effect of drawing public attention to Whitman and his work. It was, in short, good publicity. However, it was chiefly in England that his book sold, thanks to the exertions of Buchanan and Rossetti.[77] Many subscribers came to his aid by sending two or three times the price of his two volumes, among them Lord Houghton, Edward Dowden, Tennyson, Ruskin, Edmund Gosse, George Saintsbury, and Ford Madox Brown.[78] The literary and artistic élite of Great Britain gave him financial and moral support, and his reputation spread as far as Australia.[79] It was a powerful encouragement for him. As he later declared to Traubel:

I was down, down, physically down, my outlook was clouded: the appearance of that English group was like a flash out of heaven. . .[80]

Those blessed gales from the British Isles probably (certainly) saved me.[81]

Even his health was favorably influenced. The pleasure of this unexpected success must have stimulated his system and accelerated his recovery. In December, he was able to write to Peter Doyle: "I certainly am feeling better this winter, more strength to hold out, walking or like, than for nearly now four years — bad enough yet, but still *decidedly better* . . ." [82] He could now face the future with confidence. The clouds which had darkened the horizon were gone; new victories were on the way.

CHAPTER IX

NEW VICTORIES (1876–1882)

IN September 1876, someone arrived in Philadelphia, who, if Whitman had been prepared, would have changed the course of his life. This person was his great English admirer, Mrs. Anne Gilchrist. When she first read *Leaves of Grass* in 1869 she had been immediately overcome. In the distracted cry of the mockingbird from Alabama seeking his lost mate, she had heard the voice of Whitman, and being a warm-hearted widow, she felt capable of filling the painful emptiness in the poet's life.[1] It seemed to her that *Leaves of Grass* was a call, a love-letter, and she was soon passionately in love with Whitman even though she had not met him. Her modesty and her respect for the conventions prompted her at first to maintain a certain reserve. She had to content herself with singing the praises of *Leaves of Grass*,[2] but it was not the work that attracted her so much as the man, and after several months she gave way and sent him an impassioned letter expressly offering him her love. Whitman, much embarrassed by this gift for which he had no use, kept silent, probably hoping that the flame would die out for lack of fuel. But Mrs. Gilchrist, extremely worried at receiving no answer, sent him a second letter, and this time he was forced to write to her; he could no longer leave her in doubt. Therefore he addressed to her on November 3, 1871, a very brief note which was

actually nothing but a friendly acknowledgment. This calculated coolness was not enough to discourage Mrs. Gilchrist;
she continued to send long, passionate letters to which Whitman replied from time to time with a few lines informing her
of the progress of his work and inquiring after the health of
her children, which was a way of reminding her that she owed
her first duty to them. In August 1875, however, after his
paralytic attack, he committed an error. He sent her a ring
which he had worn on his finger for a number of years.[3] He
was at that time very ill and sometimes wondered whether
he was not going to die. It was therefore natural enough for
him to offer her a remembrance, but the symbolic significance
of a ring was not without its dangers.

Mrs. Gilchrist, imagining that all her hopes were now
justified, began to speak of traveling to the United States.
Whitman turned a deaf ear, but she refused to give up her
project and, one day, early in 1876, she informed him that
all her preparations had been made and that she was coming
to Philadelphia with her two youngest children. This change
of scene, she said, would be greatly beneficial to her son
Herbert, a painter, and would permit her daughter Grace to
pursue in the United States the medical studies which she
could not undertake in England.[4] Whitman immediately advised her strongly against such a move and asked her not to
make a final decision yet — to await his arrival in London, at
which time they could discuss the matter. To dissuade her he
went so far as to speak slightingly of the United States.[5] But
nothing could stop Mrs. Gilchrist, and six months later she
was in Philadelphia. No one knows how the encounter went.
But one thing is certain: Whitman must have demonstrated
admirable tact since he remained the friend of this woman
whose dream he had failed to realize. As long as the Gilchrists
remained in Philadelphia, he regularly visited their home,
even for several days at a time.[6] But he refused to let himself

be adopted; he successfully resisted the temptation to settle down and remained the incorrigible Bohemian which he had always been. His independence had been seriously threatened, but he emerged victorious from the battle.

He was too fond of solitude ever to live permanently with another person. This characteristic immediately struck Edward Carpenter, who met him for the first time during this period at Mrs. Gilchrist's: "I have seldom known anyone who, though so cordial and near to others, detached and withdrew himself at times more decisively than he did, or who on the whole spent more time in solitude." [7] He needed the company of others, but solitude was equally necessary to him; hence his taste for the attics in which he had lived in boarding-houses and in the homes of his parents and of his brother. During the years he spent in his brother's house, he probably suffered as much from the impossibility of being sufficiently alone as from the lack of friends. He therefore escaped from Camden for weeks at a time as soon as his health allowed him to travel again. He took refuge not far away at Timber Creek, on the small farm of the Staffords, whose son Harry, a printer, he had become acquainted with in Philadelphia. Beginning in 1876 he went there regularly every summer and sometimes from early spring until autumn. In *Specimen Days* he has left an account — or rather a description, since nothing ever happened there — of his visits to this enchanting spot, among trees and flowers, in the company of birds and insects.[8] His notes are entirely spontaneous, for he recorded them in notebooks which he carried with him on these walks.[9] They are still full of country odors, the rustling of leaves, the cries of quail, and the buzzing of bees. Days passed peacefully while he watched the clouds go by and listened to the song of the cicadas.[10] He relaxed deliciously, enjoying to the full his newly recovered health. The only important events were the passing of migratory birds or an encounter with a saucy squirrel com-

ing down from a tree to get a close look at him.[11] All these
fascinating sights brought back his childhood from beyond
the long years which he had spent in cities. Not being a professional naturalist, he did not observe them with the same
precise care as his friend John Burroughs, but rather tried to
absorb the "vital influences" with which they were loaded.[12]
He abandoned himself to the pleasure of feeling nature live
around him. It revived and stimulated his own vitality:

> After you have exhausted what there is in business, politics,
> conviviality, love, and so on — have found that none of these
> finally satisfy, or permanently wear — what remains? Nature
> remains; to bring out from their torpid recesses, the affinities of a
> man or woman with the open air, the trees, fields, the changes of
> seasons — the sun by day and the stars of heaven by night.[13]

He tried to be like his favorite poplar which, instead of
trying to *seem,* was content with *being.*[14] It was probably at
this time that he wrote the short poem entitled "Supplement
Hours," published posthumously in "Old Age Echoes":

> Sane, random, negligent hours,
> Sane, easy, culminating hours,
> After the flush, the Indian Summer of my life,
> Away from Books — away from Art — the lesson
>   learn'd, pass'd o'er,
> Soothing, bathing, merging all — the sane, magnetic,
> Now for the day and night themselves — the open air,
> Now for the fields, the seasons, insects, trees — the
>   rain and snow,
> Where wild bees flitting hum,
> Or August mulleins grow, or winter's snowflakes fall,
> Or stars in the skies roll round —
> The silent sun and stars.[15]

But he was not content to lead a purely vegetative or
contemplative life at Timber Creek, he also tried to shake
off the torpor of his body and to reawaken the limbs deadened

by paralysis. He exercised every day by wrestling with the trees. His favorite partner was a young hickory sapling with which he amused himself by bending the trunk and pulling with all his strength, but without roughness or jerkiness. The combat lasted about an hour and, after each round, he stopped to take a deep breath. During his walks, he similarly tested his returning vigor on low branches or saplings, along his way. It seemed to him that thanks to these "natural gymnasia" his benumbed muscles acquired the elasticity and robustness of the young trees and that the same clear sap circulated in his veins.[16]

In addition to these exercises, he had instituted a whole system of natural therapy based on sunbaths, mud-baths and nakedness, which he practiced in a well-hidden little dell, not far from the Stafford farm. The direct contact of his body with the sand, air, and water restored his vigor and made him a new man.[17]

The salutary effects of this treatment quickly made themselves felt. He was no longer a wreck stranded on the shore and slowly rotting. In 1877 he began to travel once more. He had been invited to New York by J. H. Johnston, a rich jeweler of his acquaintance, and his wife, and in March he spent several weeks with them. It was a triumphal time.[18] Receptions were given in his honor at the Liberal Club, at the Portfolio, and at the Palette Club. During one of the dinners, he delivered a speech on the question of feminism and recited some lines by Henri Murger.[19] These honors and entertainments probably did him as much good as his visits to Timber Creek. He needed warmth and sympathy in which to expand. So he visited the Johnstons again the following year on the occasion of W. C. Bryant's funeral.[20] Again he stayed in New York for nearly a month, during which he made an excursion to West Point and on up the Hudson to Esopus, where he called on his old friend John Burroughs at his country house. There he spent three delightful days, which he has recorded in *Specimen Days*.[21] On his return, he stopped again in New York. He never grew tired of the spectacle of this immense city, "bubbling and whirling and moving like its own environment of waters." [22]

He saw in this harmonious conglomerate life the best proof "of successful Democracy and of the solution of that paradox, the eligibility of the free and fully developed individual with the paramount aggregate." [23] He was an example of it himself. The "Mannahatta" which he had celebrated in 1856 had now welcomed him as a prodigal son. The New York *Tribune,* which had so often attacked him, now opened its columns to him.[24] He had been received as a celebrity, a satisfaction he highly appreciated.[25]

In 1879, his appetite for travel whetted by all these trips, he not only returned to New York [26] in order to give his first lecture on the death of Lincoln,[27] and to Esopus,[28] but he also undertook in September the longest journey of his life, traveling as far west as Colorado. He accompanied Colonel John W. Forney in order to participate in the celebration of the twenty-fifth anniversary of Kansas.[29] He went by way of Pittsburgh, Columbus, Indianapolis, and St. Louis, marveling as much at the comfort of the Pullman cars and the speed of the trains as at the wealth and immensity of the land.[30] On September 13, after a three days' journey, he arrived at Kansas City and went from there to Lawrence, where the ceremony was to take place; but he was so well entertained by the Mayor, John P. Usher, the Secretary of the Interior in Lincoln's administration, that he never got to the meeting at which he was supposed to speak. He was apparently not aware that he was expected to read a poem and had not prepared one. To make up for it, he wrote a message to the people of Kansas, which is reproduced in *Specimen Days*.[31] He then visited Topeka, the state capital, and pushing farther west, arrived at Denver on September 20. The Rocky Mountains attracted him, and he made an excursion to Pueblo, from where he was able to see Pike's Peak.[32] The Rockies did not disappoint him. These enormous piles of fantastic shapes, he thought, emanated "a beauty, terror, power, more than Dante or Angelo ever knew." [33] It seemed to him that he had found there the "law" and justification of his own poems. They had the same plenitude, the same total absence of art.[34] It was at this time that he wrote "Italian Music in Dakota," [35] "Spirit that Form'd this Scene," [36] and "The Prairie States," [37] which he was to publish in the 1881 edition of *Leaves of Grass*. Three rather slight poems were not much to show for such an impressive journey. His strength had returned, but his creative faculty was still benumbed.

On the way back, he stopped at Sterling, Kansas, to visit a Civil War veteran whom he had nursed in a Washington hospital and who had invited him to stay with him for the winter. The memory of the "wound-dresser" still lived. But Whitman continued on his way, and after a brief stay at Kansas City, arrived at St. Louis at the beginning of October. He intended to spend some time there with his brother Jeff and he stayed for three months. He was, in fact, forced by illness to prolong his visit; besides, he probably found himself short of money. As usual, he resigned himself easily to circumstances beyond his control and explored with lively interest the city where "American electricity" went so well, he thought, with "German phlegm." [38] He visited factories, schools, and slaughterhouses; he was interviewed for the local papers,[39] and he did not return to Camden until the beginning of January 1880.

He did not remain there long. In the middle of February, he went to Timber Creek for several weeks,[40] and on June 3 he was on his way to Canada to visit one of his admirers, Dr. R. M. Bucke, director of the insane asylum at London, Ontario.

On the way, he was able to see Niagara Falls from the train, and he remembered it always afterwards.[41] At the end of the trip he found himself ill again — [42] these frequent relapses show that, although he had recovered to some extent, he had not regained his former triumphant health. However, he was very well cared for, and three weeks later he was well enough to accompany his host on a long boat trip from Toronto to Quebec and even farther, since they went up the Saguenay as far as Chicoutimi.[43] They came back the same way, and in September Whitman returned to Camden with his head full of new impressions, but his work was not much richer for them. From this long trip he brought back only a thin notebook,[43] which furnished material for a few pages in *Specimen Days* [44] but not a single poem. Although more than once, as his travel notes show, he had been moved or interested, he had not felt the need to create. The sterility already evident on the occasion of his western journey was growing worse. Canada, in any case, had nothing new to offer him. The scenery was not essentially different from that of the United States, and he was not prepared by training or experience to appreciate the peculiarities of Canadian life. In the British part of the country he saw only militarism and in the French region nothing but stagnation and superstition.

All these journeys were undertaken in response to invitations, which proves that he did not lack friends or admirers, and he was warmly welcomed wherever he went. Every year large audiences attended his lecture on Lincoln to show their sympathy for him. Younger men regarded him as a master, among them Joaquin Miller, who wrote a poem in his honor in 1877,[45] and Edward Carpenter, who made a special trip to the United States to see him. Camden was beginning to attract pilgrims. Among other visitors he received Dr. Bucke in 1877 [46] and Longfellow in 1878.[47] The homage thus rendered by the author of "Evangeline" amounted to a consecration and moved him deeply. For, however great his confidence in his own genius, he did not find it displeasing to be treated as an equal by one of the most famous of the Harvard professors. Yet, Whitman was not satisfied. In an interview for a St. Louis newspaper during his western trip, he complained (on behalf of the young, but actually it was his own grievance which he was airing) that the publishing houses and the reviews were controlled by "fossils," "old fogies" like Holland and "fops" like Howells.[48] Indeed he had some ground for irritation. In spite of the success of *Leaves of Grass* in England and even in America he had never succeeded in getting his articles or his poems accepted by the reviews. He complained bitterly of it in a letter to W. S. Kennedy dated June 18, 1880:

. . . Did I tell you my last piece (poem) was rejected by the *Century* (R. W. Gilder). I have now been shut off by *all* the magazines here and the *Nineteenth Century* in England — and feel like closing house as poem writer — (you know a fellow doesn't make brooms or shoes if nobody will have 'em). . .[49]

And a year later, he noted in his Canadian diary:

Received back to-day the MS. of the little piece of "A Summer Invocation," which I had sent to H.'s [*Harper's*] magazine. The editor said he returned it because his readers wouldn't understand any meaning to it. . .[50]

The principal reason for all these rejections was simply Whitman's reputation for indecency, as this letter from J. G. Holland, the editor of *Scribner's Monthly,* shows:

I have read Stedman's paper. His treatment of Whitman's indecency is excellent, and the old wretch can no longer defend it. Without any plea for morality and purely on artistic grounds, he demolishes all the old man's defenses and leaves him without any apology for adhering to his early smut. I shall find no fault with the rest, that is, I do not criticize it, though I cannot help feeling that Whitman does not in any measure deserve the great attention we are giving him. . . I am only troubled — in regard to this paper — by the thought that we are helping to bolster a reputation that has no legitimate basis on which to stand.[51]

Holland's uneasiness was not unjustified, for according to some people,[52] Stedman's article, which was very favorable in spite of its many reservations,[53] helped to bring Whitman to the attention of James R. Osgood and Company of Boston. However, it is more likely that Whitman's visit to that city in 1881 had something to do with the offer which Osgood made him for the publication of *Leaves of Grass*. For it was in Boston that Whitman gave his lecture on the death of Lincoln that year,[54] and he spent a full week there. The day after his talk, he returned the visit which Longfellow had made to him at Camden, and he was very cordially received.[55] He went to see Quincy Shaw's collection of Millet's paintings and remained to contemplate them for hours. The elemental strength of "The Sower" vividly impressed him, and all of Millet's somber, rought-cut peasants helped him to gain a better understanding of France.[56] On Sunday, April 17, he stood meditating in Memorial Hall at Cambridge before the long list of Harvard students killed in the Civil War.[57] After sixteen years, the memory of the war still haunted him. His stay in Boston thus was uneventful, but it drew attention to him. The Massachusetts newspapers reported his smallest movements and praised his lecture in enthusiastic reviews.[57] Osgood must have thought this sterling publicity, and, in any event, a poet who was a friend of Longfellow must certainly be a respectable author and a good investment.

However, the publisher's offer did not come immediately, and Whitman had time to return to Camden and spend a vacation at Timber Creek.[58] A few weeks later, toward the end of July, he went with Dr. Bucke to revisit the places where he had spent his childhood and youth on Long Island. He returned to Long Branch and Far Rockaway, where he bathed and walked naked on the beach, reciting poetry as of old.[59] Later they went as far as West Hills to have a look at Whitman's birthplace and at the cemetery where his ancestors lay.[60] It was not a melancholy pilgrimage, but it shows that he was living more and more in the past. On the way back, he stopped for several days in New York, where he also searched out his old haunts. He visited Pfaff, with whom he called up memories of the good old days before the Civil War and all the friends now dead or scattered.[61]

In spite of his premature old age and his relative lack of success, Whitman did not give way to sadness or despair, but braced himself against them. As he declared later to Traubel: " . . . it stiffens a fellow up to be told all around that he is not wanted, that his room is better than his company, that he has a good heart — that he can nurse soldiers but can't write poetry." [62] Deep in his own mind he persisted in the belief that he was right and that the future would justify him; and the improvement which he had observed in his position during the preceding years inclined him to optimism. As a reporter wrote in the Boston *Herald* in April 1881:

> Walt Whitman has in times past been perhaps more ignorantly than wilfully misunderstood, but time brings about its revenges, and his present position goes to prove that, let a man be true to himself, however he defies the world, the world will come at last to respect him for his loyalty.[63]

It must have seemed to him that his patience was finally being rewarded when he learned through John Boyle O'Reilly that James R. Osgood and Company wanted to bring out a definitive edition of *Leaves of Grass*.[64] Of course, he accepted the offer at once, but he generously warned the publishers that "the sexuality odes about which the original row was started and kept up so long are all retained and must go in the same as ever." [65] They asked for a look at the text and were apparently not scandalized by Whitman's audacities for they accepted his conditions and promised him 12.5 per cent royalties.

In August, Whitman was in Boston again to supervise the printing of his new edition.[66] He remained for more than two months and enjoyed the visit very much. He saw Joaquin Miller almost every day and met various New England celebrities such as Longfellow, who came to see him again, O. W. Holmes, and Henry James, Sr.[67] But his greatest pleasure was to be invited to dinner at Emerson's during a visit with F. B. Sanborn at Concord.[68] The venerable philosopher, now seventy-eight years old, had completely lost his memory. He was almost incapable of taking part in a conversation and did not recognize Whitman. But physically he was still well preserved and his smiling presence was a source of great happiness to the poet of *Leaves of Grass*.

From the start, the Osgood edition had a very remarkable success. It sold about 2,000 copies during the winter of 1881–82,[69] and Whitman had reason to think that it was the end of his troubles and that he had finally succeeded. Unfortunately, on March 1, 1882, acting on a complaint of the Society for the Prevention of Vice, Oliver Stevens, District Attorney of Massachusetts, gave notice to the publisher that if he did not withdraw *Leaves of Grass* from circulation he would be prosecuted for printing and selling obscene literature.[70] Whitman was immediately informed, and not wanting to lose the support of an influential publisher, he offered to make concessions:

I am not afraid of the District Attorney's threat — it quite certainly could not amount to anything — but I want you to be satisfied, to continue as publishers of the book, (I had already thought favorably of some such brief cancellation). Yes, under the circumstances I am willing to make a revision and cancellation in the pages alluded to — wouldn't be more than half a dozen any how — perhaps indeed about ten lines to be left out & a half dozen words or phrases.[71]

But the District Attorney, upon being consulted, furnished a list of offensive passages [72] which included in addition to scattered lines three whole poems: "A Woman Waits for Me," "The Dalliance of the Eagles," and "To a Common Prostitute." This time, Whitman refused to give way: "The list whole and several is rejected by me, and will not be thought of under any circumstances." [73] The only concessions he offered were those he had already proposed: "I mail you with this a copy of L of G, with the not numerous, but fully effective changes and cancellations I thought of making: See pages 84 88 89 90 . . . The whole thing would not involve an expense of more than from 5 to $10." [73]

Thus he would have consented discreetly to censor the volume himself, but the poems which Stevens asked him to sacrifice seemed to him indispensable and irreproachable. So he felt that he had to hold fast and issue the revised volume in spite of the threat of prosecution: "My proposition is that we at once make the revision here indicated, & go on with the regular issue of the book. If then any further move is made by the District Attorney and his backer — as of course there is somebody behind it all — they will only burn their own fingers, & very badly." [74] But the publishers, wishing to avoid scandal at any price were unwilling to run this risk and suggested a compromise solution: to suppress the two most daring poems, "A Woman Waits for Me" and "To a Common Prostitute." [75] Whitman made no reply. They sent him a telegram requesting one. His answer was a refusal. [76]

At this point, the publishers had either to risk prosecution or capitulate and stop the sale of Leaves of Grass. Osgood, who was eminently respectable and did not want his name associated in the newspapers with a case involving obscene literature, preferred to give up without a fight. [77] Whitman therefore found himself again obliged to undertake the publication of his own book, which, undiscouraged, he did at once. He consoled himself by saying: "I tickle myself with the thought how it may be said years hence that at any rate no book on earth ever had such a history." [78]

Osgood having surrendered the plates of the Boston edition, Whitman made arrangements with a Camden printer to put on sale another edition exactly like the former one.[79] But the burden was too heavy for him and he soon concluded an agreement with Rees Welsh and Company of Philadelphia to publish the book. This was not a very happy choice. Several printings were quickly sold,[80] but Rees Welsh and Company printed some vulgar and ridiculous advertisements which offended Whitman's admirers.[81] As soon as he could Whitman chose another firm and had the good luck this time to find David McKay, who was to remain his publisher until his death.[82]

On the whole, Whitman had accepted Osgood's capitulation very philosophically. He had not protested against the action of the Boston District Attorney. Rather than rebelling and opposing the attack, he had preferred to shift his ground. He was stubborn, but not at all aggressive. The main thing for him was to publish *Leaves of Grass,* and as long as he succeeded, he did not care how it was done. Moreover he did not need to fight his own battle. As soon at it was known that Stevens had suppressed his book, a violent controversy broke out in the newspapers, many of which immediately supported him on the ground of freedom of thought.[83] The faithful O'Connor was of course in the front rank of his defenders, sending letter after letter to the New York *Tribune.*[84] The Reverend Mr. Morrow, a Methodist preacher in Philadelphia, supported him with equal fervor and vigorously opposed the suppression of *Leaves of Grass* in Pennsylvania.[85] But the most fanatical supporters of Whitman were the free-thinkers. Several groups in Massachusetts campaigned energetically for him, notably George Chainey, a former Baptist minister who had lost his faith and who preached free-thought every Sunday afternoon in Paine Memorial Hall in Boston. He devoted a lecture and an entire number of his journal, *This World,* to the defense of *Leaves of Grass* and particularly "To a Common Prostitute," which he quoted in its entirety. His audacity got him into trouble. The Boston postmaster refused to accept this issue of his journal on grounds of obscenity. It took an intervention by Robert Ingersoll with James H. Marr, Acting First Postmaster at Washington, to lift the embargo.[86]

Benjamin Tucker, too, launched a resounding challenge to Stevens and all the professional defenders of virtue by offering in *Liberty* to sell the proscribed book to anyone who wanted to buy it.[87] His enflamed prose suggests a thirst for martyrdom; however, he was not arrested. This good fortune came to Ezra Heywood of Princeton, Massachusetts, who published a small free-thought paper, *The Word.* Like Chainey he had printed the texts of "To a Common Prostitute" and "A Woman Waits for Me" in an issue of his periodical. Stevens had him arrested on the complaint of Anthony Comstock, Secretary of the Society for the Prevention of Vice. But when the case came to trial, Heywood was acquitted — much to Whitman's delight. "So Anthony Comstock retires with his tail intensely curved inwards," he wrote to O'Connor.[88] However, the campaign of the free-thinkers caused Whitman some discomfort. He did not want to be associated with them because he disapproved of the excesses of some of them who went so far as to advocate the practice of free-love. Therefore he kept aloof from all their activities. He even confided his doubts and hesitations to the fiery O'Connor, who was troubled with no such scruples:

As to the vehement action of the Free religious and lover folk, in their conventions, papers, &c. in my favor — and even proceedings like those of Heywood — I see nothing better for myself or friends to do than quietly stand aside & let it go on. . . I got a letter from Dr. Channing asking me to lecture in the Tilton sisters' course this winter in Boston — but I cannot lecture at present — besides I shall certainly not do anything to identify myself specially with free love.[89]

He was a poet, not a doctrinaire. It was enough for him at this time to be the author of *Leaves of Grass*. He no longer wanted to revolutionize the world. The sage of Camden had neither the enthusiasm nor the optimism of the carpenter-bard of 1855.

But what sort of book was it which had raised such a tempest of protest and such equally fanatical devotion? The fact is that the 1881 edition of *Leaves of Grass* differed little from its predecessors, at least as regards the text. As the reviewer for the *Critic* remarked.

The two volumes called *Leaves of Grass* and *The Two Rivulets* which he had printed and himself sold at Camden, N.J., are now issued in one, under the former title, without special accretion of new work, but not without a good deal of re-arrangement in the sequence of the poems. Pieces that were evidently written later and intended to be eventually put under Leaves of Grass, now find their place; some that apparently did well enough where they were have been shifted to other departments. On the whole, however, the changes have been in the direction of greater clearness as regards their relation to the sub-titles. It is not apparent, however, that the new book is greatly superior to the old in typography, although undeniably the fault of the privately printed volumes, a variation in types used, is no longer met with. The margins are narrower, and the look of the page more common-place.[90]

This uniformity and simplicity were intentional. Whitman wanted his book to have a Quakerish quality.[91] Since the war he had not tried to make an impression with the originality of his bindings and that of the 1881 edition was very conservative. The volume was bound in light yellow cloth and the front cover carried in a frame Whitman's signature in gilded letters. The backstrip naturally bore the title and the author's name and was decorated with some very simply designed blades of grass and a hand on which a butterfly was perched, a motif which had already appeared on the binding of the 1860 edition. Facing page 29, where "Song of Myself" began, was, as in most of the previous editions, a portrait of Whitman, but it was that of the 1855 volume.

There was nothing new in all this. But the table of contents showed a certain number of changes. All the poems without exception were now classified and individualized. There were no more undifferentiated sections casually entitled "Leaves of Grass" as in 1871 and 1876. Each section now had its own subtitle. This was the most highly organized edition thus far, and its arrangement of the poems was definitive; Whitman made no further changes afterwards. Curiously, the "Songs of Insurrection" had disappeared. The poems which belonged to it had been scattered among several other sections, as if Whitman had wanted to attenuate the revolutionary aspect of the book. It seems that artistic considerations had now become more important than political concerns. Most often he had gathered his poems around an image under a symbolic title such as "Sea-Drift," "Birds of Passage," "From Noon to Starry Night," [92] rather than under an explicit formula. Generally speaking, throughout the book he had been solicitous of the typographical presentation, and in particular he had completely revised the punctuation, omitting many superfluous commas and replacing dashes with commas, which gave his book a much more conventional aspect and a less personal appearance. [93]

His main concern had been with the organization; he had introduced only twenty new poems, all very short, an insignificant addition in view of the fact that he had had five years to write them and that he had made several journeys which ought to have stimulated his creative activity. [94] But, as we have had occasion to remark, he had derived only four poems from his trip to the West [95] and from his Canadian journey only a few notes. His inspiration, threatened with exhaustion since 1873, was almost completely gone. The impetuous torrent of 1855 was now reduced to a trickle. It was also symptomatic that several of these new poems had a purely literary inspiration. This is particularly true of "Roaming in Thought," subtitled "After Reading Hegel"; [96] of "The Dalliance of the Eagles," which was a paraphrase of a description by John Burroughs; [97] and of "To the Man-of-War Bird," which had been inspired by a passage from Michelet. [98] Also it seems that in order to enlarge the book he had raked up some old material. "My Picture Gallery," as Emory Holloway has shown, is a fragment of a long poem written when he was preparing the first edition of *Leaves of Grass*. [99] And, unless "Patrolling Barnegat" was a recollection of a recent excursion, it may well have been an unused sketch dating from the period of "Out of the Cradle Endlessly Rocking." [100] It has the same stormy air, the same savage and melancholy music, and in the line-endings the same repetitions of present participles. As in 1876 he included several unimpressive occasional poems, such as "What Best I See in Thee" celebrating General Grant's return from his world's tour, [101] and "The Sobbing of the Bells" written to order a few days after the death of President Garfield. [102] In addition, several other poems seem to have been composed merely in order to introduce the book or one of its sections; for instance, "Thou Reader" [103] and "As Consequent." [104]

Thus the new poems which he felt compelled to write and in which an authentic inspiration can be sensed are extremely rare. It is remarkable, however, that in spite of his illness and infirmity there is no complaint, no cry of rebellion. On the contrary, "Hast Never Come to Thee an Hour" [105] and "A Clear Midnight" [106] convey serenity and detachment. His faith remained intact. He had emerged victorious from his trials and he now awaited further events with confidence. He had formerly praised "the grandeur and exquisiteness of old age," [107] and it might be feared that after his paralytic stroke fate would give him the lie, but with patience and energy he had overcome his misfortune. Therefore old age did not disappoint him, and he did not have to renounce what he had said before his experience of it. In "Youth, Day, Old Age and Night," he solemnly reaffirmed his belief in the equality of old age and youth:

> Youth, large, lusty, loving — youth full of grace, force, fascination,
> Do you know that Old Age may come after you with equal grace, force, fascination? [108]

— a relative equality and illusory strength when we think of the poverty of his inspiration after 1871. He now only mentioned for the record the themes he had formerly chanted with so much vigor and of which "A Riddle Song" [109] is merely a rather cold inventory. Even the memory of his mother could not put warmth into "As at Thy Portals also Death," [110] which hardly echoes the great sadness her loss had caused him in 1873. And, when he undertook to sing a hymn to the sun, "Thou Orb Aloft Full Dazzling," [111] there was no trace of the fervor which once animated him in "Song of Myself." His sensuality was not altogether dead, but it was moribund. It had outlived itself.

It is not surprising therefore that he tried to tone down certain boldnesses of expression, the urgency of which he no longer felt so strongly as in his youth. Even before the controversy over the Boston edition, he had on his own initiative expurgated a certain number of poems where sexual images were not absolutely necessary. Thus, in "Year of Meteors" he suppressed some homosexual lines addressed to the Prince of Wales [112] and in "Pensive on Her Dead Gazing" an allusion to the beautiful bodies of young men.[113] He modified "Native Moments" [114] in "Children of Adam" in a similar way, and made other suppressions of that kind here and there.[115] This quiet labor of self-censorship had begun in 1871, but it had never before been carried so far. He made no mention of it, however, and was careful to let alone the more compromising poems, the absence or weakening of which would have been remarked. For he was especially anxious that these changes should not be noticed. This is clearly indicated in his letters to Osgood at the time when he was thinking of making concessions to Stevens. He insisted on the greatest secrecy: ". . . the change to be just silently made — the book, etc. at casual view all its pages to look just the same — only those minutely looking detecting the difference. . ." He specified also that "all lines and passages marked in pencil [must] come out and their places [must] be exactly filled with other matter — so that the pages will superficially present the same appearance as now." And he further requested that the copy containing his corrections be returned to him, probably so that there would be no evidence of his action.[116] An inverted form of hypocrisy, one might say — not at all. He was merely being proud and stubborn and wanted at any cost to avoid the appearance of abandoning the position which he had taken in opposition to Emerson in 1860.[117] His voluntary corrections show that he no longer insisted on his verbal audacities, but he refused to disavow his past self, thus preserving at the same time the unity of his life and the integrity of his work, his "identity," as he would have said.

In 1882, he had a volume published at Philadelphia by Rees Welsh and Company entitled *Specimen Days and Collect*, intended as a companion piece to *Leaves of Grass*,[118] the format and binding of the two books being exactly the same. He had already had the same idea in 1876 with *Two Rivulets*. But *Specimen Days* contained only prose. It included "Democratic

Vistas," "Memoranda during the War," the various prefaces of *Leaves of Grass*, a certain number of articles previously printed in periodicals, the text of his commemorative lecture on the death of Lincoln, and even, as an appendix, several juvenilia never before collected in book form. The only original material was the part of *Specimen Days* that recounted very briefly his childhood and youth, and his Civil War diary, some hundred and fifty pages in all.[119] Since 1876 he had written more in prose than in verse — a bad sign for a poet, but even in prose his output had not been abundant. This second volume definitely confirms the impression of impoverishment [120] and relative sterility given by the first.

In 1882, Whitman was sixty-three years old, and he had not yet won recognition. Thanks to Osgood and even more to the scandal occasioned by the Boston edition, *Leaves of Grass* had enjoyed a certain success, but a number of critics greeted his work with the same old sarcasms.[121] "He is a wicked Tupper; he is an obscene Ossian; he is a poetical Zola; he is — Walt Whitman," declared the New York *Examiner*.[122] He was charged with not having purified his work,[123] with having remained himself after having raised with *Drum-Taps* a momentary hope that he had reformed. This was the point made by a reviewer in the New York *Independent*:

> Whitman changed with the war. He ceased to chant the phallus; *Drum-Taps* and the like came on. His rhythms drew nearer to poetry, to the common movement of blank verse and to rhyme; but in preparing the new edition of his poems, he has preserved the old leaves and strown them all through the book.[124] Shame on the publisher who is sending them with his imprint to unsuspecting American homes.[125]

Still the same reproach of obscenity and formlessness. But some of the critics strongly defended him and completely denied these two main accusations. A reviewer in the New York *Sun* even justified his catalogues,[126] and the Reverend

Mr. Morrow, pastor of the Tabernacle Methodist Episcopal Church in Philadelphia, approved the sexual frankness of his poems.[127] The New York *Sun* review concluded that "the belief is growing in cultivated minds that in Walt Whitman we have one of the most remarkable and original individualities in literature." [128]

Even the detractors, such as the critic in the *Dial*, were obliged to recognize that Whitman had written some worthwhile poems, "Ethiopia Saluting the Colors," "O Captain! My Captain!" and "When Lilacs Last in the Dooryard Bloom'd," [129] the taste of the average reader generally running to these poems because of their patriotic and sentimental appeal and also because of their more conventional form. But the great mass of the public remained indifferent. Whitman was appreciated only by the connoisseurs. This paradox had struck the reviewer in the *Critic*: "One great anomaly of Whitman's case has been that, while he is an aggressive champion of democracy and of the working-man, in the broad sense of the term working-man, his admirers have been almost exclusively of a class the farthest possibly removed from that which labors for daily bread by manual work. . ." [130] But it could hardly have been otherwise. As a writer signing himself "Deuceace" in the St. Louis *Daily Globe Democrat* very justly remarked: "The mass of people seldom read verse (unless it be exceptionally bad, and contributed to a cheap weekly). . ." [131]

There was probably another reason, purely practical, but equally important, for Whitman's lack of popularity — namely, the lack of publicity. A New York bookseller complained about it in an interview with a reporter for the *Tribune*:

> There is some call for the book from dealers to fill orders, but I do not think the sales now are large. I guess the Philadelphia firm are trying to push it in the hope of making money out of it. The book never was well advertised, and of course that makes a difference. A book that is advertised well, is sure to sell.[132]

To console himself for the apathy of the masses and the hostility of his detractors, Whitman had the fanatic zeal of his admirers, the Whitmaniacs, as they were now beginning to be called.[133] We have seen how vigorously they supported him when the 1881 edition was attacked. In calmer times they published dithyrambic articles or even poems about Whitman.[134] They considered him, if not as a god, at least as a very great prophet. He was for them the equal of Christ, the founder of a new religion, and they were proud of being the first disciples. It was in this spirit that R. M. Bucke wrote the book on Whitman which he published in 1883,[135] and in which he included as an appendix the complete text of *The Good Gray Poet*.[136] But all this hagiographic literature could have only a very limited influence, and Whitman's more sober and judicious admirers — such as Edward Dowden,[137] Robert Louis Stevenson,[138] James Thomson,[139] and even John Burroughs [140] — who did not share this blind devotion, certainly gained more readers for *Leaves of Grass* than the noisy chorus of the enthusiasts.[141]

If Whitman's position was not precisely that which his worshipers claimed for him, neither was it that to which his detractors tried to relegate him.[142] A growing number of readers were beginning to be aware of this, as the *Critic* noted:

. . . in spite of all the things that regard for the decencies of drawing-rooms and families may wish away, he certainly *represents* as no other writer in the world, the struggling, blundering, sound-hearted, somewhat coarse, but still magnificent vanguard of Western civilization that is encamped in the United States of America. Wide [*sic*] readers are beginning to guess his proportions.[143]

Whitman realized this and looked to the future with confidence. He was sure that a more refined and spiritual civilization would eventually replace the gross commercialism of his time. He had already said so and he repeated it to his Santa Fe admirers in 1883:

The seething materialistic and business vortices of the United States, in their present devouring relations, controlling and belittling everything else, are, in my opinion, but a vast and indispensable stage in the new world's development and are certainly to be followed by something entirely different, at least by immense modifications. Character, literature, a society worthy the name, are yet to be established through a nationality of noblest spiritual, heroic and democratic attributes. . .[144]

Thus, in spite of failures, difficulties, and disappointments, his faith in himself, in democracy, and in his country won through; he was now able to face old age with serenity.

CHAPTER X

THE DECLINE (1883–1890)

THOUGH he thought for a time of leaving Camden,[1] Whitman finally decided to remain; but, in order to keep his independence, he bought in March 1884, with the money which the Philadelphia edition had brought him, a small two-story wooden house at 328 Mickle Street.[2] This was the first time that he had owned a house, a home of his own. Previously, to use his own words,[3] he had "possessed a home only in the sense that a ship possesses one." But he no longer had the courage to pursue his nomadic life, going from boarding-house to boardinghouse. The ship had been drawn up on shore, and was never again to take to sea.[4]

Mickle Street was undoubtedly democratic, but extremely ugly. There was the noise of the trains which passed on the nearby track and frequently the air brought the odor of a neighboring fertilizer factory, but Whitman was indifferent to these matters. He had never lost his Bohemian habits and the most picturesque disorder reigned in his house. He camped rather than really lived there. The furniture consisted mainly of trunks and wooden boxes, as if he were always ready to depart. The floor was littered with old newspapers, books, and piles of letters, but Whitman knew where to find what he wanted and felt perfectly happy in these almost sordid surroundings.[5] He sat with Olympian serenity in the midst of all this confusion, and his numerous visitors were struck by his beauty and nobility.[6]

He had hired as a housekeeper an elderly widow, Mary Davis, a mediocre but very devoted housewife who freed him from all material care. This arrangement gave him more independence than he had at his brother's house and more privacy, without however reducing him to complete solitude. As a matter of fact, he was visited by more and more admirers, who sometimes came from faraway places, and he welcomed them all, except the bores, with the greatest simplicity and kindness. There were actors such as Henry Irving [7] and Bram Stoker; English writers such as Edmund Gosse,[8] Ernest Rhys,[9] H. R. Haweis,[10] Edward Carpenter,[11] Sir Edwin Arnold,[12] and Oscar Wilde; [18] and more humble pilgrims such as Dr. J. Johnston,[14] Emily Faithfull,[15] and C. Sadakichi-Hartmann; [16] or even obscure students and utopians of all kinds who expected from him the consecration of their hopes.[17] Sometimes he had to pose for painters such as Thomas Eakins, Herbert Gilchrist, and J. W. Alexander, or sculptors such as Sidney Morse, who worked for weeks on a bust of him.[18] He avoided no one (on the contrary), and he offered himself with the same complacence to the demands of the photographers.[19] He had always liked to have his portrait made.

In addition to these passing visitors, Whitman also welcomed several faithful friends from Camden and Philadelphia, especially reporters such as Talcott Williams, Harrison Morris, and Thomas Donaldson,[20] and above all Horace Traubel, a clerk who every day after work came to gossip with him and keep him company. The enthusiasm of this young and rather naïve radical amused Whitman. He was not a friend or even a disciple, but a worshiper. He scrupulously recorded the slightest utterances of his idol. A minute and inexhaustible Boswell, he has left in the four fat volumes of his *With Walt Whitman in Camden* an artless account of the last years of Whitman,[21] in which the innumerable details tend to hide the man, but which constitute a valuable collection of the literary and political opinions of the aging poet. Traubel's brother-in-law, Thomas B. Harned, a lawyer in Philadelphia, was another member of the cult. Moreover, Whitman was entertained by several of the best families of the City of Brotherly Love; he frequently visited in particular the home of R. Pearsall Smith, a very strict and austere Quaker, whose daughters were great admirers of his works.[22] And on February 22, 1887, the Contemporary Club in Philadelphia gave a large reception in his honor.[23] The disgraceful author of *Leaves of Grass* was now considered, at least by some people, as an eminently respectable person.

However, in spite of all his friends and all these tokens of esteem, his material situation remained precarious. The magazines still refused to publish his poems. In 1887 he was complaining again: "I sent a little poem to Harpers — (Alden) — but it came back refused — this is the fourth refusal within a few months, & I shall try no more." [24]

He had better luck the following year, for the New York *Herald* published some of the poems which were later to appear under the title of *November Boughs*.[25] But, most of the time, his only income was from the sale of his books, which did not bring him a living. In the last half of 1885, his royalties amounted to the ridiculous sum of twenty dollars.[26] Informed of his destitution by Mrs. Gilchrist, Rossetti tried to come to his rescue. He thought at first of asking President Cleveland to intervene,[27] but realizing the inappropriateness of such a move, he launched a subscription in England which raised more than five hundred dollars.[28] This unexpected windfall permitted Whitman to wait for better times. His American friends were also active. During the same year (1885), with funds raised by a subscription limited to ten dollars per person, they offered him a horse and buggy, by means of which, in spite of his infirmity, he was able to ride about Camden. In 1886, in spite of his protests, Sylvester Baxter undertook to get him a pension in recognition of his war services.[29] A bill was introduced in the House of Representatives, but it did not pass.[30] Then a new subscription was launched, this time for the purpose of buying him a small country house so that he could get away from his sordid surroundings in Camden. The Staffords were ready to offer him a piece of land at Timber Creek. But, when he received the money, he preferred to stay where he was.[31] At his age he did not want to change, and he was probably afraid that he would have fewer visitors in the country. He preferred the warmth of human contacts to the beauty of nature.

His friends had found another very tactful way of helping him. He liked every year on the fifteenth of April to deliver his lecture on the death of Lincoln. Every year, therefore, this was an occasion for his admirers to help him. In 1887 he spoke at New York in the Madison Square Theater to an audience of over three hundred people. Mark Twain was present, and Andrew Carnegie sent a check for $350. This lecture brought him $600.[32]

These contributions enabled Whitman, in spite of his meager income as an author, to enjoy a peaceful old age free from financial worry.[33] He had at last attained complete serenity. He realized that his work was relatively unsuccessful, but he was resigned to it. He offered his *Leaves of Grass* confidently to the coming generations. It was his "carte de visite" to posterity.[34] He also looked back with satisfaction into the past "o'er Travel'd Roads." [35] In the poems of these years he evoked the memory of his parents, "precious ever-lingering memories, (of you my mother dear — you father — you, brothers, sisters, friends)." [36] He thought nostalgically of his native island:

Sea-beauty! stretch'd and basking! [37]

And he sang the sweetness of memories:

> How sweet the silent backward tracings!
> The wandering as in dreams — the meditation of old
>   times resumed — their loves, joys, persons, voy-
>   ages.[38]

He was proud of having emerged victorious from the long battles of life, like a soldier covered with scars.[39] But he did not live solely in the past and future. The present still held many pleasures for him. He was always keenly sensitive to the joy of spring, to "the simple shows, the delicate miracles of the earth," [40] namely, birds and flowers. In one poem he even celebrated the appearance of the first dandelion.[41]

But this noble serenity and these moments of quiet happiness were temporary victories over the sufferings and apathy of old age. For, over the years, the burden of his half-paralyzed body was becoming heavier.[42] A sunstroke in 1885 had aggravated his illness,[43] and in June 1888 a new paralytic stroke almost killed him. Luckily, Dr. Bucke was nearby at the time, and by means of a vigorous treatment he succeeded in bringing him through.[44] But this marked the end of his outings. He had to sell the horse and buggy and buy a wheel chair instead. He was now almost completely powerless and could move about only with the help of an attendant. His friends came to his aid and furnished the services of a male nurse so that, after a fashion, he was still able to come and go.[45] But his health was precarious. He had to fight continually against all kinds of infirmities and against the torpor of his weakened body:

> As I sit writing here, sick and grown old,
> Not my least burden is that dulness of the years,
>   querilities,
> Ungracious glooms, aches, lethargy, constipation, whim-
>   pering *ennui*,
> May filter in my daily songs.[46]

Therefore he welcomed all the more the moments of respite
which his illness left him:

> After a week of physical anguish,
> Unrest and pain, and feverish heat,
> Toward the ending day a calm and lull comes on,
> Three hours of peace and soothing rest of brain.[47]

He was still capable sometimes of a short buggy ride around
Camden.[48] "The burning fires down in [his] sluggish blood
[were] not yet extinct." He still had an "undiminish'd faith"
and "groups of loving friends." [49] But his creative power was
almost gone, as he knew very well himself; he complained of
a "strange inertia falling pall-like round" him,[50] and he confided to Traubel that "his grip [was] gone — irretrievably lost:
I seem to have lost the power of consecutive thought, work —
mental volition. . . Said he had tried to go over the Hicks
manuscript, but didn't get far along: ten minutes of it did me
up." [51]

In spite of all this he did not give up. With admirable
tenacity he forced himself to write, to scribble a few lines
whenever he felt a little better and more clear in his mind. He
resisted step by step the numbness which threatened to overcome him. He wanted to imitate the snow bird which in the
Arctic wastes sang with a blithe throat in spite of the surrounding desolation.[52] And once more he gained the victory.
In 1888, after a seven years' silence, a new volume appeared
at Philadelphia, published by David McKay: *November
Boughs*.[53] Like the *Two Rivulets* of 1876, it was a mixture of
prose and verse. It included a long preface, "A Backward
Glance o'er Travel'd Roads," [54] some sixty very short poems
(none longer than one page) collected under the title of "Sands
at Seventy," and some reprints of articles already published in
magazines or in English editions of his works. In the same
year he also published his *Complete Poems and Prose*, a thick

volume of 900 pages,[55] and during the following year (1889), for his seventieth birthday, he brought out the ninth edition of *Leaves of Grass*.[56] The text was basically the same as that of the 1881 edition, but "A Backward Glance" served as a preface and "Sands at Seventy" was added as an appendix. From this time on, all the new poems were annexed to *Leaves of Grass* instead of being truly incorporated. He no longer had the strength to rearrange his book or to modify the structure so slowly and so patiently built up. "Sands at Seventy" contained only one important poem, "With Husky-Haughty Lips, O Sea," [57] composed on the seashore in 1884. Its tone and imagery recall "Sea-Drift" (1860). In it, Whitman sang the future of the world which appeared to him as an endless battle, with the soul at the center of things perpetually trying to realize itself and in spite of all its efforts never succeeding — a battle similar to the one going on within himself. Thus he felt complete sympathy with the ocean ceaselessly tossed by winds and tempests:

> Ever the soul dissatisfied, curious, unconvinced at last;
> Struggling to-day the same — battling the same.[58]

In spite of the lethargy of his body, the battle still continued, and as usual, his soul overcame his doubts and once more he concluded:

> Life, life an endless march, an endless army, (no halt,
>   but it is duly over,)
> The world, the race, the soul — in space and time the
>   universes,
> All bound as is befitting each — all surely going some-
>   where.[59]

There was no longer any need to repress desires disapproved by social morality; his "turbulent passions" had been calmed.[60] It was no longer love that disturbed him, but the approach of death.[61] Was he afraid? Certainly he preferred to wait a little longer, not to leave his friends and the world too quickly,[62] but he no longer had to struggle so violently to achieve serenity. He resigned himself more willingly to the inevitable:

> The soft voluptuous opiate shades,
> The sun just gone, the eager light dispell'd — (I too
>   will soon be gone, dispell'd,)
> A haze — nirwana — rest and night — oblivion.[63]

He looked forward to the "halcyon days" to come.[64] He now faced the political problems which had always troubled him so much with the same optimism and the same tranquillity. The current condition of the United States did not entirely please him, but again he consoled himself with the thought that all efforts thus far had been applied to the material foundations and that the spiritual superstructure would come later. Such was the answer of "the United States to Old World critics." [65]

There is evidence therefore in "Sands at Seventy" of a still rich and varied interior life, but one that naturally lacks the power and intensity of the earlier poems. Whitman was well aware himself of the weakness and infrequency of his inspiration [66] and compared the frail poems of *November Boughs* to the sparse and lingering leaves of a tree at the approach of winter.[67] He valued them all the more, however, as they were "confirming all the rest" and were "the faithfulest, hardiest — last." [68] He was right. The remarkable thing is that this tired, paralyzed, old man renounced no part of the message of his youth [69] and, in spite of illness and suffering, continued to celebrate the joy of living. By dint of will power and tenacity — in spite of his reputation for letting himself drift lazily along — he had arrived precisely where he wanted to be. Though an invalid, he had become just such a majestic, Olympian old man, loved and respected by all, as he had described in 1855 in *Leaves of Grass*.[70] His life to the very end ran parallel to his work.

This is certainly not to say that he did not change over the years. In particular, the arrogant pride which he had displayed at the beginning had given way to an unexpected modesty and humility. After setting out in 1855 to conquer the world and imagining himself the author of the greatest masterpiece of all times, he recognized now that "not only the divine works that to-day stand ahead in the world's reading, but dozens more, transcend (some of them immeasurably transcend) all I have done, or could do." [71]

Leaves of Grass, he now maintained, had never been for him any more than an experiment, and it would take another hundred years to assess it properly. Therefore he disapproved of what he regarded as the excessive enthusiasm of O'Connor and Bucke.[72] He was now capable of a judicious detachment with regard both to himself and to others. Having outgrown his dogmatic intransigence, he had become broad-minded and tolerant. He conceded that he was not the only great poet and that "The Poetic area is very spacious — has room for all — has so many mansions!" [73] He was now philosopher enough not to be absolutely certain of anything or of any conclusion.[74] He was no longer even sure of himself; for the first time, we find him speaking humorously of his own work. He no longer presented himself as an infallible prophet and a savior of mankind, but occasionally made fun of his old man's garrulity.[75] We do not find much of this kind of mild humor in Whitman's earlier work.

His attitude toward war had also changed. He was still thinking of it: the Civil War occupied considerable space in the prose of *November Boughs* [76] and supplied the imagery of "Thanks in Old Age." [77] As in 1865, he preached the reconciliation of North and South,[78] but with the passage of years, he had forgotten the horrors of battle and now sang of the heroism and grandeur of war as he had done at first in 1860–61:

The perfume strong, the smoke, the deafening noise;
Away with your life of peace! — your joys of peace!
Give me my old wild battle-life again! [79]

What did the public think of this new Whitman? Apparently
the noble dignity of the old man had disarmed at least some of
his enemies. Only the die-hards — like the Boston *Traveller*
— [80] continued to attack him. In general, the critics were
favorable. The *Saturday Review* of London made almost complete amends for the slashing review of *Leaves of Grass* it had
published in 1855.[81] This fact alone shows how far Whitman
had come since the first edition of his book. His admirers,
realizing that his strength was declining, were lavish with
tokens of affection.[82] His birthdays became apotheoses. In
1889, to celebrate his seventieth anniversary, they gave a big
dinner in his honor at Morgan's Hall in Philadelphia, and the
newspapers of Camden and Philadelphia unanimously chanted
his praises.[83] In 1890, they did better still. Colonel Ingersoll,
the eloquent champion of free-thought, attended Whitman's
seventy-first birthday celebration and delivered a long speech
glorifying *Leaves of Grass* and, after the banquet, with reporters in attendance, disputed with Whitman about the immortality of the soul. The orator denied it, but, in spite of his
arguments, the poet refused to give up his belief in it.[84] On
October 21 of the same year, Ingersoll made another appearance. This time he delivered a lecture in Horticultural Hall in
Philadelphia [85] on Liberty in Literature;[86] it was of course a
eulogy of *Leaves of Grass,* and the poet was present on the
stage in his wheel chair. On that occasion he must have remembered that forty years earlier he had dreamed of becoming
a great orator himself. But he felt too tired to do more than
say a few words of thanks and it was the last time he was able
to appear in public.

He became more and more of a popular figure and the newspapers often mentioned him and his picturesque den in Mickle

Street. He even had a cigar named after him,[87] which in the land of publicity was a great distinction. But he still had very few readers. At the beginning of 1889, he had sold only 700 copies of *November Boughs*.[88] Nevertheless he would continue to write until the end.

CHAPTER XI

LAST MONTHS AND DEATH (1891–1892)

ON June 4, 1890, three days after his seventy-first birthday, a newspaper announced that Whitman's death was imminent.[1] The report was exaggerated, but certainly his strength was declining. He no longer went out of doors and only rarely left his room. In the summer, when the heat was stifling, he was forced to wait at his window for the evening breeze.[2] He was permanently condemned to immobility and only death could free him or put an end to this passive and patient existence.[3] Nevertheless he still had moments of happiness, for example, when the sun warmed him into life. He then felt as sportive as a wave, and he would have liked to play like a child or a young kitten: that "perfect physique" which he had sung formerly still survived in the depths of his being.[4] His seventy-second birthday was also a great occasion. Unlike the preceding ceremonies, it was celebrated privately. Some thirty of his friends gathered in the ground-floor sitting room of his house. He was so weak that he could not come down by himself and had to be carried. But the presence of his friends and the champagne which they gave him stimulated and braced him so much that he presided over the feast with spirit and gossiped indefatigably [5] for three hours.

But this was his last flurry. He soon grew worse, and Traubel called in one of the best physicians in Philadelphia, Dr. Daniel

Longaker, who has left a circumstantial account of the poet's last months.[6]

Longaker at first did not discover any particularly disturbing symptoms. Whitman mainly complained of the sleepiness which almost constantly oppressed him and which he attributed to constipation. He also suffered from an enlarged prostate and was often obliged to use a sound in order to urinate.[7] He was a model patient, very docile and courageous, who analyzed with serene lucidity the progress of the disease in his worn-out body. He noted with the greatest care for the benefit of his doctor what food and how many pills he took each day, the state of his bowels, and any pain or discomfort that he felt.[8] He seemed rather surprised that his system refused to function normally or to obey his will. He thought he saw a spiritual reason for this. He had deflected his vital powers from their proper object for too long a time; all his vitality had been absorbed by his creative work; his stomach and bowels left to themselves had gradually become inactive.[9] Open air and a little exercise would doubtlessly have done him good, but he was now too weak to apply this remedy which had succeeded so well after his first paralytic attack. If he tried to go out, he felt dizzy; he had to stay shut up in his room, his den, as he called it.[10]

However, in spite of his great weariness, he did not give up. He was still able to forget his physical sufferings and be interested in other things than his illness. He discussed the personalities and the questions of the day with his visitors and his doctors.[11] At no time, even when his condition became more serious, did he behave as a testy or peevish invalid. He declared one day to Dr. Longaker that "he thought it a grand thing to grow old gracefully," [12] and so far as he was concerned, he had managed to do so. He kept his serenity to the very end and succeeded in embodying the ideal of Olympian old age that he had always admired. This was the result of a conscious and thorough effort to keep his life in harmony with

his work in order not to betray the message of *Leaves of Grass*.
The following passage indicates his feelings:

> On, on the same, ye jocund twain!
> My life and recitative, containing birth, youth, mid-
>   age years,
> Fitful as motley-tongues of flame, inseparably twined
>   and merged in one — combining all. . .

His purpose was to preserve both the unity of his life and the
unity of his work:

> My verses, written first for forenoon life, and for the
>   summer's, autumn's spread,
> I pass to snow-white hairs the same, and give to pulses
>   winter-cool'd the same. . .[13]

He refused to give up the struggle:

> . . . Think not we give out yet,
> Forth from these snowy hairs we keep up yet the lilt.[14]

He wanted to sing "our joys of strife and derring-do to the
last." [15] In spite of the illness and paralysis of his body, he
therefore continued to write and to create. In 1891 he even
brought out a new collection of poetry and prose, *Good-Bye
My Fancy*,[16] which he had prepared during the preceding
year [17] and which later became a second annex to *Leaves of
Grass*.

But this thin volume, which was bound exactly like *November Boughs*, contained only thirty-one poems, all very short,[18]
in which Whitman hardly did more than take up again, with
less energy, some of the themes he had treated earlier.[19] He
realized this very clearly and wondered whether he should
publish them or not:

> Had I not better withhold (in this old age and paralysis of me)
> such little tags and fringe-dots (maybe specks, stains,) as follows
> a long dusty journey, and witness it afterward? I have probably

not been enough afraid of careless touches, from the first — and am not now — nor of parrot-like repetitions — nor platitudes and the commonplace. . . Besides, is not the verse-field, as originally plann'd by my theory, now sufficiently illustrated — and full time for me to silently retire? — (indeed amid no loud call or market for my sort of poetic utterance).

In answer, or rather defiance, to that kind of well-put interrogation, here comes this little cluster, and conclusion of my preceding clusters. Though not at all clear that, as here collated, it is worth printing (certainly I have nothing fresh to write) — I while away the hours of my 72nd year — hours of forced confinement in my den — by putting in shape this small old age collation.[20]

In spite of the lack of inspiration — or at least of any new inspiration — and the indifference of the public,[21] Whitman still had to keep on writing. He had no illusion about the value of his current work, but he could not persuade himself to stop. His work had become the condition of his life. He may also have seen in this activity a way of preparing for death, which was becoming more and more threatening and which he was now almost looking in the face.[22] The thought of his approaching end haunts most of the poems of *Good-Bye My Fancy*, the very title of which is a farewell to life.[23] Yet, as soon as this collection was finished, he went on to write new poems, taking advantage of the respite that death still left him. These were gathered into a posthumous annex to *Leaves of Grass*, but Whitman himself gave them their title, "Old Age Echoes," [24] which suggests that to the very end he had only one concern: the enrichment and the organization of his book. The tenth edition of *Leaves of Grass*, called the death-bed edition, the printing of which he had supervised himself in spite of his weakness, appeared almost at the time of his death.[25]

He was not only composing poems, but was still writing tirelessly to his friends, such as Bucke and especially J. W. Wallace and J. Johnston, his two faithful admirers in Lancashire. Besides informing them about the state of his health, he told them of articles being published about him, of his literary projects, of the beauty of autumn, the future of democracy, and so on.[26] His eyesight was failing, his brain more and more palpably refusing even slight tasks or revisions,[27] yet he tried to maintain contact with the mass of his readers by means of new poems and with his favorite disciples by means of letters which he awkwardly scribbled on his bed.

Nevertheless disease finally conquered this extraordinary spiritual energy. On December 17, 1891, he had a chill which quickly developed into pneumonia.[28] On the twenty-first Bucke hastened to his bedside. He was thought to be dying, but he did not do so yet. Two weeks later, to the great surprise of the doctors,[29] his worst symptoms had disappeared and his breathing and circulation had almost returned to normal. But he was not by any means cured. He was still very weak and had to stay in bed. The smallest effort exhausted him; the least conversation tired him. Still, almost every day, he had enough strength to glance through the newspapers and read his mail. He was even able to write a few more letters.[30] But he fully realized that he was condemned.[31] He was not afraid of death; he awaited it calmly and serenely. Had he not recently apostrophized it in these terms:

> Thee, holiest minister of Heaven — thee, envoy,
> usherer, guide at last of all,
> Rich, florid, loosener of the stricture-knot call'd life,
> Sweet, peaceful, welcome Death.[32]

Thus, when the time came, the man adopted the resignation of the poet. He not only accepted death, but he also bore his suffering without complaint. His body, however, had become so thin that he could no longer rest comfortably in any position. (As a last resort, his friends were obliged to put him in a water-bed.)[33] The disease progressed in proportion as his strength declined. He was soon suffering discomfort in his abdomen as well as in his chest, and at the very end he even felt severe pains in one ankle.[34] In addition, a cruel hiccup shook his body.[35] But he never had a complaint or a word of impatience for those who took care of him.[36]

Finally, in March, his long martyrdom came to an end. He died on the twenty-sixth a little before seven in the evening. He remained conscious and lucid to the last.[37]

The next day, the doctors who had cared for him and two professors of the University of Pennsylvania conducted an autopsy of his body. They made some startling discoveries. Whitman's brain during these last months had atrophied and showed symptoms of arteriosclerosis. His lungs had been ravaged by tuberculosis and only about an eighth of the right one was usable for breathing. The intestines and liver had also been attacked by tuberculosis, and tubercular abscesses, invisible from the outside, had formed under the sternum and the fifth rib and in the left foot (which explained the pains in his ankle). One of his suprarenal glands contained a cyst and his kidneys were in very bad condition. The prostate was enlarged and the bladder contained an enormous stone.[38] As Dr. Longaker concluded: "Another would have died much earlier with one-half of the pathological changes which existed in his body." [39] Only his indomitable will had enabled him to live so long in spite of all these maladies. The poet of perfect health had fought off illness and had finally been overcome by a combination of diseases the least of which would have been enough to kill another man.

He was buried on March 30 in Harleigh Cemetery, in Camden, where he had had a simple but imposing granite mausoleum built at great expense.[40] There was no religious service, but his friends had conceived a new kind of ceremony suitable for the founder of a new religion which transcended all others. At the entrance of the cemetery, before a large crowd, Francis Heward Williams read the invocation to death from "When Lilacs Last in the Dooryard Bloom'd" and quotations from Confucius, Buddha, Jesus Christ, the Koran, Isaiah, the Book of Revelation, the Zend-Avesta, and Plato. Then, Thomas B. Harned, Daniel Brinton, Dr. Bucke, and Colonel Ingersoll spoke in turn to praise the memory of the great prophet who had died.[41]

Whitman was dead, but the work in which he had embodied himself continued to live its own independent life. And we shall study it in another volume.

NOTES

ABBREVIATIONS USED IN THE NOTES

AL: *American Literature.*

AM: *Atlantic Monthly.*

CP: *The Complete Prose of Walt Whitman*, edited by Malcolm Cowley, New York: Pellegrini and Cudahy, 1948.

CW: *The Complete Writings of Walt Whitman*, 10 vols., New York: Putnam's Sons, 1902.

FC: *Faint Clews and Indirections*, edited by Clarence Gohdes and Rollo G. Silver, Duke University Press, 1949.

G of the F: *The Gathering of the Forces*, edited by Cleveland Rogers and John Black, 2 vols., New York: Putnam's Sons, 1920.

Imprints: *Leaves of Grass Imprints*, 1860.

Inc. Ed.: *Leaves of Grass,* Inclusive Edition, edited by Emory Holloway, New York: Doubleday, Doran, 1927.

In Re: *In Re Walt Whitman*, Philadelphia: David McKay, 1893.

LG: *Leaves of Grass.*

NB: *November Boughs*, 1888.

N & F: *Notes and Fragments*, edited by R. M. Bucke, London, Ontario, 1899.

N & Q: *Notes and Queries.*

NEQ: *New England Quarterly.*

RAA: *Revue Anglo-Américaine.*

SD: *Specimen Days.*

Sequel: *Sequel to Drum-Taps*, 1865.

SPL: Walt Whitman, *Complete Verse, Selected Prose and Letters*, edited by Emory Holloway, London: The Nonesuch Press, 1938.

Uncoll. PP: *The Uncollected Poetry and Prose of Walt Whitman*, collected and edited by Emory Holloway, 2 vols., 1921.

With WW in C: Horace Traubel, *With Walt Whitman in Camden*, 4 vols.

WWW: *Walt Whitman's Workshop*, edited by C. J. Furness, Harvard University Press, 1928.

NOTES

INTRODUCTION

1. *Figaro Littéraire,* September 9, 1944; reprinted in *Journal des Années Noires,* p. 51.

2. Emory Holloway and Ralph Adimari, *New York Dissected* (New York: R. R. Wilson, 1936), pp. 1–2, or "Whitman and Physique," *CW,* V, 274.

3. It should be said in fairness that the appendix of the Inclusive Edition of Leaves of Grass edited by Emory Holloway (New York: Doubleday, Page, 1927) contains a considerable number of variants collected by Oscar L. Triggs. But, unfortunately, the inventory is incomplete, and it is practically impossible to reconstruct the history of a given poem on the basis of this material.

4. "My book and I — what a period we have presumed to span! those thirty years from 1850 to '80 — and America in them!" "A Backward Glance o'er Travel'd Roads," *Inc. Ed.,* p. 525.

5. *Inc. Ed.,* p. ix, *LG 1892,* p. 2.

6. "An Executor's Diary Note," *Inc. Ed.,* p. 539.

7. Boston *Globe,* August 24, 1881, quoted by Oscar L. Triggs in *Conservator,* VIII (August 1897), 87b, and in "The Growth of Leaves of Grass," *CW,* VII, 119.

8. Interview of Whitman by J. B. S. in New York *World,* May 21, 1876, under the title of "Walt Whitman: The Athletic Bard Paralyzed and in a Rocking-Chair."

9. Letter to an unknown correspondent dated Brooklyn, July 20, 1857, *SPL,* p. 885.

10. *WWW,* p. 135.

11. *Ibid.*

12. See n. 8 above.

13. Preface to 1876 edition, *Inc. Ed.,* pp. 513–514n.

14. Preface to 1872 edition, *Inc. Ed.,* p. 510.

15. *N & F,* p. 55.

16. *WWW,* pp. 9–10.

17. *CW,* X, 101.

18. "Or from That Sea of Time," ll. 8–9, *Inc. Ed.,* p. 486.

19. Preface to 1876 edition, *Inc. Ed.,* p. 518n.

20. *Ibid.,* p. 517n.

21. "A Backward Glance o'er Travel'd Roads," *Inc. Ed.*, p. 531.
22. "A Thought on Shakspere," *NB* (1888), p. 56, *SPL*, p. 824.
23. "Ah Poverties, Wincings, and Sulky Retreats," *Inc. Ed.*, p. 398.
24. *Inc. Ed.*, p. 457.
25. "A Backward Glance o'er Travel'd Roads," *Inc. Ed.*, p. 522. In *SD* he affirms his preference for artists who have lived wildly, who have suffered disasters, but have persevered and always recovered their balance: "And yet there is another shape of personality dearer far to the artist-sense (which likes the play of strongest lights and shades), where the perfect character, the good, the heroic, although never attain'd, is never lost sight of, but through failures, sorrows, temporary downfalls, is return'd to again and again, and while often violated, is passionately adhered to as long as mind, muscles, voice, obey the power we call volition." *SD*, pp. 156–157, *CP*, p. 156.
26. "So Long!" ll. 53–54, *Inc. Ed.*, p. 418.
27. "Song of Myself," §1, l. 1, *Inc. Ed.*, p. 24.
28. "A Backward Glance o'er Travel'd Roads," *Inc. Ed.*, p. 535.
29. Reprinted in "Leaves-Droppings," *LG 1856*, p. 361.
30. *Inc. Ed.*, p. 444.
31. W. B. Yeats, *A Vision* (privately printed by T. Werner Laurie Ltd., 1925), p. 46, or *ibid.* (New York: Macmillan, 1938), pp. 113–114.
32. "Walt Whitman, an American, one of the roughs, a kosmos. . ." *LG 1855*, p. 29, "Song of Myself," §24, l. 1, *Inc. Ed.*, p. 565.
33. Esther Shephard, *Walt Whitman's Pose* (New York: Harcourt, Brace, 1938).
34. Preface to 1856 edition, *Inc. Ed.*, p. 501.
35. J. P. Sartre, *Introduction à Baudelaire — Ecrits Intimes* (Monaco: Editions du Point du Jour).
36. Frédéric Lefèvre, *Entretiens avec Paul Valéry* (Paris: Le Livre, 1926), p. 107.
37. ". . . the vagaries of my life, the many tearing passions of me. . ." "My 71st Year," *Inc. Ed.*, p. 445.
38. He very early felt this soothing influence of artistic creation. He wrote in June 1848: "You may be tired of such outpourings of spleen, but my experience tells me that I shall feel better after writing them. . ." "The Shadow and the Light of a Young Man's Soul," *Union Magazine of Literature and Art*, 11, 280–281. See also *Uncoll. PP*, I, 231.

I. YOUTH — THE UNSUCCESSFUL QUEST

1. *SD*, p. 9, *CP*, pp. 4–5.
2. *Uncoll. PP*, II, 5, 224–227, 300.

3. See "An Incident on Long Island Forty Years Ago," *Uncoll. PP,* I, 149–151.

4. "My old daddy used to say, it's some comfort to a man if he must be an ass anyhow to be his own kind of an ass!" *With WW in C,* II, 41.

5. *SD,* pp. 14–15, *CP,* p. 10.

6. "There Was a Child Went Forth," ll. 24–25, *Inc. Ed.,* p. 307.

7. John Burroughs, *Notes on Walt Whitman as Poet and Person,* quoted in *SD,* p. 12, *CP,* pp. 8–10.

8. *SD,* pp. 12–14, *CP,* pp. 8–10.

9. *Ibid.*

10. "There Was a Child Went Forth," ll. 5–18, *Inc. Ed.,* p. 306.

11. "Out of the Cradle Endlessly Rocking," l. 136, *Inc. Ed.,* p. 214.

12. *Uncoll. PP,* II, 86.

13. *Inc. Ed.,* p. 7.

14. *SD,* p. 16, *CP,* p. 11.

15. See *SD,* pp. 15, 290, *CP,* pp. 10, 297, and above all *With WW in C,* I, 96–97.

16. Many American writers started as printers: Bayard Taylor, W. D. Howells, Mark Twain, Bret Harte, J. C. Harris, Artemus Ward, Edward Eggleston, Ambrose Bierce, Stedman, Gilder, without forgetting Benjamin Franklin.

17. Van Wyck Brooks, *The Times of Melville and Whitman* (New York: E. P. Dutton, 1947), p. 126.

18. See Theodore A. Zunder, "William B. Marsh — The First Editor of the Brooklyn Daily Eagle," *American Book Collector,* IV (August 1933) 93–95. Marsh was in turn a type-setter and an editor before becoming chief editor of the Brooklyn *Eagle.*

19. *SD,* p. 15, *CP,* p. 11.

20. *Uncoll. PP,* II, 86. The date given in *SD,* p. 16, is wrong (*CP,* p. 11).

21. *Uncoll. PP,* II, 126–127.

22. *SD,* p. 16, *CP,* p. 11: "Fond of the theatre, also, in New York, went whenever I could — sometimes witnessing fine performances." See also *SD,* pp. 19–20, or *CP,* pp. 14–15.

23. *Uncoll. PP,* II, 254–255.

24. *Ibid.,* I, 229–234.

25. *Ibid.,* II, 86–87.

26. *Ibid.,* I, 48–51, 164–166; II, 319–320.

27. *CP,* pp. 336–340.

28. See "Education — Schools," etc., *Uncoll. PP,* I, 144–146, an article originally published in the Brooklyn *Eagle,* November 23, 1846.

29. "We consider it a great thing in education that the learner be

taught to rely upon himself. The best teachers do not profess to *form* the mind, but to *direct* it in such a manner and put such tools in its power — that it builds up itself." *Ibid.*, p. 146.

See "Song of Myself," §46, ll. 10-11, 24, *Inc. Ed.*, pp. 70-71:

> "Not I, not any one else can travel that road for you,
> You must travel it for yourself . . .
> I answer that I cannot answer, you must find it out for your-
> self."

30. Whitman had devoted one of his "Sun-Down Papers" to a eulogy of loafing; see *Uncoll. PP*, I, 44–46, an article reprinted from the *Long Island Democrat*, November 28, 1840.

31. *Uncoll. PP*, vol. I, pp. xxxiii–xxxiv, n. 1.

32. *Ibid.*, p. 37 (*Long Island Democrat*, September 29, 1840).

33. "Was at Jamaica and through Queens Co. electioneering in fall of 1840." MS notebook quoted in *Uncoll. PP*, II, 87.

34. See "Report of Walter Whitman's Speech in the Park, in New York City, July 29, 1841," *Uncoll. PP*, I, 51.

35. "This latter I consider one of my best experiences and deepest lessons in human nature behind the scenes and in the masses." *SD*, p. 16, *CP*, p. 11.

36. *Uncoll. PP*, I, 32–51.

37. *Ibid.*, pp. 1–16.

38. See Bliss Perry, *Walt Whitman* (1906), pp. 17–18.

39. Katherine Molinoff, *An Unpublished Whitman Manuscript: The Record Book of the Smithtown Debating Society, 1837–1838* (New York, 1941).

40. Katherine Molinoff, *Some Notes on Whitman's Family* (Brooklyn, privately printed by the author, 1941). See also the review of Frances Winwar's *Walt Whitman and His Times* by Clifton J. Furness in *AL*, XIII (January 1942), 423–432. Furness insists on the more sordid aspects of the Whitman family and quotes unpublished letters by Mrs. Whitman.

See also: "The time of my boyhood was a very restless and unhappy one: I did not know what to do." Grace Gilchrist, "Chats with Walt Whitman," *Temple Bar Magazine*, CXIII, no. 447 (February 1898), 200–212.

41. See *Uncoll. PP*, II, 87: "Went to New York in May 1841 and wrote for *Democratic Review*, worked at printing business in *New World* office. . ."

42. *Ibid.*, pp. 87–88.

43. See *The Gathering of the Forces*, ed. by Cleveland Rodgers and John Black (1920) II, 6.

44. Quoted by Bliss Perry, *Walt Whitman* (1906), pp. 22–23.

45. See Canby, *Walt Whitman* (1945), plate IV.

46. *SD*, pp. 18-19, *CP*, pp. 13-14.

47. *Inc. Ed.*, pp. 386-389.

48. John Burroughs, *Notes on Walt Whitman as Poet and Person*, quoted by Bliss Perry, *Walt Whitman*, p. 39. It has been proved that Whitman wrote himself the first chapters of Burroughs' book; see F. P. Hier, "End of a Literary Mystery," *American Mercury*, I (April 1924), 471-478. One therefore cannot trust the biographical indications which it contains. This passage in particular is as suspicious as Whitman's reply to Symonds which we shall discuss later.

49. For this period see *Uncoll. PP* and *G of the F*.

50. Canby, *Walt Whitman*, pp. 52-56.

51. "Song of Myself," §52, l. 3, *Inc. Ed.*, p. 75.

52. *Uncoll. PP*, I, 123 (Brooklyn *Eagle*, November 5, 1846).

53. "Song of Myself," §32, l. 6, *Inc. Ed.*, p. 50.

54. "A City Fire," Brooklyn *Eagle*, February 24, 1847, *Uncoll. PP*, I, 154-156.

55. "Song of Myself," §33, ll. 139-147, *Inc. Ed.*, pp. 56-57.

56. See n. 54.

57. "Philosophy of Ferries," Brooklyn *Eagle*, August 13, 1847, *Uncoll. PP*, I, 168.

58. "Crossing Brooklyn Ferry," *Inc. Ed.*, pp. 134-139.

59. Quoted by Bliss Perry, *Walt Whitman*, p. 276, n. 1.

60. W. A. Chandos, for instance, in an article entitled, "The Local Press," Brooklyn *Standard*, October 22, 1864, quoted by Holloway in *Uncoll. PP*, vol. I, p. xliii, n. 4.

61. See Emory Holloway's introduction to *I Sit and Look Out*, pp. 3-8.

62. See *G of the F*, vol. I, pp. xxvi-xxxiii.

63. *Ibid.* p. xxxiii.

64. See Whitman's own account of the event in the first number of the Camden N.J., *Courier*, quoted by Bliss Perry, *Walt Whitman*, pp. 41-42.

65. "Excerpts from a Traveller's Note-Book," *Crescent*, March 5, 6, 10, 1848, *Uncoll. PP*, I, 181-186.

66. *Ibid.*, pp. 185-186.

67. *Ibid.*, p. 187.

68. *Ibid.*, p. 185.

69. See "The West," Brooklyn *Eagle*, December 26, 1846, *Uncoll. PP*, I, 151-152.

70. See R. M. Bucke, *N & F*, pp. 41-42.

71. "From the Desk of a Schoolmaster," *Long Island Democrat*, Sept. 29, 1840, *Uncoll. PP*, I, 37.

72. *Crescent*, March 16, 1848, *Uncoll. PP*, I, 202-205.

73. *With WW in C*, II, 283.

74. "The Old Cathedral," *Crescent*, April 22, 1848, *Uncoll. PP*, I, 221–222.

75. For instance: corps de réserve (*ibid.*, p. 200); marchande des (*sic*) fleurs, em (*sic*) bon point, brune, brunette, blonde (p. 203); jolie grisette, tout à fait, nonchalance (p. 204); distingué, coiffeurs (p. 208); ecaille (*sic*) (p. 211); sans culottes (p. 212); sans froid, chaqu'un a son goût, chaqu'un a son gré (*sic*) (p. 215); bijouterie (p. 216).

76. "O Magnet-South," *Inc. Ed.*, pp. 393–394.

77. Henry Bryan Binns, *A Life of Walt Whitman* (London: Methuen, 1905), p. 51.

78. *Uncoll. PP*, vol. I, pp. xlvii–xlviii.

79. *With WW in C*, II, 316, 328, 425, 510–511; III, 80, 119–120, 140, 253, 364.

80. See above, n. 77.

81. Léon Bazalgette, *Walt Whitman, l'homme et son oeuvre* (Paris: Mercure de France, 1908), II, 80–103.

82. *Uncoll. PP*, vol. I, pp. xlii–lii. See also Emory Holloway, "Walt Whitman's Love Affairs," *Dial*, LXIX (November 1920), 473–483.

83. Emory Holloway, *Whitman, an Interpretation in Narrative* (New York: Knopf, 1926), pp. 65–71.

84. *Uncoll. PP*, II, 63–76; for the date of this notebook see p. 63, n. 1.

85. *Uncoll. PP*, II, 77–78.

86. *Ibid.*, p. 78.

87. See his letter to his mother March 28, 1848, quoted by Holloway in *Uncoll. PP*, vol. I, p. xlvi, n. 2.

88. See Canby, *Walt Whitman*, p. 78.

89. Jean Catel, *Walt Whitman* (Paris, 1929), pp. 239–241.

90. "New Orleans in 1848," *NB*, p. 102, *CP*, p. 453.

91. *Uncoll. PP*, II, 77. On Jeff's home-sickness, see n. 3.

92. *Uncoll. PP*, II, 78–79. He went sight-seeing like a tourist: "We went under the Falls, saw the whirlpool, and all the other things, including the suspension bridge" (p. 79).

93. *Uncoll. PP*, vol. I, p. liii, n. 2.

94. Catel, *Walt Whitman*, pp. 293–301.

95. "Song for Certain Congressmen," reprinted in *CP*, pp. 334–335, under the title of "Dough-Face Song."

96. *SPL*, pp. 503–504 and n., p. 1087. Whitman also reprinted this poem in *SD*, pp. 372–373 (*CP*, pp. 389–390), but for some reason or other antedated it.

97. *Uncoll. PP*, I, 27–30.

98. See Brooklyn *Freeman*, September 9, 1848. The *Catalogue of the Trent Collection* contains a facsimile of this particular number.

99. *Uncoll. PP*, vol. I, p. n. 3.

100. See chap. xvii, entitled "Slavery."

101. *SD*, pp. 258–263, *CP*, pp. 264–268.

102. These pages are not dated in *SD*. Most of them were probably written after the Civil War, but some passages — notably the one to which we allude in the next sentence — were composed much earlier. The string of abuse which Whitman fires at the delegates sent to Democratic conventions is already to be found in *The Eighteenth Presidency* which he thought of publishing in 1856 (see Clifton J. Furness, *WWW*, pp. 99–100). Furness felt that some parts of this tract had been written several years before (*ibid.*, p. 227, n. 84). All this accounts for the exceptional virulence and vigor of such passages in *SD*.

103. *SD*, p. 259, *CP*, p. 265.

104. *Selected Poems* (Oxford University Press, 1913), pp. 186–187.

105. On Emerson's attitude during all this period, see Marjory M. Moody, "The Evolution of Emerson as an Abolitionist," *AL*, XVII (March 1945), 1–21. See also his *Journal*, VIII, 185–186.

106. See Thoreau, "Slavery in Massachusetts," in *Works* (Riverside ed., 1894), Vol. X.

107. "The House of Friends," New York *Tribune*, June 14, 1850, *Uncoll. PP*, I, 26, or "Wounded in the House of Friends," *SD*, p. 373, *CP*, pp. 390–391.

108. *Ibid.*

109. "The shriek of a drowned world, the appeal of women . . .
Would touch them never in the heart,
But only in the pocket." ("The House of Friends," *Uncoll. PP*, I, 27.)

110. "Liberty, let others despair of thee,
But I will never despair of thee. . ." "Resurgemus," *Uncoll. PP*, I, 30. The very title of this poem expresses hope.

111. *Uncoll. PP*, I, 234–235.

112. "A Plea for Water," Brooklyn *Advertizer*, May 18–June 6, 1850, *Uncoll. PP*, I, 254–255.

113. See his article in the Brooklyn *Eagle*, reprinted in *G of the F*, II, 52–55.

114. *LG 1855*, p. 47, "Song of Myself," §42, ll. 22–24, *Inc. Ed.*, p. 65. After the Civil War, "wars" replaced "churches" in this list.

115. "Memorial in Behalf of a Freer Municipal Government, and against Sunday Restrictions," Brooklyn *Evening Star*, October 20, 1854, *Uncoll. PP*, I, pp. 259–264. He had already developed some of these ideas, but with less vigor, in the *Eagle* in 1846–47 (*G of the F*, II, 55–72). He took them up again in *LG*; see "To the States" (*Inc.*

Ed., p. 8) and "Poem of Remembrances for a Girl or a Boy of These States" *(ibid.*, pp. 467–468).

116. Brooklyn *Daily Advertizer*, April 3, 1851, *Uncoll. PP*, I, 241–247. He realized himself the importance of this text, for he reprinted a fragment of it in *SD*, p. 372 (*CP*, pp. 388–389).

117. *Uncoll. PP*, I, 241.

118. "Read well the death of Socrates, and of greater than Socrates." *Ibid.*, p. 246.

119. "The beautiful artist principle sanctifies that community which is pervaded by it. A halo surrounds forever that nation." *Ibid.*, p. 244.

120. "'51, '53, occupied in house-building in Brooklyn." *SD*, p. 20, *CP*, p. 15. See also *FC*, p. 49.

In "A Whitman Collector Destroys a Whitman Myth," *Papers of the Bibliographical Society of America*, LII (1958), 73–92, Charles E. Feinberg refutes the assumptions made by the editor of *FC* and very convincingly proves that Whitman was not only a carpenter, but also occasionally a contractor and a businessman. This, however, does not invalidate the testimony of George Whitman and others who saw him work — or play — at carpentering; see below n. 122.

121. O'Connor, "The Carpenter — A Story," *Putnam's Magazine*, I (January 1868), 55–90. In this tale Whitman is identified with Christ, who also worked as a carpenter before he began preaching.

122. *In Re* (Philadelphia: David McKay, 1893), p. 35.

123. Bazalgette, *Walt Whitman*, I, 112.

124. *Uncoll. PP*, I, 83–86.

125. See *The Half-Breed and Other Stories*, ed. by Thomas Ollive Mabbott (Columbia University Press, 1927).

II. THE 1855 EDITION — BIRTH OF A POET

1. Whitman probably borrowed the idea of this binding from a literary friend, Mrs. Sarah Payson Willis Parson, whose *Fern Leaves from Fanny's Portfolio* was first published in 1853 and was reprinted in 1854. This *Fern Leaves* was a duodecimo volume bound in brown or red cloth according to the edition, whereas *Leaves of Grass* was a quarto; but the cover was decorated, front and back, with a tangle of branches and roots, especially on the backstrip, where the letters of the title also had roots and were caught in the roots of a plant which branched out widely over them. Of course, the content of the book was entirely different, consisting of moralizing stories, but Whitman may have been inspired by the title. The resemblance did not escape Mrs. Parson, for she entitled the enthusiastic review of *Leaves of Grass* which she contributed to the New York *Ledger*, May 10, 1856:

"Fresh Fern Leaves: Leaves of Grass." But the borrowing — if it was one — amounted to little more than the word "leaves," which was then fashionable. Clifton J. Furness has found the word in the titles of four books, which appeared between 1852 and 1855. See his introduction to the facsimile edition of the 1855 *Leaves of Grass* (Columbia University Press, 1939).

2. Whitman even helped to set type for the book. According to his own testimony: "I had some friends in the printing business there — the Romes — three or four young fellows, brothers. They had consented to produce the book. I set up some of it myself: some call it my handiwork: it was not strictly that — there were about one hundred pages: out of them I set up ten or so — that was all." *With WW in C*, II, 471.

3. This relative anonymity elicited the following comments from the reviewer in *Putnam's Monthly* (September 1855): "As seems very proper in a book of transcendental poetry, the author withholds his name from the title-page, and presents his portrait, neatly engraved on steel, instead. This, no doubt, is upon the principle that the name is merely accidental: while the portrait affords an idea of the essential being from whom these utterances proceed. We must add, however, that this significant reticence does not prevail throughout the volume, for we learn on page 29, that our poet is 'Walt Whitman, an American, one of the roughs, a kosmos' " (*Leaves-Droppings*, pp. 368-369).

This article had been written by Charles Eliot Norton in 1855; see *A Leaf of Grass from Shady Hill*, with a review of Walt Whitman's *Leaves of Grass*, ed. Kenneth B. Murdock (Harvard University Press, 1928).

4. This portrait was a steel engraving by Samuel Hollyer, after a daguerreotype taken at Brooklyn in July 1854 by Gabriel Harrison; see Introduction to the facsimile edition of the 1855 *Leaves of Grass* by Thomas Bird Mosher, p. 10.

5. "Song of Myself," §2, l. 9, *Inc. Ed.*, p. 40.

6. *Uncoll. PP*, II, 63-76.

7. H. B. Binns, *A Life of Walt Whitman* (London: Methuen, 1905), pp. 51-52.

8. Léon Bazalgette, *Walt Whitman, l'homme et son oeuvre* (Paris: Mercure de France, 1908), I, 81-103.

9. Basil de Selincourt, *Walt Whitman, a Critical Study* (London: Martin Secker, 1914), pp. 18-24.

10. Emory Holloway, *Whitman, an Interpretation in Narrative* (New York: Knopf, 1926), pp. 64-71.

11. *Uncoll. PP*, II, 62-76.

12. In his first book, *Walt Whitman* (Philadelphia: David McKay, 1883), Bucke drew a fairly conventional portrait of the poet. It was

only after Whitman's death that he brought forward the mystical hypothesis in an essay entitled "Walt Whitman and the Cosmic Sense," which appeared in *In Re Walt Whitman* (Philadelphia: David McKay, 1893), pp. 329–347. He developed his theory in *Cosmic Consciousness: A Study in the Evolution of the Human Mind* (Philadelphia: Innes and Sons, 1901).

13. *In Re,* p. 341.

14. *Ibid.,* pp. 341–342.

15. *LG, 1855,* p. 32, *Inc. Ed.,* p. 27, "Song of Myself," §5, ll. 6–14.

16. "Prayer of Columbus," *Inc. Ed.,* pp. 352–354.

17. *Inc. Ed.,* pp. 440–441.

18. *Ibid.,* p. 449.

19. Edward Hungerford, "Walt Whitman and His Chart of Bumps," *AL,* II (January 1931), 350–384. Mark Van Doren accepted his conclusions in "Walt Whitman Stranger," *American Mercury,* XXXV (July 1935), 277–285.

20. L. N. Fowler and his brother O. S. Fowler had a phrenological office in New York (with branches in Boston and Philadelphia), which was also a bookshop and a publishing center for books on phrenology. They themselves had written a whole series of books not only on phrenology, but also on sexual education and eugenics; they were therefore in full sympathy with Whitman on at least these two points.

21. As early as November 16, 1846, he reviewed enthusiastically in the Brooklyn *Eagle* J. G. Spurzheim's *Phrenology or the Doctrine of the Mental Phenomena*. In his papers were found many clippings from the *American Phrenological Journal*; see CW, X, 75, 86, 89, 94, or N & F, pp. 205 (376), 207 (419) & (424), 210 (424). All these clippings are now in the Trent Collection of the Duke University Library (*Catalogue of the Trent Collection*, pp. 66–67).

22. *With WW in C,* II, 385.

23. *Leaves-Droppings,* p. 362.

24. *Ibid.,* p. 362. See also *In Re,* p. 25n.

25. See above, Chapter I, pp. 22–23.

26. Haniel Long, *Walt Whitman and the Springs of Courage* (Santa Fe: Writers' Editions, 1938).

27. In the 1855 Preface, among the qualities which he attributes to the great poet, are to be found precisely some of those which Fowler had detected in him: "Extreme caution or prudence, the soundest organic health, large hope and comparison . . . large alimentiveness and destructiveness and causality." *Inc. Ed.,* p. 501.

28. Quoted by Hungerford, p. 366.

29. Long, pp. 16f.

30. *Leaves-Droppings*, pp. 346–358.

31. Burroughs, pp. 16–17.

32. *SD*, p. 321. This essay had first been published in the *Literary World*, May 22, 1880.

33. *SPL*, pp. 1045–1046.

34. Bazalgette, for instance, who wrote: "L'originalité de son livre est la plus absolue peut-être qui ait été jamais manifestée en littérature." *Walt Whitman, l'homme et son oeuvre*, I, 195. See also O'Connor's introduction to R. M. Bucke's *Walt Whitman*, 1883.

35. See what he replied to Traubel when the latter reproached him with calling Emerson "Master" after having declared in "Poem of You Whoever You Are" (later "To You," *Inc. Ed.*, p. 198, l. 17), "I only am he who places over you no master, owner, better, God, beyond what waits intrinsically in yourself": "They were salad days. I had many undeveloped angles at that time. I don't imagine I was guiltless; someone had to speak for me; no one would; I spoke for myself." Horace Traubel, "Walt Whitman on Himself," *American Mercury*, III (October 1924), 186–192.

36. J. T. Trowbridge, *My Own Story with Recollections of Noted Persons* (Boston: Houghton Mifflin, 1903), pp. 360–401. See also "Reminiscences of Walt Whitman," *Atlantic Monthly*, LXXXIX (February 1902), 163–175.

37. *My Own Story*, p. 363.

38. *G of the F*, II, 270–271.

39. *Catalogue of the Trent Collection*, p. 76.

40. See Catel, *Walt Whitman*, pp. 335–336.

41. *Good-Bye My Fancy* (1891), p. 58, CP, p. 529.

42. *Pictures, an Unpublished Poem of Walt Whitman*, with an introduction by Emory Holloway (New York: June House, 1927), p. 25.

43. See above, n. 32.

44. F. M. Smith, "Whitman's Poet-Prophet and Carlyle's Hero," *PMLA*, LV (1940), 1146–1164, and "Whitman's Debt to Carlyle's Sartor Resartus," *MLQ*, III (March 1942), 51–65.

45. See *G of the F*, II, 290–293, and *Uncoll. PP*, I, 129–130.

46. See *Heroes and Hero-Worship*, Everyman's Library ed., p. 313, and also p. 281.

47. See *Heroes and Hero-Worship*, Lecture II, "The Hero as Prophet. Mahomet: Islam," and Lecture IV, "The Hero as Priest. Luther: Reformation; Knox: Puritanism."

48. Speaking of the birth of the myth of Odin, Carlyle wrote: "Fancy your own generous heart's love of some greatest man expanding till it *transcended* all bounds, till it filled and overflowed the whole field of your thought! Or what if this man Odin — since a great deep

soul, with the *afflatus* and mysterious *tide of vision* and impulse rushing on him he knows not whence, is ever an enigma, a kind of terror and wonder to himself — should have felt that perhaps he was divine; that he was some effluence of the 'Vuotan', Supreme Power and Divinity, of whom to his *rapt vision* all Nature was the awful Flame-image." *Ibid.*, pp. 261–262 (italics supplied to indicate all the words that Whitman took up in "Song of Myself," "By Blue Ontario's Shore," and in his notebooks).

49. *Ibid.*, pp. 316–323.

50. "Novalis beautifully remarks of him, that those great Dramas of his are Products of Nature too, deep as Nature herself. I find a great truth in this saying. Shakespeare's Art is not Artifice. It grows up from the deeps of Nature, through this noble sincere soul, who is a voice of Nature." *Ibid.*, pp. 339–340.

51. "Islam, like any great Faith, and insight into the essence of man, is a perfect equaliser of men. . ." *Ibid.*, p. 307. Cf. "He is the equalizer of his age and land" in the Preface to *LG 1855*, *Inc. Ed.*, p. 291.

52. *Heroes and Hero-Worship*, p. 394.

53. Lecture V.

54. "To which of these Three Religions do you specially adhere? inquires Meister of his Teacher. To all three! answers the other: To all the Three; for they by their union first constitute *the True Religion*." *Ibid.*, p. 277.

55. "To his eyes it is forever clear that this world wholly is miraculous." *Ibid.*, p. 303.

56. Smith points out in particular that the adjective "electric," which Carlyle applies to Blumine's charm, is one of Whitman's favorites.

57. "Whitman's Debt to Sartor Resartus," *MLQ*, III, 65.

58. Esther Shephard, *Walt Whitman's Pose* (New York: Harcourt, Brace, 1936). For a constructive criticism of her thesis, see Henri Roddier, "Pierre Leroux, George Sand et Walt Whitman, ou l'éveil d'un poète," *Revue de Littérature Comparée*, XXXI (January–March 1957), 5–33.

59. Shephard, p. 140.

60. *Ibid.*, p. 280.

61. *Ibid.*, p. 312.

62. *Ibid.*, p. 315.

63. *Ibid.*, p. 283.

64. *Ibid.*, p. 282.

65. *Ibid.*, p. 284.

66. *Ibid.*, p. 313.

67. *Ibid.*, p. 304, and also p. 315.

68. *Inc. Ed.*, pp. 313–316, or Preface to the 1855 edition, pp. 501–502.

69. Shephard, p. 320.

70. *Ibid.*, p. 154.

71. *Inc. Ed.*, p. 501.

72. *Uncoll.* PP, I, 135.

73. See Shephard, pp. 201–210, 420–428.

74. *Inc. Ed.*, pp. 27–28, §5.

75. Shephard, pp. 312–313.

76. Esther Shephard herself (p. 189) is obliged to admit: "Whitman, it may be like many of the rest of us, could not remember where his many seething ideas had originally come from." It is regrettable that she should not have shown the same moderation in the rest of her book.

77. There were times when Whitman judged rather severely George Sand's heroes, as when he wrote to W. S. Kennedy: "J N J [a planter who had called on him and claimed to be a great admirer of *Leaves of Grass*] is certainly crazy — a cross between Zdenko [in *Consuelo*] & something more intellectual and infernal." FC, p. 114.

78. See in particular: "Le moi que Whitman célèbre à chaque page des *Brins d'Herbe* est la projection de l'inconscient." Catel, *Walt Whitman*, p. 400.

79. Allen, pp. 61–62.

80. See above, p. 54.

81. *Uncoll.* PP, II, 63–90.

82. In the *Inc. Ed.* the punctuation of the preface has been simplified and the number of points of suspension cut down to three in all cases.

83. *Inc. Ed.*, pp. 286–299.

84. They have been taken up again only in a short passage in the poem later entitled "Song of Myself" *LG 1855*, p. 29, *Inc. Ed.*, p. 44, in "Suddenly Out of Its Stale and Drowsy Lair" *LG 1855*, pp. 87–88, *Inc. Ed.*, pp. 227–228, under the title of "Europe," in "Clear the Way There Jonathan!" (*LG 1855*, pp. 89–90, *Inc. Ed.*, pp. 225–227, under the title of "A Boston Ballad"), and finally in "Who Learns My Lesson Complete" (*LG 1855*, pp. 92–93, *Inc. Ed.*, pp. 329–330).

85. See above, Chapter I, pp. 40–41.

86. Translators have not always paid attention to this peculiarity. André Gide called *Leaves of Grass* "Brins d'Herbe," as if it had been "Blades of Grass." Only Bazalgette rendered the title correctly.

87. "Spontaneous Me" (1856), *Inc. Ed.*, p. 90, ll. 44–45. The same idea occurs in "Scented Herbage of My Breast" (1860, *Inc. Ed.*, pp. 95–97), and "You Lingering Sparse Leaves of Me" (1887, *Inc. Ed.*, p. 439). The pun is particularly unmistakable in such titles as

"Here the Frailest Leaves of Me" (1860, *Inc. Ed.*, p. 109), "A Leaf of Faces" (thus called in 1860, later entitled "Faces," *Inc. Ed.*, pp. 386–389), "A Leaf for Hand in Hand" (1860, *Inc. Ed.*, p. 110), and "Proto-Leaf" (which was, in 1860, the title of "Starting from Paumanok").

88. See above, p. 280, n. 1.

89. "So Long!" *Inc. Ed.*, p. 418, ll. 53–54.

90. Whitman purposely used the word "leaf" in its botanical sense. See what he said to Traubel; "I am well satisfied with titles — with Leaves of Grass, for instance, though some of my friends themselves rather kicked against it at the start — particularly the literary hair-splitters, who rejected it as a species of folly. 'Leaves of Grass', they said: there are no *leaves* of grass; there are spears. But *Spears* of Grass would not have been the same to me. Etymologically *leaves* is correct — scientific men use it so. I stuck to leaves, leaves, leaves, until it was able to take care of itself. Now it has got well started on its voyage — it will never be displaced." *With WW in C*, I, 186.

91. Whitman may have found the germ of this image in *Heroes and Hero-Worship*: "To us also, through every star, through every blade of grass, is not a God made visible, if we will open our minds and eyes?" (Everyman's Library ed., p. 247). It is known that he had read this book, and had reviewed it briefly in the Brooklyn *Eagle* (October 17, 1846); see *Uncoll. PP*, I, 129.

92. *LG 1855*, p. 24, *Inc. Ed.*, p. 38, §17, l. 5.

93. *LG 1855*, p. 16, *Inc. Ed.*, p. 28, §6, ll. 9–11.

94. *LG 1855*, pp. 16–17, *Inc. Ed.*, pp. 28–29, §6, ll. 13–15, 28.

95. In the introduction to the facsimile edition of the 1855 *Leaves of Grass* (Columbia University Press, 1939), C. J. Furness suggests that Whitman may have used "grass" as printer's slang meaning "a person who does casual work around the shop" or "the work such a person does." But this seems unlikely since he never mentioned the possibility when he discussed the meaning and purpose of his title with Traubel. See also Charles M. Adams, "Whitman's Use of 'Grass,' " *American N & Q*, VI (February 1947), 167–168.

96. "I celebrate myself," *LG 1855*, p. 13, "Song of Myself," *Inc. Ed.*, p. 24, §1, l. 1.

97. *LG 1855*, p. 29, *Inc. Ed.*, "Song of Myself," pp. 43–44, §24, ll. 1–4.

98. *LG 1855*, p. 44, "Song of Myself," *Inc. Ed.*, p. 62, §39, l. 1.

99. *LG 1855*, p. 44, "Song of Myself," *Inc. Ed.*, p. 62, §39, ll. 6–7.

100. *LG 1855*, p. 86, "Song of the Answerer," *Inc. Ed.*, p. 141, §1, ll. 28–29.

101. *LG 1855*, p. 39, "Song of Myself," *Inc. Ed.*, p. 56, §33, ll. 124–135.

102. *LG 1855*, p. 45, "Song of Myself," *Inc. Ed.*, p. 63, §40, ll. 17–18.

103. *LG 1855*, p. 51, "Song of Myself," *Inc. Ed.*, p. 70, §46, ll. 2–3, 6.

104. *LG 1855*, p. 18, *Inc. Ed.*, p. 31, §9.

105. *LG 1855*, p. 18, *Inc. Ed.*, p. 31, §10, ll. 16–18.

106. *LG 1855*, p. 20, *Inc. Ed.*, p. 33, §13, ll. 13–14.

107. *LG 1855*, p. 21, *Inc. Ed.*, p. 34, §14, ll. 11–13.

108. *LG 1855*, pp. 90–91, *Inc. Ed.*, pp. 90–91.

109. *LG 1855*, p. 15, "Song of Myself," *Inc. Ed.*, p. 27, §4, l. 9.

110. "Song of Myself," *Inc. Ed.*, p. 27, §2, l. 16.

111. *Inc. Ed.*, p. 616, in a variant of "Song of the Broad-Axe," dating back to 1856.

112. *LG 1855*, p. 15, "Song of Myself," *Inc. Ed.*, p. 27, §4, l. 15.

113. *LG 1855*, p. 48, *Inc. Ed.*, p. 67, §43, ll. 17–19.

114. *LG 1855*, p. 48, *Inc. Ed.*, p. 67, §43, ll. 22–23.

115. *LG 1855*, p. 39, *Inc. Ed.*, p. 56, §33, l. 136.

116. *LG 1855*, p. 43, *Inc. Ed.*, p. 61, §37, l.9.

117. See for instance *LG 1855*, pp. 32–33, *Inc. Ed.*, pp. 48–49, §28, of "Song of Myself," and *LG 1855*, p. 78, *Inc. Ed.*, "I Sing the Body Electric," p. 80, §2, ll. 5–9, 20.

118. *LG 1855*, p. 15, "Song of Myself," *Inc. Ed.*, p. 27, §4, ll. 10–14.

119. *Uncoll. PP*, II, 88–89.

120. One may even wonder if the following line is not a confession: "If you remember your foolish and outlaw'd deeds, do you think I cannot remember my own foolish and outlaw'd deeds?" *Inc. Ed.*, "A Song for Occupations," p. 179, §1, l. 17.

121. See above, n. 120.

122. See above, Chapter I, pp. 23, 38–39.

123. ". . . talking like a man unaware that there was ever such a production as a book, or such a being as a writer." Review of *Leaves of Grass* published in the *United States Review* and written by Whitman himself. See *Leaves of Grass Imprints* (1860), p. 8.

124. Here is another contradiction: he claimed that the writing of his book had been sheer joy (*N & F*, p. 63, item 37); later he had to admit that the process had been very painful and that he had been torn by doubts. See *ibid.*, p. 62, a passage which he took up in "My Book and I" and in "A Backward Glance."

125. See above, Chapter I, p. 45.

126. See "A Backward Glance," *Inc. Ed.*, pp. 523–524. In one of his early notebooks (1848–49) he was already writing: "True noble expanded American Character is raised on a far more lasting and universal basis than that of any of the characters of the 'gentlemen' of aristocratic life, or of novels, or under the European or Asian forms

of society or government. . . It is to accept nothing except what is equally free and eligible to anybody else. It is to be poor rather than rich." *Uncoll. PP*, II, 63. See the same idea in *LG 1855*, p. 29, "Song of Myself," *Inc. Ed.*, p. 44, §24, l. 11.

127. *Uncoll. PP*, II, 66.

128. *Imprints*, p. 56.

129. *Leaves-Droppings*, pp. 383–384.

130. *Ibid.*, p. 375. Whitman had actually written: "I talk wildly . . . I have lost my wits." *LG 1855*, p. 33, "Song of Myself," *Inc. Ed.*, p. 49, §28, l. 20. He was referring to a state of mystical exaltation, not to a permanent condition.

131. *Ibid.* The passage which the reviewer refers to corresponds to §5 of "I Sing the Body Electric" (*Inc. Ed.*, p. 49).

132. *Leaves-Droppings*, p. 379.

133. *Imprints*, p. 18. The reviewer was William J. Stillman.

134. *Ibid.*, p. 17.

135. *Leaves-Droppings*, pp. 381–383. See also *New York Dissected*, pp. 167–170.

136. *Imprints*, pp. 23–24.

137. *Leaves-Droppings*, pp. 368–369. For some unknown reason, W. S. Kennedy, in *Fight of a Book for the World*, pp. 12–13, classed this review among the hostile articles. But for Whitman's fanatical disciples, anything which was not unqualified praise was an attack. Norton, who was only twenty-eight years old, was already a member of the Harvard faculty. This article shows a remarkable breadth of mind on the part of the future historian and translator of Dante. It is interesting to note that Whitman, who often complained of the narrowness of academic criticism, was thus greeted by a professor at the beginning of his career — without however being aware of it, since the review was anonymous.

138. *Imprints*, pp. 3–4.

139. *Leaves-Droppings*, pp. 366–367.

140. *New York Dissected*, pp. 162–163.

141. *Ibid.*, pp. 166–167.

142. "We give a cordial welcome to *Leaves of Grass*, which we look upon as the most considerable poem that has yet appeared in our country." *Imprints*, p. 51.

143. "No one . . . can read this singular prose-poem without being struck by the writer's wonderful power of description and of word-painting . . ." Quoted by Canby, *Walt Whitman*, p. 124.

144. See *Imprints*, pp. 52–54.

145. *Leaves-Droppings*, p. 374.

146. Brooklyn *Times*, September 29, 1855, *Leaves-Droppings*, pp. 360–363, and *In Re*, pp. 23–26; *American Phrenological Journal*,

October 1855, under the title of "An English and an American Poet" (Whitman compares himself to Tennyson, to the disadvantage of the latter, naturally), *Leaves-Droppings*, pp. 369–375, and *In Re*, pp. 27–32; *United States Review*, September 1855, *In Re*, pp. 13–21.

147. The New York *Daily Times* in particular; see *Imprints*, p. 21. It is remarkable that Whitman should have reprinted this article. He was apparently indifferent to such attacks, probably because he did not feel in the least guilty.

148. "Leigh Hunt criticised his own poems. Spenser criticised himself." *CW*, VI, 119.

149. "Whitman has remarked to us that in a period of misunderstanding and abuse their publication seemed imperative." The editors of *In Re*, p. 13.

150. He once declared to Traubel: "I expected hell: I got it." *With WW in C*, II, 472.

151. "A Visit to Walt Whitman," Brooklyn *Eagle*, July 11, 1886.

152. *With WW in C*, II, 472.

153. See F. O. Matthiessen, *American Renaissance* (Oxford University Press, 1941), p. x.

154. Ralph Adimari, "Leaves of Grass, First Edition," *American Book Collector*, V (May-June 1934), 150–152. See also John T. Winterich, "Romantic Stories of Books — I. Leaves of Grass," *Publishers' Weekly*, CXII (November 1927), 1869–1873.

155. See Carolyn Wells and Alfred F. Goldsmith, *A Concise Bibliography of the Works of Walt Whitman* (Boston: Houghton Mifflin, 1922), pp. 3–5.

156. See Joseph Jay Rubin, "Carlyle on Contemporary Style," *MLN*, LVII (May 1942), 362–363.

157. *LG 1856*, p. 346.

158. *Leaves-Droppings*, p. 345.

159. For instance, in "The American Scholar" (1837), and in his essay on "The Poet" (1844).

160. He thus wrote toward the end of the Preface to the 1855 edition: "The soul of the largest and wealthiest and proudest nation may well go half-way to meet that of its poets. The signs are effectual. There is no fear of mistake . . . The proof of a poet is that his country absorbs him as affectionately as he has absorbed it." *Inc. Ed.*, p. 507.

III. THE 1856 EDITION

1. See *Imprints*, p. 2.

2. Fowler and Wells probably preferred not to have it known that they had published *Leaves of Grass*, since some critics had accused the book of obscenity. They may have been afraid of its effect on the

sale of other books bearing their imprint. But we have definite proof that they were in fact the publishers of the second edition in Whitman's letter of July 22, 1857, to an unknown correspondent, in which he complains of their ill-will — probably because of their prudence and their fear of scandal. See *SPL*, p. 885.

3. It gives a list of their agencies in the United States and abroad.

4. See above, Chapter II, p. 79.

5. Whitman was violently criticized on this count by the *Christian Examiner*; see *Imprints*, p. 7.

6. Especially in the poems now entitled "Song of Myself" and "The Sleepers."

7. This poem had already been published in 1855, but it then celebrated the human body in rather general terms; it was only in 1856 that Whitman added the very frank and bold passage which constitutes §9 of the final version (*Inc. Ed.*, pp. 85–86).

8. *Inc. Ed.*, pp. 88–90.

9. *LG 1856*, p. 356.

10. It was about this time that Whitman wrote the following note, found among his papers after his death: "Make the *Works* — Do not go into criticism or arguments at all. Make full-blooded, rich, flush, natural works. Insert natural things, indestructibles, idioms, characteristics, rivers, states, persons, etc. Be full of *strong sensual germs*" (underlined by Whitman); *CW*, VI, 7, or *N & F*, p. 57 (16). The editor, R. M. Bucke, thought that this fragment dated back to 1856.

11. See *LG 1855*, pp. 51–52, "Song of Myself," *Inc. Ed.*, pp. 70–71, §46. The theme was not new even in 1855; it was already to be found in an 1847–48 notebook (*Uncoll. PP*, II, 66–67); but the image was still very close to the banal comparison of life with a road.

12. *LG 1856*, pp. 223–239, *Inc. Ed.*, pp. 124–133.

13. *LG 1856*, pp. 124–133, *Inc. Ed.*, pp. 223–239.

14. For instance, pp. 21–24 and 35–40 in *LG 1855*, *Inc. Ed.*, "Song of Myself," pp. 34–37, §15, and pp. 51–57, §33.

15. *Leaves-Droppings*, pp. 345–346. Whitman had published this letter on October 10, 1855, in the New York *Tribune*, at the request of the editor, Charles A. Dana, who was a friend of his. He then pasted clippings from this into some of the review copies of the first edition. He also had it reprinted, and he included it as an appendix to the 1855 volume, specifying, however, that this was "Copy for the convenience of private reading only." For the publication of this letter had been violently criticized. He had in fact been guilty of discourtesy. The letter was strictly personal, and ought not to have been published without the consent of its author, who would probably have expressed himself somewhat differently if he had been writing for publication (see Bliss Perry, *Walt Whitman*, 1906, pp. 114–115).

However, Emerson, although he was sometimes taken to task for having so rashly approved such a daring book (in particular in the New York *Criterion*; see *Imprints*, pp. 55–56), never reproached Whitman for his use of the letter, and did not even speak of it when Whitman called on him a year later. Therefore, Whitman probably felt justified in publishing it as an appendix to his second edition. Moreover, he apparently found convincing arguments to justify this move. Thoreau, after his first meeting with Whitman, wrote to his friend Harrison Blake: "In his apologizing account of the matter, he made the printing of Emerson's letter seem a little thing — and to some extent throws the burden of it — if there is any, on the writer." Curiously, this sentence does not appear in the edition of Thoreau's *Letters* edited by Emerson (Thoreau, *Letters to Various Correspondents* [Boston, 1865], p. 142); it is given in Viola C. White, "Thoreau's Opinion of Whitman," *NEQ*, VIII (June 1935) 262–264.

The reviewer for the New York *Times*, otherwise favorable to Whitman, attacked him sharply for using Emerson's letter in his 1856 edition, because, he said, its praise was intended for the twelve original poems only; see *Imprints*, p. 26.

16. *LG 1856*, p. 346.

17. These poems were: "Poem of Many in One" (later "By Blue Ontario's Shore"), "Poem of the Last Explanation of Prudence" (later "Song of Prudence"), "Liberty Poem for Asia" (later "To a Foil'd Revolutionaire"), and "Poem of the Singers of the Words of Poems" (later the second part of "Song of the Answerer"). See Willie T. Weathers, "Whitman's Poetic Translations of His 1855 Preface," *AL*, XIX (March 1947), 21–40.

18. Later called "By Blue Ontario's Shore."

19. *LG 1860*, pp. 108–125.

20. A verse of the 1860 version shows the strange interconnection of the two themes: "The Many in One — what is it finally except myself?" *LG 1860*, p. 125, *Inc. Ed.*, p. 665.

21. "Whitman, the Poet," *New Republic*, October 20, 1947, p. 27.

22. See above, p. 290, n. 14.

23. *LG 1856*, p. 316, *Inc. Ed.*, p. 469.

24. *LG 1855*, pp. 89–90, *Inc. Ed.*, p. 225.

25. "Let us all, without missing one, be exposed in public, naked, monthly. . ." *LG 1856*, p. 319, *Inc. Ed.*, "Respondez," p. 471, l. 39.

26. "Let there be no God!" *LG 1856*, p. 319, *Inc. Ed.*, "Respondez," p. 471, l. 42.

27. *LG 1856*, p. 319, *Inc. Ed.*, "Respondez," p. 471, ll. 41–43.

28. *LG 1856*, pp. 318, 320, *Inc. Ed.*, "Respondez," p. 471, l. 28, and 472, l. 53.

29. *LG 1856*, pp. 321, 317, *Inc. Ed.*, p. 472, ll. 65–66, and p. 470, l. 22.

30. *LG 1856*, p. 317, *Inc. Ed.*, p. 470, ll. 13–14, 23, 26.

31. *LG 1856*, p. 321, *Inc. Ed.*, p. 472, ll. 59–62, 64.

32. *LG 1856*, pp. 317–320, *Inc. Ed.*, p. 470, l. 21, p. 471, l. 27, and p. 472, l. 50.

33. *LG 1856*, pp. 319, 321, *Inc. Ed.*, p. 471, l. 39, and p. 472, l. 63.

34. *LG 1856*, p. 255, *Inc. Ed.*, "Excelsior," p. 397, l. 4.

35. *LG 1856*, "Sun-Down Poem," pp. 216–217, *Inc. Ed.*, "Crossing Brooklyn Ferry," pp. 136–137, §6, ll. 1–12. It is to be noted that in 1860 he canceled the phrase "a solitary committer." He probably thought that it was too disquieting, and he now preferred to be considered merely as a "solitary singer."

36. *Imprints*, p. 27.

37. *Ibid.*, pp. 6–7.

38. *Ibid.*, p. 27.

39. See *I Sit and Look Out*, pp. 186–187.

40. This volume was entitled *Abbie Nott and Other Knots* (Philadelphia: Lippincott, 1856), and was the work of a mysterious "Katinka" whose identity was never established. The quoted lines came from "Song of Myself" (*Inc. Ed.*, p. 40, §20, ll. 22–24). They were taken from the 1855 edition since *Abbie Nott* appeared before the 1856 volume.

This curious book presents a problem. Some scholars have wondered whether it might have been by Whitman himself. (See John T. Winterich, "Good Secondhand Condition," *Publishers' Weekly*, March 1928, pp. 1309–1310, and Carolyn Wells, "On Collecting Whitman," *Colophon*, vol. I, no. 4, 1940.) But the problem seems insoluble. The copyright was granted under the name of Katinka (Eastern District of Pennsylvania, April 5, 1856, no. 148), and the publishers cannot give any further information, part of their record having been destroyed by a fire in 1898. One theory is that the author was Mrs. Catherine Brooks Yale (1818–1900), the wife of Linus Yale, inventor of the Yale lock. She was a writer in her spare time, publishing among other things *Nim and Cum and the Wonderland Stories* (Chicago, 1895), but there is no real evidence for this hypothesis and no close parallel between the known works of Mrs. Yale and Katinka. On the other hand, the resemblances between Katinka and Whitman are rather striking. The stories recall those which Whitman had written earlier and the sketches closely resemble descriptions in some of his articles. The same Quaker influences appear. There is frequent mention of "the inner natural light." Like Whitman, Katinka was much concerned with the problem of evil. Like him she advocated feminism (pp. 108, 216, etc.) and believed in the value of hydrotherapy (p. 96); she also describes a trip down the Mississippi (pp. 131–133), and in a chapter devoted to childhood memories she portrays an ideal mother who might have been Whitman's own (pp. 290–293). She even speaks of a poem in regular verse as a "rhythmical jingle" (p. 112). Finally, Cunningham, with whom Abbie Nott falls in love, shows a remarkable resemblance to Whitman, at least to Whitman as he would have liked to be: "He followed this interior conviction, laid aside his books and commenced his uncertain travels, following only the attraction of magnetism. Wherever he went, he scattered his rich intellectual wealth in the form of lectures and conversations." It is also remarkable that one of the terms most often used by Katinka is "magnetism" or "magnetic," which is also one of Whitman's favorites. All these are disquieting coincidences, but without further evidence, they remain inconclusive.

41. "Poem of Many in One," *LG 1856*, p. 196, *Inc. Ed.*, "By Blue Ontario's Shore," p. 296, §14, l. 16.

42. "Poem of the Sayers of the Words of the Earth," *LG 1856*, p. 331, *Inc. Ed.*, "A Song of the Rolling Earth," pp. 190–191, §4, ll. 6, 8–12.

43. See above, Chapter III, no. 2.

44. Among his papers is an article on "Egotism" clipped from *Graham's Magazine* (XXVII [March 1845] 97–103; see *Catalogue of the Trent Collection*, p. 69), in which he had underlined in pencil the following passage on Wordsworth: "His poems originally were unpopular, the principles of taste on which they are written were misrepresented and ridiculed, their faults were magnified and their merits underrated with a dishonesty almost unprecedented in the history of criticism." And further on: "A more humble spirit would have been crushed by the opposition he received and ceased to write with the condemnation of the *Lyrical Ballads*." At the bottom of this page, he wrote in ink: "See above and Beware!" which shows that he was thinking of himself. Several other passages are also underlined, including this one, two pages further on: "A great author, hated, reviled, persecuted, starved, in his own age, is almost sure of deification in the next."

It is impossible to know exactly when he read and annotated this article, but it may have been long after the date of publication, when he was beginning to work on *Leaves of Grass,* or even after he had published one or more editions.

The case of Wordsworth seems to have interested him very much, for the Berg Collection of the New York Public Library has another article on Wordsworth from an unidentified periodical, a review of Christopher Wordsworth's *Memoirs of William Wordsworth,* and of a Boston edition of Wordsworth's poems dated 1851. Whitman here also underlined several passages which he must have found encouraging; these in particular: ". . . we are always ready to ask help of him whose vision is clearer than our own. We welcome therefore the true seer [see 1855 preface, Inc. Ed., p. 492]. He is eyes for the world; he is the true keeper of keepers. . . An age of imitation never recognizes the inspired teacher who is true to his own nature. . . Happy the age in which a strong devout soul converses with the Spirit of the Universe in the hearing of men!"

Thus Wordsworth must have exerted a certain influence on Whitman, not so much through his work, which the American poet hardly knew and did not like (in the margin of the same article, next to the sentence, "Wordsworth is not equal in imagination to the greatest poets," he wrote in pencil this indignant exclamation: "Well, I should say not!"), as by his example and personality, in so far as Whitman was able to understand it through the medium of magazine articles. (See Roger Asselineau, "Whitman et Wordsworth. Etude d'une influence indirecte," Revue de Littérature Comparée, XXIX [October-December 1955], 505–512). With Whitman we must recognize in addition to the direct literary influences on his work other influences, more diffuse, but also derived from literature, which affected the development of his personality.

IV. NEW UNCERTAINTIES

1. The Journals of Bronson Alcott, ed. Odell Shepard (Boston: Little, Brown, 1938), pp. 289–290, entry for November 10, 1856.

2. See above, Chapter I, n. 40.

3. His friendship for the Broadway omnibus drivers soon became legendary. It began during his early years in New York but after Leaves of Grass had given him a certain notoriety the newspapers took it up. For example, the New York Tribune remarked in 1859: "The Boston Courier thinks it very likely that the poet Walt Whitman, as is reported, now drives a Broadway omnibus and says:

'Whitman's extraordinary abilities have always been fettered by an unconquerable laziness. The last time we saw him his dress was wonderful beyond description; high heavy boots, tight trousers, an unprecedented rough jacket, and a tapering tower of a hat. It was said last winter that he was getting up a series of lectures, but it seems that his natural indolence has conquered his poetic inspiration.' " New York Tribune, 1859, quoted in Imprints, p. 64.

A few days later the New York Constellation replied: "An omnibus driver or not? — A leading journal in this city has recently been duped by a communication or a statement manufactured in its own office into saying that Walt Whitman, the writer of Leaves of Grass, one of the most remarkable and original contributors to our literature for many years, was driving an omnibus. Now whether he has ever done so or not, we neither know nor care; but certain are we that he is not, at present, doing so, as we have repeatedly seen and conversed with him in the course of the present month. And we regard the attempt to stain the supposititious act with a ludicrous celebrity, as having been made in the worst of tastes." Quoted in *Imprints*, p. 64.

The somewhat extravagant tone of this reply would seem to indicate that the correction came from Whitman himself, and it is possible that the communication which had led the New York *Tribune* into its error was also his work. It is fairly probable that this series of articles constituted a small advertising campaign which he had engineered to attract public attention. This would have been entirely consistent with his usual practice.

4. See above, Chapter I.

5. At one time he was so short of money that he had to borrow two hundred dollars from his friend James Parton, the husband of Fanny Fern, and it seems that he had great difficulty in repaying it two months later, partly in cash, partly in kind. Parton may even have had to institute proceedings. At any rate, the two friends quarreled after this incident. Whitman was later accused by his enemies of never having paid this debt, and he thought it necessary to justify himself to posterity by explaining the whole affair to Horace Traubel (see *With WW in C*, III, 235–239).

Some of the details of this rather confused story can be found in *New York Dissected*, pp. 152–153, n, 20, p. 239; *I Sit and Look Out*, p. 211, n. 6; O. S. Coad, "Whitman vs. Parton," *Rutgers University Library Journal*, December 1940, pp. 1–8.

Coad, who was able to consult the letters of Kennedy, Harned, Traubel, and Ethel Parton (a niece of Parton's) now in the Rutgers University Library, believes that Whitman completed the payment of his debt in June 1857. Bliss Perry, however, apparently on hearsay evidence, at one time accused Whitman of having dissipated the fortune which a young man of letters, Parton, had imprudently lent him (see his *Walt Whitman*, pp. 123–124). Traubel protested violently against this unwarranted accusation ("Questions for Bliss Perry," *Conservator*, November 1906, pp. 137–138) and Bliss Perry was obliged to make a partial retractation in the appendix of the second edition. Whitman's version of the affair is very clearly given in a letter to O'Connor dated September 28, 1869 (see *SPL*, pp. 986–987).

6. In this respect he merely followed the example of Emerson, Thackeray, Dickens, Philips, and Curtis. The American public was always eager to listen to lectures. On the importance of the oratorical

tradition in the United States, see F. O. Matthiessen, *American Renaissance*, pp. 18–23.

7. *LG 1856*, p. 346.

8. *N & F*, p. 57, or *CW*, VI, 7–8. This manuscript note is dated April 24, 1857.

9. See above, Chapter I.

10. See above, Chapter I.

11. *In Re*, p. 19.

12. *In Re*, p. 35.

13. Part of this material was published by C. J. Furness in his *WWW*, pp. 33–68. See also T. B. Harned, "Walt Whitman and Oratory," *CW*, VIII, 244 ff. *New York Dissected* contains an article by Whitman (pp. 179–181) in which, after criticizing the lecturers he had heard in Brooklyn in the course of the year, he tried to define what the ideal lecturer should be. In 1851 he had himself lectured before the Brooklyn Art Union (see Brooklyn *Daily Advertizer*, April 3, 1851, *Uncoll. PP*, I, 241–247, and Bliss Perry, *Walt Whitman*, pp. 49–55).

14. See *WWW*, pp. 39–60.

15. *WWW*, pp. 66–67.

16. *WWW*, pp. 197–198, n. 31. The MS, now in the Trent Collection (see *Catalogue of the Trent Collection*, p. 58), bears the date of 1858.

As Furness remarks, the two media of expression were so closely associated in his mind that the notes which he collected were used indiscriminately for his projected lectures or for his poems. On one of the scraps of paper which he used for his rough drafts he first wrote the title "Poem-Religious" and then added: "or in lecture on Religion." Sometimes the process was reversed; materials intended for a lecture were later incorporated into a poem, as in the case of these two lines of "Starting from Paumanok" (*Inc. Ed.*, p. 16, §7, ll. 18–19):

"Nor character nor life worth the name without religion,
Nor land, nor man, nor woman, without religion."

Whitman had first written over these two lines "Lecture"; nevertheless he used them in the poem without any alteration.

17. *WWW*, p. 198, n. 31.

18. Often, moreover, in his notes, side by side with the word "lecture," he used the word "lesson." For him it was less a matter of lectures in the ordinary sense than of lay sermons. He wanted to preach above all. See *WWW*, p. 32.

19. Maurice Bucke discerned the same evolution; see *N & F*, p. vi.

20. *WWW*, p. 197, n. 31. His reason for wanting so much to

publish the text of his lectures was not merely his desire to make money; he believed profoundly in the superiority of writing over speech. In an article from the *Edinburgh Review* (Am. Ed., LXXXIX [April 1949] 149–168, see *Catalogue of the Trent Collection*, p. 80), entitled "The Vanity and Glory of Literature," he underlined the following passage: "Great as has been the influence of Socrates, he owes it almost entirely to the books he refused to write, and it might have been greater still, had he condescended to write some of his own." The article bears the date 1856 in Whitman's hand. Therefore he must have read it precisely at the time with which we are concerned. Though it may seem curious, it is possible that he may have been thinking of becoming an orator mainly for reasons of health. He had clipped and carefully preserved an article from the *American Phrenological Journal*, which contains the following statement: "This constant excitability of men of letters not unfrequently leads to inflammation, and sometimes to a softening of the brain. Dean Swift and Daniel Webster, both of whom possessed great intellects and thought profoundly, died of this affection. . . Yet, notwithstanding these evils incident to a literary life, its average duration is of a respectable length and frequently extends to great age. This was particularly the case among ancient philosophers, who alternated their time between abstruse studies in the closet and conversations and speeches in the midst of their fellow-citizens in the open air and public buildings in which they were wont to assemble. Plato died at 81, Xenocrates at 82, Thales at 89 and Democritus at 100" (*Catalogue of the Trent Collection*, pp. 66–67).

These newspaper clippings and magazine articles which Whitman so carefully annotated and underlined have not yet received the attention they deserve. A very large number have survived to give precise evidence regarding Whitman's habitual concerns and his opinions about certain literary and philosophical problems. This source of information is particularly important because Whitman read a great many periodicals and very few books, especially after 1848.

21. There are many allusions to this profession in the 1860 edition. Whitman mentions the power of the orator over crowds several times, as for example in "Poem of Joys," p. 268, §39. But in the edition of 1871 this passage has disappeared. Elsewhere ("Leaves of Grass," no. 16, pp. 189–190, later entitled "Mediums," *Inc. Ed.*, p. 399), he regards orators as mediums, as spokesmen for God. He speaks also of his intention to travel throughout the United States giving lectures or speeches ("Leaves of Grass," no. 17, pp. 190–191, later entitled "On Journeys through the States," *Inc. Ed.*, p. 8), a dream which he never gave up; in the definitive edition, the poem which expresses it is placed in the "Inscriptions," with which the

book begins, as if to give it more weight. But his finest hymn to the glory of orators was "Leaves of Grass," no. 12, pp. 183–185, later entitled "Vocalism" (*Inc. Ed.*, pp. 321–322, and variant readings, pp. 674–675).

22. *I Sit and Look Out*, p. 17.

23. He had previously resumed his journalistic activities in 1856 by contributing from time to time to *Life Illustrated*, a Fowler and Wells publication. He had in particular written a series of articles under the title of "New York Dissected," which have been collected by Emory Holloway and Ralph Adimari in *New York Dissected* (New York: R. R. Wilson, 1938). A chronological list of these articles may be found in *Catalogue of the Trent Collection*, pp. 101–102.

24. See Canby, *Walt Whitman*, Plates VI, VII, VIII. See also the description by Frederick Huene, a young German poet who came to America after the Revolution of 1848 and worked as a typographer on the Brooklyn *Times* in *I Sit and Look Out*, p. 12.

25. See *I Sit and Look Out*, p. 17. But he was only an occasional contributor.

26. The paper, however, had campaigned for Frémont, the Republican candidate in 1856, but this, as we shall see, could only please Whitman.

27. *I Sit and Look Out*, pp. 59–60.

28. *Ibid.*, pp. 47–49.

29. *Ibid.*, pp. 54–55.

30. "A Dialogue," *Democratic Review*, XVII (November 1845), 360–364, *Uncoll.* PP, I, 97–103; "Hurrah for Hanging," Brooklyn *Eagle*, March 23, 1846, *Uncoll.* PP, I, 108–110.

31. "Capital Punishment," Brooklyn *Times*, May 22, 1858, *Uncoll.* PP, II, 15–16; "The Death-Penalty," January 13, 1858, *I Sit and Look Out*, pp. 46–47.

32. "The Radicals in Council," June 29, 1858, *I Sit and Look Out*, pp. 45–46.

33. "The Temperance Movement," March 10, 1858, *ibid.*, p. 49.

34. "A Delicate Subject," June 20, 1859, *ibid.*, pp. 119–120.

35. "Reformers," *ibid.*, pp. 44–45.

36. "Our Pecuniary Difficulties," October 5, 1857, *ibid.*, pp. 169–170.

37. "We progress!" November 7, 1857, *ibid.*, p. 43.

38. See his contributions to the Brooklyn *Eagle* collected in *G of the F*, I, 240–266.

39. "The Spanish American Republics," September 10, 1858, *ibid.*, pp. 162–163.

40. Jean Catel first published it in pamphlet form: *The Eighteenth*

Presidency (Montpellier: Causse, Graille et Castelnau, 1928). C. J. Furness published a slightly different version in *WWW*, pp. 87–113. The best edition is that of Edward F. Grier, *The Eighteenth Presidency* (University of Kansas Press, 1956).

41. *WWW*, p. 92.
42. *WWW*, p. 93.
43. *WWW*, p. 95.
44. *WWW*, pp. 99–100.
45. *WWW*, p. 100.
46. *WWW*, p. 109.
47. *WWW*, p. 110.
48. *WWW*, pp. 112–113.
49. *WWW*, pp. 111–112.

50. *Inc. Ed.*, p. 236. This poem was written in 1857, probably shortly after the election of Buchanan. Whitman himself wrote this date in the copy of the 1860 edition that he used to prepare the next edition. This so-called "blue-copy" is now in the Lion Collection in the New York Public Library.

51. *Inc. Ed.*, p. 236.

52. *N & F*, p. 57 (14).

53. *SPL*, p. 885. See also Rollo G. Silver, "Seven Letters of Walt Whitman," *AL*, *VII* (March 1935), 78.

54. Yet there is one between an article published on September 30, 1857, "The Cure" (*I Sit and Look Out*, pp. 42–43), and several poems of the 1860 edition: "You Felons on Trial in Courts" (*Inc. Ed.*, p. 323), "To a Pupil" (*Inc. Ed.*, p. 327), and "Of the Visage of Things" (*Inc. Ed.*, p. 480).

55. Whitman himself wrote this article, which he probably intended to publish in a friendly periodical. The MS is now in the Yale University Library. See Canby, *Walt Whitman*, pp. 135–136.

56. Thanks to Clapp's friendship, Whitman published in the *Saturday Press* first "A Child's Reminiscence" (later "Out of the Cradle. . .") on December 24, 1859, and on January 7, 1860, an anonymous article entitled "All about a Mocking-Bird," which was a reply to an attack of the Cincinnati *Commercial* of December 28, 1859 (reprinted in *Imprints*, pp. 57–59). In this article he triumphantly announced the approaching publication of the third edition of *Leaves of Grass*. On May 19, 1860, the *Press* published a very favorable review of his book — which he had written himself. See T. O. Mabbott and Rollo G. Silver, *"A Child's Reminiscence by Walt Whitman"* (University of Washington Bookstore, 1930).

57. On Whitman and the New York Bohemia, see Van Wyck Brooks, *The Times of Melville and Whitman* (New York: Dutton,

1947), pp. 192–216; W. S. Kennedy, "Notes on the Pfaffians," *Conservator*, March 1897; Charles I. Glicksberg, "Walt Whitman and Bayard Taylor," *N & Q, CLXXIII* (July 3, 1937), 5–7.

58. W. D. Howells, *Literary Friends and Acquaintances*, 1900, p. 74.

59. *Uncoll. PP*, II, 93.

60. *With WW in C*, I, 417.

61. *Uncoll. PP*, II, 91. This notebook dates back to 1859. This fragment has been used partly in "That Shadow My Likeness," *Inc. Ed.*, p. 112. (*LG 1860*, "Calamus" no. 40, p. 376). The same idea is to be found in "Song of Myself," *Inc. Ed.*, p. 27, §4, ll, 10–14.

62. See introduction to *I Sit and Look Out*, pp. 13–17.

63. *I Sit and Look Out*, pp. 119–120.

64. *Ibid.*, pp. 120–122.

65. *Uncoll. PP*, II, 91, n. 1.

66. *Ibid.*; Holloway, *Whitman*, p. 164, and *I Sit and Look Out*, p. 16.

67. Canby, *Walt Whitman*, p. 130.

68. *SD*, p. 20, *CP*, pp. 15–16. There is nothing on the years between 1857 and 1860.

69. *Uncoll. PP*, II, 91.

70. He may have been for some time ready to defy public opinion; see his article in the Brooklyn *Times* on February 4, 1858 (*I Sit and Look Out*, p. 172).

71. The poem which best expresses this obsession is "To You" (*LG 1860*, p. 403, *Inc. Ed.*, p. 479) which was also suppressed in 1867. Other characteristic poems are: "A Glimpse" (*LG 1860*, "Calamus" no. 29, p. 371, *Inc. Ed.*, p. 109), "Among the Multitude" (*LG 1860*, "Calamus" no. 41, p. 376, *Inc. Ed.*, p. 112). In the "Poem of Joys" (*LG 1860*, p. 261, §§13–14, *Inc. Ed.*, "A Song of Joys," p. 610, in the variant readings) there is a discreet allusion to his secret desires: "O the young man as I pass! O I am sick after the friendship of him who, I fear, is indifferent to me. . . The memory of one only look — the boy lingering and waiting." This revealing passage was suppressed in 1881.

72. The date 1858–59 which we suggest is based on no document; it is however extremely probable, for if we may believe "Long I Thought that Knowledge. . ." (*Inc. Ed.*, pp. 477–478), the sentimental crisis was posterior to the political crisis. The latter, as we have seen, occurred in 1856–57. Fredson Bowers, after a careful study of Whitman's MSS, has reached exactly the same conclusion; see *Whitman's Manuscripts — Leaves of Grass 1860* (University of Chicago Press, 1955), pp. xli–l, and Fredson Bowers, *Textual and Literary Criticism* (Cambridge University Press, 1959), pp. 35–65.

73. *LG 1860*, "Calamus" no. 8, pp. 354–355, *Inc. Ed.*, "Long I Thought that Knowledge," pp. 477–478, ll. 5–12.

74. *LG 1860*, "Calamus" no. 26, p. 369, *Inc. Ed.*, p. 108.

75. *LG 1860*, "Calamus" no. 9, pp. 355–356, *Inc. Ed.*, pp. 478–479.

76. *LG 1860*, pp. 269–277, *Inc. Ed.*, p. 210 ("Out of the Cradle Endlessly Rocking").

77. *LG 1860*, p. 276 (30), *Inc. Ed.*, p. 637, variant reading of l. 150.

78. G. W. Allen, *Walt Whitman Handbook*, pp. 143–144.

79. *Inc. Ed.*, p. 212, l. 74, p. 213, ll. 111–112, 115.

80. *Inc. Ed.*, p. 638, variant reading of ll. 158ff. The passage was canceled in 1881. It was quite out of place since it expressed the despair of Whitman in 1858–59 rather than the feelings of the child.

81. *LG 1860*, pp. 195–199, *Inc. Ed.*, pp. 216–218.

82. *LG 1860*, pp. 410–411, *Inc. Ed.*, p. 377, under the title of "Thought," ll. 9–10. See also "Yet, yet, Ye Downcast Hours," *Inc. Ed.*, p. 372, l. 4 (*LG 1860*, p. 422).

83. *LG 1860*, "Calamus" no. 17, pp. 362–363, *Inc. Ed.*, p. 372. In his various editions of *Leaves of Grass*, Emory Holloway erroneously gives 1871 as the first publication date of this poem. See my article, "A propos de Walt Whitman," *Langues Modernes*, 42ème Année, no. 4, p. 65 (August–October, 1948).

84. *LG 1860*, p. 425, *Inc. Ed.*, p. 373 ("As if a Phantom Caress'd Me").

85. *LG 1860*, "So Long!" p. 464 (15), and 456 (23), *Inc. Ed.*, p. 417, l. 33, pp. 418–419, ll. 64–71, and variant readings, p. 704.

86. *LG 1860*, p. 423, *Inc. Ed.*, p. 482.

87. *LG 1855*, p. 55, *Inc. Ed.*, p. 75, "Song of Myself," §50, l. 10.

88. "A Word out of the Sea," *LG 1860*, p. 276 (31), *Inc. Ed.*, p. 638, "Out of the Cradle Endlessly Rocking," variant reading of ll. 158f.

89. *Walt Whitman*, trans. Evie Allison Allen, with an introduction by Gay W. Allen (New York: Columbia University Press, 1951), pp. 160–179.

90. *Ibid.*, p. 143. Schyberg believes that his period of dissipation ended on April 16, 1861, on which day Whitman recorded the following resolution in one of his notebooks: "Thursday, April 16, 1861, I have this hour, this day resolved to inaugurate a sweet, clean-blooded body by ignoring all drinks but water and pure milk — and all fat meats, late suppers — a great body — a purged, cleansed, spiritualized invigorated body."

However, Schyberg's thesis is greatly weakened by the fact that these dietary rules do not imply that Whitman had previously led a life of debauchery. There are several other similar resolutions in his notebooks, some of which are even more disquieting than this one, notably that which he took on July 15, 1868 or 1869 (*Uncoll. PP*, II, 95).

91. See C. J. Furness, "Walt Whitman Looks at Boston," *NEQ*, July 1928, pp. 353, 370. See also *SD*, p. 183, W. S. Kennedy, *The Fight of a Book for the World*, p. 15, and J. T. Trowbridge, "Reminiscences of Walt Whitman," *Atlantic Monthly*, LXXXIX (February 1902), 163–175.

92. See above, n. 85.

v. THE 1860 EDITION

1. As this passage in *Fourteen Thousand Miles Afoot* (New York, 1859) shows: "Nothing can more clearly demonstrate the innate vulgarity of our American people, their radical immodesty, their internal licentiousness, their unchastity of heart, their foulness of feeling, than the tabooing of Walt Whitman's *Leaves of Grass*. It is quite impossible to find a publisher for the new edition which has long since been ready for the press." (Quoted in *Imprints*, pp. 51–52.)

2. See Chapter IV, n. 56.

3. According to Kennedy, it was Col. Richard J. Hinton who gave Thayer and Eldridge the idea of publishing *Leaves of Grass* (*The Fight of a Book for the World*, p. 242).

4. See C. J. Furness, "Walt Whitman Looks at Boston," *NEQ*, I, (July 1928), 353–370.

5. See *NB*, pp. 47–49, *CP*, pp. 399–401.

6. Frank Sanborn himself recalled the incident in a letter to the Springfield *Republican* (April 19, 1876). See Furness, "Walt Whitman Looks at Boston," *NEQ*, I (July 1928), and Holloway, *Whitman*, pp. 164–165.

7. *Atlantic Monthly*, April 1860.

8. "Reminiscences of Walt Whitman," *ibid.*, LXXXIX, 163–175, later reprinted in *My Own Story* (Boston: Houghton Mifflin, 1903), pp. 360–401.

9. After the failure of Thayer and Eldridge in 1861, the plates were bought by an unscrupulous publisher, Richard Worthington, who later printed thousands of fake copies of the third edition (10,000 according to Kennedy). The copies of this spurious edition can easily be distinguished from the genuine ones by their coarser binding and the absence on p. 2 of the indication: "Electrotyped at the Boston Stereotype Foundry," the mention of which would have enabled Whitman to take legal action against Worthington. See *With WW in C*, I, 195–196, 250–251, 255–256; W. S. Kennedy, *The Fight of a*

Book for the World, p. 243, and Carolyn Wells and Alfred F. Goldsmith, *A Concise Bibliography of the Works of Walt Whitman* (Boston: Houghton Mifflin, 1922), p. 107.

10. The name of the author, however, is given on the backstrip, but, unlike the title, is not gilded.

11. This butterfly reappeared in *SD*, which contains between pages 122 and 123 a fine photograph showing Whitman with a butterfly on his forefinger. Esther Shephard (*Walt Whitman's Pose*, pp. 250–251 and plate 16, p. 212) has proved that this protograph was a fake. She has found among Whitman's papers a cardboard butterfly which he probably tied to his finger with a piece of wire on that occasion. But this does not detract from the symbolic value of the picture.

12. See above, Chapter IV, n. 53.

13. The 45 poems of "Calamus" were new and so were 12 or 15 of the poems which made up "Enfans d'Adam" — 57 in all. It is probable that the poems entitled "Chants Democratic" were composed earlier, in 1856–57 when Whitman went through his political crisis — and so were most of the longer poems (for the date of "Proto-Leaf," see below, n. 38).

14. *LG 1860,* p. 13, "Proto-Leaf," §34, *Inc. Ed.,* p. 17, "Starting from Paumanok," §10, ll. 3–5. He also announced "Calamus":
> "And sexual organs and acts! do you concentrate in me —
> For I am determined to tell you with courageous clear
> voice, to prove you illustrious."

LG 1860, p. 10, "Proto-Leaf," §21, *Inc. Ed.,* p. 18, "Starting from Paumanok," §12, l. 11.

15. From an article published anonymously by Whitman in the New York *Saturday Press* (January 7, 1860), reprinted in Mabbott and Silver, *A Child's Reminiscence by Walt Whitman* (University of Washington Press, 1930).

16. From a letter dated July 20, 1857; see *SPL,* p. 885.

17. *LG 1860,* p. 239, *Inc. Ed.,* p. 475, "So Far and So Far and On Toward the End."

18. *LG 1860,* pp. 451–456, *Inc. Ed.,* pp. 416–419.

19. He wanted his book to look like a Bible. All the longer poems are divided into numbered paragraphs so that it is possible to give chapter and verse, so to speak, for any quotation.

20. *LG 1860,* p. 29, *Inc. Ed.,* p. 44, "Song of Myself," §24, ll. 20–22.

21. *LG 1855,* pp. 77–82, *Inc. Ed.,* pp. 79–86, "I Sing the Body Electric."

22. "Poem of Women," *LG 1856,* pp. 100–102, *Inc. Ed.,* p. 327–328, "Unfolded out of the Folds"; "Poem of Procreation," *LG 1856,* pp. 240–243, *Inc. Ed.,* pp. 86–88, "A Woman Waits for Me"; "Bunch

Poem," *LG 1856*, pp. 309–312, *Inc. Ed.*, pp. 88–90, "Spontaneous Me."

23. He said so himself in *LG 1860*, p. 11, "Proto-Leaf," §22, *Inc. Ed.*, p. 15, "Starting from Paumanok," §6, ll. 21–23.

24. In a letter to Harrison Blake, *Thoreau's Familiar Letters* (Boston: Houghton Mifflin, 1894), p. 345.

25. He already aimed at this kind of symmetry in the fifth poem of *LG 1855*, *Inc. Ed.*, pp. 79–86, "I Sing the Body Electric."

26. *N & F*, p. 169 (63).

27. See above, Chapter IV, pp. 107–113.

28. *LG 1855*, p. 79, *Inc. Ed.*, p. 81, "I Sing the Body Electric," §4, l. 165.

29. *LG 1856*, pp. 240–243, *Inc. Ed.*, pp. 86–88, "A Woman Waits for Me."

30. *LG 1856*, p. 312, *Inc. Ed.*, p. 90, "Spontaneous Me," l. 42.

31. This was in 1856 the beginning of the first line of "Poem of Procreation."

32. Is it not symptomatic that all the poems that make up "Calamus" were published in 1860, while several of the more important poems in "Enfans d'Adam" date from the first two editions? It proves that he became aware of the abnormal character of his instincts only in 1859–60.

33. *SD*, p. 191, *CP*, p. 189.

34. *LG 1867*, p. 7, *Inc. Ed.*, p. 12, "Starting from Paumanok," §1, ll. 3–4. As early as 1860 he declared:

> "See in my poems, old and new cities, solid, vast, inland, with paved streets, with iron and stone edifices, and ceaseless vehicles and commerce."

LG 1860, p. 21, "Proto-Leaf," §63, *Inc. Ed.*, p. 22, "Starting from Paumanok," §18, l. 6.

35. "Calamus" no. 10, *LG 1860*, p. 356, *Inc. Ed.*, p. 593, among the variant readings of "Recorders Ages Hence."

36. "Calamus" no. 8, *LG 1860*, p. 354, *Inc. Ed.*, "Long I Thought that Knowledge," p. 478, l. 4.

37. *LG 1860*, p. 105.

38. "Proto-Leaf," *LG 1860*, p. 5 (1), *Inc. Ed.*, p. 557. This poem, the exuberance and optimism of which are so close to those of the first edition, may have been written as early as 1856, since Whitman declared:

> "In the Year 80 of the States. . .
> I, now thirty-six years old. . ."

LG 1860, p. 8 (11), *Inc. Ed.*, pp. 548–549, variant reading of §3. The year of Independence, 1776, plus 80, equals 1856.

39. *Ibid.*

40. "Leaves of Grass" no. 20, *LG 1860*, p. 239, *Inc. Ed.*, p. 475.
41. *LG 1860*, pp. 451–456, *Inc. Ed.*, pp. 416–419.
42. "Apostroph," *LG 1860*, pp. 105–106, *Inc. Ed.*, pp. 473–475. This poem was suppressed in 1867, probably because it expressed unwarranted fears and also because it was extremely awkward with all its "O" 's. Besides, in 1860 it served mainly as a prologue to "Chants Democratic" and in 1867 these poems were dispersed.
43. "Proto-Leaf," *LG 1860*, p. 10 (20), *Inc. Ed.*, "Starting from Paumanok," p. 14, §6, ll. 7–9.
44. From a notebook dated 1860–61 now in the Library of Congress.
45. See above, Chapter IV.
46. *LG 1860*, p. 286, *Inc. Ed.*, p. 398, ("Thought," ll. 1–4, 8–10).
47. *LG 1860*, pp. 179–180 ("Chants Democratic" no. 9), *Inc. Ed.*, p. 408 ("Thoughts," §1, ll. 1–2, 5–8).
48. *LG 1860*, pp. 182–183 ("Chants Democratic" no. 11), *Inc. Ed.*, p. 409 ("Thoughts," §2, ll. 1, 9, 11, 15).
49. See the title page: "Year 85 of the States (1860–1861)."
50. *LG 1860*, p. 179 ("Chants Democratic" no. 9), *Inc. Ed.*, p. 408 ("Thoughts," §1, l. 3).
51. See above Chapter III.
52. *LG 1860* ("Leaves of Grass" no. 13), *Inc. Ed.*, p. 323 ("You Felons on Trial in Courts"), and variant readings, pp. 675–676.
53. *LG 1860*, pp. 237–238 ("Leaves of Grass" no. 18), *Inc. Ed.*, pp. 395–396 ("All is Truth," ll. 6–8, 16–17).
54. *LG 1860*, p. 236 ("Leaves of Grass" no. 17), *Inc. Ed.*, p. 232 ("I Sit and Look Out," ll. 1, 9–10).
55. *Ibid.*, l. 2.
56. *LG 1860*, pp. 361–362 ("Calamus" no. 16), *Inc. Ed.*, p. 479 ("Who Is Now Reading This," ll. 1–2, 5–7).
57. See for instance "Calamus" no. 36, *LG 1860*, p. 374, *Inc. Ed.*, p. 110.
58. *LG 1860*, p. 343 ("Calamus" no. 2), *Inc. Ed.*, p. 96 ("Scented Herbage of my Breast," ll. 10–11, 14).
59. "As the Time Draws Nigh," *Inc. Ed.*, p. 405 and 697, which gives the text of the original poem entitled "To My Soul" in 1860.
60. *LG 1860*, pp. 5–22, *Inc. Ed.*, "Starting from Paumanok," pp. 12–23.
61. *LG 1860*, pp. 259–268, *Inc. Ed.*, "A Song of Joys," pp. 149–155.
62. "Leaves of Grass" no. 10, *LG 1860*, pp. 224–226, *Inc. Ed.*, "Myself and Mine," pp. 201–202, ll. 2–4, 30–33, and variant readings p. 633.

63. ". . . full of life now. . ." "Calamus" no. 45, *LG 1860*, p. 378, *Inc. Ed.*, p. 113, l. 1. "I, forty years old. . ." he added; so the poem was written in 1859.

64. *Walt Whitman Handbook*, pp. 143–144, where Schyberg's views are summed up. See Frederik Schyberg, *Walt Whitman* (Copenhagen: Gyldendalske Boghandel, 1933), or the translation by Evie Allison Allen (Columbia University Press, 1951).

65. *LG 1860*, p. 196, "Leaves of Grass" no. 1, §4, *Inc. Ed.*, "As I Ebb'd with the Ocean of Life," p. 216, §2, ll. 5–6.

66. *LG 1860*, p. 342 ("Calamus" no. 2), *Inc. Ed.*, pp. 95–96 ("Scented Herbage of My Breast," ll. 3–5).

67. *LG 1860*, p. 359 ("Calamus" no. 13), *Inc. Ed.*, p. 593 among the variant readings of "Roots and Leaves Themselves Alone."

68. "Whitman: the Poet," *New Republic*, October 20, 1947, p. 27.

69. *LG 1855*, p. 55, *Inc. Ed.*, p. 74, "Song of Myself," §50, l. 4.

70. *LG 1860*, p. 277, §33, *Inc. Ed.*, p. 215, "Out of the Cradle Endlessly Rocking," ll. 165–173.

71. *LG 1860*, p. 268, §41, *Inc. Ed.*, p. 155, "A Song of Joys," ll. 157–161, and p. 612.

72. *LG 1860*, p. 14 (39), *Inc. Ed.*, p. 18, "Starting from Paumanok," §11, l. 4.

73. For example in "Calamus" no. 10 (*LG 1860*, pp. 356–357, *Inc. Ed.*, p. 102, "Recorders Ages Hence"), "Calamus" no. 11 (*LG 1860*, pp. 357–358, *Inc. Ed.*, pp. 102–103, "When I Heard at the Close of the Day"), "Calamus" no. 19 (*LG 1860*, p. 364, *Inc. Ed.*, p. 105, "Behold This Swarthy Face"), "Calamus" no. 29 (*LG 1860*, p. 371, *Inc. Ed.*, p. 109, "A Glimpse"), and "Calamus" no. 20 (*LG 1860*, pp. 364–365, *Inc. Ed.*, p. 106, "I Saw in Louisiana a Live-Oak Growing").

74. See "Calamus" no. 2, *LG 1860*, p. 343, *Inc. Ed.*, p. 96, "Scented Herbage of My Breast," l. 21.

75. *LG 1860*, p. 353 ("Calamus" no. 7), *Inc. Ed.*, p. 101, "Of the Terrible Doubt of Appearances," ll. 14–16.

76. See in particular "Calamus" no. 20, l. 9, *LG 1860*, p. 365, *Inc. Ed.*, p. 106, "I Saw in Louisiana a Live-Oak Growing."

77. "Calamus" no. 39, *LG 1860*, p. 375–376, *Inc. Ed.*, p. 111, "Sometimes with One I Love."

78. See "Proto-Leaf," §22, *LG 1860*, pp. 10–11, *Inc. Ed.*, p. 15, "Starting from Paumanok," ll. 18–26; "Calamus" no. 5, *LG 1860*, pp. 349–351, *Inc. Ed.*, pp. 200–201, "For You O Democracy," and pp. 266–267, "Over the Carnage Rose Prophetic a Voice," and p. 476, "States"; "Calamus" no. 23, *LG 1860*, p. 367, *Inc. Ed.*, p. 107, "This Moment Yearning and Doubtful"; "Calamus" no. 35, *LG 1860*, p. 374, *Inc. Ed.*, p. 111, "To the East and to the West"; "Calamus" no.

37, LG *1860*, p. 375, *Inc. Ed.*, p. 110, "A Leaf for Hand in Hand"; "Calamus" no. 33, LG *1860*, p. 373, *Inc. Ed.*, p. 109, "No Labor-Saving Machine"; "Calamus" no. 34, LG *1860*, p. 373, *Inc. Ed.*, p. 110, "I Dream'd in a Dream."

79. "Calamus" no. 45, LG *1860*, p. 450, *Inc. Ed.*, p. 113, "Full of Life Now." Gay W. Allen in *The Solitary Singer* (New York: Macmillan, 1955, or Grove Press, 1959), p. 257, points out that the MS version of this poem gives Whitman's age as thirty-eight. But the fact that the poet later changed it to forty shows that he thought his statement was still valid two years later.

80. "To My Soul," LG *1860*, p. 450, *Inc. Ed.*, p. 405, "As the Times Draws Nigh," 1. 8.

81. "Quicksand Years that Whirl Me I Know not Whither," *Drum-Taps*, p. 30, *Inc. Ed.*, p. 374. Though this poem was published only in 1865, it is obvious that it applies to the prewar years and was probably composed toward the end of 1860 or in 1861.

82. "Leaves of Grass" no. 18, LG *1860*, p. 191, *Inc. Ed.*, p. 9, "Me Imperturbe."

83. "Leaves of Grass" no. 20, LG *1860*, p. 239, *Inc. Ed.*, p. 475, "So Far and So Far and On Toward the End."

84. LG *1856*, pp. 211–212, *Inc. Ed.*, pp. 134–139, "Crossing Brooklyn Ferry."

85. For example in "Chants Democratic" no. 14, pp. 186–187, *Inc. Ed.*, p. 11, "Poets to Come," and variant readings, pp. 546–547.

86. See end of "Chants Democratic" no. 11, p. 183, *Inc. Ed.*, p. 409, "Thoughts," §2 ll. 15–18, and: "The market needs to-day to be supplied — the great West especially — with copious thousands of copies" (anonymous article entitled "All about a Mocking-Bird," published in New York *Saturday Press* on January 7, 1860; reprinted in Mabbott and Silver, *A Child's Reminiscence by Walt Whitman*).

87. LG *1860*, pp. 391–403.

88. "To Him That Was Crucified," p. 397, *Inc. Ed.*, pp. 322–323.

89. LG *1860*, p. 398, *Inc. Ed.*, p. 376.

90. LG *1860*, p. 399, *Inc. Ed.*, p. 324.

91. See *Uncoll.* PP, II, 66, 69, 71–72.

92. "Proto-Leaf," §25, LG *1860*, p. 11, *Inc. Ed.*, p. 16, "Starting from Paumanok," §7, ll. 8–10.

93. *Uncoll.* PP, II, 91–92.

94. According to Trowbridge, Whitman occasionally played the Redeemer's part in everyday life. This is how he described his first encounter with the poet in 1860 at Boston: "We found a large, gray-haired and gray-bearded, plainly dressed man, reading proof-sheets at a desk in a dingy little office, with a lank, unwholesome looking lad at his elbow, listlessly watching him. . . . After he had gone out,

Whitman explained: 'He is a friendless boy I found at my boarding-place — I am trying to cheer him up and strengthen him with my magnetism.' " "Reminiscences of Walt Whitman," *Atlantic Monthly*, LXXXIX (February 1902), 164.

95. Many parodies, in particular, were written. Mabbott and Silver give a list of ten in *A Child's Reminiscence by Walt Whitman*. Whitman reprinted one in his *Imprints*, pp. 61–62. See also Mabbott and Silver, "William Winter's Serious Parody of Walt Whitman," *AL*, V (March 1933), 63–66, and Charles I. Glicksberg, "Walt Whitman Parodies Provoked by the 3rd Edition of *Leaves of Grass*," *American N & Q*, VII (March 1948), 163–168. The richest collection of these parodies is Henry S. Saunders, *Parodies on Walt Whitman*, preface by Christopher Morley (New York: American Library Service, 1923). Some are to be found in *The Antic Muse*, ed. Robert P. Falk (New York: Grove Press, 1955), pp. 115–126.

96. *Southern Field and Fireside*, June 9, 1860.

97. Reprinted in *Imprints*, p. 58.

98. For instance in the Brooklyn *Times* of July 5, 1860: "In the studied taste and expensiveness of this edition, the publishers have proclaimed the high value they have set upon Mr. Whitman's effusions, whatever divisions of opinions may exist in the rest of the world about them. Years ago we knew him as New York editor and for several years later he has been a miscellaneous contributor to the Press; and during all this time his writings were like other men's, no more strikingly marked with individuality of style. . . . We make no doubt that the singularity of the Leaves is a matter of principle with their author, the embodiment of a piece of profound sagacity."

The Brooklyn *Standard* of November 24, 1860, was still more enthusiastic: "We are not disposed to review or criticize these Leaves because we like them in toto and that's enough. We have read them lovingly and reverently like a true Brooklynite."

99. In the New York *Saturday Press* in particular; see Mabbott and Silver, *A Child's Reminiscence by Walt Whitman*. A list of reviews of the 1860 edition is to be found in W. S. Kennedy, *The Fight of a Book for the World*, pp. 14–15.

100. Reprinted in Charles I. Glicksberg, "A Friend of Walt Whitman," *American Book-Collector*, VI (March 1935), 91–94.

101. Quoted by Kennedy, *The Fight of a Book for the World*, p. 14.

102. "Walt Whitman and *Drum-Taps*," *Galaxy*, II, 606–615.

103. The best proof of this is probably the fact that Thayer and Eldridge planned to publish another collection of poems by Whitman under the title of "Banner at Daybreak." This book was announced as being "in preparation" in O'Connor's *Harrington*, in 1860, p. 560, and also in two issues of the *Liberator*, an antislavery paper, on

November 2 and 9, 1860: "A new volume of poems by Walt Whitman — a handsome brochure of 150 pages — 1 volume 16mo." It is therefore probable, as the title suggests, that this volume had a strong abolitionist bias. See Goodale, "Some of Walt Whitman's Borrowings," *AL*, X (May 1938), 205.

There is no way of establishing the contents of this abortive volume. But "Song of the Banner at Daybreak" would probably have had a prominent place in it, as it did at the beginning of *"Drum-Taps"* and also in the definitive edition of *Leaves of Grass*. It was probably this poem which gave the volume its title. It is not about the Civil War, but about the irreconcilable ideological conflict which divided the North and the South. It is likely also that Whitman would have included all of the poems not specifically about the Civil War which later appeared in *Drum-Taps*. They were probably written at this time, with the exception of "The Centenarian's Story," which was probably composed at the same time as the series of historical articles on Brooklyn that Whitman contributed to the Brooklyn *Weekly Standard* in 1861 (*Uncoll. PP*, II, 222–321). The table of contents might therefore have included the following titles:

"Rise O Days from Your Fathomless Deeps," *Drum-Taps*, p. 35, *Inc. Ed.*, p. 247; "Pioneers! O Pioneers!," *Drum-Taps*, p. 25, *Inc. Ed.*, p. 194; "Year of Meteors," *Drum-Taps*, p. 51, *Inc. Ed.*, p. 202; "Quicksand Years that Whirl Me I Know not Whither," *Drum-Taps*, p. 30, *Inc. Ed.*, p. 374; "When I Heard the Learned Astronomer," *Drum-Taps*, p. 34, *Inc. Ed.*, p. 230; "A Child's Amaze," *Drum-Taps*, p. 37, *Inc. Ed.*, p. 233; "Mother and Babe," *Drum-Taps*, p. 41, *Inc. Ed.*, p. 234; "Did You Ask Dulcet Rhymes from Me," *Drum-Taps*, p. 50, *Inc. Ed.*, p. 272 ("To a Certain Civilian"); "The Torch," *Drum-Taps*, p. 52, *Inc. Ed.*, p. 331; "Years of the Unperform'd," *Drum-Taps*, p. 53, *Inc. Ed.*, p. 405 ("Years of the Modern"); "The Ship," *Drum-Taps*, p. 60, *Inc. Ed.*, p. 9 ("The Ship Starting"); "A Broadway Pageant," *Drum-Taps*, p. 61, *Inc. Ed.*, p. 206; "Flag of Stars, Thick-Sprinkled Bunting," *Drum-Taps*, p. 65, *Inc. Ed.*, p. 402 ("Thick-Sprinkled Bunting"); "Old Ireland," *Drum-Taps*, p. 66, *Inc. Ed.*, p. 307; "Look Down Fair Moon," *Drum-Taps*, p. 66, *Inc. Ed.*, p. 270; "Out of the Rolling Ocean the Crowd," *Drum-Taps*, p. 67, *Inc. Ed.*, p. 91; "Others May Praise What They Like," *Drum-Taps*, p. 68, *Inc. Ed.*, p. 329; "Solid, Ironical, Rolling Orb," *Drum-Taps*, p. 68, *Inc. Ed.*, p. 483; "Shut not Your Doors to Me Proud Libraries," *Drum-Taps*, p. 8, *Inc. Ed.*, p. 11; "Beginning My Studies," *Drum-Taps*, p. 18, *Inc. Ed.*, p. 7.

Two of these poems, if we agree that they were composed in 1860, strongly confirm the hypothesis of Whitman's moral regeneration in 1859–60; for "Out of the Rolling Ocean the Crowd" is a remarkably

appropriate answer to the cry of despair of "Out of the Cradle Endlessly Rocking," and "Solid, Ironical, Rolling Orb" expresses a complete and unreserved reconciliation with the world.

104. It was only in 1881 that James R. Osgood and Company
offered to publish *Leaves of Grass*.

VI. THE WOUND DRESSER

1. "Leaves of Grass" no. 20, *LG 1860*, p. 239, *Inc. Ed.*, "So Far
and So Far and On Toward the End," p. 475, ll. 9–12.

2. "Messenger Leaves," *LG 1860*, p. 399, *Inc. Ed.*, p. 232.

3. *SD*, p. 21, *CP*, p. 16.

4. Quoted by Emory Holloway, *Whitman*, p. 185.

5. "Give Me the Splendid Silent Sun," *Drum-Taps*, pp. 48–49, §3,
Inc. Ed., pp. 264–265.

6. Quoted by Jean Catel, "Whitman et la Guerre Civile," *Revue
Anglo-Américaine*, II (June 1934), 437.

7. *Uncoll. PP*, II, 222–321.

8. *Ibid.*, pp. 1–5.

9. *SD*, pp. 22–25, *CP*, pp. 18–20.

10. *Uncoll. PP*, II, 306–321.

11. In "First O Songs for a Prelude," *Drum-Taps*, p. 5 (under the
title of "Drum-Taps"), *Inc. Ed.*, pp. 237–239; "Eighteen Sixty-One,"
Drum-Taps, p. 17, *Inc. Ed.*, pp. 239–240; "Beat! Beat! Drums!"
Drum-Taps, p. 38, *Inc. Ed.*, p. 240.

12. "(I am more and more surprised at the very great proportion
of youngsters from fifteen to twenty-one in the army). . ." *SD*, p.
28, *CP*, p. 22. See DeWolfe Miller's refutation of Higginson's charges
in his introduction to his facsimile of *Drum-Taps* (Gainesville, Florida:
Scholars' Facsimiles and Reprints, 1959), p. xv.

13. *Drum-Taps*, p. 18, *Inc. Ed.*, pp. 240–241, ll. 1–2, 9–11.

14. Preface to 1855 edition, *Inc. Ed.*, p. 491; see "Poem of Many
in One," *LG 1856*, p. 189, "By Blue Ontario's Shore," *Inc. Ed.*,
p. 292, §10, l. 9. Whitman liked this idea so much that he took it up
again in 1860; see "Calamus" no. 31 (2), *LG 1860*, p. 372, "What
place is besieged?" *Inc. Ed.*, p. 10.

15. See his letter to his mother dated July 15, 1863: "I have had
it much on my mind what could be done if it should so happen that
Jeff should be drafted of course he could not go without its being the
downfall almost of our whole family. . ." *SPL*, p. 912.

16. See Emory Holloway, "Some New Whitman Letters," *American
Mercury*, XVI (February 1929), 187.

17. *SPL*, p. 940.

18. *SPL*, p. 888.

19. *SD*, p. 26, *CP*, p. 21.

20. *Ibid.*

21. *SD*, pp. 26–27, *CP*, pp. 21–22.

22. *Uncoll. PP*, II, 21.

23. *SD*, pp. 27–28, *CP*, pp. 22–23. In *SD* Whitman says he came back from Falmouth in January 1863, but this is an error. In 1882 he did not remember the exact date. In fact he was back in Washington as early as December 29, 1862. He wrote a letter to his mother from there on that day; see *SPL*, p. 888.

24. *SD* pp. 26–27, *CP*, pp. 21–22.

25. This is the title which he gave in 1898 to a collection of letters sent by Whitman from Washington during the war. Whitman himself had used the phrase as a title for one of his poems, called "The Dresser" in 1867 (*Drum-Taps,* p. 31), and later, in 1881, "The Wound-Dresser," *Inc. Ed.*, p. 261.

26. Dr. D. B. St. John Roosa, a house surgeon of the old New York Hospital, wrote in 1896 an interesting account of Whitman's visits there which was printed in the Philadelphia *Evening Telegraph,* June 30, 1896, under the title "Recollections of Whitman." The article had also been published by the New York *Mail and Express* with the following subtitle: "Dr. D. B. St. John Roosa writes of the poet's visits to the New York Hospital — Fond of stage drivers — The young physician never took his poetry seriously and thought him a crank — His sympathetic nature." See Bliss Perry, *Walt Whitman,* p. 131.

27. Quoted by Canby, *Walt Whitman,* pp. 217–218.

28. "I am the only one that doles out this last [i.e., tobacco] and the men have grown to look to me." Letter to W. S. Davis, October 1, 1863, *SPL*, p. 919.

29. See *SD*, pp. 27–28, *CP*, p. 23: "Then went thoroughly through ward 6, observ'd every case in the ward, without, I think, missing one." See also letter to Mrs. Margaret S. Curtis, October 4, 1863, *SPL*, p. 922.

30. Some of these notebooks are now in the Library of Congress; *A Catalog Based upon the Collections of the Library of Congress,* 1955, p. 19. See also *SD*, pp. 57–58, *CP*, pp. 32–34, 54.

31. See the second volume of this study (in preparation), or Roger Asselineau, *L'Evolution de Walt Whitman,* Part II, Chapter V.

32. Many of the letters sent to Whitman after the war by young soldiers he had cared for are now in the Berg Collection. Whitman must have kept them religiously. One of these young men, E. D. Fox, wrote to him: ". . . you know I used to call you Father or 'Pa' and I still think of you as such for I am sure no Father could have cared for their [*sic*] own child better than you did me. . ." Another, Joe Harris,

began his letter, "Dear Uncle Walt. . ." See also *Catalogue of the Trent Collection*, p. 60.

33. *SD*, p. 29, *CP*, p. 24.

34. "Hospitals Visits," July 1863, quoted by Canby, *Walt Whitman*, p. 218.

35. "October 1st (1863) — Among other things in my visits to hospitals I commence reading pieces." Notebook in the Library of Congress.

36. See above, p. 138.

37. *LG 1855*, p. 45, *Inc. Ed.*, "Song of Myself," p. 63, §40, ll. 21-23, and §41, l. 1.

38. "The doctors tell me I supply the patients with a medicine which all their drugs and bottles and powders are helpless to yield." *SPL*, p. 920.

39. Letter to his mother, June 30, 1863, *SPL*, pp. 908-909.

40. Letter to his mother, September 8, 1863, *CW*, IV, 195.

41. Letter to his mother, April 15, 1863, quoted by Canby, *Walt Whitman*, p. 220.

42. *CW*, IV, 158.

43. Letter to his mother, June 30, 1863, *SPL*, p. 908.

44. Letter to Mrs. Abby Price, October 11, 1863, *SPL*, p. 926.

45. One of the notebooks in the Library of Congress, dated 1863, contains the fellowing entry:
"Nov. 5: am home these days.
Dec. 2nd: Returned to Washington."

46. "Nelly . . . I got home about 8 in evening — was up bright and early to the polls next morning . . . I shall probably stay five or six days longer . . . I have been several times to the Opera and the French Theatre . . ." Letter to Mrs. O'Connor, November 15, 1863, now in the Berg Collection.

47. Letter to Elijah Fox, November 21, 1863, *SPL*, p. 935.

48. One night, however, it was thought that the Confederates were going to attack, but nothing happened; see letter to Trowbridge, February 8, 1864, quoted by Bliss Perry, *Walt Whitman*, p. 145.

49. Letter to his mother, February 12, 1864, *SPL*, p. 937.

50. "I am well as usual; indeed first rate every way." Letter to his mother, April 10, 1864, *SPL*, p. 941.

51. Letter to his mother, June 3, 1864, *ibid.*, pp. 943-944.

52. Letter to his mother, June 7, 1864, *ibid.*, p. 945.

53. The first letter in which he mentioned his ill-health was dated March 31, 1863: "I have felt well of my deafness and cold in my head for four days or so, but it is back again bad as ever this morning." *SPL*, p. 900. See also letter to his mother, June 9, 1863, *ibid.*, p. 905;

letter to Lewis Kirk Brown, August 1, 1863, *ibid.*, p. 914, and letter to his mother, June 14 and 17, 1864, *ibid.*, pp. 947–948.

54. Letter to O'Connor, January 6, 1865, *SPL*, pp. 949–950.

55. Two letters help us to reconstruct his stay in Brooklyn at this time:

"The political meetings in New York and Brooklyn are immense. I go to them as to shows, fireworks, cannons, clusters of gaslights, countless torches, banners, and mottos [*sic*], 15, 20, 50, 100 people. Per contra I occasionally go riding into the country, in quiet lanes, or a sail on the water, and many times to the seashore at Coney Island." Letter to Charles Eldridge, October 8, 1864, Berg Collection.

"There is a hospital here, containing a couple of hundred soldiers, it is only a quarter of a mile from our house, and I go there a good deal — am going this afternoon to spend the afternoon and evening.

"Strange as it may seem days after days elapse without their having any visitors — so you see I am still in business — some of the cases are very interesting." Letter to O'Connor, September 11, 1864, Berg Collection.

56. *SD*, p. 76, *CP*, pp. 72–73; *NB*, pp. 116–117, *CP*, pp. 467–468; and letter to his mother, January 1, 1867, in *Letters Written by Walt Whitman to His Mother*, with an introductory note by Rollo G. Silver (New York: Alfred Goldsmith, 1936), p. 21. His visits to the hospitals lasted at least until April 16, 1867. This is the date of the last letter to his mother in which they are mentioned. See *ibid.*, p. 43.

57. See *SD*, p. 57, *CP*, pp. 53–54. At the end of the war he claimed that he had distributed thousands of dollars in the hospitals. See also *SPL*, pp. 893, 919–920, 921–923, 953.

58. Letter to Mrs. Abby H. Price, *SPL*, p. 927. He tried at first to find a job in a government service, but without success. He told his office-hunter's disappointments to Jefferson Whitman in a letter dated February 13, 1863, *SPL*, pp. 893–894. In August he still had found nothing; see letter to Lewis Kirk Brown, August 1, *SPL*, p. 914, and his letter to Nat and Fred Gray, May 19, 1863, *SPL*, p. 898. In the meantime, however, he must have found his part-time job with Major Hapgood, for he finished writing the letter last mentioned in the office of the latter: "Friday Morning 20th — I finish my letter in the office of Major Hapgood, a paymaster, and a friend of mine." He had apparently already worked as a copyist, for in *Lain's Brooklyn Directory* for 1860 one could read: "Walt Whitman, copyist"; see *Uncoll. PP*, II, 23, n. 2.

59. To the Brooklyn *Daily Union* in particular (see *Uncoll. PP*, II, 26–29) and to the New York *Times* (*ibid.*, pp. 29–36). He also sent some articles to the Brooklyn *Eagle*, but they edited them and

then refused to publish them any longer; see his letter of May 26, 1863, *CW*, IV, 161. Raymond of the New York *Times* sent him $50 for one of his articles; see *With WW in C*, III, 77.

60. Letter to his mother, May 5, 1863, *SPL*, p. 902.

61. Letter to his mother, June 9, 1863, *SPL*, p. 907. See also letters to the same, July 15, 1863, *SPL*, p. 912, and March 2, 1864, *The Wound Dresser*, 1898, p. 153.

62. His correspondence contains no allusions to this project, but several documents now in the Yale University Library show that he thought of it very seriously. He had already found a title:

MEMORANDA
OF A YEAR
(1863)
by Walt Whitman.

And here is the rough draft of the letter he sent to Redpath (October 21, 1863) to tell him of his project:

"At all events the year 1863 is the most important in the history of America. And this book with its framework jotted down on the battlefield in the shelter tent or by the wayside amid the rumble of passing artillery train or the march of cavalry . . . I should think two or three thousand sell out to be certainly depended on, here in hospitals in Washington, Army Depts and etc. My idea is a book of handy size and form 16mo or smallish 12mo first rate paper (this is indispensable) ordinary binding strongly stitched. It should be got out immediately I think — an edition elegantly bound might be pushed off for books for presents etc. for the holidays, if advertised for that purpose — it would be very appropriate. I think it is a book that would please women. I should expect it to be popular with the trade.

"Of course I propose the affair to you publisherially — as something to invest in, to make out (for both of us). I take it it would be a very handsome speculation only it is to be done while the thing is warm, namely *at once*. I have been and am in the midst of these things. I feel myself full of them and I know, and would readily absorb and understand my memo — wherefore let us make and publish this book and out with it so as to have it for sale by middle or 20th of November."

Unfortunately these War Memoranda were to come out only in 1876 in *Two Rivulets*.

63. See above, n. 58.

64. See "Where I Lived, and What I Lived For" in *Walden*.

65. Letter to his mother, June 9, 1863, *SPL*, p. 906.

66. J. T. Trowbridge, "Reminiscences of Walt Whitman," *Atlantic Monthly*, LXXXIX (February 1902), 164–168.

67. He lived at first with the O'Connors, 394 L Street, then, in

October 1863 he moved to an attic, 456 Sixth Street (see letter dated October 20, 1863, CW, IV, 210–220); it is there that Trowbridge visited him. Finally, in May 1864, he moved to 502 Pennsylvania Avenue (see letters dated May 23, 1864, CW, IV, 267, and June 7, 1864, SPL, p. 947).

68. He had not renounced beer however; see letter to Hugo Fritsch, August 7, 1863, SPL, pp. 916–917.

69. See his letter to his mother, June 14, 1863: "My boarding place, 502 Pennsylvania av., is a miserable place, very bad air . . . " SPL, p. 947.

70. See above, Chapter IV, p. 313, n. 58.

71. He saved money even on his clothes and wore shirts made by his mother and old suits: "How welcome the shirts were — I was putting off, and putting off, to get some new ones . . . and the coats too, worn as they are, they come in very handy . . ." Letter to his mother, May 19, 1863, SPL, p. 903.

72. See "First O Songs for a Prelude," Drum-Taps, pp. 5–7, Inc. Ed., pp. 237–239.

73. Drum-Taps, p. 45, Inc. Ed., p. 263, "Long, Too Long America."

74. Drum-Taps, p. 7 (8), Inc. Ed., p. 239, "First O Songs for a Prelude," ll. 54–57.

75. See this MS note in the Library of Congress: "Battles and death condense a nationality."

76. "Eighteen Sixty-One," Drum-Taps, p. 17, Inc. Ed., pp. 239–240. The last line, however, contains the word "sad."

In 1846–47, during the Mexican War, he had similarly extolled war in the Brooklyn Eagle (see G of the F, I, 242). Whatever may have been the circumstances at the beginning, the American cause was, in his opinion, just; because the United States represented democracy, whereas the Mexican government was nothing but a ridiculous and odious parody of it (Brooklyn Eagle, June 6, 1846, G of the F, I, 244). Thus it seemed to him quite proper for the United States simply to annex if not all Mexico, at least all of the territory down to the peninsulas of Yucatan and California, not for imperialistic reasons, but in order to bring the benefit of democracy to oppressed and badly governed people (Brooklyn Eagle, June 6, 1846, G of the F, I, 242). These naïve views have also been expressed by two historians: Justin H. Smith, in War with Mexico, and more recently by Alfred Hoyt Bill, in Rehearsal for Conflict: The War with Mexico, 1947.

Whitman nevertheless condemned war: "But war is a dreadful evil, in any event and under any circumstances . . ." (G of the F, I, 248). But he soon qualified this condemnation: "War is a horrible evil: so is anarchy but as the latter is less horrible than despotism so is war far less in its evils than quieter, but deeper dangers" (*ibid.*, p. 256).

He reacted in the same way in 1861. Though by nature opposed to violence, he willingly resigned himself to its use to assure the victory of democracy and to preserve his country from the "quieter but deeper dangers" which had threatened it since 1850. No doubt, the Mexican War having been fought far to the west, occasioned a much less complex and human reaction than Whitman had to the Civil War. The editor of the Brooklyn *Eagle* theorized about remote events, the author *Drum-Taps* responded as a man to his own experience among the suffering wounded soldiers.

77. "Did you ask dulcet rhymes from me?" *Drum-Taps*, p. 50, *Inc. Ed.*, p. 272, under the title "To a Certain Civilian."

78. "Drum-Taps," *Drum-Taps*, p. 7 (5), *Inc. Ed.*, "First O Songs for a Prelude," pp. 238–239, ll. 47, 49.

79. "The Veteran's Vision," *Drum-Taps*, p. 56, *Inc. Ed.*, p. 268, "The Artilleryman's Vision."

He took up the same theme much later in "The Dying Veteran" (1888), although this may have been a rejected poem dating from the time of the Civil War. But even if it was written in his old age, it need not surprise us, because, even after having experienced all the horrors of war, he still remained very responsive to its heroic aspect. In "Some War Memoranda" published in *NB*, he mentions several acts of extraordinary bravery (pp. 80–112, *CP*, pp. 432, 462–463).

He never rejected the poems written during the time when he believed that war was heroic and which he printed in *Drum-Taps* side by side with those expressing his sadness and disillusion. He clung to these contradictions imposed by the complexity of life. Always primarily preoccupied with the future, he never tried to erase the past. After 1855, his evolution was accomplished without revolution.

Jean Catel in "Walt Whitman et la Guerre Civile" (*RAA*, XI [June 1934], 434–439) accuses Whitman of having disseminated false propaganda at the beginning of 1862 in reassuring articles on the military hospitals, which he published in the New York *Leader*; but Whitman was sincere in writing them; they were composed at the same time as the patriotic and warlike poems of *Drum-Taps*. The fact that he used the pseudonym of Velsor Brush and that he never mentioned these articles to anyone does not prove that he was ashamed of them. He generally preferred to have his journalistic work remain anonymous, for he had no illusions concerning its value.

Curiously, although Whitman formed a much more accurate idea of war after December 1862, and described it much more realistically, he never in his poems or in his memoirs talked about fear. This omission is the more surprising as he was much concerned with the question of deserters. Evidently the "wound-dresser" never completely supplanted the belligerent poet of 1861. At any rate, *Drum-Taps*, in spite of the profound pity which inspires many poems, still presents to some extent an idealized picture of war.

80. "Poem of Joys," *LG 1860*, pp. 263–264 (23), *Inc. Ed.*, pp. 151–152, "A Song of Joys," ll. 65–72.

81. See "Beat! Beat! Drums!" *Drum-Taps*, p. 38, *Inc. Ed.*, p. 240. This poem was first published in *Harper's Weekly* on September 28, 1861, and on the same day in the New York *Leader* (*SPL*, p. 1071). This proves that it was written at the very beginning of the war. From the same period we have "Old Ireland," which seems out of place in *Drum-Taps*, but Whitman probably wrote it to stimulate the patriotic ardor of the Irish in New York and to encourage them to engage in the defense of their new country. The poem first appeared in the New York *Leader*, November 2, 1861 (see *SPL*, pp. 1074–1075).

82. "I would like to see *every man* in the land — I would like to see the people embodied en masse . . . for that will be something like our nation getting itself up in shape." Letter dated March 1863; see E. Holloway, "Some New Whitman Letters," *American Mercury*, XVI (February 1929), 187.

83. See above Chapter V, n. 103.

84. "Song of the Banner at Daybreak," *Drum-Taps*, p. 16 (18), *Inc. Ed.*, p. 246, l. 139.

85. "Song of the Banner at Daybreak," *Drum-Taps*, p. 12 (12), *Inc. Ed.*, p. 243, l. 63.

86. ". . . O Libertad! arm'd Libertad!" in "Shut not Your Doors to Me Proud Libraries," *Drum-Taps*, p. 8, *Inc. Ed.*, p. 546, among the variant readings.

87. "Rise O Days from Your Fathomless Deeps," *Drum-Taps*, p. 35, *Inc. Ed.*, pp. 247–248, esp. §§2 and 3.

88. "Song of the Banner at Daybreak," *Drum-Taps*, p. 12 (12), *Inc. Ed.*, p. 244, l. 75.

89. *Drum-Taps*, p. 26 (9), *Inc. Ed.*, p. 195, ll. 33–36.

90. *Drum-Taps*, p. 25 (2), *Inc. Ed.*, p. 194, l. 7.

91. The period of enthusiasm lasted from April 13, 1861, when Fort Sumter was bombarded, until July 20–21, 1862, the date of the first battle of Bull Run, which clearly showed that the war would be longer and harder than anyone had thought and that the Union could not be sure of winning. But it may have lasted until December 1862, since the passage in *SD* in which Whitman describes the arrival of the retreating army in Washington is not an eye-witness report. He probably did not realize the full horror of war until he

had seen it close up on the Rappahannock. His point of view changed along with that of the Northern public. In this respect he was the spokesman of his time. He summarized the history of the Civil War on a scrap of paper, preserved in the Library of Congress, in this way: "the electric uprising of the North in vast paroxysm of contempt and astonishment and rage — the first Bull Run the utter cast-down shock and dismay — the call for troops — the chaos of divided counsel and then followed the war in full-blood — the war with all its hope — holocaust of death four years of fratricidal war."

92. "The Wound-Dresser," *Inc. Ed.*, p. 261, ll. 4–6. These three lines were added in 1881; they admirably sum up his evolution during the war. He became conscious of it afterwards.

93. Ellen M. Calder (ex-Mrs. O'Connor), "Personal Recollections of Walt Whitman," *Atlantic Monthly*, XCIX (June 1907), 833.

94. Letter to his mother, September 8, 1863, *CW*, IV, 193.

95. See "Vigil Strange I Kept on the Field One Night," *Drum-Taps*, p. 42, *Inc. Ed.*, pp. 257–258, and "A Sight in Camp in the Daybreak Gray and Dim," *Drum-Taps*, p. 46, *Inc. Ed.*, p. 259, esp. the last three lines.

96. See "A March in the Ranks Hard-Prest and the Road Unknown," *Drum-Taps*, p. 44, *Inc. Ed.*, pp. 258–259.

97. See "In Clouds Descending in Midnight Sleep," *Sequel to Drum-Taps*, p. 20, *Inc. Ed.*, p. 402, under the title "Old War-Dreams."

98. See "Come up from the Fields Father," *Drum-Taps*, p. 39, *Inc. Ed.*, pp. 255–257. He may have used a real incident; see *SPL*, pp. 1071–1072.

99. "One of the drifts [of his *Memoranda of a Year*] is to push forward the very big and needed truth that our national military system needs entirely shifting and revolutionizing and made to tally with democracy — the people — The officers should almost invariably rise from the ranks. The entire capacity keenness and courage of our army are in the ranks. There is an absolute want of democratic spirit exclusively . . ." From the rough draft of a letter to Redpath dated October 21, 1863 (Yale University Library). See also *SD*, pp. 24–25, *CP*, pp. 19–20.

100. *SD*, pp. 24–25, *CP*, pp. 19–20.

101. *Drum-Taps*, p. 54, *Inc. Ed.*, pp. 260–261.

102. Letter to his mother, September 8, 1863, *CW*, IV, 193.

103. Letter to his mother, April 10, 1864, *SPL*, p. 940.

104. Letter to Tom Sawyer, April 21, 1863 (Berg Collection).

105. Letter to his mother, July 15, 1863, *SPL*, pp. 911–912.

106. Letter dated August 18, 1863, *CW*, IV, 183.

107. *Drum-Taps*, pp. 42, 46, *Inc. Ed.*, pp. 257, 259.

108. "Pensive on her dead gazing, I heard the mother of all," *Drum-Taps*, p. 71, *Inc. Ed.*, p. 412.

109. See "Over the Carnage Rose Prophetic a Voice," *Drum-Taps*, p. 49, *Inc. Ed.*, p. 266. He incorporated in this poem almost word for word, a fragment from "Calamus" no. 5 (*LG 1860*, p. 349, *Inc. Ed.*, pp. 476–477, under the title of "States").

110. He made significant additions to some of the 1860 poems. Thus, in 1871, he added to "Thoughts" (*Inc. Ed.*, pp. 408–409) the clause printed below in italics (l. 14):

"And how all people, sights, combinations, the democratic masses too, serve — and how every fact, *and war itself; with all its horrors, serves* . . . "

111. Military parades even aroused his warlike enthusiasm: "I tell you, mother, it made everything ring — made my heart leap . . . I tell you it had the look of *real war* — noble-looking fellows; a man looks so proud on a good horse and armed . . . Alas! how many of these healthy handsome rollicking young men will lie cold before the apples ripen in the orchard." (Letter to his mother, June 30, 1863, *SPL*, pp. 910–911.) He would not have added the note of pity in 1862, though.) A more sober description of the same parade is given in *SD*, pp. 39–40, *CP*, p. 35.

112. See "Lo, Victress on the Peaks," *Sequel to Drum-Taps*, p. 23, *Inc. Ed.*, p. 273, ll. 7–9; "Camps of Green," *Drum-Taps*, p. 57, *Inc. Ed.*, pp. 413–414; and "Hymn of Dead Soldiers," *Drum-Taps*, pp. 59–60, *Inc. Ed.*, "Ashes of Soldiers," pp. 406–408.

113. See "Turn O Libertad," *Drum-Taps*, p. 70, *Inc. Ed.*, pp. 274–275, ll. 10–12.

114. "Years of the Unperform'd," *Drum-Taps*, pp. 53–54, "Years of the Modern," *Inc. Ed.*, pp. 405–406, ll. 1–3, 7, 25, 29–30.

115. *SD*, p. 32, *CP*, p. 28. See also *NB*, p. 81, *CP*, p. 433.

116. *SD*, p. 80, *CP*, p. 76.

117. *SD*, p. 78, *CP*, p. 74, and also *SD*, p. 48, *CP*, pp. 43–44. He took up the subject again in *Democratic Vistas* (*CP*, pp. 219–221). See also a letter to his mother, September 15, 1863, *The Wound-Dresser*, 1949, p. 116.

118. The Civil War had the same happy influence on Melville.

119. "Reconciliation," *Sequel*, p. 23, *Inc. Ed.*, p. 271. See also the last two lines of "To the Leaven'd Soil They Trod," *Sequel*, p. 24, *Inc. Ed.*, p. 275.

120. See his letter to his mother, April 10, 1864, *SPL*, p. 940. Almost the same passage occurs in *NB*, p. 111, *CP*, p. 462. See also this sentence from a letter to Lewis Kirk Brown, August 15, 1863

(now in the Library of Congress): "I agree with you that a rebel in the Southern army is much more respectable than a Northern copperhead."

121. *SD*, p. 78, *CP*, pp. 74–75.

122. "A Secesh Brave," *SD*, p. 33, *CP*, p. 28.

123. "The Dresser," *Drum-Taps*, p. 31, "The Wound-Dresser," *Inc. Ed.*, p. 261, l. 8.

124. "Camps of Green," *Drum-Taps*, p. 57, *Inc. Ed.*, pp. 413–414, ll. 20–21.

125. Article published in *Army Square Hospital*, May 20, 1865, and reprinted by E. Holloway in *Colophon*, Part I, 1930, under the title of "Whitman on War's Finale."

126. *Sequel*, pp. 15–17, *Inc. Ed.*, pp. 370–372.

127. F. DeWolfe Miller has established the exact date in the introduction of his facsimile edition of *Drum-Taps* (Gainesville, Florida: Scholars' Facsimiles and Reprints, 1959), p. l.

128. Whitman did not follow a chronological order in this volume, except for the first few poems, which are undoubtedly the earliest. For the remainder, he was guided by purely aesthetic and sometimes even typographical criteria. In order to obtain an attractive typographical arrangement on the page and at the same time to include the largest amount of material in the smallest number of pages — for the sake of economy perhaps — he added here and there some very short poems, such as "Cavalry Crossing a Ford" (p. 8), "By the Bivouac's Fitful Flame" (p. 16), "Beginning My Studies" (p. 18 — this is an extreme case; its theme makes it irrelevant here, and Whitman later placed it in "Inscriptions"), "A Child's Amaze" (p. 37), "Mother and Babe" (p. 41), etc. Sometimes he placed poems together because they had similar titles. Three poems, the titles of which begin with "Year" or "Years," are thus grouped together toward the end of the volume, although "Year of Meteors" would be better placed at the beginning and "Year that Trembled and Reel'd beneath Me" serves as a sort of tail-piece to "Years of the Unperform'd," which should be the last of the three since it phophesies the future.

129. Letter to his mother, March 31, 1863, *SPL*, p. 900.

130. Letter to his mother, April 10, 1864, *SPL*, p. 941.

131. Trowbridge, "Reminiscences of Walt Whitman," *Atlantic Monthly*, LXXXIX (February 1902), 171.

132. Letter to O'Connor, January 6, 1865, *SPL*, pp. 949–950.

133. *Ibid.*

134. The great metaphysical themes were almost completely absent from it. They reappeared only in "When Lilacs Last . . ." and "Chanting the Square Deific," which both belong to *Sequel*.

135. Letter to O'Connor, January 6, 1865, *SPL*, pp. 949–950.

136. Other things being equal, there is the same difference between *Leaves of Grass* and *Drum-Taps* as between nonrepresentational and traditional painting.

137. Letter to O'Connor, January 6, 1865, *SPL*, pp. 949–950.

138. *Ibid.*

139. This collection of poems was never published separately. See Wells and Goldsmith, *A Concise Bibliography of the Works of Walt Whitman*, p. 11.

140. *SD*, pp. 43–44, *CP*, pp. 38–39.

141. *Drum-Taps*, p. 69, *Inc. Ed.*, pp. 284–285.

142. *Sequel*, pp. 3–12, *Inc. Ed.*, pp. 276–283.

143. By Swinburne, in particular, in "Under the Microscope" (1872); by Bliss Perry (*Walt Whitman*, 1906, p. 157); and by Canby (*Walt Whitman*, p. 240). A dissenting voice is that of Malcolm Cowley (see *The Complete Poetry of Walt Whitman*, 1948, pp. 34–36). The beauty of the poem has, on the contrary, been extolled by Richard P. Adams in "Whitman's 'Lilacs' and the Tradition of Pastoral Elegy," *PMLA*, LXXII (June 1957), 479–487.

144. "I Heard You, Solemn-sweet Pipes of the Organ," *Sequel*, p. 17, *Inc. Ed.*, pp. 93–94; "Not my enemies . . . ," *Sequel*, p. 17, *Inc. Ed.*, p. 484; "O Me! O Life!" *Sequel*, p. 18, *Inc. Ed.*, p. 231; "Ah poverties . . . ," *Sequel*, p. 18, *Inc. Ed.*, p. 398.

145. In fact, we know that "I Heard You Solemn-Sweet Pipes of the Organ" was first published in the New York *Leader* (October 12, 1861) under the title of "Little Bells Last Night" (*SPL*, pp. 1066–1067). The other poems may very well date from the same time. They are perfectly consistent with what we know of the spiritual crisis that Whitman underwent shortly before publishing the third edition of *Leaves of Grass*. "I Heard You . . ." is a poem of love and regret. "O Me! O Life!" and "Ah Poverties . . ." are both very melancholy and express the grief of a broken heart, but they end on a note of resignation and courageous acceptance. "This Day, O Soul" corresponds to a recovery and a reconciliation with the world. The whole conclusion of the 1859–60 crisis is therefore summarized in these few poems, if our hypothesis is correct. "Not My Enemies . . ." seems to have a more general meaning, having to do with the homosexual tendencies that continued to trouble Whitman secretly throughout the war, in spite of the apparent propriety of his behavior.

146. *Sequel*, p. 13, *Inc. Ed.*, p. 284.

147. *Sequel*, pp. 15–17, *Inc. Ed.*, pp. 370–372.

148. See above, n. 62.

149. Kennedy in *The Fight of a Book for the World*, pp. 16–18, gives a list of reviews of *Drum-Taps*.

150. *Ibid.*, p. 16.

151. *Ibid.*
152. *Galaxy*, II (December 1866), 612–613.
153. *Round Table*, November 1865, pp. 147–148.
154. This review has been reprinted in *Views and Reviews*, 1908, pp. 101–110.
155. See above, n. 145.
156. For instance, "Drum-Taps" (later "First O Songs for a Prelude"), "Song of the Banner at Daybreak," "1861," "Pioneers! O Pioneers!" "Rise O Days from Your Fathomless Deeps," "Beat! Beat! Drums!" "City of Ships," "Long, Too Long, O Land," and "Give Me the Splendid Silent Sun."
157. *Drum-Taps*, pp. 19–24, 68, *Inc. Ed.*, pp. 250–254, 267.
158. See "Cavalry Crossing a Ford" (*Drum-Taps*, p. 8, *Inc. Ed.*, p. 254); "Bivouac on a Mountain-side" (*Drum-Taps*, p. 68, *Inc. Ed.*, p. 267); and "The Most Inspiriting of All War's Shows" (*SD*, pp. 39–40, *CP*, p. 35). See also "The Veteran's Vision" (*Inc. Ed.*, pp. 268–269), and the beginning of "Hymn of Dead Soldiers" (*Drum-Taps*, p. 59, *Inc. Ed.*, pp. 406–407, under the title "Ashes of Soldiers").
159. *SPL*, pp. 949–950.
160. See above, p. 157.
161. *The Poems of Wilfred Owen* (London: Chatto and Windus, 1933), p. 40.
162. There was no contemporary collection of poems or even of memoirs in which any attempt was made to give a realistic account of the fighting. This was not done until much later. General John Beatty's *Memoirs of a Volunteer* appeared only in 1879 (see critical edition by Harvey S. Ford, with an introduction by Lloyd Lewis, New York, 1946) and Ambrose Bierce's *Tales of Soldiers and Civilians* in 1891. The bitter and disillusioned letters of Oliver Wendell Holmes, Jr., the son of the Autocrat of the Breakfast Table, whose reaction to the horrors of infantry combat resembled those of Siegfried Sassoon during World War I, were not published until 1946.
163. As the title indicates, most of the poems describe battles or celebrate generals. Melville, as a poet, was not interested in ordinary soldiers.
164. Letter to O'Connor, January 6, 1865, *SPL*, pp. 949–950.
165. O. L. Triggs, "The Growth of Leaves of Grass," *Conservator*, VIII (August 1897), 84–88.
166. *NB*, p. 13, *Inc. Ed.*, p. 531.
167. *Ibid.*
168. See "So Long!" *LG 1860*.
169. See above, Chapter V, p. 130.
170. He was not unaware of the existence of evil and did not try to conceal it. See for example his description (*SD*, pp. 55–57, *CP*,

pp. 52–53) of the atrocities committed by a band of Southern raiders. See also the passage on Southern prison camps (SD, pp. 54–55, CP, pp. 50–51). He was also aware of the sadism of the punishments inflicted on some of the Union soldiers: there are jottings on the subject in some of his notebooks now in the Library of Congress. Even in the hospitals, as he knew, the soldiers were sometimes robbed and the corpses rifled. There were times when he almost lost faith in humanity; see letter to his mother, March 29, 1864, SPL, p. 939. But his despair did not last; the heroism of the wounded soldiers made up for all these failings. See also his letter to his mother, March 8, 1863, quoted by Rollo G. Silver in "Thirty-One Letters of Walt Whitman," AL, VIII (January 1937), 417–418.

171. See above, p. 93.

172. See above, Chapter IV, p. 104.

173. This struck W. D. Howells; see above, Chapter IV, p. 105.

174. See above, Chapter V, p. 132.

175. Many were published in The Wound Dresser, A Series of Letters Written from the Hospitals in Washington by Walt Whitman, ed. by R. M. Bucke (Boston: Maynard, 1898), reprinted with an introduction by Oscar Cargill (New York: The Bodley Press, 1949).

176. See above, p. 144.

177. "Whoever You Are Holding Me Now in Hand," Inc. Ed., p. 98, l. 20.

178. Letter to Mrs. Abby H. Price, October 11, 1863, SPL, p. 927, or letter to Hugo Fritsch, August 7, 1863, SPL, p. 916. Also letter to W. S. Davis, October 1, 1863, SPL, p. 918, and letter to Nat and Fred Gray, March 19, 1863, SPL, p. 896. Strangely enough he never mentioned this to his mother, and there are hardly any allusions to it in SD.

179. "Pioneers! O Pioneers!" Drum-Taps, p. 27 (10), Inc. Ed., p. 195, l. 38.

180. "The Dresser," Drum-Taps, p. 33, Inc. Ed., "The Wound-Dresser," p. 263, §4, l. 7.

181. "First O Songs for a Prelude," Drum-Taps, p. 6, Inc. Ed., p. 238, ll. 32–33.

182. "Pensive on Her Dead Gazing, I Heard the Mother of All," Drum-Taps, p. 71, Inc. Ed., p. 701, among the variant readings.

183. For instance, this is what he wrote from Brooklyn on November 21, 1863, to Elijah Fox, a young wounded soldier: "Dearest son: it would be more pleasure if we could be together just in quiet, in some plain way of living, with some good employment and reasonable income, where I could have you often with me, than all the dissipations and amusements of this great city." SPL, p. 935.

184. "Vigil Strange I Kept on the Field One Night," Drum-Taps,

pp. 42–43, *Inc. Ed.*, pp. 257–258, ll. 3–4, 23. He may have been thinking of an episode described in *SD*, p. 37, *CP*, p. 32.

185. Letter to Benton Wilson, April 15, 1870, *SPL*, p. 988.

186. *Drum-Taps*, p. 67, *Inc. Ed.*, p. 91. Such an encounter is recorded in one of Whitman's notebooks; see *Uncoll. PP*, II, 93.

187. See above, nn. 178 and 183.

188. "Calamus" no. 5, *LG 1860*, pp. 349–351, *Inc. Ed.*, "States," pp. 476–477.

189. "As I Lay with My Head in Your Lap Camerado," *Sequel*, p. 19, *Inc. Ed.*, p. 272, ll. 10–11.

190. *LG 1860*, p. 277 (33), *Inc. Ed.*, p. 215, l. 168.

191. *LG 1860*, p. 275 (28), *Inc. Ed.*, p. 214, l. 133.

192. *LG 1860*, p. 276 (31), *Inc. Ed.*, p. 638 in the variant readings of l. 158.

193. "When Lilacs Last. . ." *Sequel*, pp. 9–10 (28 and 31), *Inc. Ed.*, p. 281, §14, ll. 28, 40–43.

194. See, for instance, *NB*, pp. 111, 113, *CP*, pp. 462, 464. Hence his conclusion: "Then I should say, too, about death in war, that our feelings and imaginations make a thousand times too much of the whole matter. Of the many I have seen die, or known of, the past year, I have not seen or known one who met death with terror. In most cases I should say it was a welcome relief and release." *NB*, p. 112, *CP*, p. 463.

195. "Death's Valley," *Inc. Ed.*, p. 462, ll. 5–6. This poem was published in 1892 only.

196. Letter to Nat and Fred Gray, March 19, 1863, *SPL*, p. 897.

197. "When Lilacs Last. . . ," *Sequel*, p. 11, §18 (39), *Inc. Ed.*, p. 283, §15, ll. 18–20.

198. See above, n. 170.

199. See above, n. 145.

200. *Sequel*, p. 6, §8 (12), *Inc. Ed.*, p. 278, §8, l. 6.

201. *Sequel*, p. 6, §4 (7), *Inc. Ed.*, p. 277, §4, ll. 7–8.

202. *Drum-Taps*, p. 69, *Inc. Ed.*, p. 399, ll. 1, 5–8.

VII. HAPPY BUREAUCRAT AND TORMENTED POET

1. Ellen M. Calder, "Personal Recollections of Walt Whitman," *Atlantic Monthly*, XCIX (June 1907), 825.

2. See "Walt says he had a prospect of getting a good berth in Washington." Letter from George Whitman to his mother, January 22, 1863, *Faint Clews and Indirections*, ed. Clarence Gohdes and Rollo G. Silver (Duke University Press, 1949), p. 155. See also above, Chapter VI, n. 58.

3. See Dixon Wecter, "Walt Whitman as Civil Servant," *PMLA*, LVIII (January 1943), 1094–1109.

4. Letter to O'Connor, January 6, 1865, *SPL*, p. 949.

5. It was a copy of the third edition. He mentioned it in a letter to his mother, March 31, 1863 (*SPL*, p. 900). This copy is now in the Lion Collection, New York Public Library.

6. See Bliss Perry, *Walt Whitman*, p. 165.

7. For a detailed study of Whitman's career as a civil servant, see Wecter, "Walt Whitman as a Civil Servant," *PMLA*, LVIII 1094–1109.

8. *The Good Gray Poet: A Vindication* (New York: Bunce and Huntington, 1866 — but the text itself is dated September 2, 1865), reprinted in R. M. Bucke, *Walt Whitman* (Philadelphia: MacKay, 1883), pp. 99–130. See also *In Re*, pp. 149–157, which gives under the title of "The Good Gray Poet: Supplemental," a long letter dated January 22, 1866, which O'Connor had sent to the Boston *Transcript*, but which this paper did not print. It vigorously sums up the main ideas of his pamphlet.

9. See Bliss Perry, *Walt Whitman*, p. 176.

10. In January, according to Kennedy, *The Fight of a Book for the World*, p. 18.

11. In particular, in the *Round Table*, January 20, in which Stoddard wrote that it was "one of the most extraordinary things we ever encountered." For the reception of *The Good Gray Poet*, see Kennedy, *The Fight of a Book for the World*, p. 19.

12. Whitman was even amused at times by O'Connor's zeal: "He grows stronger and fiercer in his championship of Leaves of Grass — no one can ever say a word against it in his presence without a storm," he wrote to his mother on December 4, 1866, *Letters Written by Walt Whitman to His Mother, 1866–1872*, with an introductory note by Rollo G. Silver (New York: Alfred Goldsmith, 1936), p. 17.

13. "I have an agreeable situation here — labor moderate and plenty of leisure." Letter to his mother, August 1, 1866, "Letters of Walt Whitman to His Mother and an Old Friend," *Putnam's Monthly*, V (November 1908), 167.

14. See above, n. 1.

15. Letter to Jefferson Whitman, January 30, 1865, *SPL*, p. 952.

16. Letters to his mother, January 22 and March 12, 1867, *Letters Written by Walt Whitman to His Mother*, pp. 26, 38.

17. All his letters are dated: "Attorney General's Office. . ." and in one of them he wrote: "Mother I am writing at my table, by the big window I have mentioned several times in former letters — it is very pleasant indeed — the river looks so fine and the banks and hills in the distance — I can sit sometimes and look out for a long time —

It is mighty lucky for me I fell in with such a good situation." *Letters Written by Walt Whitman to His Mother*, 1936, p. 37. See also the letters dated March 26, 1867, and February 2, 1869, *ibid.*, pp. 39–41, 67.

He kept repeating that he had very little to do: "We have not much to do in the office" (August 13, 1868, *ibid.*, p. 58). "I am sitting at my desk writing this — there is not much to do to-day in the office" (February 2, 1869, *ibid.*, p. 67). He sometimes jested about it: ". . . since I began this letter, I have been sent for by the Cashier to receive my pay for the arduous and invaluable services I have already rendered to the government" (letter to Jefferson Whitman, January 30, 1865, *SPL*, p. 952; he was referring here to his first month's salary). In the Indian Bureau he worked as a mere copyist, but in the General Attorney's office he was sometimes assigned more complex tasks (see letter dated August 1, 1866 in "Letters of Walt Whitman to His Mother and an Old Friend," *Putnam's Monthly* V [November 1908]). So in December 1871 he could write to his mother: "The new Attorney Gen'l, Mr. Williams, has assigned me there [the office of the Solicitor of the Treasury] but several important bits of work have had to be done just now and to-day and yesterday I have had to do them — (as the old ladies say, I guess they'll miss me a good deal more than they 'spected)" (*SPL*, p. 999).

18. Letter to O'Connor, April 17, 1865, *SPL*, p. 954.

19. In August-September 1866 he prepared in Brooklyn the publication of the fourth edition of *Leaves of Grass* (see letter to O'Connor, August 26, 1866, Berg Collection). Same thing in 1870 when he prepared the fifth edition (see letter to Peter Doyle, September 6, 1870, *SPL*, p. 993). In 1872 he beat all his previous records. He was in Brooklyn from the middle of February to the beginning of April, and again from June to the middle of July. See Wecter, "Walt Whitman as a Civil Servant," *PMLA*, LVIII, 1094–1109.

20. Letter to his mother, November 16, 1866, *SPL*, p. 960.

21. "I have lots of money — in fact untold wealth." Letter to Mrs. Price, September 14, 1866, *Putnam's Monthly*, V (November 1908), 168. "I can send you whatever money you need, dear mother, any time." *Letters Written by Walt Whitman to His Mother*, p. 45.

22. Letters to his mother, February 12, 1867, *ibid.*, p. 31.

23. Letters to his mother, March 5 and 12, 1867, *ibid.*, pp. 35–38. Later, however, he was less enthusiastic (letter dated August 24, 1868, *ibid.*, p. 60).

24. This letter, now in the Berg Collection, was written by Whitman himself, but it was meant to be sent and signed by O'Connor. It was probably composed at the end of 1866 when there was already some question of publishing an English edition of *Leaves of Grass*.

Whitman must have intended to send in this roundabout way information that W. M. Rossetti could use in his preface. This letter may have been sent. There is a passage in Rossetti's preface which seems to echo it: "His ordinary appearance is masculine and cheerful: he never shows depression of spirits, and is sufficiently undemonstrative, and even somewhat silent in company." *Poems By Walt Whitman,* 1868, p. 14.

25. *Inc. Ed.,* p. 488.

26. It might be objected that he purposely toned down his portrait to reassure potential English readers; but it is a fact that his vitality had decreased and that he had become a stay-at-home.

27. See letter to his mother, June 29, 1866, *Letters Written by Walt Whitman to His Mother,* pp. 8–9, and *ibid.,* p. 13, or *SPL,* p. 961.

28. Letter to Peter Doyle, August 21, 1869, *SPL,* p. 984, and letter to the same, September 3, 1869, *Calamus,* 1897, p. 56.

29. See letter to his mother, June 29, 1866, *Letters Written by Walt Whitman to his Mother,* pp. 8–9.

30. Letter to Peter Doyle, September 6, 1870, *SPL,* p. 993.

31. Letter to Peter Doyle, June 27, 1872, *Calamus,* p. 96, and letter to the same, July 12, *ibid.,* p. 98.

32. Letter to George Whitman, October 23, 1872, Rollo G. Silver, "Thirty-One Letters of Walt Whitman," *AL,* VIII (January 1937), 421.

33. Later Whitman mixed up dates. Thus in *SD* (p. 81, *CP,* p. 78) he wrote that his stroke occurred in February. But the date of January 23 is given by Bucke in his *Walt Whitman* and also in the letter that Whitman scribbled in pencil the next day for his mother (this letter is now in the Yale Library).

34. See R. M. Bucke, *Walt Whitman* (Philadelphia; MacKay, 1883), pp. 45–46.

35. *In Re,* p. 115.

36. *Inc. Ed.,* p. 538. See also letter to Peter Doyle, September 3, 1869, *Calamus,* p. 56: "The doctor says it is all from that hospital malaria, hospital poison absorbed in the system years ago."

37. Burroughs protested against this allegation in the New York *Evening Post,* March 28, 1892 (reprinted in the *Nation,* April 7). See Clara Barrus, *Whitman and Burroughs: Comrades* (Boston: Houghton Mifflin, 1931), p. 297.

38. Eduard Bertz, *Der Yankee-Heiland* (Dresden: Carl Reissner, 1906), p. 30.

39. On Whitman's family, see Katherine Molinoff, *Some Notes on Whitman's Family* (privately printed, Brooklyn, 1941), and Josiah C. Trent, "Walt Whitman — A Case History," *Surgery, Gynecology and Obstetrics,* LXXXVII (July 1948), 113–121.

40. *Ibid.*

41. Whitman seems to have had several premonitory strokes. See Mrs. Whitman's letter to Mrs. Price quoted in "Letters of Walt Whitman to His Mother and an Old Friend," *Putnam's Monthly*, V (November 1908), 169. "He had a very slight attack soon after the war, but it seemed to pass over."

42. Letter dated May 16, 1866, and quoted in Florence Hardiman Miller, "Some Unpublished Letters of Walt Whitman's Written to a Soldier Boy," *Overland Monthly*, XLIII (January 1904), 62.

43. *Ibid.*

44. See above, Chapter II, p. 66.

45. At least after 1867, and anyway he could visit them only on Sundays now.

46. See letter to his mother, May 4, 1868, *SPL*, p. 976. He told his mother he was happy (letter from Mrs. Whitman to Walt Whitman, August 19, 1868, *FC*, p. 198). But a little later he had to confess: "You say you think I like Washington so much — Well I am satisfied here, but not particularly attached to the place — only I think it is better for me as things are, & better all round — if it could only be so that I could come home for a little while, & frequently, I should want nothing more — but one mustn't expect to have everything to suit perfectly" (Letter to his mother, August 24, 1868, *Letters Written by Walt Whitman to His Mother*, p. 61.) He felt happy and safe only at home with his mother, and that is why he went back to Brooklyn as often as possible. After his stroke, he took refuge with his brother George in Camden, and he hoped to proceed from there to Brooklyn (see his letter to his mother quoted in *FC*, p. 78).

47. "Leaves of Grass" no. 2, *LG 1867*, pp. 249–250, *Inc. Ed.*, "Tears," p. 218.

48. See O'Connor's testimony quoted by R. M. Bucke in his introduction to *Calamus*, p. 18, and Burroughs's, *ibid.*, p. 16.

49. *Uncoll. PP*, Vol. I, p. lviii, n. 15.

50. Frances Winwar, *American Giant: Walt Whitman and His Times* (New York: Harper, 1941).

51. See his review of Frances Winwar's book, *AL*, XIII (January 1942), 423–432. Furness, in particular, proves that Whitman could have known the Beaches only in New York before the Civil War.

52. *Whitman: An Interpretation in Narrative* (New York: Knopf, 1926).

53. *Uncoll. PP*, II, 95–96.

54. See above, the beginning of Chapter VI.

55. See, for instance, "Song of Myself," §28, *Inc. Ed.*, pp. 48–49, and ". . . the furious storm through me careering. . ." in "From Pent-up Aching Rivers," *Inc. Ed.*, p. 78, l. 31. Also: "The torment,

the irritable tide that will not be at rest. . ." in "Spontaneous Me," *Inc. Ed.*, p. 89, l. 29.

56. "Leaves of Grass" no. 3, *LG 1867*, p. 250, *Inc. Ed.*, pp. 219–220, ll. 3–8, 10–11.

57. I have examined this MS in the Library of Congress. It is written in pencil and "him" and "his" are still very clearly legible under "her."

58. *Uncoll. PP*, II, 95. As to the two mysterious numbers 16 and 164, Edward Hungerford thinks that they are the numbers attributed by Fowler to "Hope" and "Adhesiveness"; see "Walt Whitman and His Chart of Bumps," *AL*, II (January 1931), 350–384.

59. See "To You," *LG 1860*, p. 403, *Inc. Ed.*, p. 479.

60. *LG 1860*, "Enfans d'Adam" no. 6, p. 309 (6), *Inc. Ed.*, "One Hour to Madness and Joy," p. 90, l. 19.

61. *Sequel*, p. 18, *Inc. Ed.*, p. 398.

62. *Uncoll. PP*, II, 95.

63. *Sequel*, "Not My Enemies Ever Invade Me," p. 17, *Inc. Ed.*, p. 484, l. 4.

64. See above Chapter VI, n. 145.

65. *Uncoll. PP*, II, 94.

66. *Ibid.*, p. 97.

67. See *Calamus*, p. 23.

68. Letter to Peter Doyle, July 30, 1870, *Calamus*, p. 61.

69. *Passage to India*, p. 15, *Inc. Ed.*, p. 351, §9, ll. 19–20, 22, 25–26, 29–31. The idea of this passage to India was already in germ in "Enfans d'Adam" no. 10, *LG 1860*, p. 312, *Inc. Ed.*, p. 94, "Facing West from California."

70. *Passage to India*, p. 84, §6, *Inc. Ed.*, p. 221, ll. 25, 30–32.

71. "Warble for Lilac Time," *Passage to India*, p. 97, *Inc. Ed.*, p. 318, ll. 16–20. The same aspirations are expressed in "The Last Invocation," *Passage to India*, p. 69, *Inc. Ed.*, p. 378; "Now Finale to the Shore," *Passage to India*, p. 117, *Inc. Ed.*, p. 416; "Joy, Shipmate, Joy!" *Passage to India*, p. 120, *Inc. Ed.*, p. 415.

72. *Passage to India*, p. 50–51, §15, *Inc. Ed.*, p. 154, ll. 126–133.

73. "Poems bridging the way from Life to Death. . ." in "Proud Music of the Storm," *Passage to India*, p. 24, §15 (32), *Inc. Ed.*, p. 342, §6, l. 21.

74. "Leaves of Grass" no. 3, *LG 1867*, p. 250, *Inc. Ed.*, p. 219, "Aboard at a Ship's Helm."

75. *Passage to India*, p. 120, *Inc. Ed.*, p. 415.

76. *Passage to India*, p. 117, *Inc. Ed.*, p. 416.

77. "The Untold Want," *Passage to India*, p. 118, *Inc. Ed.*, p. 415.

78. "Shut Not Your Doors. . ." *Passage to India*, p. 118, *Inc. Ed.*, p. 415.

79. See above, p. 182.
80. *As a Strong Bird on Pinions Free*, p. xi, *Inc. Ed.*, pp. 484–485.
81. *Leaves of Grass*, New York, 1867, 338 pp. + *Drum-Taps*, New York, 1865, 72 pp. + *Sequel to Drum-Taps*, Washington, 1865–66, 24 pp. + *Songs before Parting*, no place or date, 36 pp.
82. Wells and Goldsmith, *A Concise Bibliography of the Works of Walt Whitman*, p. 114.
83. Gay W. Allen in his *Walt Whitman Handbook* lists one too many: "Not the Pilot" was already included in the edition of 1860, p. 425.
84. *LG 1867*, p. 5, *Inc. Ed.*, p. 434, "Small the Theme of My Chant."
85. *LG 1867*, p. 214, *Inc. Ed.*, p. 233.
86. *LG 1867*, pp. 249–250, *Inc. Ed.*, p. 218.
87. *LG 1867*, p. 250, *Inc. Ed.*, pp. 219–220.
88. *LG 1867*, p. 268, *Inc. Ed.*, p. 7.
89. *LG 1867*, p. 284, *Inc. Ed.*, pp. 308–309.
90. *LG 1867*, p. 284.
91. *LG 1867*, "Starting from Paumanok," p. (7), §1, *Inc. Ed.*, p. 12, §1, l. 5.
92. In "By Blue Ontario's Shore" for instance; see *Inc. Ed.*, p. 659, variant reading of §6, ll. 40–41, and p. 661, variant reading of §12, l. 10.
93. "Chants Democratic" no. 1, *LG 1860*, pp. 108–125, "As I Sat Alone by Blue Ontario's Shore", *LG 1867*, pp. 4–21, *Inc. Ed.*, pp. 286–299.
94. The importance of the poet was further reduced in 1871. See, for instance, the 1867 version of §1 (*Inc. Ed.*, pp. 656–657) and that of 1871 (*Inc. Ed.*, p. 286), esp. ll. 4–6.
95. He thus added §§1, 7, 11, 19, and 20. Besides, he added between parentheses at the end of pre-existing paragraphs groups of verses devoted to democracy, which he personified and called "Mother"; this image is one of the leit-motifs of the poem.
96. *Songs before Parting*, §22 (70), *Inc. Ed.*, p. 666, variant readings of ll. 9–13 of §20.
97. See *Inc. Ed.*, p. 658, an 1856 reading of l. 9 of §6. The word "defections" disappeared in 1867.
98. *LG 1856*, "Poem of Many in One," p. 196, *Inc. Ed.*, p. 662, variant reading of l. 4 of §14, and *Songs before Parting*, 1867, "As I Sat Alone by Blue Ontario's Shore," p. 16, §14 (45), *Inc. Ed.*, p. 295, §14, l. 4.
99. *Songs before Parting*, "As I Sat Alone by Blue Ontario's Shore," *Inc. Ed.*, p. 286, §2, ll. 10–11. These two lines were added in 1867.
100. *Songs before Parting*, "As I Sat Alone by Blue Ontario's

Shore", p. 5, §4 (11–12), *Inc. Ed.*, p. 657, variant reading of ll. 7f of §3.

101. *LG 1860*, pp. 354–355, 355–356, 361–362, *Inc. Ed.*, pp. 477–478, 479.

102. "Calamus" and "Children of Adam," however, were expurgated too. See, for instance, *Inc. Ed.*, p. 585, variant readings of ll. 3 and 4 of §11 of "I Sing the Body Electric," and p. 588, variant readings of "A Woman Waits for Me," etc.

103. "Walt Whitman," *LG 1860*, p. 51 (118), *Inc. Ed.*, p. 562, variant reading of §21.

104. "Walt Whitman," *LG 1860*, p. 86 (276), *Inc. Ed.*, p. 576, variant reading of §41.

105. See, for instance, the variant readings of l. 19 of "There Was a Child Went Forth. . ." *Inc. Ed.*, p. 668. See also the variant readings of l. 12 of §10 of "Starting from Paumanok," *Inc. Ed.*, p. 550.

106. At the same time he dropped a number of lines in which he had claimed to be not the Messiah but a John the Baptist preparing the way; see Gay W. Allen, *Walt Whitman Handbook*, p. 186. J. T. Trowbridge was the first critic to draw attention to this discreet process of expurgation; see "Reminiscences of Walt Whitman," *Atlantic Monthly*, LXXXIX, 174.

107. In this selection the emphasis was laid on Whitman, the poet of democracy. The two sections entitled "Chants Democratic" and "Drum-Taps" took up nearly one half of the book. The others were entitled: "Walt Whitman," "Leaves of Grass," "Songs of Parting" (and not "Songs before Parting," for Rossetti already knew of some of the changes which were to take effect in the next edition).

108. They are: "Whoever you are holding me now in hand" (which Rossetti entitled "Fit Audience"), "These I singing in spring" (entitled "Singing in Spring"), "Not heaving from my ribb'd breast only" (entitled "Pulse of my life"), "For you O Democracy" (entitled "Love of Comrades").

109. See Whitman's letter to M. D. Conway, July 24, 1867, *SPL*, p. 963. Rossetti used the text of the 1867 edition. Whitman sent him a copy of it with manuscript revisions. In *WWW*, Furness gives the text (pp. 150–154) and tells the story (pp. 141–149) of an introduction, probably written by Whitman himself but signed by O'Connor, which Whitman wanted Rossetti to use. This introduction came too late and could not be printed. It was better in any case for the English public to have a qualified presentation by Rossetti than an extravagant eulogy by O'Connor.

110. Letter to Conway, November 1, 1867, *SPL*, p. 964.

111. Letter to W. M. Rossetti, December 3, 1867, *SPL*, pp. 966–967.

112. *Ibid.*, p. 967.
113. See his prefatory notice, pp. 20–23.
114. See *With WW in C*, II, 447–448. Traubel quotes several letters from F. S. Ellis.
115. *With WW in C*, II, 420.
116. *Galaxy*, December 1867, pp. 919–933.
117. *Ibid.*, May 1868, pp. 540–547.
118. *Democratic Vistas* (Washington, 1871).
119. "In Cabin'd Ships at Sea," *LG 1871*, p. 9, §2, *Inc. Ed.*, p. 2, l. 15.
120. See *CP*, pp. 214–215.
121. *LG 1871*, "Respondez," pp. 333–334, *Inc. Ed.*, p. 470, ll. 17–20.
122. The date of the copyright is 1870. The book was probably printed during Whitman's stay at Brooklyn from July 25 to October 1, 1870. See letter to Peter Doyle, September 6, 1870: "I am at the printing-office several hours every day. . ." *Calamus*, p. 72, or *SPL*, p. 993.
123. The copyright notice reads: "Entered according to Act of Congress in the year 1870. . ." The book may even have been ready as early as the beginning of 1869, if we are to believe an article in the Washington *Commercial*, May 9, 1869, which was probably inspired by Whitman if not written by him. See Emory Holloway, "Whitman as His Own Press-Agent," *American Mercury*, XVIII (December 1929), 482–488.
124. Whereas the pages on the right bear the title "Passage to India," those on the left bear the title "Leaves of Grass."
125. *After All Not to Create Only*, Boston: Roberts Bros., 1871, vii + 24 pp.
126. The 1872 edition was merely a reprinting: "I have attended to the bringing out the new edition of my book, but as the plates were all ready before, it is not much of a job." Whitman to Peter Doyle, March 4, 1872, *Calamus*, p. 89.
127. *LG 1867*, p. 273, §5 (14), *Inc. Ed.*, p. 610, last line of the passage following l. 31 in 1860.
128. *LG 1867*, p. 258, *Inc. Ed.*, p. 479. This poem dated back to 1860 (*LG 1860*, p. 403).
129. The 1865 *Drum-Taps* were now split into three groups: "Drum-Taps," "Marches Now the War is Over," and "Bathed in War's Perfume," separated by groups of poems entitled "Leaves of Grass." There was a fourth group of former "Drum-Taps" in *Passage to India* under the title of "Ashes of Soldiers."
130. *LG 1871*, pp. 337–338, *Inc. Ed.*, p. 274.
131. "Proud Music of the Storm," *Passage to India*, p. 17, §1, *Inc. Ed.*, p. 337, §1, ll. 10–11.

132. Same poem, *Passage to India*, p. 18, §3 (5), *Inc. Ed.*, p. 338, §2, ll. 13–15.

133. *After All Not to Create Only*, p. 17, §8, *Inc. Ed.*, p. 170, §7, ll. 1–3 ("Song of the Exposition"). See also "The Mystic Trumpeter," *Inc. Ed.*, p. 391, §6, ll. 1–4, in which he depicts war as one of the evils which afflict mankind.

134. See "Virginia — The West," *As a Strong Bird on Pinions Free*, p. 15, *Inc. Ed.*, pp. 248–249. See also the end of *After All Not to Create Only*, pp. 23–24, §§ 13–14, *Inc. Ed.*, "Song of the Exposition," pp. 173–174, §9. In the Preface to the edition of 1872 he expressed the hope that the wounds caused by the war would soon be healed; see *Inc. Ed.*, p. 511.

135. *LG 1871*, p. 11–12, *Inc. Ed.*, pp. 3–4. See also *Inc. Ed.*, p. 409, §1, 1.14, and variant readings, p. 699. In the same year he added to "Song of the Banner at Daybreak," the following line (*Inc. Ed.*, p. 647):
"The war is over — yet never over. . . out of it, we are born to real life and identity."

136. "As I Ponder'd in Silence," *LG 1871*, p. 8, §2, *Inc. Ed.*, p. 2, ll. 13, 15–16.

137. *LG 1871*, p. 309.

138. See above, Chapter VI, pp. 160, 174.

139. *LG 1867*, p. (5), *Inc. Ed.*, p. 1. The 1867 poem subsists in the definitive edition (*Inc. Ed.*, p. 434); Whitman included it in his "Sands at Seventy."

140. *LG 1867*, p. (5), "Inscription."

141. *Inc. Ed.*, pp. 511–512.

142. *LG 1871*, pp. 363–369.

143. *LG 1871*, p. 363, *Inc. Ed.*, p. 10.

144. Mark Twain and C. D. Warner, *The Gilded Age: A Tale of Today*, 1873.

145. *WWW*, p. 229, n. 95.

146. The title page bears the following indication: "Recited by Walt Whitman on invitation of Managers American Institute, on Opening their 40th Annual Exhibition, New York, noon, September 8, 1871."

147. The germ of this poem was already contained in "Enfans d'Adam" no. 10, in *LG 1860*. This poem was later entitled "Facing West from California's Shores."

148. *Passage to India*, pp. 108–111, *Inc. Ed.*, "Outlines for a Tomb," pp. 319–320.

149. *Passage to India*, pp. 94–96, *Inc. Ed.*, pp. 316–318.

150. *Passage to India*, pp. 87–93, *Inc. Ed.*, pp. 301–306, "The Return of the Heroes."

151. There were eleven new poems in all in 1871: "One's Self I

Sing," "As I Ponder'd in Silence," "In Cabin'd Ships at Sea," "To Thee Old Cause," "For Him I Sing," "Still though the One I Sing," "The Base of all Metaphysics," "Ethiopia Saluting the Colors," "Delicate Cluster," "Adieu to a Soldier," plus "After All Not to Create Only," though it was published separately.

Passage to India also contained some new poems: "Gliding o'er All," "Passage to India," "Proud Music of the Storm," "To a Certain Civilian," "This Dust Was Once a Man," "Whispers of Heavenly Death," "Darest Thou Now O Soul," "A Noiseless Patient Spider," "The Last Invocation," "As I Watch'd the Ploughman Ploughing," "Pensive and Faltering," "On the Beach at Night," "A Carol of Harvest for 1867" (later "The Return of the Heroes"), "The Singer in the Prison," "Warble for Lilac Time," "Sparkles from the Wheel," "Brother of All with Generous Hand" (later "Outlines for a Tomb"), "Gods," "Lessons," "Now Finale to the Shore," "Thought" (later "As They Draw to a Close"), "The Untold Want," "Portals," "These Carols," "Joy, Shipmate Joy."

152. As a Strong Bird on Pinions Free and Other Poems (Washington, D.C., 1872), XIII + 16 pp. This booklet contained the following poems: "One Song, America, before I Go," "Souvenirs of Democracy" (later "My Legacy"), "As a Strong Bird. . ." (later "Thou Mother with Thy Equal Brood"), "The Mystic Trumpeter," "O Star of France," "Virginia — The West," "By Broad Potomac's Shore."

153. For the circumstances of this invitation, which seems to have originated in a practical joke that the students of Dartmouth wanted to play on the faculty, see Bliss Perry, Walt Whitman, pp. 203–210. But in a letter to Peter Doyle June 27, 1872 (SPL, pp. 1007–1008), Whitman declared: "All went off very well." And in the Burlington Free Press and Times there appeared on July 1, 1872, a flattering account of the poet's performance — which may have been written by Whitman himself.

154. He himself announced on p. 5 of As a Strong Bird. . . : "The Mystic Trumpeter, and O Star of France, and indeed all Walt Whitman's other pieces since 1871–72, follow."

155. As a Strong Bird. . . pp. 13–14, Inc. Ed., pp. 331–332. He hated Napoleon III, but loved the French, see his letter to Peter Doyle, September 6, 1870, SPL, p. 993.

156. Inc. Ed., pp. 507–508.

157. See above, p. 182.

158. Letter to Peter Doyle, September 6, 1870, SPL, pp. 993–994.

159. Inc. Ed., p. 508.

160. Inc. Ed., pp. 484–485.

161. LG 1871, pp. 8–9, Inc. Ed., pp. 2–3, ll. 1–2, 4–6, 10, 12, 15, 17, 19.

162. Letter to O'Connor, September 27, 1867 (Berg Collection).
163. See above, p. 199.
164. Later entitled "The Return of the Heroes," *Inc. Ed.*, pp. 301–306.
165. See Portia Baker, "Walt Whitman's Relations with Some New York Magazines," *AL*, VII (November 1935), 274–301.
166. A review signed "C." in the *Round Table*, January 19, 1867.
167. *Nation*, January 2, 1868, p. 8.
168. On Whitman's reception in Great Britain, see Harold Blodgett, *Walt Whitman in England* (Cornell University Press, 1934).
169. "Walt Whitman's Poems," London *Chronicle*, July 6, 1867. Robert Buchanan a little later published a very warm article in his turn in the *Broadway Magazine*, November 1867. He reprinted it the following year in *David Gray and Other Essays*.
170. Letter to J. C. Hotten, April 24, 1868, *SPL*, p. 974.
171. Letter to M. D. Conway, February 17, 1868, *SPL*, pp. 969–970.
172. See above, n. 169.
173. Swinburne had already compared Whitman to Blake in his essay on the latter in 1867. In 1871, in his *Songs before Sunrise*, he greeted him as the prophet of Liberty in a poem entitled "To Walt Whitman in America." But in 1872, in *Under the Microscope*, he began to qualify his praises, and in 1887 he attacked Whitman violently in the *Fortnightly Review*. See G. W. Allen, *Walt Whitman Handbook*, pp. 477–478.
174. In *The Poetry of the Period* (London: R. Bentley, 1870).
175. This article has been reprinted in *In Re*, pp. 41–55. The quotation is borrowed from p. 48.
176. Thus Robert Buchanan's article in the *Broadway Magazine*, November 1867, was immediately reprinted in the New York *Citizen*, November 2, and in the Washington *Sunday Morning Chronicle*, November 10. In the same way, Rossetti's article in the London *Chronicle*, July 6, 1867, was reprinted in the New York *Citizen* as early as August 10.
177. Ferdinand Freiligrath's three articles on Whitman (*Wochenausgabe der Augsburger Allgemeine Zeitung*, May 10 *et seq.*, 1868) were later reprinted in his complete works, *Gesammelte Dichtungen* (Stuttgart, 1877), IV, 75 ff.
178. *Revue Britannique*, May 1868.
179. *Revue des Deux Mondes*, XLII (June 1, 1872), 556–577.
180. *Renaissance Littéraire et Artistique*, III, no. 7 (June 8), no. 11 (July 6), and no. 12 (July 13, 1872).
181. "Walt Whitman det amerikanske Demokratis Digter," *For Ide og Virkelighed*, I, 152–216.

182. Thus a translation of Freiligrath's articles was published in the Boston *Commonwealth* as early as July 4 and in the July issue of the *New Eclectic*. Mme Bentzon's article, though less favorable, was published in the New York *Spectator and Weekly Commercial Adviser* of July 19, 1872, under the title of "A French Opinion of Walt Whitman." The same journal had published in April a translation of Rudolf Schmidt's article. Whitman was so proud of this Danish tribute that he gave a summary of it among the advertisements printed at the end of *As a Strong Bird on Pinions Free*. The full article was later printed in *In Re*, pp. 231–248.

183. Such was the conclusion drawn by R. J. H. (R. J. Hinton) in "The Poet Walt Whitman — His Fame and Fortunes in Europe and America," Rochester *Evening Express*, March 17, 1868. This article was reprinted in the *Kansas Magazine* in December 1872. Whitman alluded to it in a letter to his mother (April 28, 1868, *SPL*, p. 975).

Most English critics insisted on the essentially American quality of his personality and art: "Walt Whitman is by far the most original product of his time, the sum and expression of the great democracy of the West . . ." (Review of Rossetti's edition, *Academia*, March 21, 1868, p. 278) "He is the first characteristic writer that the United States have produced . . . Whitman's very faults are national. The brag and bluster, and self-assertion of the man are American only . . ." (*Chambers's Journal*, July 4, 1868). But most of his compatriots refused to recognize themselves in the mythical American character whom English critics discovered in *Leaves of Grass*. The *New Eclectic* was even indignant: "That he is an American, in one sense, we must admit. He is something no other country could have produced. He is American as certain forms of rowdyism and vulgarity, excrescences on American institutions, are American. But that he is American in the sense of being representative of American taste, intellect, or cultivation, we should be very sorry indeed to believe." *New Eclectic*, July 1868.

184. *As a Strong Bird* . . . , p. xiii, *Inc. Ed.*, p. 412, which, however does not give the original version of the poem.

185. "Most readers will be surprised at the tone of unqualified, panegyric which runs through this little volume." An anonymous review, New York *Tribune*, July 20, 1867.

186. See F. P. Hier, "End of a Literary Mystery," *American Mercury*, I (April 1924), 471–478.

187. "The Carpenter," *Putnam's Magazine*, I (January 1868). This tale was later reprinted in *Three Tales* (Boston: Houghton Mifflin, 1892), pp. 211–320.

188. Letter to Peter Doyle, July 16, 1871, *SPL*, p. 996.

189. "The Poetry of Democracy: Walt Whitman," *Westminster Review*, XCVI (July 1871), 33–68. See Harold Blodgett, "Whitman and Dowden," *AL*, I (May 1929), 171–182.
190. Letter to O'Connor, July 14, 1871, *SPL*, p. 995.
191. John C. Dent, "America and Her Literature," *Temple Bar*, Vol. XXXVII, no. 147, p. 401.

VIII. THE HEROIC INVALID (1873–1876)

1. "I call myself a half-paralytic these days, and reverently bless the Lord it is not worse . . ." *SD*, p. 82, *CP*, p. 78.
2. See Josiah C. Trent, "Walt Whitman — A Case History," *Surgery, Gynecology and Obstetrics*, LXXXVII (July 1948), 3; see also letter to his mother, May 11, 1873, in *Wake* 7, pp. 14–15.
3. Letter to Peter Doyle, August 28, 1873, *Calamus*, p. 109.
4. Preface to *Two Rivulets*, p. 7n, *Inc. Ed.*, p. 514n.
5. Martha was Jeff's wife; she died of tuberculosis at St. Louis, where the couple had settled after the war.
6. See Dixon Wecter, "Walt Whitman as Civil Servant," *PMLA*, LXVIII (January 1943), pp. 1094–1109.
7. *In Re*, p. 114.
8. Letter to Peter Doyle, July 7, 1873, *Calamus*, pp. 102–103.
9. July 24, 1873, *ibid.*, p. 104.
10. September 5, 1873, *ibid.*, p. 112.
11. "I am going to try to get down to the ferry boat, and cross to Philadelphia — so you see I am not altogether disabled — but it is awful tough work." August 28, 1873, *ibid.*, p. 110. See also letter to Mrs. Abby H. Price and Helen Price, January 1874, *SPL*, p. 1017.
12. ". . . but I have so many times got a little better, only to fall back again as bad as ever, or worse . . ." (September 12, 1873, *Calamus*, p. 112). ". . . the worse of my case is these *fall backs* — But I have been out a little to-day. My walking does not improve any at all. (Then to make things more *cheerful*, there are many deaths here about from paralysis)" (October 16, 1873, *ibid.*, p. 112).
13. October 13, 1873, *ibid.*, p. 119.
14. "I keep a bully good heart, take it altogether . . ." (January 19, 1874, *ibid.*, p. 140). See also letter of April 16, 1874, *ibid.*, p. 152. After April 1874 he had other worries. Owing to lack of exercise, he suffered from dyspepsia (letters to Peter Doyle, May 22 and April 30, 1874, and December 3, 1875, *Calamus*, pp. 153, 160, 163).
15. See letters to Peter Doyle, September 26, 1873, March 26, 1874, and 1875, *Calamus*, pp. 116–117, 150, 159.
16. Letter to Peter Doyle, October 3, 1873, *SPL*, p. 1014.

17. Letter to Peter Doyle, January 30, 1874, *Calamus*, p. 141.
18. *Two Rivulets*, pp. 25–26, *Inc. Ed.*, pp. 392–393.
19. See above, n. 6.
20. "I don't fret about being discharged — I wonder it didn't come before." July 10, 1874, *Calamus*, p. 155.
21. *SD*, p. 93, *CP*, p. 89.
22. First published in *Harper's Monthly Magazine*, XLVIII (March 1874), 524–525, and then in *Two Rivulets*, pp. 21–23.
23. *Two Rivulets*, p. 21, *Inc. Ed.*, p. 682. Whitman himself realized the autobiographical value of the poem: ". . . as I see it now I shouldn't wonder if I have unconsciously put a sort of autobiographical dash in it." Letter to Mrs. O'Connor, February 3, 1874, Berg Collection.
24. *Inc. Ed.*, p. 352, ll. 1, 4, 6, 15–19.
25. *Ibid.*, pp. 352–353, ll. 27–30.
26. *Ibid.*, p. 353, ll. 51–55.
27. *Ibid.*, l. 46.
28. "Song of the Redwood Tree," *Inc. Ed.*, p. 175, §1, ll. 6–7.
29. *Ibid.*, p. 176, §1, ll. 39–40.
30. *Ibid.*, p. 177, §1, l. 62.
31. Preface to *Two Rivulets*, p. 7n, *Inc. Ed.*, p. 514n.
32. Whitman seems, at this time, to have been little interested in the social problem, which, however, had reached an acute stage in 1873–1876. In his letters to Peter Doyle (January 16, 1874, *Calamus*, p. 139; February 6, 1874, *ibid.*, p. 142 or *SPL*, p. 1019) he sometimes alluded to the sufferings of the unemployed, but never mentioned the matter in print. In 1871 (see Newton Arvin, *Whitman*, p. 138) he thought of prefixing a violent protest against "the more and more insidious grip of capitalism" to his "Songs of Insurrection" (*WWW*, p. 229, n. 95), but he eventually gave up the idea.
33. *Inc. Ed.*, p. 460, ll. 1–4.
34. *Ibid.*, p. 461, ll. 11–12, 17–18.
35. Letter to Mrs. O'Connor, March 22, 1874, Berg Collection.
36. From an article published in a series entitled " 'Tis But Ten Years Since," which appeared in the *Graphic* from January 27 to March 7, 1874. Whitman reprinted it partially in his *Memoranda during the War*. The passages which he left out are to be found in Thomas Mabbott and Rollo G. Silver, " 'Tis But Ten Years Since," *AL*, XV (March 1943), 51–62. The passage quoted above occurs on p. 52.
37. "Song of the Redwood Tree," *Two Rivulets*, p. 15, *Inc. Ed.*, p. 178, §3, ll. 8–11.
38. Preface to *Two Rivulets*, p. 14, *Inc. Ed.*, p. 521.
39. "Wandering at Morn," *Two Rivulets*, p. 28, *Inc. Ed.*, p. 334

40. "Prayer of Columbus," *Two Rivulets*, p. 23, *Inc. Ed.*, p. 354, ll. 64–66.
41. See letter to Peter Doyle, December 3, 1875, *Calamus*, p. 163.
42. See letter to Einstein, November 26, 1875, *SPL*, p. 1023, and *SD*, pp. 157–158 (*CP*, p. 157).
43. Letter to Mrs. Gilchrist, *SPL*, p. 1024.
44. Letter to Einstein, November 26, 1875, *SPL*, p. 1023.
45. *Two Rivulets* (Camden, N.J., 1876, 384 pp.) contained:
1. "Two Rivulets," 32 pp., which included fourteen new poems: "Two Rivulets," "Or from That Sea of Time," "Eidólons," "Spain, 1873–74," "Prayer of Columbus," "Out from behind This Mask," "To a Locomotive in Winter," "The Ox Tamer," "Wandering at Morn," "An Old Man's Thought of School," "With All Thy Gifts," "From My Last Years," "In Former Songs," "After the Sea-Ship."
2. "Democratic Vistas," 84 pp.
3. "Centennial Songs," 18 pp., which included "Song of the Exposition" (first published in 1871 as "After All Not to Create Only"), "Song of the Redwood Tree," "Song of the Universal," "Song for All Seas, All Ships," the last three being new poems.
4. "As a Strong Bird on Pinions Free," X+16 pp. (first published in 1872).
5. "Memoranda during the War," 68 pp.
6. "Passage to India," 120 pp.
As usual, the title page did not give the author's name. Some parts of the volume were printed in New York and others in Camden on different kinds of paper.
The 1876 edition of *Leaves of Grass* was an exact reproduction of the 1871–72 volume, but in some copies, notably those sent to English purchasers, some of whom paid three or four times the price of the book, and to whom Whitman wanted to give something extra, a few new poems were inserted. These additional poems had originally been printed on a single sheet intended to be cut in such a way as to permit the various poems to be glued to the page indicated in a supplementary table of contents. One of these sheets is preserved in the Carolyn Wells Houghton Collection of the Library of Congress and contains the following poems:
"The Beauty of the Ship," *Inc. Ed.*, p. 485.
"As in a Swoon," which was never printed again and is not included in *Inc. Ed.*:

> "As in a swoon, one instant,
> Another sun, ineffable, full-dazzles me
> And all the orbs I knew — and brighter, unknown orbs;
> One instant of the future land, Heaven's land."

"When the Full-grown Poet Came," *Inc. Ed.*, pp. 451–452. This poem was not included in the 1881 edition of *Leaves of Grass*; it reappeared only in *Good-Bye My Fancy* in 1891. "After an Interval," *Inc. Ed.*, p. 485.

These poems were to be glued respectively on pages 207, 247, 359, and 369, to fill the blanks left at the bottom of each of these pages. As we have had occasion to notice with the 1860 edition, Whitman hated to leave blank spaces.

Thus, *Two Rivulets* contained seventeen new poems and *Leaves of Grass* four. Since the 1871–72 edition, Whitman had written twenty-one new poems, as well as "To the Man-of-War Bird," which appeared in the *Athenaeum* on April 1, 1876.

46. ". . . the present melange," Preface to 1876 edition, *Inc. Ed.*, p. 512.

47. See letter to Edmund C. Stedman, June 17, 1875, *SPL*, p. 1021, and Preface to *Two Rivulets*, p. 6, *Inc. Ed.*, p. 513. See also "Two Rivulets," *Inc. Ed.*, pp. 485–486.

48. Preface to *Two Rivulets*, p. 5n, *Inc. Ed.*, p. 513n.

49. Preface to *Two Rivulets*, p. 6n, *Inc. Ed.*, p. 513n; see also "In Former Songs," *Two Rivulets*, p. 31, *Inc. Ed.*, p. 487.

50. Preface to *Two Rivulets*, p. 5n, *Inc. Ed.*, p. 513n.

51. *Two Rivulets*, pp. 17–20, *Inc. Ed.*, pp. 4–7.

52. "The Ox Tamer," *Two Rivulets*, pp. 27–28, *Inc. Ed.*, pp. 332–333.

53. *Centennial Songs*, p. 16, *Inc. Ed.*, p. 192, §2, ll. 7–10.

54. Preface to *Two Rivulets*, p. 7, *Inc. Ed.*, pp. 514–515.

55. Preface to *Two Rivulets*, p. 7, *Inc. Ed.*, p. 514n.

56. *Two Rivulets*, p. 24, *Inc. Ed.*, p. 321, ll. 4–5, 7. Line 7 is a Biblical reminiscence; see Revelation 9:2. Mrs. O'Connor recounts the following incident which may have inspired the poem: "It was about this time [during Whitman's stay in Washington] that one evening . . . he was accosted by a policeman and ordered to remove that 'false face', his name for a mask. Walt quietly assured him that the only face he wore was his very own, but added, 'Do we not all wear false faces?' " Ellen M. Calder, "Personal Recollections of Walt Whitman," *Atlantic Monthly*, XCIX (June 1907), 831.

57. Preface to *Two Rivulets*, p. 11n, *Inc. Ed.*, p. 518n.

58. *Ibid.*

59. *Ibid.*, p. 520.

60. *Ibid.*, p. 517.

61. "After an Interval," *LG 1876*, p. 369, *Inc. Ed.*, p. 485, ll. 5–6.

62. *Inc. Ed.*, p. 400. This poem was inspired by the proclamation of the Republic in Spain under the presidency of Emilio Castelar.

63. *Two Rivulets*, p. 29, *Inc. Ed.*, pp. 333–334.

64. *Two Rivulets*, "Centennial Songs," pp. 15–17, *Inc. Ed.*, pp. 192–194.

65. See letter to Mrs. O'Connor, June 10, 1874, Berg Collection.
66. Letter to Robert Buchanan, May 16, 1876, *SPL*, pp. 1027–1028.
67. *The Hour*, March 1876.
68. New York *Independent*, June 29, 1876.
69. This article was entitled "Walt Whitman — True Reminiscences of His Writings." A few months earlier, the same paper had published an article in which, almost in the same terms, Whitman complained of being boycotted (January 26, 1876); see *WWW*, pp. 245–248, n. 220.
70. See above, nn. 22 and 28.
71. In 1873, the New York *Graphic* had published "Nay,Tell Me Not To-day the Publish'd Shame" (March 5); "The Singing Thrush" (March 15 — later "Wandering at Morn"); "Spain 1873–'74" (March 23); "'Tis But Ten Years Since" (January 27–March 7); "An Old Man's Thought of School" (November 3); "A Christmas Garland," (Christmas number), which was composed of "In the Wake Following" (later "After the Sea-Ship") and "The Ox-Tamer."
The Camden *New Republic* had published "Song of the Universal" on June 20, 1874.
72. London *Athenaeum*, March 11, 1876.
73. He referred to American poets as "rooks" and "caws" and called Whitman "a sick eagle." Two days earlier, the same paper had published an article by its special correspondent in the United States on Whitman's difficult situation: ". . . while the stories of his extreme poverty and suffering which recently obtained circulation, are, I am glad to say, untrue, he has fallen into obscurity, if not into positive neglect, and apparently into a mood of sorrow." It was probably this report which, coming after the article in the *Athenaeum*, provoked Buchanan's letter. The public quickly responded to his appeal. On March 14 and 15, he thanked the generous donors who had immediately sent contributions, but on March 16 the *Daily News*, probably somewhat worried, tried in an editorial to calm the American public, maintaining that after all it was free to ignore a poet whom, from the start, it had refused to recognize. According to Traubel, Whitman granted the justice of this view; see *With WW in C*, I, 343–344.
74. New York *Tribune*, March 31, a note by E. C. Stedman on O'Connor's part in the Harlan affair; April 12, a new attack by Taylor charging Whitman with obscenity; April 13, an article by Burroughs; April 22, an article by O'Connor, "Walt Whitman; Is He Persecuted?"; July 10, an occasional poem by Whitman, "A Death-Sonnet for Custer" (later "From Far Dakota's Cañons"; on the origin of this poem, see *SD*, pp. 187–188, *CP*, pp. 184–185); July 13, "Robert Buchanan and Walt Whitman in Court," on the action for libel

brought by Buchanan against P. A. Taylor, the owner of the *Examiner*, who had published Swinburne's attack against Whitman.

75. New York *Herald*, April 2, 1876.

76. See W. S. Kennedy, *The Fight of a Book for the World*, p. 27. On the English subscription, see Clarence Gohdes, "The 1876 English Subscription for Whitman," *MLN*, L (April 1935), 257–258.

77. See letters to Buchanan, May 16 and September 4, 1876, *SPL*, pp. 1026–1028, and to W. M. Rossetti, March 17, *ibid.*, pp. 1024–1025. He was justly proud of the dignity of his attitude throughout this affair and quoted the last-mentioned letter in *SD*, pp. 316–317 (*CP*, pp. 324–325); see also *With WW in C*, I, 344–347.

78. See Bliss Perry, *Walt Whitman*, pp. 217–218.

79. See Robert Dudley Adams, "Walt Whitman, the American Poet," Sydney *Evening News*, May 20, 1876.

80. *With WW in C*, I, 343.

81. Quoted by Bliss Perry, *Walt Whitman*, p. 217.

82. Letter to Peter Doyle, December 13, 1876, *Calamus*, p. 165.

IX. NEW VICTORIES (1876–1882)

1. See *The Letters of Anne Gilchrist and Walt Whitman*, ed. with an introduction by T. B. Harned (New York: Doubleday, Doran, 1918).

2. See above, Chapter VII, p. 209.

3. Letter to Anne Gilchrist, August 17, 1873, *SPL*, p. 1013.

4. See E. Holloway, *Whitman*, pp. 290–293.

5. Letter to Anne Gilchrist, March 17, 1876, *SPL*, p. 1023.

6. Letter to John R. Johnston, June 20, 1877, *SPL*, pp. 1029–1030.

7. "A Visit to Walt Whitman in 1877," *Progressive Review*, I, no. 5 (February 1897), 413.

8. *SD*, pp. 82–123, *CP*, pp. 78–121.

9. *SD*, pp. 82–84, *CP*, pp. 78–80.

10. See "Bumble-Bees," "Summer Perfume — Quail — Notes — The Hermit-Thrush," "The Sky — Days and Nights — Happiness," "Colors — A Contrast," *ibid.*

11. See "Birds Migrating at Midnight," "Autumn Side-Bits," *ibid.*

12. "I sit here amid all these fair sights and vital influences . . ." *SD*, p. 92, *CP*, p. 86.

13. *SD*, p. 82, *CP*, p. 78.

14. "The Lesson of a Tree," *SD*, p. 89, *CP*, p. 86.

15. *Inc. Ed.*, p. 461, l. 6, echoes the title of a chapter in *SD*, "The Sky — Days and Nights — Happiness," which confirms the fact that the poem was in all likelihood composed at Timber Creek.

16. *SD*, pp. 104–105, *CP*, pp. 101–102.

17. *SD*, pp. 103–104, *CP*, pp. 99–101. On his health at the end of his second summer at Timber Creek, see letter to Peter Doyle, June 20, 1877, *Calamus*, p. 167, and letter to Tennyson, August 9, 1878, *SPL*, p. 1032. On his stays at Timber Creek, see Sculley Bradley, "Walt Whitman on Timber Creek," *AL*, V (November 1933), 235–246.

18. See Camden *Daily Post*, March 29, 1877: "Walt Whitman — He visits New York after 5 years' absence — High Tone Society now takes him to its bosom — Yet he rides again atop of the Broadway Omnibuses and fraternizes with drivers and boatmen — He has a new book under way — He is better in health."

19. See Baltimore *American*, March 17, 1877: "Our New York Letter: . . . Walt Whitman on the Woman Question . . . he talked in an easy delightful way regarding the new social and political aspects which life had taken since his banishment from its activities and seemed to feel very much as if he had gone to sleep ten years ago in New Jersey . . . Mr. Whitman recited with his old fire some lines from Henry Murger, the French Bohemian poet, called the 'Midnight Visitor.' They were very sad." The text of this poem will be found in Traubel, "Walt Whitman and Murger," *Poet Lore*, VI (October 1894), 484–491. It was an adaptation of "Ballade du désespéré," in *Les Nuits d'Hiver*.

20. *SD*, pp. 113–114, *CP*, pp. 110–111.

21. *SD*, pp. 114–115, *CP*, pp. 111–112.

22. *SD*, p. 117, *CP*, 114.

23. *SD*, p. 117, *CP*, 115.

24. See "A Poet's Recreation," New York *Tribune*, July 4, 1878, and "Gathering the Corn," *ibid.*, October 24.

25. See *Walt Whitman's Diary in Canada*, p. 55.

26. Letter to George Whitman, June 15–17, 1878, *SPL*, pp. 1030–1031.

27. *SD*, p. 306, *CP*, p. 315.

28. *SD*, pp. 129–133, *CP*, pp. 127–131.

29. He was the guest of the Old Settlers of Kansas Committee.

30. *SD*, p. 142, *CP*, pp. 140–141. On his western journey, see R. R. Hubach, "Walt Whitman and the West," a digest of a doctoral dissertation, Indiana University, 1943.

31. *SD*, pp. 141–142, *CP*, pp. 139–140.

32. *SD*, pp. 147–148, *CP*, p. 146.

33. *SD*, p. 145, *CP*, p. 144.

34. *SD*, p. 143, *CP*, p. 142.

35. *Inc. Ed.*, p. 334–335.

36. *Inc. Ed.*, p. 403.

37. *Inc. Ed.*, p. 336. He may also have composed at this time the poem entitled "Mirages," to which he prefixed the following note: "Noted verbatim after a supper talk outdoors in Nevada with two old miners." But he published it only in 1891 in *Good-Bye My Fancy*.

38. *SD*, p. 155, *CP*, pp. 154–155. On his stay in St. Louis, see also letter to Peter Doyle, November 5, 1879, *Calamus*, pp. 170–172, and R. R. Hubach, "Walt Whitman visits St. Louis," *Missouri Historical Review*, XXXVII (July 1943), 386–394. See also "Plate Glass Notes," *NB*, pp. 78–79, *CP*, pp. 430–431.

39. R. R. Hubach, "Three Uncollected St. Louis Interviews of Walt Whitman," *AL*, XIV (May 1942), 141–147.

40. *SD*, p. 159, *CP*, p. 158–159.

41. *SD*, pp. 160–161, *CP*, p. 160. ". . . a remembrance always afterwards."

42. Letter to Peter Doyle, July 24, 1880, *Calamus*, p. 172.

43. See above, n. 25.

44. *SD*, pp. 161–165, *CP*, pp. 160–166.

45. "To Walt Whitman," *Galaxy*, January 1877, p. 29.

46. See *Calamus*, p. 10.

47. *SD*, p. 180, *CP*, pp. 179–180.

48. St. Louis *Post Dispatch*, October 17, 1879; see above, n. 39.

49. Trent Collection, Duke University.

50. *Walt Whitman's Diary in Canada*, pp. 58–59.

51. Letter from J. G. Holland to R. W. Gilbert, September 19, 1880, quoted in Johnson, *Remembered Yesterdays* (Boston, 1923), pp. 337–338.

52. See Portia Baker, "Walt Whitman's Relations with Some New York Magazines," *AL*, VII (November 1935), 274–301.

53. E. C. Stedman, "Walt Whitman," *Scribner's*, XXI (November 1880), 47–64. This article was reprinted by Stedman in his *Poets of America* (Boston and New York: Houghton, Mifflin, 1885), pp. 349–395.

54. *SD*, p. 179, *CP*, p. 178.

55. *SD*, p. 180, *CP*, pp. 179–180.

56. *SD*, pp. 181–182, *CP*, pp. 180–181.

57. For instance, in the Boston *Herald*, April 18, 1881: "Walt Whitman — His second visit to the New England Metropolis — A cordial welcome in literary circles — Sketch of his life and poetic characteristics." See also, Boston *Evening Traveller*, April 16, 1881: "Walt Whitman on the death of Lincoln."

58. *SD*, pp. 182–183, *CP*, p. 182.

59. *SD*, pp. 185–186, *CP*, pp. 182–183. See also New York *Tribune*, August 4, 1881, "Letter from Walt Whitman — Week at

West Hills," and Mrs. Mary Wager-Fisher, "Walt Whitman," *Long Islander*, August 5, 1881.
60. *SD*, pp. 9–10, *CP*, pp. 5–6.
61. *SD*, pp. 186–187, *CP*, pp. 183–184.
62. *With WW in C*, I, 60.
63. Boston *Herald*, April 18, 1881.
64. Thomas B. Harned, "Walt Whitman and His Second Boston Publishers," *CW*, V, 275–300.
65. *Ibid.*, 276.
66. "I was in Boston from August 19 to October." MS note in Trent Collection, Duke University; see *Catalogue*, p. 49, no. 34.
67. Letter to Burroughs, September 24, 1881, *SPL*, p. 1039.
68. *SD*, pp. 189–190, *CP*, pp. 186–187.
69. See letter quoted by Harned, *CW*, V, 288.
70. *Ibid.*, 289–290.
71. *Ibid.*, 290.
72. Bucke gives the list in his *Walt Whitman*, p. 149.
73. Letter to Osgood quoted by Harned, *CW*, V, 294. The poems which Whitman intended to censor were: "I Sing the Body Electric" (§§5 and 8), "A Woman Waits for Me," and "Spontaneous Me."
74. *CW*, V, 294.
75. *Ibid.*, p. 295.
76. *Ibid.*, p. 296.
77. *Ibid.*
78. Letter to O'Connor, May 25, 1882, Berg Collection.
79. The only difference was that the title page bore the indication: "Camden, Author's Edition."
80. "They are now on their fourth Philadelphia edition of *Leaves of Grass*." Postcard to O'Connor, September 17, 1882, Berg Collection. See also letter to Burroughs, *SPL*, p. 1042.
81. See Springfield *Republican*, September 24, 1882: "It is to be regretted that Whitman had not the patience to wait for some firm of consequence to take up the task Osgood so feebly laid down. The Philadelphia firm advertise in this fashion in the Philadelphia *Press*: 'Leaves of Grass by Walt Whitman, is not an agricultural book in the haymakers' parlance; but it is a daisy, and don't you forget it.' "
82. This edition is identical with the Osgood, Author's, and Rees Welsh editions.
83. A few periodicals approved the suppression of *Leaves of Grass*: *The Literary World* (June 3, 1882), the New York *Tribune*, and the Boston *Advertiser* (May 24), the latter in an article entitled "Dirt in Ink." But there were many protests: in the Boston *Globe* (May 31), a letter from Dr. Bucke in the Springfield *Republican* (May 23), the

Camden _Post_ (May 22), the _Critic_ (June 3), the Boston _Commonwealth_ (September 23), an article entitled "Old Obscenity Comstock" in the Washington _Capital_ (July 23), _Man_, "a liberal journal of progress and reform," September 1 ("The liberties of this country ar [_sic_] not worth a brass copper when its citizens hav [_sic_] to beg or hire distinguished lawyers and politicians to intercede with the Heads of Departments to get rights that have been unlawfully and arbitrarily refused . . ."), and _Dr. Foote's Health Monthly_ (July and August 1882).

84. He sent three letters: on May 25, June 18, and August 27. See _With WW in C_, I, 52–54.

85. See New York _Tribune_, July 15: "Whitman's _Leaves of Grass_ — Movement in Philadelphia to suppress the work — Opinion of a prominent clergyman" and Philadelphia _Press_, same date: "Walt Whitman's Work — The Society for the Prevention of Vice to stop the sale — A clergyman defends the poet — He thinks that the Association will make a mistake — Rev. James Morrow, a prominent Methodist, invited to write a review of the poems for the author's edition."

86. See _This Word_, III, no. 13 (April 1, 1882): "We need some of the Gospel of Walt Whitman, who grandly and heroically dares to say: 'Divine am I, inside and out' . . ." In no. 24 (June 17), under the title of "Keep off the Grass," Chainey printed the full text of "To a Common Prostitute"; and in no. 26 (July 1), Chainey told the story of the difficulties raised by Tobey, the Boston postmaster, and published a letter of thanks which Whitman had sent him: "My dear friend, I to-day mail you a copy of _Leaves of Grass_ as a little gift and testimonial of thanks. Please send me a word if it is safely received. I sent you a little package of printed sheets last week by mail." It was a rather cold and noncommittal letter. O'Connor, on the other hand, had sent an impassioned missive.

87. See _Liberty_, July 22, 1882.

88. Letter to O'Connor, April 14, 1883, Berg Collection; see also letter to the same, November 12, 1882, _SPL_, pp. 1042–1043.

89. _Ibid._

90. _Critic_, I (November 5, 1881), 303; reprinted in _Essays from the Critic_ (Boston: Osgood, 1882), pp. 175–185.

91. Letter to Osgood, May 27, 1881, _CW_, V, 278.

92. "Birds of Passage" was not an original title. Whitman may have borrowed it from Longfellow.

93. Here is an example:

1876:
"One's-self I sing — a simple, separate Person;
Yet utter the word Democratic, the word En-masse.

Of Physiology from top to toe I sing;
Not physiognomy alone, nor brain alone, is worthy for the
   muse — I say the Form complete is worthier far;
The Female equally with the Male I Sing."
1881:
"ONE'S-SELF I sing, a simple, separate person,
Yet utter the word Democratic, the word En-Masse.
Of physiology from top to toe I sing,
Not physiognomy alone nor brain alone is worthy for the
   Muse, I say the Form complete is worthier far,
The Female equally with the male I sing."

94. Here is the list of the twenty new poems: "Thou Reader,"
"Youth, Day, Old Age and Night," "To the Man-of-War Bird,"
"Patroling Barnegat," "The Dalliance of the Eagles," Roaming in
Thought," "Hast Never Come to Thee an Hour," "As Consequent,"
"Italian Music in Dakota," "My Picture-Gallery," "The Prairie States,"
"Paumanok Picture," "Thou Orb Aloft Full-Dazzling," "A Riddle
Song," "From Far Dakota's Cañons," "What Best I See in Thee,"
"Spirit That Form'd This Scene," "A Clear Midnight," "As at Thy
Portals also Death," "The Sobbing of the Bells."

However, "Youth, Day, Old Age and Night" was not really new; it
was a fragment from "Great Are the Myths" and thus dated from
1855.

95. "Italian Music in Dakota," "The Prairie States," "From Far
Dakota's Cañons," and "The Spirit That Form'd This Scene." One
might add to these "A Paumanok Picture," which Whitman probably
wrote during his trip to Long Island with Dr. Bucke in 1881.

96. *LG 1881*, p. 216, *Inc. Ed.*, p. 233.

97. *LG 1881*, p. 216, *Inc. Ed.*, pp. 232–233. See Clara Barrus,
Whitman and Burroughs: Comrades, p. xxiv.

98. *LG 1881*, pp. 204–205, *Inc. Ed.*, p. 219. See Adeline Knapp,
"Walt Whitman and Jules Michelet; Identical Passages," *Critic*, XLIV,
467–468, and Gay W. Allen, "Walt Whitman and Jules Michelet,"
Etudes Anglaises, I (May 1937), 230–237.

99. *LG 1881*, p. 310, *Inc. Ed.*, p. 335. See *Pictures*, an unpublished poem by Walt Whitman, with an introduction and notes by
E. Holloway (New York: June House, 1927), pp. 9–10.

100. *LG 1881*, pp. 208–209, *Inc. Ed.*, p. 223. See "Out of the
Cradle Endlessly Rocking," §1, ll. 130–143 (*Inc. Ed.*, p. 214).

101. *LG 1881*, p. 368, *Inc. Ed.*, p. 403.

102. *LG 1881*, p. 378, *Inc. Ed.*, p. 414. According to Joaquin
Miller ("An Anecdote on Whitman," *Poet Lore*, X [1898], 618),
Whitman had at first declined to write a poem on Garfield in spite
of an offer of $100 from a Boston editor. Yet Whitman did write one

eventually, and it was published in the Boston *Globe*, September 27, 1881. He must have finally yielded to temptation. Moreover, he knew Garfield personally (see *With WW in C*, I, 324), and there is among his papers in the Library of Congress a note describing the President's death and the emotion of the American people: "All this while . . . the silent half-light through which everything else is seen, is the condition of President Garfield lying low on his bed there at the White House with death lurking stealthily nigh and sometimes almost showing his grisly visage while as gallant a struggle as was ever made against him is day and night dauntlessly kept up by the surgeons and doctors to say nothing of the splendid endurance of the patient himself.

"Besides the personal and technically political points of this whole affair, I often think of it in its bearings upon the American people, the whole fifty millions of them — giving them a common centre, essentially human, eligible to all, where they can all and each agree and where the warmest and best emotions of the heart are identified with abstract patriotism, union, nationality and made one."

When writing "The Sobbing of the Bells," Whitman probably remembered the last line of Poe's poem entitled "The Bells": "To the sobbing of the bells . . ." He was aware of it himself and for this reason was reluctant to include this piece in *Leaves of Grass*; see *With WW in C*, III, 129.

103. *LG 1881*, p. 18, *Inc. Ed.*, p. 11.

104. *LG 1881*, pp. 277–278, *Inc. Ed.*, pp. 300–301. Lines 13–33 of this poem originally belonged to "Two Rivulets" and so date back to 1876. Lines 13–15 were part of "Two Rivulets" proper (*Inc. Ed.*, p. 486); ll. 22–23 were §1 of "Or from That Sea of Time," and ll. 13–21 were §2 of the same poem, which thus should not have been placed among the "Rejected Poems" in the *Inc. Ed.*

105. *LG 1881*, p. 218, *Inc. Ed.*, p. 235.

106. *LG 1881*, p. 369, *Inc. Ed.*, p. 404.

107. "Chants Democratic" no. 8, *LG 1860*, p. 177 (4), "Song at Sunrise," *Inc. Ed.*, p. 410, l. 20.

108. "Youth, Day, Old Age and Night," *LG 1881*, p. 180, *Inc. Ed.*, p. 191. This is all that Whitman kept in 1881 of the long poem entitled in 1867 "Great Are the Myths," which dated back to 1855.

109. *LG 1881*, pp. 362–363, *Inc. Ed.*, pp. 396–397.

110. *LG 1881*, p. 376, *Inc. Ed.*, p. 412.

111. *LG, 1881*, p. 352, *Inc. Ed.*, pp. 385–386.

112. This poem was written in 1860 but included in *LG* only in 1867. The canceled passage is quoted in *Inc. Ed.*, p. 634 (after l. 13).

113. See *Inc. Ed.*, p. 701, for variant reading of l. 11.

114. He thus canceled l. 7: "I take for my love some prostitute." *Inc. Ed.*, p. 590.

115. Thus, in "The Sleepers," he canceled all the description of an erotic dream (*Inc. Ed.*, p. 683, after §1); in "To Think of Time," a line in §6 (*Inc. Ed.*, p. 686, before l. 3); and in "A Song of Joys," a whole passage that he had already toned down in 1867 (*Inc. Ed.*, p. 610, after l. 31).

116. Letter to Osgood, March 7, 1882, *CW*, V, 291–294.

117. The reviewer in the New York *Tribune*, November 19, 1881, was quite aware of Whitman's dilemma: "Of late years we believe that Mr. Whitman has not chosen to be so shocking as he was when he had his notoriety to make, and many of his admirers, the rational ones — hoped that the *Leaves of Grass* would be weeded before he set them out again. But this has not been done; and indeed Mr. Whitman could hardly do it without falsifying the first principle of his philosophy, which is a belief in his own perfection, and the second principle, which is a belief in the preciousness of filth . . ."

118. Whitman was already planning this book in 1879; see letter to Mrs. Gilchrist, *SPL*, p. 1033. He had thought of other titles before choosing the present one: "Nota Benes — Note-Posts of a Life in the New World in the nineteenth century — Dawns noons and (starry) nights of a half-paralytic — Only some days and nights of a half-paralytic — Resumes, notes and recallés [*sic*] of a half-paralytic — Odds and omnes — Far and near at 64 — Omnes" (a MS note in the Library of Congress). In March 1882, in a letter to Osgood, he spoke of "Specimen Days and Thoughts" (*CW*, V, 292–293).

119. For the memories of his childhood and youth, see *SD*, pp. 7–21 (*CP*, pp. 3–16), and for his diary from 1865 to 1882, *SD*, pp. 81–200 (*CP*, pp. 77–206).

120. The more so since this prose volume merely skimmed the surface of the subject, as Whitman himself knew very well: "Do you know what *ducks and drakes* are? Well S.D. is a rapid skimming — over the pond-surface of my life, thoughts, *expressions* that way — the real are altogether untouched, but the flat pebbles making a few dips as it flies and flits along — enough at least to give some living touches and contact points — I was quite willing to make an immense negative book." Letter to O'Connor, November 12, 1882, *SPL*, p. 1043.

121. As the reviewer in *Papers for the Times* (no. 22, April 1886, p. 181), noted, most critics did not even take the trouble to read his book: "These opponents may be divided into two classes: persons who honestly object to Whitman's plainness of speech, because they regard it as unnecessary and unfitting . . . These persons we can respect; their opinion is honest and intelligible. The other class we cannot respect. It consists for the most part of hack writers to the press who think it no portion of their duty to know anything of the works they

are paid to review." And he gave the following example: "For instance here is a Saturday Reviewer boldly denouncing Whitman, who does not even know the name of Whitman's book — Blades of Grass he calls it."

122. New York *Examiner*, January 19, 1882.

123. No critic seems to have been aware of the discreet work of expurgation carried out by Whitman since 1867. E. P. M. thus wrote in the New York *Sun*, November 19, 1881: "Of this side of the matter it is enough to say that if the new edition is a triumph for the poet, it has been achieved without any concession on his part. He has modified nothing. He has canceled no objectionable line or offensive phrase. He has confessed no sin against good taste or decency."

124. See above, n. 123.

125. "Walt Whitman's Leaves of Grass Redivivus," New York *Independent*, December 29, 1881. There were other attacks in *The Dial*, January 1882; the New York *Tribune*, November 19, 1881; the New York *Evangelist*, January 26, 1882; the *Literary World*, June 3, 1882; and the Detroit *Free Press*, January 7, 1882.

126. New York *Sun*, November 19, 1881.

127. His answer to the Philadelphia officers of the Society for the Suppression of Vice was quoted in the New York *Tribune*, July 15, 1882: "Walt Whitman is robust and virile but not obscene . . . The book, were its publication unobstructed, would speedily find its own level and its circulation would be limited to that level . . ."Other vindications of *Leaves of Grass* appeared in an article by B. W. Ball entitled "Two American Poets" in *The Index*, January 12, 1882; *The Scottish Review*, Vol. II, no. 4, pp. 281–300; *The Pioneer Press*, December 12, 1881; the Philadelphia *Times*, December 3, 1881; *The Mace*, March 21, 1882; an article by G. E. M. entitled "Whitman, Poet and Seer," New York *Times*, January 22, 1882; the Springfield *Republican*, September 24, 1882; the Boston *Herald*, May 24, 1882; an article by G. C. Macaulay in the *Nineteenth Century*, December 1881, pp. 903–918. See also in the *Iconoclast* (Indianapolis, Indiana), November 11, 1882, an article by Elmira, "the Quaker Infidel": "Suggestions and Advice to Mothers," in which the author advised mothers to make their children read *Leaves of Grass* because Whitman sang the body with admirable purity.

128. A review by E. P. M. in the New York *Sun*, November 19, 1881.

129. "In view of his savage contempt for anything musical in poetry, it will be a fine stroke of the irony of fate if he should be destined to be remembered only by the few pieces which are marked by the 'piano-tune' quality that he derides — the true and tender

lyric of My Captain and the fine poem on Ethiopia Saluting the Colors. These pieces with the magnificent threnody on Lincoln — When Lilacs Last in the Dooryard Bloomed — and a few others in which there is an approach to metrical form . . . are likely to be preserved in memory . . ." *The Dial*, January 1882, p. 219.

130. *Critic*, November 5, 1881, pp. 177–178. The reviewer in the London *Nineteenth Century* offered the following explanation: "The mass of his countrymen were not and are not strong enough to accept him. They have too little confidence in their own literary originality to appreciate duly one from among themselves who breaks through all the conventional usages of literature . . . It is necessary perhaps that this writer . . . should be first accepted in the Old World before he can be recognized by the New, which at present can see nothing in literature but by reflected light." G. C. Macaulay, "Walt Whitman," *Nineteenth Century*, XII, December 1882.

131. Deuceace, "Walt Whitman, Rhapsodist and Loafer," St. Louis *Daily Globe Democrat*, July 2, 1882.

132. New York *Tribune*, August 6, 1882.

133. O'Connor claimed the paternity of the word in a letter to Dr. Bucke (February 23, 1883), now in the Harris Collection of Brown University Library: "I wrote once, gaily, to the fellows in New York, that I was a Hugolater and a Whitmaniac. Soon after I saw in some of the ring papers sneers at us Whitmaniacs! . . . They are indebted to us for even their epithets of abuse . . ."

134. For instance: Joaquin Miller, "To Walt Whitman," *Galaxy*, January 1877; Robert Buchanan, "To Walt Whitman" (a sonnet), *Progress*, April 3, 1880; Linn B. Porter, "Walt Whitman," Boston *Transcript*, April 18, 1881; Walter R. Thomas, "A Sonnet to Walt Whitman," Boston *Index*, December 20, 1883, etc.

135. Richard Maurice Bucke, *Walt Whitman* (Philadelphia: David McKay, 1883).

136. O'Connor made a few alterations in the original text at Whitman's own request: ". . . I have been looking through the GGP as Dr. B sent it in his copy and it comes to my soul over the dozen years more eloquent and beautiful than ever — seems to me . . . it deserves to stand just as it is — two passages in the last page only might be left out — and I should so suggest. Seems to me all that is wanted is a brief prefatory dated present time, distinctly confirming your faith etc. That is without diminution (it couldn't have 'increase') . . ." Letter to O'Connor, February 19, 1883, Berg Collection.

137. Dowden's *Studies in Literature*, 1789–1877 (London: C. Kegan Paul, 1878), contained a chapter entitled "The Poetry of Democracy: Walt Whitman," pp. 468–523.

138. Stevenson's *Familiar Studies of Men and Books* (London,

1882), contains a chapter on Whitman, pp. 104-136, on which W. S. Kennedy passed the following comment: "R. L. Stevenson discussed Whitman . . . in a tone of frigid admiration, mingled with semi-sneering flippant detraction" (*The Fight of a Book for the World,* p. 32). Whitman, on the contrary, was perfectly satisfied with it: "Yes, he was complimentary to the Leaves; not outrightly so — saying yes with reservations: but being a man in whom I dare not waits upon I would he does not state his conviction unequivocally . . . His wife assured me that he felt far more strongly on the subject than he wrote." *With WW in C,* I, 145-146.

139. Thomson, "Walt Whitman," *Cope's Tobacco Plant,* II (May, June 1880), 471-473, 483-485. These two essays were reprinted with an introduction by Bertram Dobell in James Thomson, *Walt Whitman, the Man and the Poet* (London 1910).

140. Burroughs, *Birds and Poets* (Boston: Houghton Mifflin, 1877), pp. 185-235. This is how Whitman judged Burroughs' attitude toward him: "John is a milder type — not the fighting sort — rather more contemplative: John goes a little more for usual, accepted things, respectable things, than we do . . . though God knows he is not enough respectable to get out of our company." *With WW in C,* I, 334.

141. About this time, however, he was violently attacked by Sidney Lanier, who took him to task for his inverted dandyism and concluded: "The truth is, that if closely examined, Whitman, instead of being a true democrat, is simply the most incorrigible of aristocrats, masquing in a peasant's costume; and his poetry, instead of being the natural outcome of a fresh young democracy, is a product which would be impossible except in a highly civilized society." *The English Novel and the Principle of Its Development* (New York: Scribner's Sons, 1883).

Yet Lanier had written a very friendly letter to Whitman in 1878 with an order for a copy of *Leaves of Grass* (see *With WW in C,* I, 208). It is true that at that time he made some reservations concerning the form of Whitman's poetry. This passage from enthusiasm to disillusionment was not unusual among Whitman's admirers. He accepted it serenely (*ibid.,* 209). We might note, however, that Mrs. Lanier protested against the omission by W. D. Browne, the editor of her husband's papers, of a whole passage favorable to Whitman. In 1897 she published a complete edition of this posthumous work.

142. In 1884 the *Critic* conducted a poll of its readers in order to establish a list of forty authors who deserved to be members of an imaginary American Academy. Whitman was placed twentieth on the list. To be sure, the *Critic* had always been favorable to him. See Portia Baker, "Walt Whitman's Relations with Some New York Magazines," *AL,* VII (November 1935), 274-301.

143. *Critic*, November 5, 1881, pp. 177–178.
144. Philadelphia *Press*, August 5, 1883.

X. THE DECLINE (1883–1890)

1. "I shall break up from here in the spring and leave Camden — I don't know where . . ." Letter to Harry Stafford, January 2, 1884, Berg Collection.
2. See Bliss Perry, *Walt Whitman*, p. 245.
3. George Selwyn, "Walt Whitman in Camden," *Critic*, February 28, 1885, reprinted in *Uncoll. PP*, II, 58.
4. See "The Dismantled Ship," *NB*, p. 37, *Inc. Ed.*, p. 440. On the origin of this poem, see *With WW in C*, I, 390. An earlier version is included in "Walt Whitman; Unpublished Notes," *Wake* 7, p. 9.
5. *Uncoll. PP*, II, 60.
6. See, for instance, Stuart Merrill, *Walt Whitman* (Toronto: Henry S. Saunders, 1922), pp. 6–8, a reprint of an article in *Masque*, Series II, no. 9–10, pp. 303–307. Edmund Gosse, who visited Whitman in 1885, had the same impression; see E. Gosse, "A Note on Walt Whitman," Littell's *Living Age*, May 26, 1894, p. 498.
7. See "Mr. Irving's Second Tour of America," *The Theatre*, April 1885.
8. See above, n. 6; also "The Poet and His Guests," Camden *Post*, January 8, 1885, and "A Poet's Symposium: Edmund Gosse brings Walt Whitman kind words from Tennyson," *ibid.*, January 7, 1885.
9. See *With WW in C*, I, 161–163. Rhys had published a rather timid selection of *Leaves of Grass* in England: *Poems by Walt Whitman* (London: Canterbury Poet Series, 1886); see also E. Rhys, "The portraits of Walt Whitman," *Scottish Art Review*, June 1889.
10. H. R. Haweis, "A Visit to Walt Whitman," *Pall Mall Budget*, no. 930, January 14, 1886, reprinted in the *Critic*, February 27, 1886.
11. Edward Carpenter, *Days with Walt Whitman and Some Notes on His Life and Works* (London, 1906). He visited Whitman twice, in 1877 and in 1884.
12. "Arnold and Whitman," Philadelphia *Press*, September 15, 1889; "Arnold and Whitman; The Light of Asia Visits the American Poet — Kind Greetings sent by Browning and Rossetti to the Good Gray Poet," Philadelphia *Times*, September 15, 1889. See also Edwin Arnold, *Seas and Lands* (London, 1892), pp. 78–84.
13. Wilde's visit dated back to 1882; see "The Aesthetic Singer Visits the Good Gray Poet: He asks the advice of the latter and is told to go ahead in his missions to shatter the ancient idols," Phila-

delphia *Press*, January 19, 1882. See also Helen Gray Cone, "Narcissus in Camden," *Century*, November 1882.

14. J. Johnston, *Notes of a Visit to Walt Whitman* (privately printed, Boston, 1890), and J. Johnston and J. W. Wallace, *Visits to Walt Whitman in 1890–91 by two Lancashire Friends* (London, 1917; New York, 1918).

15. Emily Faithfull, *Three Visits to America* (New York: Fowler and Wells, 1884), pp. 94–96.

16. C. Sadakichi-Hartmann, "Notes of a Conversation with the Good Gray Poet by a German Poet and Traveller," New York *Herald*, April 14, 1888. See also his *Conversations with Walt Whitman*, (New York: E. P. Coby, 1895). Whitman protested against the unreliability of these interviews in a letter to Kennedy, August 4, 1890; see *FC*, p. 139.

17. See, for instance, "The Good Poet's Guest — A Southern Admirer Visits Walt Whitman — John Newton Johnson travels from his cotton plantation to call on Nature's bard . . ." New York *Tribune*, June 5, 1887. On this picturesque character, see Sidney Morse, "My Summer with Walt Whitman," *In Re*, pp. 376–377.
". . . have some nice visitors — sometimes foreigners — two or three American girls now and then — great comfort to me" (postcard to O'Connor, January 26, 1885, Berg Collection). Whitman enjoyed such visits very much; see *With WW in C*, I, 71.

18. Sidney Morse, "My Summer with Walt Whitman, 1887," *In Re*, pp. 376–391.

19. Whitman was also frequently interviewed by journalists; see, for instance, Richard Hinton in New York *World*, April 14, 1889, or J. L. G. "A Visit to Walt Whitman's Shanty," *Critic*, November 28, 1891.

20. Thomas B. Donaldson, *Walt Whitman, the Man* (New York: Harper, 1896).

21. *With Walt Whitman in Camden*, in 3 volumes of over 500 pages each, appeared from 1906 to 1914. A fourth volume edited by Sculley Bradley was published in 1953 by the University of Pennsylvania Press (reprinted in 1959); a fifth one is in the press. These four volumes cover only about a year of the poet's life.
In 1890 Traubel founded a monthly review with philosophical pretensions, *The Conservator*, and after Whitman's death, he devoted it to the worship of his hero and made it the organ of the fanatical Whitmaniacs. It continued to appear until 1919, but during the last years of its existence articles on Whitman became less and less frequent, and Traubel spoke increasingly as a prophet of socialism rather than the high priest of the Whitman cult.

22. See above, n. 15.

23. See Bliss Perry, *Walt Whitman*, p. 251. Several members of the Club resigned in protest; see L. D. Morse, "Dr. Daniel Brinton on Walt Whitman," *Conservator*, November 1899, p. 134.

24. Letter to Kennedy, September 14, 1887, *FC*, p. 115. However, the Springfield *Republican* had accepted "The Dying Veteran" for $25, and the *Critic* sent him $10 for "Twilight" (see postcard to Kennedy, July 9, 1887, *FC*, p. 113); and on August 18, 1886, Whitman wrote to O'Connor: ". . . have been writing somewhat busily for me in the last three or four weeks — articles, generally ordered one — *Century* — *North American Review* and *Lippincott's* — a little bit about Shakespeare in last *Critic*" (Berg Collection). See also postcard to *Century Magazine* in *SPL*, p. 1045. He also received $25 for an article of reminiscences in the New Orleans *Picayune*, January 25, 1887, for the centenary of this paper.

In February 1886 he delivered his Lincoln lecture at Elkton, Maryland; see Rollo G. Silver, "Walt Whitman's Lecture in Elkton," *N & Q*, March 14, 1936, pp. 190–191.

25. "My writing for the *Herald* continues on — they have lately written to me to continue — they have paid me so far dol. 165, wh' I call first rate, 25 for Whittier bit, also enclosed." Letter to O'Connor, April 18, 1888, Berg Collection.

26. "My last half-annual return of royalties for both my books just rec'd — dol. 20.71 cts." Letter to O'Connor, January 22, 1886, Berg Collection. See also: "I get a miserable return of royalties from McKay my Philadelphia publisher — not dol. 50 for both books Leaves of Grass and Specimen Days for the past year." Letter to Burroughs, December 21, 1885, Berg Collection.

27. See letters of W. M. Rossetti to Mrs. Gilchrist, June 15, July 5, August 28, 1885, and letters of the same to Herbert Gilchrist, December 23, 1885 and May 9, 1886.

28. "The English 'offering' (through Rossetti and Herbert Gilchrist) will am't over 500 dollars — the principal part of which has already been sent to me — and on which I am really living this winter." Letter to O'Connor, January 22, 1886, Berg Collection. The first subscription took place in 1885, but there was a second one in December 1886, launched by the *Pall Mall Gazette*; see Whitman's letter to the editor of this magazine, *SPL*, pp. 1048–1049.

29. See Whitman's letter to S. Baxter, December 8, 1886, Berg Collection: "I thank you deeply and Mr. Lovering also — but do not consent to being an applicant for a pension as spoken of — I do not deserve it. Send word to Mr. Lovering or show him this . . ."

30. See postcard to Kennedy, January 26, 1887, *FC*, p. 106.

31. Sylvester Baxter, "Walt Whitman in Boston," *New England Magazine*, August 1892, pp. 720–721.

32. Letter to Eldridge, April 21, 1887, quoted by Bliss Perry, *Walt Whitman*, pp. 252–253. In 1886 his Lincoln lecture had been delivered at Philadelphia (*ibid.*, p. 251) and the last one was also delivered in Philadelphia at the Contemporary Club, in 1890.

33. He still sometimes complained of his poverty, though: see "To the Pending Year," which was published in the *Critic*, (January 5, 1889, under the title of "To the Year 1889" (*Inc. Ed.*, p. 447).

34. *Inc. Ed.*, p. 522.

35. See title of the preface to *NB*.

36. *NB*, p. 19, *Inc. Ed.*, p. 435, l. 3.

37. "Paumanok," *NB*, p. 19, *Inc. Ed.*, p. 420, l. 1.

38. "Memories," *NB*, p. 21, *Inc. Ed.*, p. 423. See also "By That Long Scan of Waves," *NB*, pp. 24–25, *Inc. Ed.*, pp. 426–427.

39. See "True Conquerors," *NB*, p. 31, *Inc. Ed.*, p. 434. See also: "Result of seven or eight stages and struggles extending through nearly thirty years . . ." "A Backward Glance . . . ," *Inc. Ed.*, p. 522.

40. "Soon Shall the Winter's Foil Be Here," *NB*, p. 33, *Inc. Ed.*, p. 436, l. 6.

41. "The First Dandelion," *NB*, p. 21, *Inc. Ed.*, p. 423.

42. See the photograph of him at seventy in *Uncoll. PP*, II; the dissymmetry of the face caused by paralysis became more and more marked as he grew older.

43. See postcard to Kennedy, August 5, 1885, *FC*, p. 100. He had had a sunstroke in 1858; see letter to Lewis Kirk Brown, August 1, 1863, *SPL*, p. 914.

44. See letter to O'Connor, June 14, 1888, Berg Collection: ". . . Have been pretty ill, indeed might say pretty serious, two days likely a close call — but Dr. Bucke was here and took hold me [*sic*] without gloves . . ."

45. See E. Holloway, *Whitman*, pp. 311–312. His first nurse was a medical student, Eddie Wilkins; he was succeeded by Frank Warren Fritzinger, a young sailor and Mrs. Davis' adopted son. Whitman was very fond of him: "Frank Warren Fritzinger, my friend and gillie," he called him in a letter to J. W. Wallace, September 22, 1890, *SPL*, p. 1053. See Elizabeth L. Keller, *Walt Whitman in Mickle Street*, 1921.

46. *NB*, p. 20, *Inc. Ed.*, p. 422.

47. "An Evening Lull," *NB*, p. 37, *Inc. Ed.*, p. 441. See *With WW in C*, I, 354.

48. "Drove down yesterday three or four miles to Gloucester, on the Delaware below here, to a fine old public house close to the river, where I had four hours and a good dinner of planked shad and champagne . . . enjoyed all and was driven back to Camden at sundown — so you see I get out and have fun yet — but it is a

dwindling business." Letter to O'Connor, April 25, 1888, Berg Collection.

49. "A Carol Closing Sixty-Nine," *NB*, p. 20, *Inc. Ed.*, p. 421, ll. 8-9.

50. *Ibid.*, l. 7.

51. *With WW in C*, I, 354.

52. "Of that blithe throat of thine," *NB*, p. 28, *Inc. Ed.*, p. 430.

53. *November Boughs*, Philadelphia: David McKay, 1888, 140 pp.

54. See *Walt Whitman's Backward Glances*, ed. Sculley Bradley and John A. Stevenson (University of Pennsylvania Press, 1947).

55. *Complete Poems and Prose of Walt Whitman, 1855-1888*, Philadelphia: published by the author, 1888, 900 pp.

56. *Leaves of Grass* with *Sands at Seventy* and *A Backward Glance O'er Travel'd Roads*, Philadelphia, 1889, 422 pp.

57. *NB*, p. 26, *Inc. Ed.*, p. 428. This poem was written during a stay at Ocean Grove with Burroughs in 1884; see *Walt Whitman's Diary in Canada* (Boston: Small, Maynard, 1904), p. 63, n. 1, and *With WW in C*, I, 406.

58. "Life," *NB*, p. 30, *Inc. Ed.*, p. 433, ll. 5-6.

59. "Going Somewhere," *NB*, p. 31, *Inc. Ed.*, p. 433, ll. 6-8.

60. "Halcyon Days," *NB*, p. 22, *Inc. Ed.*, p. 424, l. 3. The change struck Sidney Morse, who had done his bust and saw him again eleven years later in 1887; see *In Re*, p. 372.

61. "Queries to my Seventieth Year," *NB*, p. 21, *Inc. Ed.*, p. 422.

62. "After the Supper and Talk," *NB*, p. 38, *Inc. Ed.*, p. 142, esp. l. 11.

63. "Twilight," *NB*, p. 35, *Inc. Ed.*, p. 439. According to Traubel, some of Whitman's admirers protested against this poem, especially on account of the last word which they considered inconsistent with the rest of his work. See *With WW in C*, I, 140-141. The poem is not really inconsistent with the rest of *Leaves of Grass*; it merely expresses a mood and is not a philosophical pronouncement.

64. "Halcyon Days," see above, n. 60.

65. *NB*, p. 32, *Inc. Ed.*, p. 434. See also "Not Meagre, Latent Boughs Alone," *Inc. Ed.*, p. 439.

66. As in the 1876 and 1881 editions there is a high percentage of occasional poems, which shows the weakening of his inspiration: "Abraham Lincoln," "Election Day, November 1884," "Death of General Grant," "Red Jacket," "Washington's Monument," "The Dead Tenor," "Orange Buds by Mail from Florida," "The Dead Emperor." He also used old poems. Thus, "Small the Theme of My Chant," which had been included in *Leaves of Grass* in 1867, now reappeared after an eclipse.

67. "You Lingering Sparse Leaves of Me," *NB*, p. 36, *Inc. Ed.*, p. 349

68. *Ibid.*, ll. 5–6.

69. On the contrary, he congratulated himself on having made no concessions: "I had my choice when I commenc'd. I bid neither for soft eulogies, big money returns, nor the approbation of existing schools and conventions . . . unstopp'd and unwarp'd by any influence outside the soul within me, I have had my say entirely my own way, and put it unerringly on record . . ." *Inc. Ed.*, p. 523.

70. For instance, in "Song of Myself," *LG 1855*, p. 51, *Inc. Ed.*, p. 69, §45, l. 11; and in "Debris," *LG 1860*, p. 423, *Inc. Ed.*, p. 482, ll. 9–11.

71. *Inc. Ed.*, p. 527.

72. *Ibid.*, p. 523.

73. *Ibid.*, p. 530.

74. *Ibid.*, p. 523.

75. "Continuing the subject, my friends have more than once suggested — or may be garrulity of advancing age is possessing me." *Ibid.*, p. 529. Also: ". . . garrulous to the very last . . ." in "After the Supper and Talk," *NB*, p. 38, *Inc. Ed.*, p. 422, last line.

76. "Some War Memoranda," "Abraham Lincoln," and "Last of the War Cases."

77. *NB*, p. 32, *Inc. Ed.*, p. 435, particularly ll. 11–14.

78. "While Not the Past Forgetting," *NB*, p. 33, *Inc. Ed.*, pp. 436–437.

79. "The Dying Veteran," *NB*, p. 34, *Inc. Ed.*, p. 437, ll. 16–18.

80. "If there are readers who find intellectual greatness and spiritual uplifting in Walt Whitman, we can only say that for those who enjoy this kind of 'poetry', it is poetry that they will enjoy . . ." Boston *Traveller*, January 17, 1889.

81. "That work . . . was reviewed in the earliest days of the *Saturday Review* by a very eminent hand. We shall not say that it was unjustly reviewed, nor do we think so. From certain points of view Walt Whitman deliberately laid himself open to what he has abundantly received, the process known technically as 'slating' . . . Now it seems to us that Walt Whitman's unfavorable critics hitherto have failed to distinguish between the faults which false premises to start from and misconceived aim tend to have produced in him on the one side, and the faculties, and even to a certain extent the accomplishments as a poet, which in spite of all these evil influences he has displayed on the other . . . let us none the less confess that this strayed reveller, this dubiously well-bred truant in poetry, is a poet still, and one of the remarkably few poets that his own country

has produced." Review of *NB* in *Saturday Review* (London), March 2, 1889, pp. 260–261.

82. Thus an admirer sent him orange-buds by mail from Florida; see the poem on this subject, *NB*, p. 35, *Inc. Ed.*, pp. 438–439.

83. The Camden *Post* in particular published an article entitled "Camden Honors Him — Poet Whitman's 70th Birthday" (June 1, 1889) and announced on May 10: "A Camden Compliment — On Walt Whitman's 70th Birthday — An Imposing Celebration — Morgan's Hall has been secured for dinner which will be attended by prominent literary characters." The speeches delivered on that occasion were published by Horace Traubel under the title *Camden's Compliment to Walt Whitman*.

84. See Philadelphia *Press*, June 1, 1890: "The old poet talks across table on immortality with the agnostic — A dinner of intimate friends in honor of the Camden sage's seventy-second [*sic*] birthday."

85. If we are to believe the local newspapers, the organizers of this ceremony encountered difficulties: "Refused to Col. Ingersoll — Walt Whitman's testimonial benefit cannot be held in the Academy — Horticultural Hall chosen — Directors will not allow the famous atheist to lecture on 'art and morality' — What President Baker says." Philadelphia *Press*, October 5, 1890.

86. *In Re*, pp. 253–283.

87. "In fact, his personality had such advertising value that an enterprising manufacturer in 1889 named a cigar after him." C. Gohdes, "Walt Whitman and the Newspapers of His Day," *Library Notes, a Bulletin Issued for the Friends of the Duke University Library*, I, no. 2, (October 1936), 3–4.

88. ". . . of *November Boughs* over 700 have been sold." Postcard to O'Connor, February 16, 1889, Berg Collection.

XI. LAST MONTHS AND DEATH (1891–1892)

1. "Walt Whitman's End — It seems to be approaching rapidly now." London, Ontario, *Free Press*, June 4, 1890.

2. "To the Sunset Breeze," *Good-Bye My Fancy*, p. 12, *Inc. Ed.*, p. 449.

3. ". . . nothing left but behave myself quiet, and while away the days yet assign'd . . ." Preface Note to 2nd Annex, *Inc. Ed.*, p. 538.

4. *Ibid.*, p. 548.

5. *In Re*, pp. 297–327.

6. *Ibid.*, pp. 393–411. See also letter to J. Johnston, June 1, 1891, *SPL*, p. 1057.

7. *In Re*, pp. 394–395.
8. *Ibid.*, p. 395.
9. *Ibid.*, p. 396.
10. *Ibid.*, p. 397.
11. *Ibid.*, p. 398.
12. *Ibid.*
13. *Good-Bye My Fancy*, p. 8, *Inc. Ed.*, p. 444, ll. 1–3, 10–11. See also "L of G's Purport," *ibid.*, p. 456, ll. 6–9.
14. "Sounds of Winter," *Good-Bye My Fancy*, p. 13, *Inc. Ed.*, p. 451, ll. 6–7.
15. "Old Age's Ship and Crafty Death's," *Good-Bye My Fancy*, p. 10, *Inc. Ed.*, p. 446, l. 4.
16. Some of these poems had already appeared in magazines in 1890 and some of them even as early as 1889. Thus, "My 71st Year" was first published in the *Century Magazine* in November 1891; "Old Age's Ship and Crafty Death's" in the same magazine in February 1890; "To the Pending Year" in the *Critic*, January 5, 1889, under the title "To the Year 1889"; "Bravo, Paris Exposition!" in *Harper's Weekly*, September 28, 1889; "Interpolation Sounds" in the New York *Herald*, August 12, 1888 (see *With WW in C*, II, 125); "To the Sunset Breeze" in *Lippincott's Magazine*, December 1890; "Old Chants" in *Truth*, March 19, 1891; "A Twilight Song" in *Century Magazine*, May 1890; "Osceola" in *Munson's Illustrated World*, April 1890; "A Voice from Death" in the New York *World*, June 7, 1889; "The Commonplace" in *Munson's Illustrated World*, March 1891; and "The Unexpressed" in *Lippincott's Magazine*, March 1891. As for "Sail Out for Good, Eidólon Yacht," it had appeared in *Lippincott's* as early as March 1881.
17. ". . . I shall put in order a last little six or eight page annex (the second) of my L of G and that will probably be the finish . . ." Letter to Kennedy, June 18, 1890, *Rains Catalogue*, p. 79.
18. Among them, as in *November Boughs*, there were several occasional poems: "My 71st Year," "To the Pending Year," "Bravo Paris Exposition!" "Interpolation Sounds," "A Christmas Greeting" (to Brazil), "Osceola," and "A Voice from Death." To this list might be added "For Queen Victoria's Birthday," which was published in the *Critic*, May 24, 1890, but was never incorporated in *Leaves of Grass*. At this time of his life, Whitman often spoke as the poet laureate of the United States.
19. Thus "When the Full Grown Poet Came" took up an idea already expressed in "Passage to India" in 1876.
20. *Good-Bye My Fancy*, p. 5, *Inc. Ed.*, p. 537. See also letter to J. Johnston, March 30, 1891, *SPL*, p. 1055.

21. As usual, he put all his hope in the judgment of posterity; see "Long, Long Hence," *Inc. Ed.*, p. 447.

22. See "L of G's Purport," *Inc. Ed.*, p. 456, ll. 11–12.

23. See in particular: "Sail Out for Good, Eidólon Yacht!" "Lingering Last Drops," "Good-Bye My Fancy," "Old Age's Ship and Crafty Death's," "Osceola," "A Voice from Death," and "L of G's Purport."

24. See "An Executor's Diary Note," *Inc. Ed.*, p. 539.

25. *Leaves of Grass*, Philadelphia: David McKay, 1892, 438 pp. It was a very plain edition; the volume was bound in green cloth, and the backstrip bore the following indication: "Leaves of Grass, Complete, 1892" and a facsimile of Whitman's signature. It included, besides *Leaves of Grass* proper (i.e., the text of the 1881–82 edition), "Sands at Seventy," "Good-Bye My Fancy," and "A Backward Glance o'er Travel'd Roads."

26. The last one that he sent to J. Johnston was dated February 6, 1892; see *SPL*, pp. 1058–1059.

27. Preface to 2nd Annex, *Inc. Ed.*, p. 537.

28. See Daniel Longaker, "The Last Sickness and the Death of Walt Whitman," *In Re*, pp. 398–399.

29. *Ibid.*, p. 402.

30. The last letter that he wrote was dated March 17, 1892, and was addressed to his sister, Hannah Heyde; see *In Re*, p. 432.

31. "He did not, as is usual with consumptives, entertain any hopes of recovery . . ." *Ibid.*, p. 404.

32. "Death's Valley," *Inc. Ed.*, p. 463, ll. 18–20.

33. "Walt just put in his water-bed . . ." J. W. Wallace (quoting a letter from Traubel), "Last Days of Walt Whitman," *In Re*, p. 433.

34. "March 18 . . . the severe pain in W.'s left ankle increases." *Ibid.*, p. 433.

35. *Ibid.*, p. 403.

36. *Ibid.*, p. 410.

37. See *In Re*, pp. 434–435 and R. M. Bucke, "Memories of Walt Whitman," *Walt Whitman Fellowship Papers*, May 1897, pp. 35–42. On the exact time of his death, see "Virbius," "Walt Whitman's Death," *N & Q*, CLXVII (August 18, 1934), 116.

38. See the notes of the post-mortem examination in *In Re*, pp. 406–409, and Josiah C. Trent, "Walt Whitman — A Case History," *Surgery, Gynecology and Obstetrics*, LXXXVII (July 1948), 113–121.

39. *In Re*, p. 409.

40. This grave became a topic of controversy. Whitman's enemies accused him of feigning poverty in order to save up enormous sums which were swallowed up in his mausoleum. He was in particular accused of stinginess and ingratitude toward Mrs. Davis, notably by

Elizabeth Leavitt Keller (his nurse during his last illness) in *Walt Whitman in Mickle Street* (New York: Mitchell Kennerley, 1921). These accusations were taken up by Frances Winwar in *American Giant: Walt Whitman and His Times*, but C. J. Furness in his review of this book in *AL*, XIII (January 1942), 423–432, justified Whitman by quoting passages from Thomas B. Harned's diary. It seems that Whitman did not spend more than $1,500 on his tomb and let himself be drawn too far by unscrupulous contractors. For a vindication of Whitman's generosity, see Helena Born, "Whitman's Altruism," *Conservator*, September 1895, pp. 105–107.

41. *In Re*, pp. 437–452.

GENERAL INDEX

INDEX OF POEMS AND PROSE-WRITINGS